The Synergy Theory on Economic Growth: Comparative Study Between China and Developed Countries

Jianhua Liu · Zhaohua Jiang

The Synergy Theory on Economic Growth: Comparative Study Between China and Developed Countries

Science Press
Beijing

Springer

Jianhua Liu
School of Management Engineering
Zhengzhou University
Zhengzhou, Henan, China

Zhaohua Jiang
Faculty of Humanities and Social Science
Dalian University of Technology
Dalian, Liaoning, China

ISBN 978-981-13-1884-9 ISBN 978-981-13-1885-6 (eBook)
https://doi.org/10.1007/978-981-13-1885-6

Jointly published with Science Press, Beijing, China

The print edition is not for sale in China Mainland. Customers from China Mainland please order the print book from: Science Press.

Library of Congress Control Number: 2018950203

This Springer imprint is published by the registered company Springer Nature Singapore Pte Ltd.
The registered company address is: 152 Beach Road, #21-01/04 Gateway East, Singapore 189721, Singapore

Preface

Over the past thousands of years of human civilization, the average annual economic growth of more than 2% only happened in western developed countries (such as the United Kingdom, France, Germany, the United States, and other countries) in the past 200 years. Prior to this, every country's economy often developed at a very low growth rate. China's high growth after the reform and opening up is a miracle in the history of human economic development.

How to explain economic growth, or analyze economic growth quantitatively? In economics, it has started since the classical economic growth theory of Adam Smith and David Ricardo, who put forward the classical labor value theory. Marx's *Das Kapital* and labor value theory paved the way for a quantitative analysis of economic growth. Then, Keynes put forward the four-sector theory of the national economy. On the basis of this theory, Harold and Domar established the economic growth model of capital determinism. Then, Solow emphasized the role of scientific and technological progress based on the four-sector theory of Keynes, although the scientific and technological progress is only a "surplus" in his opinion. In the 1980s, the Arrow-Sheshinski model and new growth theories of Romer, Lucas, and Schumpeter began to be the mainstream. These theories generally emphasized the role of innovation in economic growth and weakened the role of capital, resulting in a lot of controversies. For example, Jorgenson's economic growth theory is inclined to capital determinism. On the other hand, Coase and North's new institutional economics theories and methods have also been introduced into the study of economic growth.

Now, there are lots of production functions and economic growth models in the international academic community. The scholars study economic growth from their own perspectives and on some theoretical basis. As a result of the authors' exploration over the years, this book analyzes a dozen countries' drivers of economic growth from the perspective of the synergy theory. In terms of theoretical basis, the economic growth models are established, and the empirical results of more than a dozen countries are analyzed. The synergy theory neither tends to capital determinism nor to innovation determinism. It tends to show that material capital, human capital, science and technology, institution, labor force, and the economic environmental externalities determine economic growth together. Of course, the contributions of these factors in the economic growth are different in different countries and periods. For example, since 1982, the contributions of technological innovation (scientific and technological progress), human capital innovation (improvement of per-capita years of schooling), and institutional innovation have been more than 60% in the United States. Therefore, the United States' economy is driven by innovation. From 1978 to 2000, the contribution of capital (physical capital stock and investment in physical capital) to China's economic growth was 53% while from 2001 and 2012, this number reached 78%.

This book makes a comparative study of economic growth in China and 14 developed countries over the past decades, and also builds a theoretical framework of synergy theory of economic growth. Subsequently, on the basis of the detailed data, this book establishes economic growth models for the 15 countries and measures the contribution of physical capital stocks, investment in physical capital, labor, science and technology, institutions, and economic externalities to the economic growth of these countries respectively. Furthermore, it summarizes the experiences of economic growth among these countries over the past decades, such as United States, Japan, the United Kingdom, South Korea, and Singapore. And based on the synergy theory, this book also establishes dynamic stochastic general equilibrium model groups for economic growth in South Korea and China, and studies the relationship among science and technology, economy, and ecological environment in the process of structural reforms (such as urbanization, informatization, and industrialization), which further expands the research scope of economic growth. On the basis of studies mentioned above, this book conducts a new analysis of China's gradual dual-track system reform, structural reform, and innovation-driven strategy.

This book is the result of a project of the Henan Department of Science and Technology, a project of the Henan Department of Transportation, a project of the National Natural Science Foundation of China, a project of Innovation working methodology of Ministry of Science and Technology of China, a project of the State Intellectual Property Office of China, a key project of the Chinese Academy of Engineering, a key project of the National Social Science Fund of China, and projects of the National Natural Science Foundation of China.

This book is the result of the cooperation among two teachers and some students over the years. Meng Zhan, Ma Jiao, Li Wei, Pan Song, Ma Ruijundi, Wang Mingzhao, Pu Junmin, Obaid Ullah, Wang Xianwen, Yang Ming, Jiang Chaoni, Xu Guoquan, Li Yafei, etc., as graduate students, participated in the studies. In addition, Dr. Hu Mingyuan from the School of Public Administration, Tsinghua University, Prof. Wang Jinfeng from the School of Management Engineering, Zhengzhou University, Prof. Yang Mingxing from the School of Foreign Languages, Zhengzhou University, and Mr. Chen Zhongwu from the Mount Song Think Tank also participated in the writing and translation of this book. Thanks again for guidance and support from leaders and teachers of Zhengzhou University and Dalian University of Technology.

Zhengzhou, China Jianhua Liu
Dalian, China Zhaohua Jiang

Contents

Chapter 1
Introduction

1.1 The Proposition of the Problem

New growth theories have been a hot topic in the research of economic growth since 1980, but there have been considerable empirical evidences proposing the questions to "new growth theories". Mankiw et al. (1992) pointed out that Solow-Swan neo-classical model, which included exogenous technological change and marginal return to capital, could explain the majority of cross-country difference in output per-capita, while the new growth theories cannot do this, and Neo-Schumpeter model, as a branch of the endogenous growth theory which emphasized the technology innovation and R&D, had received serious queried. The analysis result on growth accounting carried out by Jorgenson and Zhong (1989) showed that, compared to the capital accumulation, the technological change was not the main source of economic growth. According to Jones (1995) marked, after World War II, the R&D expenditure increased hugely, but the rise of productivity did not speed up, which objected to the new Schumpeter growth theory and supported the viewpoint that population growth rate was the only decisive factor in the long-term economic growth rate (Gaspar et al. 2014). Therefore, the economic growth theory needs new developments and breakthroughs (Hosoya 2012), and we need to investigate the economic growth in the new way of the new view (Liu 1998). To this end, based on the analyses of studies on China's economic growth by domestic and foreign scholars, this book establishes a new economic growth model including scientific and technological progress, human capital and other factors on the basis of the synergy theory of economic growth.

Practically, China urgently needs to transform its economic development mode. Currently, China's medium-high speed growth mainly relies on investment, and has been characterized by the extensive growth mode with hi gh levels of material consumption, energy consumption, land consumption, and water consumption. China faces the increasingly acute shortage of energy and resources, pressure on the environment etc., and China also cannot keep the high speed growth rate for a long

J. H. Liu and Z. H. Jiang, *The Synergy Theory on Economic Growth: Comparative Study Between China and Developed Countries*,
https://doi.org/10.1007/978-981-13-1885-6_1

time. Therefore, China's economy urgently needs transformation, which requires to carry out an empirical study with a new theory of economic growth, which is combined with China's reality, to find the scientific approach.

About these theoretical and practical problems, we need to explore the relationship between China's economic growth and those following factors: the growth of physical capital stock, the growth of investment in physical capital, science and technological progress, improvement on the quality of human capital, the growth of labor force, institutional innovation, and economic externalities, and then establish the empirical model of China's economic growth based on the relevant data. Thus, we continue to analyze these economic growth factors to test the new theory and guide China's economic transition[1].

To establish a new economic growth model, we firstly need to analyze the existing problems of the original model. Therefore, the study of this chapter aims to theoretically review the development of economic growth theory and analyze its existing problems.

1.2 Literature Review on Economic Growth

The modern economists' theory on economic growth originated from *The General Theory of Employment, Interest and Money* of J.M. Keynes. On this basis, the first generation of economic growth model represented by Harrod-Domar model and the second generation of economic growth model[2] represented by Solow-Swan model were established. The current mainstream model is the new growth theory model represented by Romer and Lucas (the third generation of economic growth model).

1.2.1 Harrod-Domar Model

Research on the role of science, technology, knowledge, information, and innovation in economic growth can be traced back to Smith (1972), the founder of the British classical economics. In his masterpiece *The Wealth of Nations*, he gave a high degree of recognition to the role of science and technology in production. Smith used the development of distribution of workload as a breakthrough point for the research questions. He discussed that the specialization of production would facilitate the applications of science and technology in the production, which could

[1]China proposed transformation from investment-driven to innovation-driven, then how to measure the role of innovation in the economy has become a problem that we need to study well.

[2]The basic assumption of Harrod-Domar model and the Solow-Swan model is the two-sector equilibrium model of the Keynes which means that the investment is equal to savings. On this basis, the economic growth model was derived. This section is written according to related works.

improve the labor productivity significantly. Finally, he illustrated the role of science and technology playing in the production.

Influenced by British classical economics, Marx (1978) also paid great attention to the role of science and technology played in the economic growth. He thought that science and technology progress played an important role in enhancing productivity, thus made the economic growth increased. Marx treated the high-developed of science and technology as the motivational power of all types of social progress.

The classical economics have not yet put forward a comprehensive economic growth theory model. Complete economic growth theory models have been built up in the dynamic development of Keynes macroeconomic theory during 1940s to 1950s, among which the most classical models were independently proposed by the British economist Harrod and American economist Domar. Harrod (1981) and Domar (1983) tried to integrate economic growth factors into Keynes's analysis.

The Harrod-Domar Model in economic growth theory (Harrod 1981) is derived from the basic premise of "investment = saving" under the equilibrium condition:

$$\because I = S \tag{1.1}$$

$$\therefore \frac{\Delta Y}{Y} = \frac{\Delta Y}{I} \cdot \frac{I}{Y} = \frac{\Delta Y}{I} \cdot \frac{S}{Y} \tag{1.2}$$

$s = \frac{S}{Y}$ is called as savings rate, $v = \frac{I}{\Delta Y}$ is called as capital-output ratio, and $\frac{\Delta Y}{Y}$ is written as G_W (economic growth rate under the equilibrium condition)

Then

$$G_W = s/v \tag{1.3}$$

This is the condition for achieving steady growth of the whole economy (Domar 1983).

Harrod-Domar model obscures the fact that capital-output ratio of economic development is unbalanced in various economic sectors by using a simple mathematical transformation technique and Keynes's a prior equation $I = S$. On the other hand, Harrod-Domar model assumes that the capital-output ratio in all sectors are same and constant, and this assumption does not conform to reality. Due to the different levels of factors that determine economic growth, their capital-output ratios are not same. Furthermore, Harrod-Domar model does not take into accounting the role of science and technological progress in economic growth. The model shows that in the short and medium term, there is no obvious progress in science and technology. However, long-term is only accumulation of short term and medium term, and if scientific and technological progress in short-term and medium-term is not considered, and how a long-term scientific and technological progress can exist? This contradicts the rapid development of modern science and technology. The progress of modern science and technology in economic management, economic forecasting and decision, new product development, the quality of human capital, et al., is updating every day, and this plays an important role in economic development. The neoclassical model overturns some of the metaphysical hypotheses of Harrod-Domar theory and suggests that there exists science and technological progress, and holds the idea that everything is dynamic.

1.2.2 Solow-Swan Model and Production Function Method

1.2.2.1 Solow-Swan Model

The main drawbacks of Harrod-Domar model lie in the two assumptions of constant capital coefficients and no in scientific and technological progress. In response to the problems of the Harrod-Domar model, economists represented by Solow (1989) proposed a neoclassical growth model.

The neoclassical growth model introduced the technological changes into the basic model. When there was a neutral technology change in the economy, total output growth rate, total consumption growth rate, and capital growth rate were equal to the sum of technology change rate and labor growth rate;

Income per-capita growth rate was equal to technology change rate, which suggested that income per-capita growth was caused by exogenous technology change.

Accordingly, Solow-Swan model drew the following conclusions:

(1) There was a balanced growth path in the economy.
(2) No matter the initial state of the economy, the economy would eventually return to the balanced growth path, thus the solution of balanced growth was stable.
(3) The long-term growth rate of total output had nothing to do with the savings rate. The change in the savings rate changed the income level. Therefore, the change in the savings rate only made a horizontal effect, but not a growth effect.

1.2.2.2 Solow Residual Method: Measuring the Contribution of Science and Technology Progress in Economic Growth

The so-called production function, in the opinion of the American famous economist Samuelson (1992a, b), was a kind of technical relationship which used to illustrate that how much the maximum possible output with the combination of specific inputs (production factor). The different economists tended to construct different forms of production function.

If Y represents output, K and L respectively represent capital input and labor input calculated by “physical” units. Then total production function can be written:

$$Y = F(K, L, t) \tag{1.4}$$

Solow pointed out the reason for the occurrence of t in F was to consider technological change. He pointed out that this was the technological change used in short-term expressive meaning and it expressed any types of changes in the production function, such as deceleration, acceleration, and so on.

Solow further argued that if the changes in the production function made the marginal rate of substitution between labor and capital keep constant, and only simply made the amount of output attained by a given input increase or decrease (Hu 2012), this change would be neutral technological change (Hicks Neutral Change). In this case, the form of the production function (1.4) becomes

$$Y = A(t)f(K(t), L(t)) \tag{1.5}$$

$A(t)$ is technical level.

Differential on both sides of the above formula is

$$\frac{dY}{dt} = f\frac{dA}{dt} + A\frac{\partial f}{\partial K}\cdot\frac{dK}{dt} + A\frac{\partial f}{\partial L}\cdot\frac{dL}{dt} \tag{1.6}$$

The both sides of the above formula are divided by $Y = Af$.
Then,

$$\frac{dY}{Ydt} = \frac{dA}{Adt} + \frac{A}{Y}\cdot\frac{\partial f}{\partial K}\cdot\frac{dK}{dt} + \frac{A}{Y}\cdot\frac{\partial f}{\partial L}\cdot\frac{dL}{dt} \tag{1.7}$$

Namely,

$$\frac{dY}{Ydt} = \frac{f}{Af}\cdot\frac{dA}{dt} + \frac{A}{Af}\cdot\frac{\partial f}{\partial K}\cdot\frac{\partial K}{dt} + \frac{A}{Af}\frac{\partial f}{\partial L}\cdot\frac{dL}{dt} \tag{1.8}$$

That is

$$\frac{dY}{Ydt} = \frac{dA}{Adt} + \frac{K}{f}\frac{\partial f}{\partial K}\cdot\frac{dK}{Kdt} + \frac{L}{f}\frac{\partial f}{\partial L}\cdot\frac{dL}{Ldt} \tag{1.9}$$

In the above formula, make

$$\alpha = \frac{K}{f}\frac{\partial f}{\partial K}, \quad \beta = \frac{L}{f}\frac{\partial f}{\partial L} \tag{1.10}$$

Then,

$$\frac{dY}{Ydt} = \frac{dA}{Adt} + \alpha\frac{dK}{Kdt} + \beta\frac{dL}{Ldt} \tag{1.11}$$

Make

$$a = \frac{dA}{Adt}, z = \frac{dK}{Kdt}, w = \frac{dL}{Ldt}, y = \frac{dY}{Ydt}$$

$$y = a + \alpha z + \beta w \tag{1.12}$$

This is the famous Solow economic growth equation. The contribution of science and technology progress is

$$\frac{a}{y} = \frac{y - \alpha z - \beta w}{y} = 1 - \alpha\frac{z}{y} - \beta\frac{w}{y} \tag{1.13}$$

The method by using model (1.13) to measure contribution of scientific and technological progress in economic growth is called Solow residual method.

Kendrick called a as the contribution of total factor productivity. Total factor productivity, in concept, is a kind of surplus including science and technology factor, policy factor, natural factor, institutional factor, management factor, and so on. For example, Yuan (1991) thought that the total factor productivity included: (1) science and technological progress. It provided a material basis to make capital and labor reach the appropriate efficiency level. (2) Policy. It affected the efficiency of capital and labor by influencing the enthusiasm of laborers. (3) Market. Supply of raw materials, fuel, outsourcing, etc., and products sales would directly affect the using efficiency of capital and labor. (4) Natural and other random factors. They could also affect the efficiency of capital and labor.

He pointed out that science and technological progress and policy were the most significant in economic growth, and science and technological progress was particularly important, so the total factor productivity could be used as a measure of generalized science and technology progress.

As a result, many people attempt to measure the total factor productivity using the production function method and separate out the science and technological progress from the total factor productivity.[3]

1.2.2.3 Cobb-Douglass Production Function

As for C-D productive function, it takes the form of $Y = AK^{\alpha}L^{\beta}$. This productive function reflects some hypotheses:

(1) Production function is homogeneous, that is, if $K' \Rightarrow \lambda K, L' \Rightarrow \lambda L$, then $Y' \Rightarrow A(\lambda K)^{\alpha}(\lambda L)^{1-\alpha} = A\lambda^{\alpha}K^{\alpha}\lambda^{1-\alpha}L^{1-\alpha} = \lambda Y$. That is to say, the growth rate of output Y keep the same with the growth rate of K and L.

[3]It is generally assumed that if science and technological progress, human capital, and institution are not included in the model, then these factors are included in total factor productivity.

(2) The productive subjects to the law of diminishing returns, which is, if the number of one factor remains constant, the increase of the other factors will make incremental production less and less.
(3) The technological change is neutral. This means that technological change will cause the two production factors increasing at the same rate, thus, marginal rate of substitution (the ratio of the marginal production) is constant. That is

$$\frac{\partial Y}{\partial K} = \alpha \frac{Y}{K} \tag{1.14}$$

$$\frac{\partial Y}{\partial L} = \frac{Y}{L}(1-\alpha) \tag{1.15}$$

Then,

$$\left(\frac{\partial Y}{\partial K}\right) / \left(\frac{\partial Y}{\partial L}\right) = \frac{\alpha}{1-\alpha} \cdot \frac{L}{K} \tag{1.16}$$

That is to say, it is nothing to do with technological change.
Otherwise, we can rewrite this productive function as

$$Y = A\left(\frac{L}{K}\right)^{1-\alpha} K \tag{1.17}$$

This is almost similar to the Harrod-Domar model except for $\tau = A\left(\frac{L}{K}\right)^{1-\alpha}$. However, the conclusion is that the capital coefficient will increase driven by the science and technological progress and the labor-capital ratio.

According to Cobb-Douglas model, it can be concluded that if $\dot{Y}/Y = \dot{K}/K$, which is the same as $y = z$, that is to say total output growth rate equals to the growth rate of capital, then

$$y = a(1-\alpha)^{-1} + w \tag{1.18}$$

This is the so-called long-term equilibrium growth condition. However, if $a = 0$, then

$$y = w \tag{1.19}$$

In this way, the total output growth rate is equal to the growth rate of labor.

1.2.2.4 Constant Elasticity of Substitution (CES Model)

The general form of CES is

$$Y = A[\delta_1 K^{-\rho} + \delta_2 L^{-\rho}]^{-r/\rho} \tag{1.20}$$

In (1.20), $\delta_1 + \delta_2 = 1, r \leq 1, \rho \geq -1$, where ρ and r are respectively called substitute parameter and scale parameter, and δ_1 means distribution rate.

If $\delta_1 = \alpha$, then Formula (1.20) becomes

$$Y = A[\alpha K^{-\rho} + (1-\alpha)L^{-\rho}]^{-(r/\rho)} \tag{1.21}$$

In (1.21), if $\rho \to 0$, the C-D function model is obtained. Therefore, the C-D function is a special case of the CES function. If $A = A_0 e^{\alpha t}$, and taking the natural logarithm on both sides of model (1.21), we can obtain

$$\begin{aligned} \ln Y &= \ln A - r/\rho \ \ln[\alpha K^{-\rho} + (1-\alpha)L^{-\rho}] \\ &= \ln A_0 + \alpha t - r/\rho \ \ln[\alpha K^{-\rho} + (1-\alpha)L^{-\rho}] \end{aligned} \tag{1.22}$$

The above equation is expanded for ρ by Taylor series in the vicinity of $\rho = 0$, and omit the high order infinitesimal, finally,

$$\ln Y = \beta_0 + \alpha t + \beta_1 \ln K + \beta_2 \ln L + \beta_3 \ln(K/L) \tag{1.23}$$

In the (1.22), $A_0 = \exp(\beta_0), \alpha = \beta_1/(\beta_1 + \beta_2), r = \beta_1 + \beta_2$, and $\rho = -2\beta_3(\beta_1 + \beta_2)/\beta_1 \cdot \beta_2$.

The parameters can be obtained by regression method through (1.23). The bilateral differential of (1.23) can obtain the formula as the following:

$$y = \alpha + \beta_1 z + \beta_2 w + \beta_3 \frac{dK/L}{K/L} = \alpha + \beta_1 z + \beta_2 w + \beta_3 (z - w) \tag{1.24}$$

If $z = w$, then

$$y = \alpha + (\beta_1 + \beta_2)w = \alpha + rw \tag{1.25}$$

If $\rho = r = 1$, which is to say returns to scale and substitute parameters are constant, and then

$$Y = A\left[\alpha K^{-1} + (1-\alpha)L^{-1}\right]^{-1} \tag{1.26}$$

Therefore,

$$A = \alpha(Y/K) + (1 - \alpha)(Y/L) \tag{1.27}$$

If Y/K is constant, then

$$\frac{dA}{dt} = (1 - \alpha)\frac{d\frac{Y}{L}}{dt} \tag{1.28}$$

That is to say the growth of labor productivity is determined by the science and technological progress.

1.2.2.5 Stochastic Frontier Function

The general form of this function is

$$Y = f(x_1, x_2, \ldots x_n)\exp(v - u) \tag{1.29}$$

v has a symmetry feature and obeys normal distribution $N(0, \sigma_v^2)$, u obeys the truncated normal distribution.

The natural logarithmic form of Eq. (1.29) is

$$\ln Y = \ln f(x_1, x_2, \ldots x_n) + v - u \tag{1.30}$$

When $u = 0$, the production reaches the frontier. At this time,

$$\ln Y = \ln f(x_1, x_2, \ldots x_n) + v \tag{1.31}$$

$\ln f(x_1, x_2 \ldots x_n)$ can be written by the form of trans-logarithm.

$$\ln f = \alpha_0 + \sum_i (\alpha_i \ln x_i) + \frac{1}{2}\sum_i \sum_j \beta_{ij} \ln x_i \ln x_j \tag{1.32}$$

Equation (1.32) includes CES as its special case.

1.2.2.6 Jorgenson Function

We assume that the capital stock is K, the labor force is L, the time is T, and the added value is Y. Then

$$Y = F(K, L, T) \tag{1.33}$$

The trans-log production function form of Eq. (1.33) is

$$Y = \exp[\alpha_0 + \alpha_K \ln K + \alpha_L \ln L + \frac{1}{2}\beta_{KK}(\ln K)^2 + \beta_{KL} \ln K \ln L + \beta_{KT}(\ln K)T + \frac{1}{2}\beta_{LL}(\ln L)^2 + \beta_{LT}(\ln L)T + \frac{1}{2}\beta_{LL}T]^2 \quad (1.34)$$

In Eq. (1.34), α, β are undetermined parameters which satisfy the following assumptions. Therefore, the following can be estimated by the econometric method with the support of historical data:

$$\begin{aligned} \alpha_K + \alpha_L &= 1 \\ \beta_{KK} + \beta_{KL} &= 0 \\ \beta_{KL} + \beta_{LL} &= 0 \\ \beta_{KT} + \beta_{LT} &= 0 \end{aligned} \quad (1.35)$$

1.2.2.7 Problems of Production Function Method

As mentioned above, we have discussed a number of well-known production functions. In fact, as Samuelson said, there is incalculable production function. There are many excessively strict assumptions on these production function methods, which are seriously divorced from reality and affect its applicability. For example, in Solow-Swan model, there are the following three assumptions:

(1) There are only two production factors including capital and labor, and the two production factors can replace each other.
(2) Science and technological progress is neutral.

Intuitively, this assumption separated the link among *A*, *K*, and *L*. According to the idea of Solow, it should be

$$Y = F(A, K, L, t) \quad (1.36)$$

Then

$$\frac{dY}{dt} = \frac{\partial F}{\partial A} \cdot \frac{dA}{dt} + \frac{\partial F}{\partial K} \cdot \frac{dK}{dt} + \frac{\partial F}{\partial L} \cdot \frac{dL}{dt} \quad (1.37)$$

So

$$\frac{\frac{dY}{dt}}{Y} = \frac{\frac{\partial F}{\partial A}}{Y} \cdot \frac{dA}{dt} + \frac{\frac{\partial F}{\partial K}}{Y}\frac{dK}{dt} + \frac{\frac{\partial F}{\partial L}}{Y} \cdot \frac{dL}{dt} \quad (1.38)$$

Namely

$$\frac{\frac{dY}{dt}}{Y} = \frac{A}{Y}\frac{\partial F}{\partial A} \cdot \frac{\frac{dA}{dt}}{A} + \frac{K}{Y}\frac{\partial F}{\partial K}\frac{\frac{dK}{dt}}{K} + \frac{L}{Y}\frac{\partial F}{\partial L}\frac{\frac{dL}{dt}}{L} \quad (1.39)$$

Namely

$$\frac{\dot{Y}}{Y} = \alpha_1\frac{\dot{A}}{A} + \alpha_2\frac{\dot{K}}{K} + \alpha_3\frac{\dot{L}}{L} \quad (1.40)$$

In the equation,

$$\begin{aligned} \alpha_1 &= \frac{A}{Y}\frac{\partial Y}{\partial A} \\ \alpha_2 &= \frac{K}{Y}\frac{\partial Y}{\partial K} \\ \alpha_3 &= \frac{L}{Y}\frac{\partial Y}{\partial L} \end{aligned} \quad (1.41)$$

In this way, it is not $\alpha_2 + \alpha_1 = 1$, but

$$\alpha_1 + \alpha_2 + \alpha_3 = \frac{A}{Y}\frac{\partial Y}{\partial A} + \frac{K}{Y}\frac{\partial Y}{\partial K} + \frac{L}{Y}\frac{\partial Y}{\partial L} \quad (1.42)$$

(3) Returns to scale are unchanged.

In addition, the model also assumes that capital and labor are fully utilized at all times and that economic growth is under full competition condition.

The definition of substitution elasticity is

$$\sigma = [d \ln(K/L)]/[d \ln(F_L/F_K)] \quad (1.43)$$

In the equation, $F_L = \partial F/\partial L, F_K = \partial F/\partial K$. F stands for production functions. *C-D* production function assumes that $\sigma = 1$ is not only inconsistent with most of the production phenomena, but also difficult to run an in-depth theoretical analysis on the production function.

The basic assumptions of *CES* are that substitution elasticity and the returns to scales are constant, and the input factors and products are in a perfectly competitive market. Consequently, Revandar, Hoffman, et al., put forward the variable elasticity of substitution (*VES*).

Furthermore, the main difficulty of the production function method is the problem of parameter. As Song and Tang (1992) pointed out, "the current methods of estimating α and β (such as distribution method, proportion method, empirical method, regression analysis, etc.) have either economic or mathematical assumptions, and these methods cannot be used in any case. These methods have their own advantages and disadvantages. Additionally, different methods may lead to different results. Moreover, they generally statically assume that α and β are constants. Sometimes $\alpha(t)$ appears as a negative value which makes no sense of practical significance. Therefore, the final results (estimation of α and β) will be low in reliability and instability."

Shi et al. (1988) who earlier introduced and studied China's production function method pointed out that, scholars at home and abroad have carried out extensive researches on this issue (estimation of α and β), and put forward a number of estimation methods. However, in all, they can be divided into three types including proportional method, econometric analytic approach, and rule of thumb. The above three methods have their own advantages and disadvantages, and none of them is perfect. The method of proportion requires strong economic hypothesis is not always suitable in China's case. Econometric analytic approach assumes that the rate of technological progress is constant. The rule of thumb with a certain degree of subjectivity is a more practical method of estimating the parameters.

1.2.3 New Growth Theory

New growth theory was symbolized by Paul Romer's paper *Increased Returns and Long-term Growth* published in 1986 and Lucas' paper *On the Economic Development Mechanism* published in 1988. New growth theory did not have the basic theoretical models as the neoclassical growth theory, which was mutually accepted by most economists. However, it was a loose aggregate composed of many economic growth models which were put forward by some economists who hold the same or similar views (Zhu 1999). We give some reviews of the important models:

1.2.3.1 Arrow-Sheshinski Learning by Doing Model

(1) Arrow model

The Economic Implications of Learning by Doing by Arrow (1962) is an initial attempt to make technological progress as an endogenous factor of growth model and also the ideological source of the endogenous growth theory. This book aims to propose a theory of knowledge change. Its important contribution is that it introduces the concept of "learning by doing". In Arrow model, there are two basic assumptions. Firstly, learning by doing or knowledge is the by-product of investment. Improving a manufacturer's physical capital stock will result in a corresponding increase in its knowledge stock.[4] Secondly, knowledge is a public

[4]This assumption implies that the technological progress of the manufacturers are the result of the learning by doing, and then formed the function of its physical capital stock. In terms of quantification, technology can be expressed as a function of investment, so that technology becomes an endogenous variable, thus it opening up a precedent for endogenous growth theory.

product which has a "spillover effect". Therefore, any given manufacturer's productivity is suited for the increasing function of total investment accumulated by the total industry. With the conduct of the investment and production, new knowledge will be appear and form increased returns.

Arrow believed that technological progress was a learning process, which mainly learned from the experience. However, experience was mainly derived from the "doing", so we needed "learning-by-doing". To this end, he amended model (1) and wrote the production function as

$$Y = AK^{\alpha}[b(t)L]^{1-\alpha} \tag{1.44}$$

In the equation, A is a constant. $b(t)$ is labor efficiency determined by Arrow learning function B. If there do not have depreciation, then

$$b(t) = B[K(t)] \tag{1.45}$$

According to Arrow's ideas, the following production function can also be constructed.

$$Y = A(aK)^{\alpha}(bL)^{\beta} \tag{1.46}$$

In (1.46), a and b are respectively technical innovation coefficient and learning coefficient. The two gather together represent the role of science and technology progress. A is a constant.

(2) Arrow-Sheshinski model

Sheshinski (1967) simplified and extended the structure of Arrow model in *the Optimal Accumulation with the Learning By Doing* in 1967 and proposed a simplified Arrow model known as the Arrow-Sheshinski model. The defect of this model is that the economic growth depends on exogenous technological progress which is similar to the neoclassical growth model. However, the economic growth depends on exogenous population growth. Obviously, this conclusion is incompatible with the observed truth. Nevertheless, Arrow-Sheshinski model's contributions are to make the technological progress exogenous and to establish the dynamic models of increased returns and competitive equilibrium, which have become an important theoretical basis for endogenous growth theory.

1.2.3.2 Uzawa's Optimal Technological Change Model

Uzawa (1965) described an optimal growth model that human capital and physical capital both have the ability of production in the paper of *the Optimal Technological Change in the Aggregate Model of the Economic Growth* in 1965, which based on the two-sector model. In this model, the linear output of human capital leads to an unlimited economic growth. The important contribution of

Uzawa's model is to provide a possible attempt to explain the endogenous technological changes, and it becomes an important theoretical basis for Lucas' human capital accumulation growth model as well as Romer's endogenous technological change model. The basic idea of Uzawa's model is: technological change is derived from the education sector that produces ideas. If a certain amount of social resources are allocated to the education sector, new knowledge (human capital) is produced. The new knowledge will enhance the productivity and be zero-cost assessed by other sectors. It will further improve the output of the production sector. Therefore, in the Uzawa's model, the accumulation of human capital can lead to sustaining growth of income per-capita without an external "growth engine" (Xu 2006).

1.2.3.3 Romer Model

Romer (1986) gave a step forward to Arrow model.

The four assumptions of Romer's endogenous technological change model are:

- Population and labor supply remains unchanged.
- The total human capital stock remains unchanged, and its market share also remains unchanged.
- The forgone consumption is equivalent to the transfer of resources from the consumer sector to the capital sector.
- The economy consists of three sectors: research department, it takes their human capital and knowledge as investment, and gets new designs as output (new products, new technology, etc.). Intermediate product sectors take the existing product and new designs as input, and get durable capital equipment as output. And finally, final product sectors take labor, human capital and durable capital equipment as input, and consumer goods as output (including goods used for producing new capital goods).

Hence the production function can be written

$$Y = H^{\alpha} L^{\beta} \sum_{i=1}^{A} X_i^{1-\alpha-\beta} \tag{1.47}$$

In the equation, H denotes the human capital of the final product (measured by cumulative effect of formal education or in-service education). L is Labor force (measured by the number of employees). X_i is the durable capital equipment, $i = 1, 2, \ldots$, and A is the number of equipment. Assuming that i is a continuous variable, then Romer's endogenous production function (1.47) can be expressed as

$$Y = H^{\alpha} L^{\beta} \int_{0}^{A} x(i)^{1-\alpha-\beta} di \tag{1.48}$$

1.2.3.4 Lucas' Professional Growth Model of Human Capital Accumulation

In 1988, Lucas (1988) published *on the Mechanism of Economic Development* in the *Journal of Monetary Economics*, modified the technological progress equation of Uzawa and also established a growth model of human capital. Lucas' model consists of two sub-models. The first is the "Two Periods model"; the second is the "Two Sector Model". The "Two Periods Model" divides capital into two forms: physical capital and human capital. Human capital is divided into "specialized human capital" and "primitive labor". The "Two Periods Model" thinks that the specialized human capital is the real driving force for the economic growth. Since human capital is entirely formatted outside the production process in this model, it cannot represent all the circumstances obtained by the human capital. Therefore, Lucas also proposed the second human capital model which was established on the basis of "learning by doing": "Two Sector Model". "Two Sector Model" insists that the decisive factor of output growth is the specialized human capital (specialized labor skills) which is required by the production of a commodity. There are two ways to improve human capital: school education and practical learning. The specialized human capital is mainly obtained through "learning by doing". The model emphasizes the difference between internal effects and external effects on human capital (Xu 2006).

Supposing that N represents laborers in the economy, and h represents the same level of human capital or technology for each labor. u represents a part of each worker's working time for production in the current period while $1-u$ represents the remaining part of time for each labor to accept school education, that is, human capital investment. In addition, the improvement of human capital not only has the internal effect that enhances their own production capacity, but also has the external effect that enhances the overall production capacity of society: $h_a^\gamma = h^\gamma$. In this way, Lucas expresses the form of the production function as (Shen 2003):

$$Y = A \cdot K(t)^\beta [u(t)h(t)N(t)]^{1-\beta} h_a(t)^\gamma = N(t)c(t) + dK(t)/dt \tag{1.49}$$

Thus, the form of output used by Lucas includes an assumption of increasing returns to scale: an increase in the proportion of physical capital and human capital will result in the increase in output. This output is higher than the proportion of growth due to an external spillover effect of human capital.

At the same time, the formation of human capital is not subject to the assumption of diminishing returns, and it takes a linear form of production:

$$dh(t)/dt = h(t) \cdot \delta[1 - u(t)] \tag{1.50}$$

The total utility of infinite horizon families is still represented in the following form:

$$\int_0^\infty e^{-\rho t} \cdot [(c^{1-\theta} - 1)/(1-\theta)] \cdot N(t)dt \tag{1.51}$$

The dynamic optimization problem at this time is to maximize the total utility of the household under the constraint of (1.49) and (1.50). Establishing the Current-Value Hamilton Function:

$$\begin{aligned} H(K, h, \theta_1, \theta_2, c, u, t) &= [(c^{1-\theta} - 1)/(1-\theta)] \cdot N \\ &+ \theta_1 \cdot [A \cdot K^\beta (uhN)^{1-\beta} h^\gamma - Nc] + \theta_2 \cdot [\delta h(1-u)] \end{aligned} \tag{1.52}$$

The necessary condition of dynamic optimal first-order is that (c and u are the control variables, K and h are state variables):

$$\partial H/\partial c = 0 \Rightarrow c^{-\theta} = \theta_1 \tag{1.53}$$

$$\partial H/\partial u = 0 \Rightarrow \theta_1(1-\beta)AK^\beta(uhN)^{-\beta}Nh^{1+\gamma} = \theta_2\delta h \tag{1.54}$$

$$\begin{aligned} &\partial H/\partial K = \rho\theta_1 - (d\theta_1/dt) \Rightarrow \\ &(d\theta_1/dt) = \rho\theta_1 - \theta_1\beta AK^{\beta-1}(uhN)^{1-\beta}h^\gamma \end{aligned} \tag{1.55}$$

$$\begin{aligned} &\partial H/\partial h = \rho\theta_2 - (d\theta_2/dt) \Rightarrow \\ &(d\theta_2/dt) = \rho\theta_2 - \theta_1(1-\beta+\gamma)AK^\beta(uN)^{1-\beta}h^{-\beta+\gamma} - \theta_2\delta(1-u) \end{aligned} \tag{1.56}$$

After deriving both sides of (1.53), we substitute the result into (1.55), obtaining:

$$\beta AK^{\beta-1}(uhN)^{1-\beta}h^\gamma = \rho + \theta\gamma_c \tag{1.57}$$

According to (1.49) and (1.57), we get:

$$N(t)c(t)/K(t) + [dK(t)/dt]/K(t) = (\rho + \theta\gamma_c)/\beta \tag{1.58}$$

In the steady state, γ_c and $\gamma_K = [dK(t)/d(t)]/K(t)$ are constant, so $N(t)c(t)/K(t)$ is also constant. Furthermore, we can obtain:

$$\gamma_K = [dK(t)/dt]/K(t) = [dN(t)/dt]/N(t) + [dc(t)/dt]/c(t) \tag{1.59}$$

If we let λ be labor growth rate, then $\gamma_K = \gamma_c + \lambda$. Assuming that labor remains unchanged ($\lambda = 0$), then, the growth rate of per-capita physical capital equals to the growth rate of per-capita consumption, that is $\gamma_K = \gamma_c$.

After taking the natural logarithm and derivation to both sides of (1.57), we obtain:

$$\gamma_k = \gamma_c = [(1 - \beta + \gamma)/(1 - \beta)] \cdot \gamma h \tag{1.60}$$

This shows that the growth rate of per-capita physical capital and per-capita consumption level are positively dependent on the growth rate of human capital. The investment in education and the accumulation of human capital will significantly increase the growth rate of physical capital and consumption level.

1.2.3.5 Stokey's Knowledge Spillover of New Product Introduction Endogenous Growth Model

Stokey (1988) added "new product introduction" to his model, and solved the problem that the effect of knowledge spillover or learning by doing would eventually fade and lose its status of being a growth engine as time went by. The continuous introduction of new products, continuous elimination of old products, and the learning by doing, these processes above have produced spillover effects on various products. In this way, as long as new products are continually introduced, learning by doing will continue, and thus the economy will be able to maintain sustainable growth. Stokey claimed that the only source of economic growth was knowledge spillovers, and emphasized that the investment of human capital was a key factor of introducing new products (Xu 2006).[5]

1.2.3.6 Young's Limited Growth Model of Learning by Doing

The model (Young 1991) further highlighted the limitation of learning by doing and stressed that only continuous technological progress could maintain continuous learning by doing. Otherwise, knowledge spillovers would lose the nature of the growth engine. The model constructed the hybrid model of interaction between learning by doing and invention, and the research on externalities was further expanded. In addition, uncertainties were introduced to the invented model.

Through the review of literature, we can find the difference between the new growth model and the traditional one. The traditional growth model classifies the technological change as a residual term that without being able to explain further, while the new growth model closely links the economic growth rate with the various decomposition of technical items (knowledge, human capital and endogenous technology growth) (Xu 2006).

---

[5]This is consistent with a basic view of this book (technological progress and investment, human capital promotion is in a co-relationship).

1.2.3.7 New Development of New Economic Growth Theory

The R&D endogenous economic growth model began from Romer's endogenous model proposed in 1990 and believed that an increase in intermediate input could achieve productivity growth of R&D sector. However, Jones (1995) studied the role that the R&D of OECD countries played in the productivity growth after World War II. He then found that R&D expenditure of OECD countries increased sharply after the war, and there was no substantive evidence for its improvement effect to their productivity. Thus, Jones (1995) inherited the thought of Arrow's (1962) learning by doing and established an R&D endogenous growth model. The model retained the two-sector model framework including the final output sector and the R&D sector in endogenous growth theory, so as to preserve the essential characteristics that knowledge spillovers effect over time. However, it abandoned strong assumptions conditions that the endogenous accumulated factors had a constant return to scale, and obtained the conclusion of scale-free. In Jones's two-sector model, the output elasticity of knowledge stock was no longer set to 1 as same as Romer model, but assumed to be less than 1. This assumption implied that the contribution of the population or knowledge stock to their own accumulation was not as big as the envisaged by R&D endogenous growth model.

Jones and Williams (1998) provided an approach to measure social return to R&D. They established a functional relationship between the social return rate and the proportion of R&D input in economic output, and held that the distortions of market (patent right, taxes and monopoly power) affected the proportion of R&D input in economic output, and the share did not have a relation with the function.

1.2.3.8 Other Relevant Models

(1) Technical content productive function

This productive function[6] treats technology as a means to transform a kind of resource into another kind, in other word, the conversion between inputs and outputs is achieved by the technology in the production. The technology is a combination of technoware T, humanware H, inforware I and orgaware O, namely

$$TCC = (T, H, I, O) \tag{1.61}$$

"Technical content coefficient" TCC can be defined as

$$TCC = T^{\alpha_1} H^{\alpha_2} I^{\alpha_3} O^{\alpha_4} \tag{1.62}$$

In (1.62), $0 \leq \alpha_1, \alpha_2, \alpha_3, \alpha_4 \leq 1$.

---

[6]This is the method recommended by the United Nations, which is similar to the Index System Method, but it uses the measurement form of the production function.

If $\sum_{i=1}^{4} \alpha_i = 1$, returns to scale is constant; if $\sum_{i=1}^{4} \alpha_i < 1$, then returns to scale decreases progressively; if $\sum_{i=1}^{4} \alpha_i > 1$, returns to scale increases progressively.

Deriving on Eq. (1.62), thus we can obtain the following:

$$\frac{dTCC}{TCC} = \alpha_1 \frac{dT}{T} + \alpha_2 \frac{dH}{H} + \alpha_3 \frac{dI}{I} + \alpha_4 \frac{dO}{O} \tag{1.63}$$

(2) Knowledge-based production function

The form of this production function (created by Posner, Gomulka and Cornwall and inherited by Fagerberg) is

$$Y = A_0 O^{\alpha_1} T^{\alpha_2} C^{\alpha_3} \tag{1.64}$$

In it, A_0 is a constant. O means the knowledge level on abroad. T is domestic knowledge level. C is the ability of using knowledge.

From (1.64), we can get

$$\frac{dY}{Y} = \alpha_1 \frac{dO}{O} + \alpha_2 \frac{dT}{T} + \alpha_3 \frac{dC}{C} \tag{1.65}$$

According to the above equation, economic growth depends on knowledge level on abroad (namely the technology introduction, et al.), depends on the growth of indigenous technical knowledge, and depends on growth of their ability to take advantage of knowledge.

1.3 Studies on the Relationship Between Institutional Innovation and Economic Growth

Institutional change theory in the new institutional economics starts with the point of "rational man" paradigm in neoclassical economics, taking the property right theory and the transaction costs theory as the theoretical background, and devotes to analyze the institutional functions and mechanisms and processes of institutional change (Pu 2007), attempting to explain the role and status of institution and the reasons for institutional change, as well as the relationship among these reasons in the social and economic development. Researching in this area, North made a seminal contribution; he carried out the research that combined history and experience to show the idea: The economic revolution in the history was not just caused by the technological revolution, but the institutional change paved the way for the technological revolution. A good institutional environment was an indispensable factor of economic growth. The effect of institutions on economic growth was mainly in its services and coordination functions. Institutional changes that adopted the requirements of production development would provide a good development environment for technological change and economic growth.

North put forward institutional innovation theory in *Institutional Change and American Economic Growth* (1971) of his book and analyzed the relationship between institutional innovation and economic growth. He argued that institutional innovation was a change in the existing institution that enabled innovators to gain additional benefits. The motive of institutional innovation was maximized in their personal interest. The essence was that the innovator could grasp the new chance brought by the adjustment and change of the institution to achieve the expected profit growth. The result of institutional innovation was institutional equilibrium. Institutional innovation is a variable, and institutional equilibrium may also be broken under the new external conditions and potential benefits, and thus the process of institutional change is the process of institutional equilibrium and institutional innovation alternately. The economic growth of some countries (such as the United States) can be explained through the institutional innovation process (Wang and Chen 2006).

New institutional economics believes that property right institution plays the most important role in the institution, and the causes and motivations of institutional change respectively are the definition and change of property rights. Since the state plays an irreplaceable role in the institutional innovation, government optimizes the property right structure through the implementation of institutional innovation, which is an effective way to achieve economic growth (Hou 2008).

1.3.1 The Studies of the Relationship Between Institutional Change and Economic Growth: from Kuznets to Acemoglu

Simon Kuznets emphasized the importance of the institution on the analysis of sources of economic growth. He gave a comprehensive analysis of various factors based on a large number of statistics and described the trend of economic growth from the quantitative and structural aspects. He described the institution's role in economic growth and hold the idea that a country's economic growth could be defined as "a long-term increase in production capacity of economic goods that people needs", while the enhancement of production capacity was based on an advanced technological foundation, and it needed the adjustment of institution and ideology (Dai 2008).

In an earlier study, Schultz (1968) name the institution as an endogenous variable in economic institution. He criticized that the neoclassical economics only focused on the largest oriented paradigm and never took the system and organizational conditions of maximization into account. Schultz believed that there was an intrinsic link between economic growth and structure of the economic institution. The changes of the economic institution will not only occur one time, but are constantly taking place; these things, like that people make the choice of institutional change and innovation of organizational institution, are to promote economic efficiency and economic welfare (Jin 2008).

Kormendi and Meguire (1985) and Scully (1988) respectively explored the relationship between the Gastil index, which reflected the political freedom (including the civil liberties and political rights), and economic growth in their article in recent studies and found that civil liberties slightly affected economic growth.

Knack and Keefer (1995) first used a level of property security to analyze the relationship between institution and economic growth in the economic growth literature. Their research results showed that, the protection of property rights was the key factor that affected economic growth. Mauro (1995) studied the role of the healthy institution in economic growth. His study suggested that, corruption would hinder economic growth. The institutional variable he used was the corruption index which was the mean of ICRG and BI, where BI was country risk index provided by a company called Business International (Wang and Chen 2006).

In recent years, more and more researchers have used the Economic Freedom Index to analyze the relationship between institutions and economic growth. Economic Freedom Index is provided by the Heritage Foundation and Fraser Institute in Canada. The Economic Freedom Index consists of more than a dozen economic indicators and more than 50 economic variables and its scores range from 1 to 5, and the lower scoring means a higher level of economic freedom (Wang and Chen 2006).

Barro (1996) found that, democracy had a weak negative effect on economic growth, and there was a non-linear relationship between democracy and economic growth. That is to say that if the political freedom keeps at a low level, the greater democracy freedom will promote economic growth. However, once the political freedom arrives at a reasonable level, the greater democracy freedom will hinder the economic growth. Accordingly, Barro concluded that the western developed countries should deliver their economic institution (especially the property rights institution and free market philosophy) to the poor countries to improve the welfare of these countries, rather than deliver the political institution to these countries. The reason of the conclusion is very simple: when the living standards of these poor countries have risen to a reasonable level, their political institution will be developed naturally. Early democracy can promote economic growth. However, when the economy develops to a certain extent, the democracy will have a negative impact on economic growth. Under these circumstances, the economic growth depends on the democratic institutions, and this situation often appears in the Southeast Asian countries. Jurajda and Mitchel (2001) had proved that the redistribution institution is the most important factor affecting economic growth on a global scale.

Ali (1997) found that, economic freedom affected economic growth more than political freedom and democratic power. Dawson's (1998) studies had shown that, economic freedom and economic growth had a positive correlation. Easton and Walker (1997) found that, economic freedom was an important explanatory variable in terms of steady-state level of income, and adding economic freedom to the neoclassical growth model would improve the explanation force of the model, and under the influence of a limited government's political institution, economic freedom could promote the economic growth (Wang and Chen 2006).

In recent studies, Kwan and Chiu (2015) used nine indicators to measure the institutional level: whether the country or economy has a stable political environment; whether public and civilian services is of a high quality; whether the public governance is good; whether the press is free, whether it establishes the legal protection of the rule of law, property rights, and labor protection, whether it has a convergence policy that promotes the development of the private sector; whether the business environment is beneficial to entrepreneurship business. Finally, they came to a conclusion that, there was an interaction between institutional changes and human capital, and these two factors cooperate together to promote economic growth.

According to Yang's (2015) study on foreign institutional innovation and economic growth in recent years, the current main research results include: based on the ICRG and WGI databases, Law et al. (2013) used the Granger method found that there was a two-way causal relationship between institution and economic growth in more than 60 countries. The institutional innovation was an important reason to promote economic growth in high-income countries, while economic growth was an important reason for enhancing the quality of the institution in low-income countries. Compton et al. (2013) considered "economic freedom" as a proxy variable of institution, and found that economic freedom has a positive effect on the growth of income.

Acemoglu et al. (2002), one of the representatives of the new institutional economics, studied the income reversal among countries colonized by European powers during the past 500 years, for example, countries which were relatively rich like India and Mexico are poor now, while countries which were relatively poor like Canada and the United States are extremely rich now. The study found that urbanization patterns and population density in 1500 affected income per capita through institutional changes. Thus, "the institutions hypothesis" can be proved more effectively, that is, the reason for the income reversal among countries colonized by European powers during the past 500 years is the institutional reversal. Accordingly, Acemoglu drew up the idea of "system is essential (institution matters)", denied the "geography hypothesis" (a theory holds that differences in wealth among countries are mainly determined by geographical, climatic or ecological differences) which was widely accepted before, and finally put forward the "institutions hypothesis".

Subsequently, based on his previous studies, Acemoglu et al. (2005) established a dynamic theoretical framework of institutional and long-term growth:

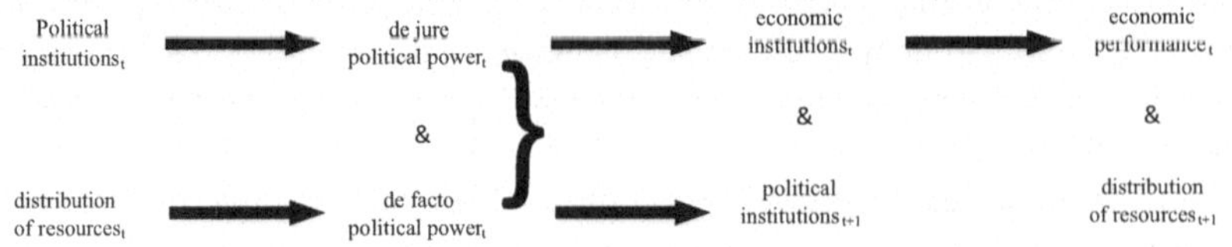

Acemoglu added the political institutions and allocation of resources to the dynamic theoretical framework of institution and long-term economic growth as the basic national variables to study the relationship between institutional and long-term economic growth. He believed that these variables basic could affect the economic institutions with the flow of time elements and ultimately have an impact on economic performance.

Acemoglu et al. (2005) first analyzed the underlying causes of the rise of Europe during 1500–1850 by establishing mathematical models. He found that the rise of Western Europe after 1500 was largely due to growth of countries access to the Atlantic Ocean and growth of substantial trade with the New World, Africa, and Asia via the Atlantic. Subsequently, he verified the relationship between the political institutions and the Atlantic trade. Through the empirical research, Acemoglu pointed out that the Atlantic trade changed the economic institutions by changing the distribution pattern of political rights and eventually promoted the rise of Europe. Accordingly, he puts forward the "social contradiction theory" decided by the institutions, that is, the different interest groups have different choices of economic institutions because of their different preferences. However, the decision of the institutions depends on the distribution of political rights in the society. Acemoglu's contributions to the new institutional economics include establishing a dynamic model of institutional change and long-term economic growth and putting forward the "social contradiction theory" decided by institutional, as well as the empirical research on the relationship between income and democracy (Acemoglu et al. 2008). Based on the study of Acemoglu and Rodrik (2004) demonstrated the relationship between economic growth, "limited" government and institutional constraints, finally he concluded that, to some extent, "limited" government and institutional constraints could promote economic growth.

1.3.2 Chinese Scholars' Studies on the Relationship Between Economic Growth and Institutional Innovation

The studies on the relationship between institutional innovation and economic growth in China mainly include: the policy of reform and opening up, empirical analysis and theory construction.

Liu and Li (2001) put forward structural analysis methods, and pointed out that, the most fundamental change in economic system was the change of ownership structure. The most prominent change in ownership structure was the increase in the proportion of non-state economy. The increase of the proportion of non-state economy improved the efficiency of labor and capital in the whole society. When the non-state economic sector expanded, the change in output elasticity of factors was determined by institutional innovation, especially the output elasticity of capital would increase significantly. Then, they constructed a production function that includes institutional innovation (the proxy variable was the proportion of non-state-owned). This study based on the mechanism of that institution affected the production factors allocation efficiency, used institutional variables (such as the proportion of non-state-owned) to construct the production function, and studied China's reform and opening up and economic growth. Especially, the research put forward the thought that the institutional innovation determined the output elasticity of factors, which became the foundation of quantitative research on the institutional innovation.

Jin (2001) believed that, from 1978 to 1999, Chinese macroeconomic institutional changes were mainly represented by the following four aspects: property right institutional change, the process of marketization, distribution pattern change and the opening up degree. On the basis of this, he defined these four institutional variables: the rate of denationalization, marketization index, the proportion of national fiscal revenues in GDP and the degree of opening up. He got the following conclusions through the method of dynamic interconnection analysis: the influence of marketization degree ranked first in China's economic growth from 1978 to 1999, and the next one was the influence of property right institutional reform (Xu 2009).

Wang et al. (2002) believed that, the main factors affecting a country's economic growth were: institution, industrial structure, labor and capital. Then, they designed four institutional variables to stand for institutions: the rate of denationalization, marketization index, the proportion of market-oriented income and the degree of opening up. They used principal component analysis to analyze the institution's contribution to economic growth (Xu 2009).

Liu (2003) summarized and criticized on relevant research results of the role of capital factor in the economic growth, and established an econometric model that used to measure the capital allocation efficiency, and then empirical analysis of capital allocation efficiency in China's economic growth. The analysis results showed that institutional defects of Chinese capital allocation made no sense of the capital allocation. In order to rationalize the Chinese capital allocation, we must innovate and improve the institutional arrangements, so that capital allocation institution would transform from "government-oriented" to "market-oriented".

Ye (2004) also constructed four similar institutional variables for empirical analysis on China's economic growth. These four institutional variables respectively were the degree of denationalization, the marketization index, the degree of social wealth possession and the degree of opening up. The result of regression analysis showed that science and technological progress and institutional innovation played an important role in China's economic growth after the reform and opening up, and they also improved the efficiency of factors. Technological and institutional innovation jointly promoted the productivity, and contributed 42.4% of economic growth and promoted 3.25% points of economic growth (Wang and Chen 2006).

Jiang and Bian (2004) adopted the quantitative indicators of institutional change, and carried out an empirical analysis on the relationship between institutional change and economic growth in Shandong province since 1978, and they found that the institutional changes had a significant contribution to economic growth in Shandong province, and the contribution was as high as percent 25.2.

Wang and Zhu (2004) used the following indexes to measure institutional change: the proportion of total imports and exports in GDP, the proportion of population in urban areas in the total population, the proportion of non-state gross industrial output value in gross industrial output value, the proportion of non-state economy sector investment in physical capital in the total social investment in physical capital, and the proportion of the number of employees in secondary and tertiary industries in the total employment. The empirical analysis of the study also shows that institutional change play a key role in affecting economic growth in Henan province, since the implement of reform and opening up. They found that the institutional change had a significant contribution to economic growth in Henan province, and its contribution was 23.17%, which showed that institutional change was an important variable to promote economic growth in Henan province, finally they gave some useful suggestions about the economic system reform (Xu 2009).

Wang and Du (2005) studied economic growth in China after the implementation of reform and opening up. Using the augmented Solow model, combined with endogenous growth theory and new institutional economics, they analyzed the mechanism of China's economic growth. Based on the data from 1978 to 2001, the panel data method was used to empirically analyze the economic growth in China. The results showed that the influence intensity of the income share of physical capital, the income share of human capital, the income share of labor, institutional change to economic growth respectively were 0.41, 0.56, 0.03 and 0.147. It can be seen that investment in education is important, and institutional change has a significant effect on the economy.

Chen (2005) used denationalization rate to stand for institutional factors (denationalization rate was calculated by the proportion of total output value of non-state industry in total industrial output value). Based on Cobb-Douglas production function, he established an econometric model by introducing variable to represent institutional factors. According to the regression analysis on the data from 1978 to 2003, he concluded that if the denationalization rate increased 1%, the production scale of economy would expand 0.23%. This showed that impact of institution on China's economic growth was evident. Therefore, it could give the suggestions on the issue of using institution to promote the western region's economic growth in exploring the western development.

Studies from Zhang (2005) adopted Jin's quantitative indicators of institutional change to establish a China's economic growth model that including institutional factor, and analyzed these factors according to corresponding indicators. Through empirical analysis of the data from 1983 to 2001, he concluded that impact of institutional factors on China's economic growth was significant. In addition, he also analyzed the role of these institutional variable in China's economic growth by the gray correlation analysis method, and got a number of useful suggestions to the government.

Song and Zhao (2005) took Jilin province as an example to calculate the influence of these following three variables on economic growth: non-public economic development levels, the degree of market-oriented and the degree of opening to outside world. Subsequently, they established a comprehensive regression model, which explained institutional factors of Jilin province and China, how to affect economic growth.

In the framework of the new classical genre, Guo (2006) analyzed the impact of institutions on economic growth, and tried to quantify the institutional factors by SEM (Structural Equation Modeling) and he concludes that the impact of labor inputs on the economy is less important than the capital investment and institutional factors to China's economic growth. Institutional factors influenced economic growth mainly through capital investment and labor input. The institutional factors played a direct negative role in economic growth, but institutional factors played a positive role in economic growth on the whole.

Based on the data from 1985 to 2003 in Ningxia, Han and Zuo (2006) used Cobb-Douglas production function to study, and they got the result that the institutional factors had significant contribution (the contribution was 7.15%) to economic growth among all these factors.

Gao and Sun (2006) chose capital, labor and institution as three factors that influenced economic growth to build a three-factor model by using the panel data from 1978 to 2003 of the 28 provinces and econometric methods to estimate and test the econometric model. Then, they had proved that the difference of institutional change was the main reason of inter-regional differences in economic growth.

Starting from the Cobb-Douglas production function, Yang (2006) established a quantitative relationship model between economic growth and the growth of other factors. Combined with Chinese specific circumstances, he introduced some variables (human capital, R&D capital, industrial structure, property rights institution, marketization degree and the degree of opening up) to this model. Based on the relevant data from 1978 to 2003, he calculated these influencing factors' contribution to economic growth, which further demonstrated the relationship between various factors and economic growth. The contribution of marketization degree and the degree of opening up (these two factors on behalf of institutional changes) to economic growth respectively were 16.91 and 15.14%, which meant that the improvement of marketization degree and the degree of opening up would improve China's economic growth.

Based on quantitative analysis on economic growth factors in Changsha City, Wu (2006) concluded: capital stock, the government expenditure, labor input and marketization degree were important factors of economic growth in Changsha, and the impact coefficient of marketization degree on economy was 0.5565.

Li (2005) used a similar model to conduct a quantitative analysis on determining factors of economic growth in Hubei province. He calculated the contribution of capital factors, institutional factors and labor factors to economic growth. The degree of opening up and marketization degree contributed to economic growth at the rate of 1.42 and 12.81% respectively in Hubei Province.

Deng and Li (2006) did the similar work that established an econometric model for economic growth, in which including the number of labor input, the industrial structure change index, institutional change index, physical capital stock, human capital stock and labor productivity. They also gave an empirical analysis on the contribution of the institutional change, industrial structure change, capital and other factors to economic growth in Hunan province. And they found that the institutional factors contributed 7.49% to economic growth (Xu 2009).

Based on Chinese data from 1982 to 2004, Huang (2007) used factor analysis and principal component regression method to give an empirical analysis on China's economic growth factors. He argued that these following five factors is the most important factors to economic growth: government consumption, the institutional changes, physical capital, domestic residents' consumption and R&D. The regression coefficients of these five factors were as follows: 0.17912, 0.11636, 0.11103, 0.10954 and 0.09277. Therefore, the effect of institutional change on economic growth ranks second among these factors (Xu 2009).

He (2007) made a regression analysis on these relevant factors of economic growth, based on the statistical data from 1953 to 2004, and concluded that the correlation coefficients of capital and labor inputs with economic growth were 0.6739 and 0.4223, while correlation coefficient between institutional variables and economic growth was 0.0176. He thought that long-term impetus to China's economic growth came mainly from the factor input, and the efficiency of factor inputs was related to a number of non-economic factors that were made by the economic development strategy.

At present, Chinese research on the contribution of institutional innovation to economic growth during the period of China's reform and opening up is represented by Liu's structural analysis method. The main idea of structural analysis method is selecting variables of institutional innovation at first, such as the increased proportion of non-state-owned, increased marketization degree, distribution pattern changes and expansion of opening up, and then constructing the production function. In the production function, the institutional innovation determines the change of the factor output elasticity. This method is first proposed by Chinese scholars in the international academic field, which lays the foundation for the quantitative research of institutional innovation. On the basis of this, the institution determines the allocation efficiency of production factors, the scholars calculate the contribution of institutional innovation to economic growth by the method of non-parametric Data Envelopment Analysis (Jiang 2003). Scholars not only get the results consistent with the actual (1978–2012 China, 1992–2002 the United States, 1980–2010 the United Kingdom, 1987–2000 New Zealand, 1980–2000 Ireland, etc.), but also find the reasons why the production factors allocation efficiency of the country increases (or decrease).

Based on the basic principle of structural analysis that institution determines the allocation efficiency, the calculation method of this book adopts the objective measurement method (DEA method does not need to estimate the parameters), which only needs these data as follows: physical capital stock, human capital stock and labor stock and GDP. In a word, this method is more simple and practical, and in particular the measured results are in line with the economic reality. Therefore, DEA method can be used for empirical measurement and further analysis of a country or region or industry. And, the method of structural analysis adopts “the proportion of non-state-owned” as the proxy variable to measure the contribution of institution, the measurement results are consistent with the resource allocation efficiency of production factors measured by this book. For example, in 1977–2012, the resource allocation efficiency of production factors is mainly determined by “the proportion of non-state-owned”. The structural analysis method can figure out the reasons, determined factors and path of institutional innovation, therefore, it can be better to analyze the contribution of institutional innovation to economic growth with the method of efficiency analysis (DEA).

The measurement results of this book in China show that institutional innovation plays an important role in China’s economic growth after the reform and opening up. The contribution of institutional innovation to economic growth has reached to 31% on average during 1978–2000, and has reached to 5% at an average from 2001 to 2012. In the current state that the new economy enters into the new normal, only by deepening reform comprehensively and conducting vigorous institutional innovation can we achieve the goal of sustained and rapid economic growth.

1.4 The Analysis of Mapping Knowledge on the Evolution of Economic Growth Theory

This book selects the network version of Web of Science database constructed by American Institute for Scientific Information (ISI). It reveals the inherent relationship among economic growth literature by Web of Science Citation Index, and reflects the evolution of the economic growth theory.

The book searches in three citation databases of SCI-EXPANDED, SSCI, A & HCI in the Web of Science, and sets timespan = all years. The retrieval type is Topic = (“economic * growth” and model *), and the refine result is Categories = (ECONOMICS). Finally, the research draws a total of 3341 data records (each data record includes title, author, summary and citations of the literature). Considering that the analysis on evolution of economic growth theory requires a longer period of time to observe, according to the characteristics of downloaded data and the development stage of economic growth model, the data can be divided into two periods of 1957–2000 and 2001–2010. CiteSpace software developed by professor Chen Chaomei in Information Science and Technology Institute of United States Drexel University,[7] is used to draw knowledge map (Chen 2010).

---

[7]At present, CiteSpace software developed by Professor Chen Chaomei has been widely used in mapping knowledge graph of all kinds of natural science theory and social science theory. Therefore, the theoretical leading edge and hot spots are revealed.

1.4.1 Main Representative and Their Important Works

Make a citation analysis on literature in 1957–2000 years. The key nodes in the citation network represent representatives and their important works in the development of economic growth model. The earliest key node in the map is "Towards a Dynamic Theory. *Some Recent Developments of Political Economic and Their Applications to Policy* published by Harrod in *Economic Journal* in 1939. In this article, Harrod proposed the famous Harrod model. There are two key nodes closely linked to Harrod model. One is the book of *A Neo-classical Theory of Economic Growth* published by James E. Meade in 1961 and the other is the article of *Neutral Inventions and the Stability of Growth Equilibrium* published by Uzawa in 1961. As it is shown in citation network map, *A Contribution to the Theory of Economic Growth* published by Solow in 1956 takes the form of a purple circle in the map. Its betweenness centrality is the highest and it is 0.22, which indicates that the structural property of the literature is high. Therefore, the Solow model proposed in the literature becomes a key node in the model evolution (Fig. 1.1).

1.4.2 Development Vein of Economic Growth Theory

The economic growth theory studies the role that each growth factor in economic system plays in economic growth. According to its development vein and internal relations, the economic growth theory has gone through three stages: capital determinism, exogenous knowledge (technological progress) determinism and

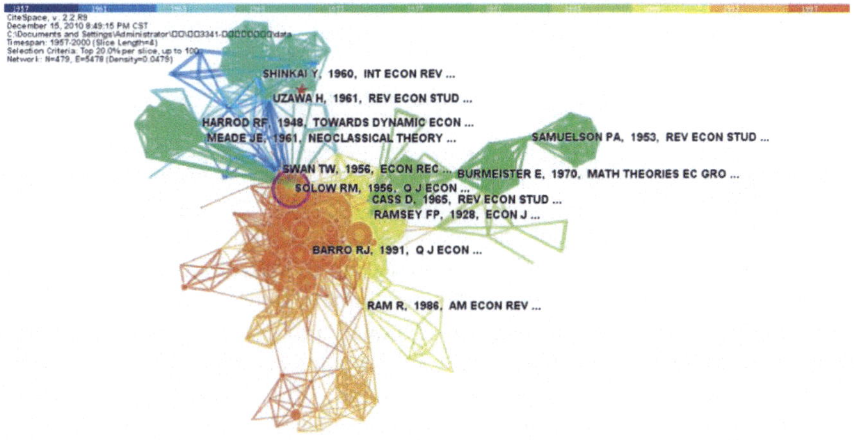

Fig. 1.1 Citation network of economic growth (1957–2000)

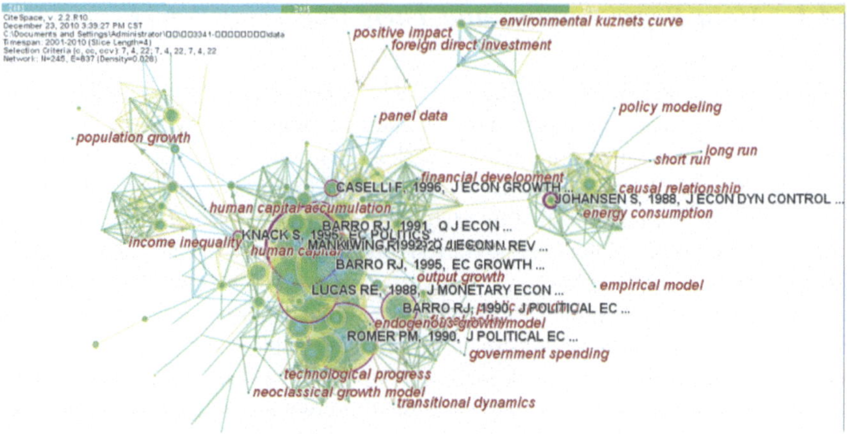

Fig. 1.2 Citation network of economic growth (2001–2010)

endogenous knowledge (technological progress) determinism (Xu 2006). Among them, the capital determinism is represented by Harrod-Domar model of classical growth theory. The exogenous knowledge (technological progress) determinism is represented by the Solow model of neoclassical growth theory. The endogenous knowledge determinism is represented by endogenous growth theory, including knowledge spillovers model of Romer and human capital spillover model of Lucas. From Fig. 1.2, it can be seen, representatives' papers of endogenous growth theory, such as Barro, Lucas, Romer, etc. occupy the central position in citation network.

1.5 The Inclusive Evolution of Economic Growth Model

1.5.1 Evolution Type of Scientific Theory

1.5.1.1 Game Evolution

The thought of game evolution can trace back to mid-20th century, and Nash's "explanation of group behavior" is considered to be the earliest achievement of evolutionary game theory (Wang 2009). It is a new theory which combines the game theoretic analysis with dynamic evolutionary process analysis. Its basic idea is that players engage in repeated games activities in game group of a certain size. Due to limited rationality, players cannot find the optimal balance point in every game. Therefore, the best strategy he thought is to imitate and to improve the most advantageous strategy of themselves and others in the past (Zhu and Zhang 2010).

1.5.1.2 Kuhn Evolution

Kuhn evolution is also known as paradigm evolutionary.[8] Paradigm defined by Kuhn is a common belief of a scientific community in a profession or discipline, which defines their common basic views, basic theory and basic methods, and provides them with a common theoretical models and frameworks to solve the problem, thus becoming a common tradition of the science, and providing a common direction for the development of the discipline. Kuhn evolution follows the rule: proto-science → conventional science → anomaly and crisis → scientific revolution → new normal science (Li 2013).

1.5.1.3 Inclusive Evolution

Inclusive evolution follows a common methodology and framework in the course of evolution. The theory of new stage contains important theoretical results of the previous stage theory, and the development based on the results. The connotation of inclusive evolution can be examined as the following:

(1) Inclusiveness reflects the accommodation to existing theoretical views. In the process of inclusive evolution, all the schools have the same theoretical foundation and ideology. That is to say scholars have reached an agreement on the basic theoretical concepts. The development of theory is not skeptical and controversial to the basic theory, but to further research on the related theory and continue to integrate into their own new ideas on the basis of the existing theories. Therefore, dominant performances of inclusiveness are accommodation, perfection and improvement of the current views (Li 2013).
(2) Inclusiveness reflects the affirmation to exist research methods. The specific performance is that inclusive evolution has a strong path dependence. Path dependence was first used to explain the evolution of the economic institution. The path dependence refers to the process of theoretical development, when scholars choose a research method, due to the drive of inertia force, this method will be made self-reinforcing, which makes it difficult for the later researchers to get out of the theoretical model. North believed that the path dependence was similar to "inertia" in physics. Once a path is chosen, it is possible to depend on the path. Predetermined direction of a path will be self-reinforcing in the future development. The selections people used to make determine their current and future possible options (Li and Wang 2009). When the selections enter the locked state, it is very difficult to set up new paths. For researchers with different emphases, in the process of inclusive evolution, they will accept the

---

[8]Kuhn's paradigm theory is one of the most important theories in philosophy of science. His scientific evolution theory is based on a systematic study on the history of scientific development and a large number of case studies. There are similar studies, such as Popper's perjury, Lakatos's the methodology of scientific research programs, and so on.

ways and theoretical models used by scholars to study the issue at the present stage, and follow a common guiding ideology. In short, there is consistency existing in the framework and thinking used to solve problem.

Inclusive evolution includes the following four characteristics:

(1) From the point of the assumption, inclusive evolution includes the evolution of the basic assumptions. It is a process of "gradually assume → gradually progress → close to reality". Because the development of various theories is based on certain assumptions to draw a conclusion by logical deduction and reasoning process, more realistic assumptions will promote the conclusion closer to reality. If with hypothetical evolution as the logical starting point, development path can be attributed to four different stages including neoclassical economics, information economics, new institutional economics and sustainable development economics. The basic of neoclassical economics analysis is hypothesis of rational man (to minimize the economic costs which are used to pursue the maximum economic benefit), complete information hypothesis (full information between two transactions sides in the economy), scarcity hypothesis (resources cannot meet the growing demand), established market economy institution hypothesis, etc.; information economics amendments make information hypothesis more realistic. That is to say that the information owned by two transactions sides in realistic economy is asymmetric; the new institutional economics treats the information as a scarce and expensive commodity, so the access to information is also a kind of transaction, and the access of it needs to pay some fees—"information costs", as part of the transaction costs. In addition, the new institutional economics also makes three amendments for rational man hypothesis. First one is the limited rationality of people. Second, people's behavior is not only for the pursuit of wealth maximization. Third is people's opportunism behavior tendency. Since the premise of new institutional economics assumptions is closer to reality, thus there is more explanatory power to the real problem (Chen and Rao 2005). The sustainable development economics makes amendments for rational man hypothesis and scarcity hypothesis. There are some alternatives between different resources in neoclassical economics while irreplaceability of resources in sustainable development economics is restricted largely. The irreplaceability of some scarce resources poses a challenge to sustainable development of human. At the same time, human is no longer "rational man" that plunders nature infinitely to pursue profit maximization, but "environmentalists" with long-term development vision. The inclusive evolution in this study developed original theory through continuous improvement of the assumptions which do not match the reality. Therefore, theoretical achievement developed has a greater capacity to solve practical problems than the former.

(2) From the view of variables needed by model, inclusive evolution is a process that maintains existing variables and constantly add new explanatory variables, and at the same time, evolution implies endogenous of kernel variables.

Namely, kernel variables in the model transform from exogenous to endogenous. Firstly, we need to distinguish variables between endogenous and exogenous variables. The endogenous variable in the theoretical model is determined by a given economic system model itself. The exogenous variables in the theoretical model cannot be decided by economic system model, if other factors other than the model. That is to say, in the theoretical model, when a variable is used to explain other variables, but its own cannot be explained by the other variables in the model, this variable is exogenous variable; the variables that can be explained by the other variables in the model are endogenous variables (Wang 2008). On the one hand, inclusive evolution constantly adds new variables in the model. On the other hand, we integrate new variables into the model to achieve endogenous interpretation of the original kernel variables.

(3) From the perspective of the production function, inclusive evolution is a process that model species increase constantly. Production function embodies the relationship between the maximum output and the amount of a variety of production factors used to reach the output in a given period and a particular level of technology. When the existing production function can make a reasonable explanation for continuous growth of economy, inclusive evolution based on the original production function will seek changes in types of the production function to increase the explanatory power. In the process of inclusive evolution, in the proposition of the new assumptions and constant introduction of new factors, scholars make variables of the production function change.

(4) In terms of the future development of model, modeling and theoretical basis of inclusive evolution need a breakthrough. Because inclusive evolution is based on the existing framework and theoretical model, research is much overcautious, and construction of the model lacks of innovation. The theoretical basis that the model relies on has not been out of the constraints of original standard, and it lacks of a comprehensive comparison with other methods, so that the further development is limited. At the same time, strong path dependence also develops a psychological contract in researchers' hearts. When the thought contrary to the original theoretical basis appears, it will be rejected and resisted by the researchers. Therefore, this concept of inertia makes it difficult for evolution to make a breakthrough to new theoretical approaches.

1.5.2 *Inclusive Evolutionary Tracks of Economic Growth Model*

Though the above analysis on the evolution of representative economic growth mode, we get the following four tracks and directions of the evolution:

(1) The model assumptions are closer to reality, and adaptability is stronger.

Harrod-Domar model only includes two production factors: capital and labor. Supposing the capital-labor ratio constant, constant production returns to scale, diminishing marginal returns of factors, and production technology unchanged; Solow-Swan model relaxes the assumption existed in Harrod-Domar model, and thinks that capital and labor can substitute for each other, and the capital-labor ratio is variable. At the same time, the model takes the impacts of technological progress on economic growth into account, and assumptions on economic growth are closer to reality; Arrow model treats knowledge as a by-product of the investment, and assumes that knowledge as public goods has "spillover effect". The model sees the technological progress as an endogenous variable determined by investment; Uzawa model assumes that there is education sector in economics, which endogenizes partial effects of exogenous technological progress in the Solow model; Romer inherits the "spillover effect" idea of Arrow and thinks that knowledge is the byproduct which results from profit-seeking firms' investment; Lucas improves the two-sector model of Uzawa and assumes that each producer not only works on production but also improves human capital by learning. Finally, Uzawa has revealed that human capital is the continuing root of the sustained economic growth, which is in line with economic development status; The model including institutional factors introduces institutional assumptions into the process of economic growth, to make an explanation on economic development of developing countries in context of complex institution; economic growth model including ecological capital increases assumption about ecological capital, and highlights the role of environmental factors in economic growth. Therefore, from the overall point of view, the development of the model is also a process that assumptions are closer to reality (Li 2013).

(2) More factors are considered to establish the model, and variables are increasingly abundant.

Harrod-Domar model sees capital and labor as important factors of economic growth, and thinks that the fundamental force of economic growth is the accumulation of physical capital. Solow-Swan model introduces technical factors into the analysis of growth model on the basis of Harrod-Domar model, and draws the final conclusion that the per-capita output of the labor force is determined by technology, investment rate and population growth rate; Arrow model not only confirms the promotion of technological progress on economic growth but also achieves a part of the endogenous interpretation of technological progress from the perspective of the knowledge accumulation; Romer introduces directly the human capital factor into the model, while human capital spillover model of Lucas achieves the endogenous technological progress from the point of human capital; the model containing institutional factors is gradually aware of the promotion and inhibition of institution on economic growth, and introduces variable of institution into the model, which begins to demonstrate that the some policies of government can promote economic growth, but some policies will play an impedimental role in economic growth; the economic growth model including ecological capital stresses the influence of ecological environment on economic growth, which is closer to the current status of economic development. The specific process of factors endogenesis is shown in Fig. 1.3 (Li 2013).

(3) From the point of the production function, there are more and more different types of models.

In the evolution of the economic growth model, the increments of the production function model are shown in the following aspects: firstly, the inclusion of factors lead to the growth of model categories. The Solow-Swan model and Arrow model introduce technological progress factors. Lucas' human capital spillover model establishes the relationship between human capital and technological progress, and the economic growth model including institutional factors and ecological capital also adds the research of relationships among institutions, ecological capital and macro production function. Secondly, the endogenesis of core factors in the model causes the amount of model types increasing. In the process of the factor endogenesis in the model, endogenous factors become critical for economic development. It keeps evolving with the development of economy, and the economists explain from endogenesis of exogenous variables in terms of knowledge, human

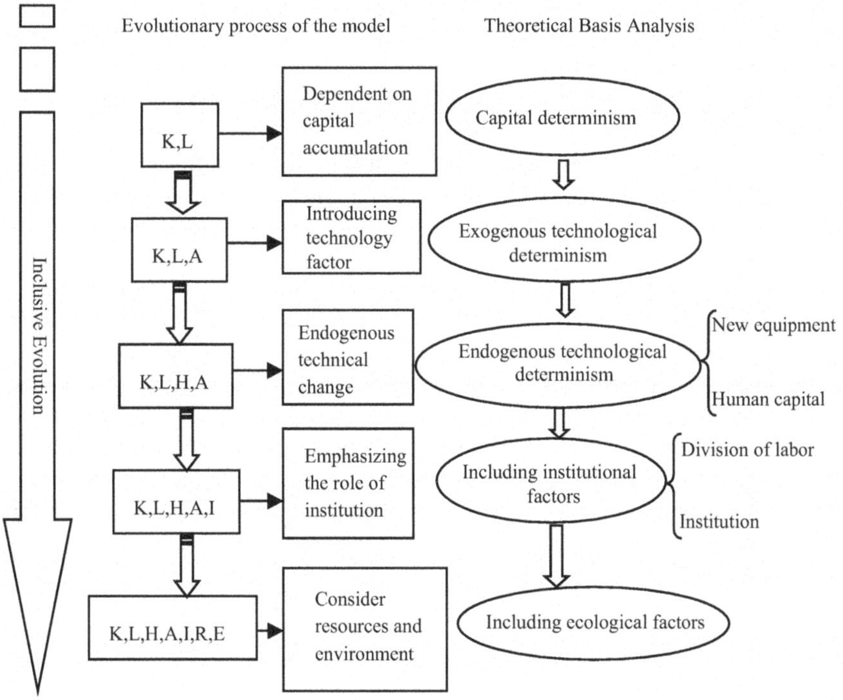

Fig. 1.3 Inclusive evolutionary analysis framework of economic growth model (Wang and Niu 2005)

capital, etc., which respectively leading to growth of model types. Thirdly, the division of the productive sectors results in the increase of the model types. For example, Uzawa model assumes that there is the education sector in economic systems except the production sector, and Romer divides it into research sectors, intermediate goods sector and the consumer goods sector. This division of the economic sectors can also get different production function types. Thus, in the evolutionary of the economic growth model, with the continuous improvement of assumptions, the successive introduction of economic variables, achievement on endogenesis of core factors and meticulous division of economic sectors, the number of model types also tends to increase (Li et al. 2013).

(4) From the perspective of modeling, the construction of phasing model depends on a common theoretical framework.

From classical economic growth model to the neoclassical economic growth model, they are based on Cobb-Douglas production function. In the process of evolution, the model incorporates different economic growth factors at different stages, and transform exogenous variables into endogenous constantly, so they adopt the consistent modeling method; in the new growth theory, since the dynamic equilibrium problems of economic decentralization began to be focused, dynamic general equilibrium analysis is introduced; the model including institutional factor and the model containing ecological capital are still based on Cobb-Douglas productive function. Thus, the evolution of the economic growth model urgently needs new theoretical framework as a support. In the future development of the economic growth model, the modeling method and theoretical basis need further breakthroughs.

Table 1.1 shows the evolutionary track from Harrod-Domar model to the model including ecological capital, evolutionary path of the model in assumptions and production function, and improvement and history defects comparing with the former model.

This section proposes a new evolutionary way—inclusive evolution, which is based on the game evolution and Kuhn evolution. In terms of assumptions, modeling factors, production functions, and modeling variables, they satisfy the features and mechanism of inclusive evolution though the analysis on the typical economic growth models, and which prove that the evolution of the economic growth model is a kind of inclusive evolution. The evolution of the economic growth model is badly in need of new theoretical framework as a support. In the future development of the economic growth model, modeling method and theoretical basis need further breakthroughs.

Table 1.1 The evolution of economic growth model

Items		Models	Assumptions	Production function	Improvements relative to the former
Capital determinism model	Harrod-Domar model	The equilibrium growth rate depends on the savings rate and the capital-output rate	$G_w = s/v$		Assume that savings will be fully turned into invested; Solely emphasize on the impact of capital increase on economic growth
Exogenous technological determinism	Solow-Swan neo-classical model	Capital and labor can replace each other; capital-labor ratio is variable	$Y = A(t)f(K, L)$	Consider the impact of technological progress on economic growth	The equilibrium growth rate is determined by the natural growth rate of population; technological progress is exogenous variable
Endogenous technological determinism model	Arrow model	Knowledge is a by-product of investment; Knowledge is public goods, which has the "spillover effect"	$A(t) = BK(t)^{\beta}, B > 0, \beta > 0$ $Y(t) = K(t)^{\alpha}[A(t)L(t)]^{1-\alpha}, 0 < \alpha < 1$	Consider technological progress as an endogenous variable for investment decisions	Equilibrium growth rate is determined by the natural growth rate of population
	Uzawa H model	Improve the simple Solow production department model; Assume that there is an education sector in the economy	$A = G(A, L_E)$ $Y = F(K, AL_p)$	Endogenize the partial action of exogenous technology advancement in Solow model; it is the earliest human capital growth model	Equilibrium growth rate is determined by the natural growth rate of population
	Romer's effect model of knowledge spillovers	Endogenous technological progress is the core of economic growth; assume that there are three sectors in the economy: the research department, the intermediate product sector, the consumer goods sector; knowledge is the product of investment; knowledge spillovers effect	$Y_i = AK_i^{1-\alpha-\beta} H_i^{\beta} \sum_{j=1}^{N} x_{ij}^{\alpha}$ $0 < \alpha < 1, 0 < \beta < 1$	It expands the extension of capital and introduces the human capital factors into the model	Lack of institutional research; lack of analysis of human learning mechanisms; it still uses the dynamic general equilibrium model
	Lucas model	Improve Uzawa's Two-Sector Model; assuming that each producer is engaged in production, and	$Y(t) = K(t)^{\alpha}[u(t)h(t)N(t)]^{1-\alpha} h_E^{x}(t)$ $dh/dt = h(t)\delta[1 - u(t)]$	It reveals that human capital is the source of sustained economic growth	

(continued)

Table 1.1 (continued)

Items		Models	Assumptions	Production function	Improvements relative to the former
		improves human capital through learning			
	Becker and Murphy model	The increase of specialization or knowledge stock will improve the level of per-capita output; the evolution of division of labor is limited by the cost of coordination; the growth of human capital (knowledge), the progress of technology and the decrease of coordination cost will promote economic growth	$y = AY^{\alpha}n^{\theta} - \lambda n^{\beta}$ $C = \lambda n^{\beta}$ $Y = AH^{\alpha}n^{\theta}$	The division level of labor is determined by the cost of coordination and the level of social knowledge; the mutual promotion of evolution of labor division and knowledge accumulation determines economic growth	
	The model of direct introduction of institutional factors	Social endowment is units of labor and units of human capital; labor is only involved in the production of the final product; part of human capital engaged in institutional innovation, and the other is engaged in technological innovation	$Y = AK^{\alpha}H^{\beta}(IL)^{1-\alpha}$ $dA/dt = \theta(H - H_1)A$	It introduces the institutional factors into the economic growth model	
Model of ecological capital		Assume that the ecological capital model is similar to the physical capital model; the ecological capital loss caused by nature is zero; ecological capital stock is not less than its rigid threshold	$Y(t) = K(t)^{\alpha}H(t)^{\beta}E(t)^{\gamma}[A(t)L(t)]^{1-\alpha-\beta-\gamma}$ $E(t) = s_E Y(t) = mE(t)$ $E(t) = E(N, P, Y, P_d, C, \ldots)$	The ecological capital is embedded into the model as endogenous variable	Ecological factors and capital factors are not in the same category

1.6 The Structure of Economic Growth Model and Its Methodology of Evolution

In this chapter, we elaborates the structure of the knowledge system based on certain cognitive models firstly, including the paradigm concept set and three basic concept sets. Then, we put forward the concept of modules and illustrate the relationship between modules, paradigm concept set and basic concept sets. From the view of J-system theory, we conclude various kinds of structure and evolution modes of economic growth model. On this basis, we discuss the construction of conceptual coordinate system of economic growth theory from the view of J-system theory and method.

1.6.1 Structure of Knowledge System

The unity of various scientific knowledge systems and their models in the structure and form is a research focus of general system theory (Seising 2010). R. L. Cansey, an American scholar, who has long been engaged in the study of the unity of science, pointed out that people were always interested in a unified science for a long time that may provide general descriptions of all kinds of natural phenomena and social phenomena (Haken 1992). In fact, pursuing the unity of science to a certain extent, the basic direction of the general system theory pioneered by Bertalanffy (1973).

However, J-system theory proposed by Jiang in 1990s extents one element set which proposed by Bertalanffy into three elements set (according to a certain pattern, the system is defined as an overall composed of three elements sets) (Jiang and Liu 1989). More detail theoretical research is "*J-system Reconstruct Ability: A Formalized Study*", which is published in "*International Journal of General Systems*" (Jiang 2000).

By means of case analysis, J-system theory investigated the composition of scientific knowledge system deeply and found that many knowledge systems consist of a paradigm concept set and three basic concept sets according to a certain cognitive pattern. This is a form definition of knowledge system defined by J-system theory. The so-called "J-system" satisfies the following conditions.

$$J = [P]([A],[B],[C]) \tag{1.66}$$

Or

$$J = ([A],[B],[C],[P]) \tag{1.67}$$

Or

$$J = [A]O_1[B]O_2[C] \quad (1.68)$$

where in formula (1.66)–(1.68), O_1 and O_2 are mutual actions among the three basic concept sets $[A]$, $[B]$ and $[C]$.

The paradigm concept set $[P]$ of J-system determines the way of connection among three basic concept sets, regulates the movement forms of the three basic concept sets and the connection between this system and other systems simultaneously. In other words, $[P]$ actually represents the qualitative regularity of the system.

Paradigm concept set $[P]$ is synthesized by two parts generally, that are the cognitive subject pattern K_p and the cognitive subject pattern Z_p. The object cognitive pattern is of pure quality which no subject participated in and exist objectively. According to Kant's words, it is a self-being, self-making and natural quality, and it is abundant, pure and innocent; However, no matter in the past, present and future, what we human beings are faced is not and will never be simple, but that we human beings has been practiced or detected indirectly by means of experience, feelings or theoretical concepts. So the thing is not pure itself, it is what we can take advantage of and it infiltrated with people's consciousness. Thus, there is a Z_p in the cognitive pattern which marks the factors, printed marks, and values of human consciousness. Z_p means the essential characteristics of the ways of people observing issues, doing scientific research and engaging in productive activities, and it is the quality of ideological program or behavioral manner. Therefore, Z_p is impacted by human cultural traditions, thinking mode and basic knowledge. In philosophy of science, Kuhn calls the cognitive pattern "paradigm", Lakatos calls it "research program" and Lao Dan calls it "research tradition".

As for the concept sets $[A]$, $[B]$ and $[C]$, the component elements possesses a certain relationship, sequence and structure. In general, the concept sets are provided with dynamic, integral and orderly nature.

Thus, a given J-system defined as

(1) The concept set the subset, main elements, elements of the concept set $[A]$ are written as a_i, $[A] = \{a_1, a_2, \ldots, a_n\}$
(2) The concept set the subset, main elements, elements of the concept set $[B]$ are written as b_i, $[B] = \{b_1, b_2, \ldots, b_n\}$
(3) The concept set the subset, main elements, elements of the concept set $[C]$ are written as c_k, $[C] = \{c_1, c_2, \ldots, c_n\}$
(4) The three basic concepts are combined into some kind of cognitive mode pattern $[P]$, which is described by other concept sets $[P] = \{p_1, p_2, \ldots, p_n\}$;

This is a completely formal definition, and "some" conveys the information that there may be various sorts of $[P]$, and each of the specific $[P]$ corresponds to the concrete three concept sets thereby corresponds to a sort of knowledge system.

1.6.2 Multiform Models of Economic Growth Theory

Thus, beginning with the formal analysis of many specific scientific models, J-system theory further abstracts the various types of formal models and sums them up into five kinds of simple formal models. And we find that many models can be regarded as one, made up of three or four modules.

1.6.2.1 Module

(1) The concept of module

Module is composed of several conceptual variables and it is an integrated body of symbols with specific meaning. For example, the three modules in Newtonian mechanics of rigid motion are M (inertia), F (torque), $\frac{d^2x}{dt^2}$ (acceleration). The module has a clear "physical meaning" or "chemical meaning" etc. that they contain specific and scientific meaning in model.

(2) The relationship between the module and the model

Model simply consists of modules, while modules can be very complex. If we compared the model to the furniture assembled by building blocks, the building blocks are the modules.

In Cobb-Douglas' production function model $Y = aK^{\alpha}L^{\beta}$ of economic growth theory, a, K^{α} and L^{β} are the three modules (Romer 1999), while $K(\mathrm{t})^{\alpha}$, $[A(t)]^{1-\alpha}$, $[L(t)]^{1-\alpha}$ are the three modules in Arrow model $Y(t) = K(t)^{\alpha}[A(t)L(t)]^{1-\alpha}$.

Jones and Manuelli (1990) constructed a productive function model as follows

$$Y = AK + \Omega(K, L)$$

A simple form is

$$Y = AK + BK^{\alpha}L^{\beta}$$

It is incomplete from the point of view that we discuss. And the complete model should consist of three modules.

(3) Model is constructed by module

A knowledge system is constructed by three basic concept sets ($[A]$, $[B]$ and $[C]$) and a paradigm concept set ($[P]$) according to the cognitive pattern. Modules are intermediate products in constructing model. A, B, C and P are the "module" that integrated by some elements in $[A]$, $[B]$, $[C]$ and $[P]$ through some mathematical operations, referred as block A, block B, block C, block P. The model is constructed by the module A, B, C and P.

In general, modules A, B, C and P are codetermined by $[A]$, $[B]$, $[C]$ and $[P]$, and there is no simple corresponding relation between them. However, in usual, A is determined by $[A]$ largely and generated based on $[A]$. Similarly, B is determined by $[B]$ largely and is generated based on $[B]$; C is determined by $[C]$ largely and is generated based on $[C]$; P is determined by $[P]$ largely and is generated based on $[P]$. A more detailed description is shown in Fig. 1.4.

1.6.2.2 The Wholes and Parts Model

There are totally 5 categories of formalized models in J-System: the whole and parts model, causal model, control model, optimization model and evolutionary model.

The whole and parts model reflects the relationship between the entirety and the portion. Its formal model is:

$$J = (A, B, C) \tag{1.69}$$

The three more specific forms of (1.69) are

$$J = Ao_1Bo_2C \tag{1.70}$$

$$J = A \pm B \pm C \tag{1.71}$$

$$J = A \cdot B \cdot C \tag{1.72}$$

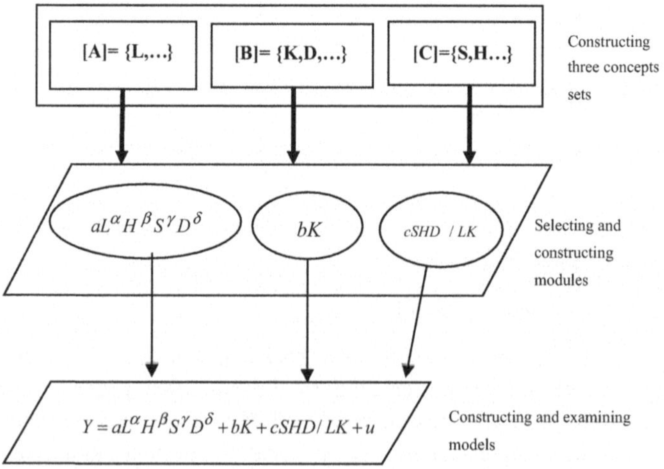

Fig. 1.4 Logic of economic growth modeling based on synergy theory

As for (1.71), a well-known example in economics is GDP = consumption + investment + net exports; as for (1.72), another well-known example in economics is Cobb-Douglas production function model $Y = aK^{\alpha}L^{\beta}$ which includes three modules a, K^{α} and L^{β}, while Y (GDP) is an integral nature of economic system. However, the economic growth model based on synergy theory has the form of $J = A + B + C$.

1.6.2.3 Causal Model

Causal model reflects the causal relationship among the three sets which constitute the system. Its formal model is:

$$BOA \Rightarrow C \tag{1.73}$$

In (1.73), O is the interaction between A and B.

Depending on different explanations for "O" and "⇒", formula $BOA \Rightarrow C$ has different specific forms, for instance:

$$A \pm B = C \tag{1.74}$$

$$B \cdot A = C \quad \text{or } C = A/B \tag{1.75}$$

Harold-Thomas model (Harrod 1981) in Economic Growth Theory has such a form:

$$G_w = s/v \tag{1.76}$$

1.6.2.4 Optimization Model

Many optimization problems in the field of science, engineering project, society and economy can be ultimately summarized as solving a function optimization problem with a constraint. The general form of the optimization model can be written as

$$\begin{aligned} &\min C \\ &s.t. A \leq B \end{aligned} \tag{1.77}$$

where C is the optimization function, A and B are the constraints.

The general equilibrium problem based on the economic growth theory has such a form. For example, the optimal function of the optimal design problem of China's sustained economic growth and transformation in 2015–2020 discussed in the previous chapter is

$$\int_{0}^{\infty} \frac{C^{1-\theta}}{1-\theta} e^{-pt} dt \tag{1.78}$$

A constraint model is a transforming form of economic growth model which is

$$\dot{K} = a(HL)^{\alpha}(SD/L)^{\beta} + bK + cHSD/K^2 + u - C - \delta K - C_1 \tag{1.79}$$

1.6.2.5 Control Model

The general control model is the following nonlinear system:

$$\frac{dx}{dt} = f(x, u, t) \tag{1.80}$$

$$y = g(x, u, t)$$

where $x = (x, x, \ldots, x^{n-1})^T \in R^n$ is the state vector of the system, and u $\in R, y \in R$ are respectively the input (economics calls it an exogenous variable or a random variable) and output (economics calls it an endogenous variable or a controlled variable) of the system. $f(x)$ is a smooth vector field of R^n, $h(x)$ is the smooth function of R^n.

The authors of this book in the *Innovation Driven and Upgraded in the New Normal: A Case Study of Henan Province* set up a linear solution of the model DSGE (Dynamic Stochastic General Equilibrium), which has such a form. And there are two major linear forms of the model

$$\begin{aligned} 0 = & -y_t + a_1 k_{t-1} K/Y + a_2(d_t + s_{t-2} - k_{t-1})DS/YK + a_3 DS/YL(d_t + s_{t-2} - l_t) \\ & + (DS/L)^{\alpha_1} \cdot (ELL)^{\alpha_2}(\alpha_1 d_t + \alpha_1 s_{t-2} - \alpha_1 l_t + \alpha_2 e_t + 2\alpha_2 l_t)/Y \end{aligned} \tag{1.81}$$

$$0 = -new_t + a_3 p_t + a_4 zf_t + a_5 n_t + a_6 p_{t-1} \tag{1.82}$$

Equation (1.81) is the linearization of economic growth model, and (1.82) is the relationship model between the patent and the new product. Where $Y_t = Y(1 + y_t)$, Y indicates the trend value of Y_t and y_t indicates the deviation of the fluctuating component of the variable from the trend value Y. In the model system of (1.82), $[P_t]$ is the deviation of the fluctuation component of the state variable from the trend value, $[y_t, e_t, l_t, d_t, s_{t-2}, new_t]$ is the deviation of the fluctuation component of the control variable from the trend value, and $[k_{t-1}, n_t, zf_t]$ is the deviation of the fluctuation component of the random variable from the trend value.

1.6.2.6 Evolutionary Model

The general form of the evolutionary model can be written as

$$\frac{dC}{dt} = f(A, B, C) - g(A, B, C) \tag{1.83}$$

In (1.83), f represents the promotion and recognition to evolution, and g represents the suppression and denial to evolution.

One important result of these discussions above is that many model can be seen as a composition of four modules (A, B, C, P) or simply composed of three modules (A, B, C) while the module is complex.

1.6.3 Construction of Economic Growth Model

By means of the research towards a large number of evolutionary cases of economic growth models, the following ways of constructing economic growth models are summarized.

1.6.3.1 Analog Modeling

In the process of new model design and development process, scientists use many techniques or skills to form and define a new and good module, and in order to quicken the pace they usually depend on previous knowledge, experience and examples of models or applies analogy method intentionally or unintentionally. Analog modeling helps researchers with limited experience construct a reasonable model and solve the problem more quickly.

1.6.3.2 Inclusive Modeling

This is a process of keeping the existing variables maintained and adding new explanatory variables. Meanwhile, the evolution implies the process of core element's endogenesis, that is the core variable in the model transformed from exogenous to endogenous. From the perspective of assumptions, inclusive evolution includes the evolution of the basic factors. The process begins with gradual assumption, then successive progression, and finally closes to the reality. As the development of various kinds of theories is based on certain assumptions, and concluded by logical deduction and reasoning process, therefore, the closer the assumptions are to the reality, the closer the conclusions will be promoted to the reality.

For example, constructing a productive function according to Arrow's idea is as follow

$$Y = A(aK)^{\alpha}(bL)^{\beta} \tag{1.84}$$

where a and b are science and technological process coefficient and learning coefficient, and both of them represent the role of technological progress while A is a constant. This is an extension of the Cobb-Douglas production function essentially.

1.6.3.3 Transformation Modeling

Transformation modeling makes the structure or form of a model changed by transformation. For example, Cobb-Douglas production function is changed into

$$Y = A\left(\frac{L}{K}\right)^{1-\alpha} K \tag{1.85}$$

This is similar to Harold-Thomas model $Y = \tau K$ while $\tau = A\left(\frac{L}{K}\right)^{1-\alpha}$.

1.6.3.4 Restructuring Modeling

"Restructuring modeling" refers to the model which adds more than two new elements or variables on the original model. The general form of CES (Constant Elasticity of Substitution) is

$$Y = A[\delta_1 K^{-\rho} + \delta_2 L^{-\rho}]^{-r/\rho} \tag{1.86}$$

where $\delta_1 + \delta_2 = 1, r \leq 1, \rho \geq -1, \rho$ and r are alternative parameter and size parameter, and δ_1 is distribution rate. This can be thought of a restructure of the Cobb-Douglas production function.

1.6.3.5 Integration Modeling

Integration is an overlapping and integrated process. In scientific modeling, the integration of two or several forms of models leads to a new generation of models.

For example, the transcendental logarithm model of economic growth is a integration model

$$Y = \exp[\alpha_0 + \alpha_K \ln K + \alpha_L \ln L + \frac{1}{2}\beta_{KK}(\ln K)^2 + \beta_{KL} \ln K \ln L \\ + \beta_{KT}(\ln K)T + \frac{1}{2}\beta_{LL}(\ln L)^2 + \beta_{LT}(\ln L)T + \frac{1}{2}\beta_{LL}T^2] \tag{1.87}$$

1.6.4 Conceptual Coordinate System of Economic Growth Theory

1.6.4.1 The Production Process of Scientific Knowledge

Knowledge hierarchy is composed of the following six levels: the first level is information (data, facts); the second level is concept system; the third level is module; the fourth level is model group; the fifth-level, is theory (which consists of the concept set, module, model group and reasoning rules); the sixth level is inference, which are the conclusion, forecast (Zhao and Liu 2011) and program derived under some initial conditions and boundary conditions with the help of a variety of concepts and according to the model.

The basic path of knowledge discovery based on J-system theory (the concept proposition, the model selection and construction) and knowledge production are as follows. For the scientific question generated by an information field, firstly, a group of models is selected from a type of example model library under the frame of the formal model, according to the nature of the problem; and according to some criteria for testing, some models are eliminated, while others are persevered. Secondly, the other models are selected from the other types of example model libraries under the other frame of the formal model; and according to the criteria for testing; some models are eliminated, while others are persevered. Thirdly, the still other models are selected from the rest example model library under the rest frames of the formal model; and according to the criteria for testing, some models are eliminated, while others are persevered. Finally, the models remained on the aforementioned are improved, reconstructed and innovated; and according to the criteria for testing, some models are eliminated, while others are persevered. If the scientific, explanatory ability and foresee ability of the remained models are satisfactory, the models are regarded as the base of further research by the professional researcher, who decides which model should be adopted (Fig. 1.5).

1.6.4.2 The Conceptual Coordinate System of Synergy Theory

First the J-system method presents the four concept sets in the four quadrants of the "conceptual coordinate system," and then explores the relationship between these concepts. The two "axes" of the "conceptual coordinate system" represent the two fundamental, mutually corresponding and "contradictory" contradictions of the

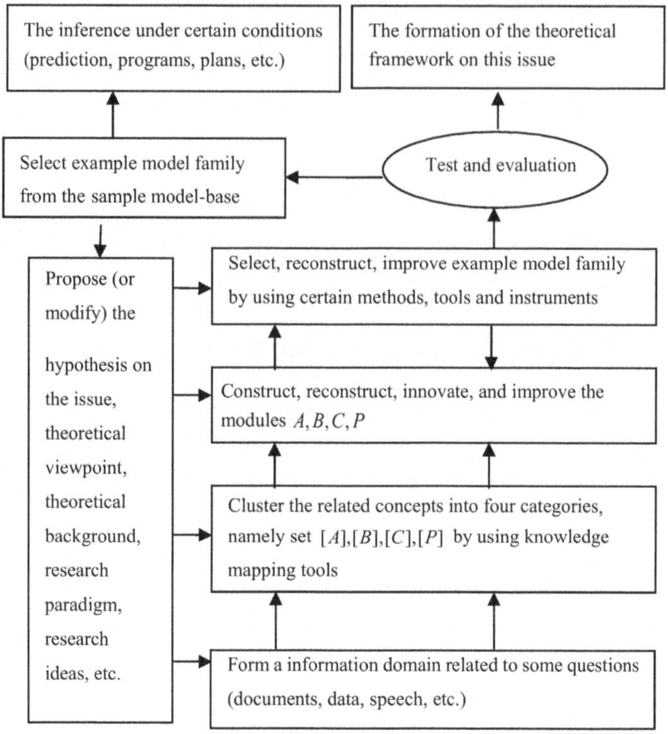

Fig. 1.5 Production process of scientific knowledge based on J-system theory

problem of study. For example, "quantity" and "price" in the market structure question are the two coordinate axes of its conceptual coordinate system; the "entity factor" and "relational element" in the economic growth question are the two coordinate axes of its conceptual coordinate system. Details are shown in Fig. 1.6.

1.6.5 Conclusion

This chapter is devoted to studying the formal structure and evolution of the economic growth model. The main conclusions are as following.

(1) By means of case analysis, J-system theory investigated the composition of scientific knowledge system deeply and found that many knowledge systems consist of a paradigm concept set and three basic concept sets according to a certain cognitive pattern. This is a formal definition of knowledge system defined by J-system theory.

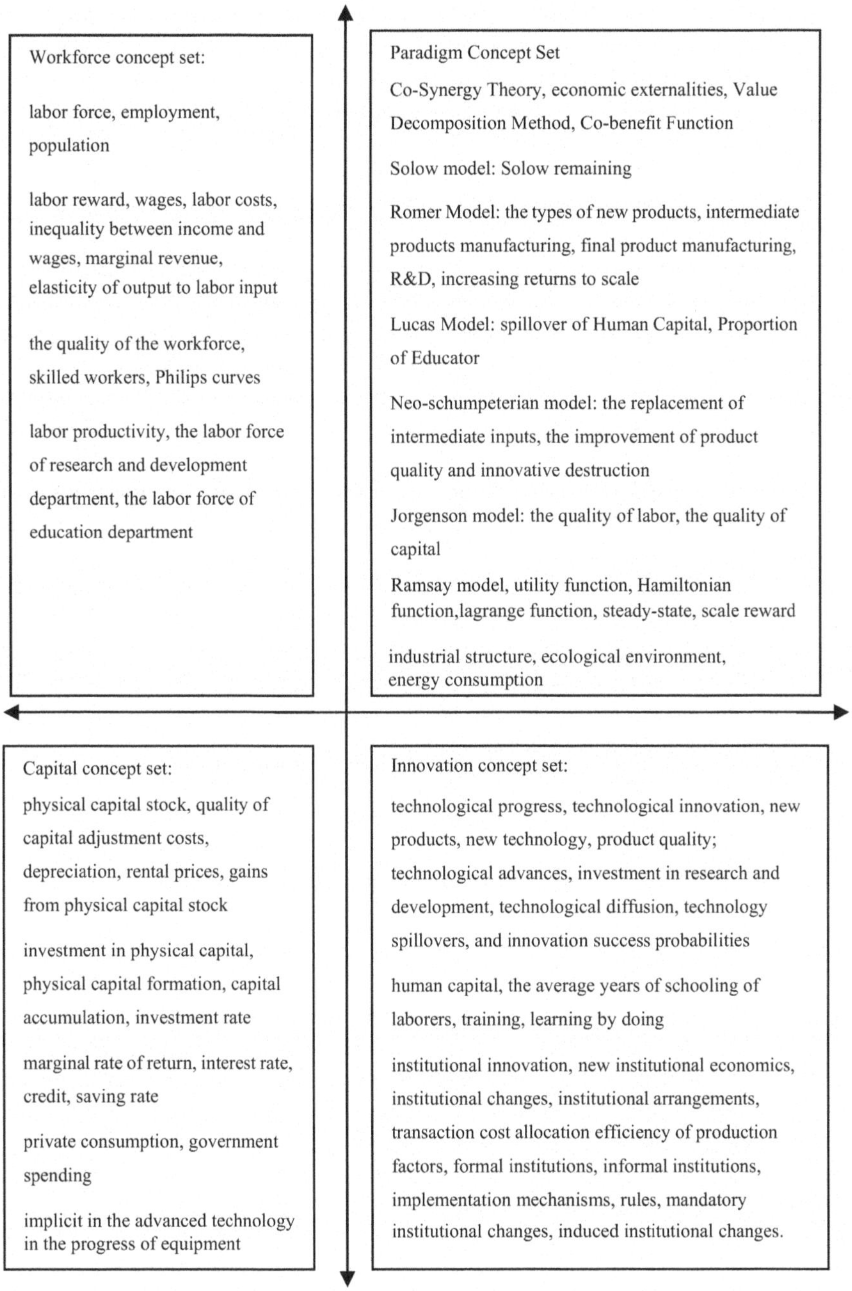

Fig. 1.6 Conceptual coordinate system of economic growth theory

(2) Scientific models in different fields are often exactly the same or similar in the form or structure, many models can be seen as a model by simply composed of three or four modules. The key of scientific discovery is tantamount to utilize and revise the previous case model. J-system theory is based on a large number of scientific case models, and its formal model highly abstracts various types of scientific models. The synergy theory of economic growth model appears to be complicated. In fact, there are three modules simply constituted, although each module itself is complicated.
(3) Based on the evolution of J-system model family, we absorb various previous scientific achievements and wisdom. It is the wisdom (reference model) that inspired us to select construction, improve, eliminate and foster groups of promising model. Compared to some of the existing knowledge discovery methods (such as self-organizing data mining), knowledge discovery (modeling) based on J-system has the advantage that the selection of experimental model is not limited to polynomial function, the experimental model which J-system selected can be combinations of various scientific functions and expressions. In the theory of economic growth, the Cobb-Douglas model is such a reference model.
(4) The "four concept sets analysis method" (concept coordinate system method), which is put forward by J-system theory, provides a scientific evolutionary analysis tools. Establishing two mutually contradictory axes is the basis for establishing a conceptual coordinate system. The model, however, is merely some mathematical combination of the concepts of four quadrants (or three quadrants) according to a certain paradigm.

1.7 The Methods and Innovations of the Research

1.7.1 Research Methods

Based on the database of economic growth in China, the United States, Japan and other countries, this book uses comparative case study method, econometric method and data envelopment analysis, etc. to absorb the important results of new growth theory and new institutional economics. Based on the synergy theory, the economic growth models of these countries are established, the contribution of each factor is calculated and some conclusions are summarized. The basic research ideas and methods of this book are shown in Fig. 1.7.

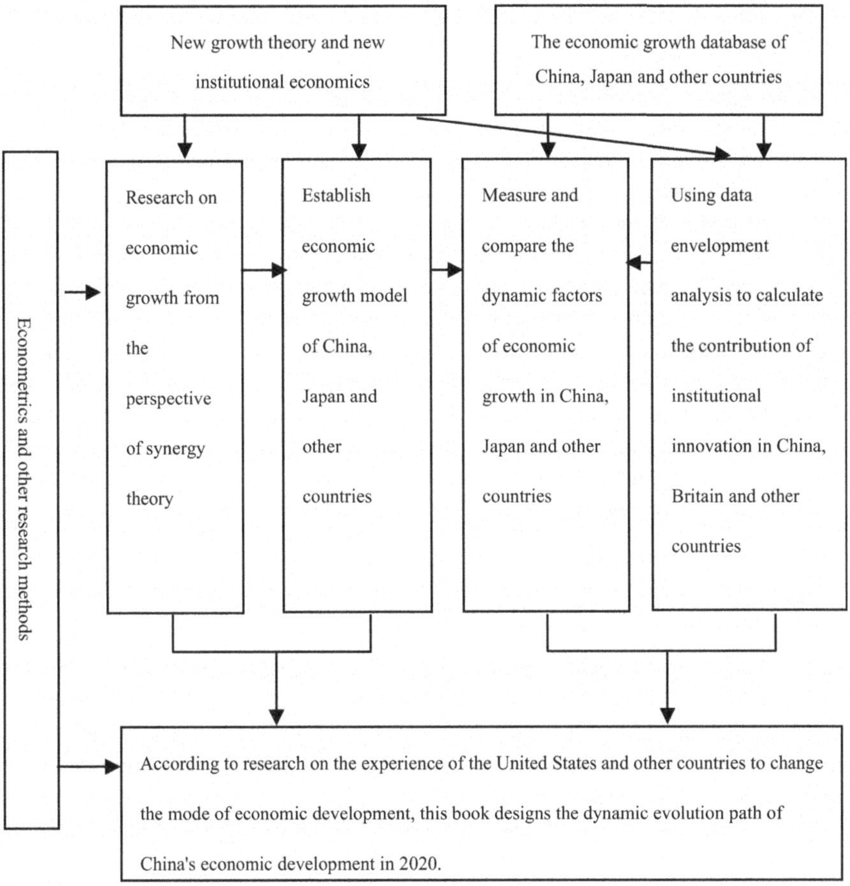

Fig. 1.7 The basic ideas and methods of this book

1.7.2 Innovations

In this book, there are the new explorations mainly in the following three aspects.

(1) This book studies the various determining factors of economic growth.

In addition to the labor, physical-capital (physical capital stock and investment in physical capital), human capital, science and technology, and institutional factors, the economic externalities (including the externalities of natural environment, social environment, market environment, and policy environment, etc.) is also an important factor that decides and affects economic growth. This book not only studies the determination method and contribution calculation method of the labor, physical-capital (physical capital stock and investment in physical capital), human capital, technology and institution to economic, but also studies on the influence of economic externalities on economic growth. And this book also puts forward the residual value method to estimate the economic growth.

(2) This book constructs the synergy theory framework and the modeling method of economic growth.

This book studies economic growth from the perspective of cooperation on science and technology, human capital and investment. It divides GDP into compensation of employees, capital gains and synergy benefits, and establishes a new economic growth model. After that, the sufficient conditions for the endogenous economic growth are deduced on the basis of the new economic growth model. The basic characteristic of equilibrium is given as follows: per-capita consumption level, per-capita capital stock and the growth rate of per-capita output are equivalent to the same positive constant. At the same time, the applicable conditions of the three hypotheses which are common in contemporary economic theory, namely, output-depletion hypothesis, decomposition hypothesis (all output is decomposed into capital gains and compensation of employees), marginal revenue hypothesis (under the conditions of profit maximization, the price of production factors is equal to its marginal output) are studied. From the perspective of synergy theory of economic growth, the book reveals the limitations of these assumptions.

(3) This book uses data envelopment analysis to measure the allocation efficiency of production factors resources, and thus establishes the calculation formula to measure contribution of institutional innovation.

Judging from the mechanism, the most fundamental and essential role of institutional innovation to economic growth is to improve the allocation efficiency of production factors. Thus, the efficiency analysis can be used to assess the contribution of institutional innovation to economic growth. Data Envelopment Analysis (DEA) is precisely such a method (Jiang 2004). By using this method, this book takes labor, physical capital stock, and human capital as input and takes GDP as output to get the relative productivity of DMU (Decision Making Units, take each year as a sample point). On this basis, the calculation formula of the contribution of institutional innovation to economic growth is deduced.

(4) The construction of economic growth model and the analysis of economic growth factors in several countries.

Based on empirical data, this book constructs economic growth models of China, Japan, South Korea, Britain, France, Canada, Singapore, Italy, Finland, Sweden, Australia, New Zealand, Ireland and other countries in the framework of synergy theory, and analyzes economic growth factors of these countries.

(5) An optimized analysis on China's innovation-driven force and the transformation of economic development.

This book establishes China's economic growth model and pollutant emissions—energy consumption—environmental protection input model, constructs Hamilton function, and determines the optimal growth rate and the relationship among the important indicators including the GDP, investment, science and technology investment, pollution control investment, energy consumption etc., which achieve the transformation of economic development in 2020 and the optimal growth rate.

References

Acemoglu, D., Johnson, S., & Robinson, J. (2002). Reversal of fortune: geography and institutions in the making of the modern world income distribution. Quarterly Journal of Economics, (118), 1231–1294.

Acemoglu, D., Johnson, S., & Robinson, J. (2005). Institutions as the fundamental cause of long-run growth. North Holland: Elsevier.

Acemoglu, D., Johnson, S., & Robinson, J., et al. (2008). Income and Democracy? American Economic Review, 98(3), 808–842.

Ali, A. (1997). Economic freedom, democracy and growth. Journal of Private Enterprise, 13(1), 1–20.

Arrow, K.J. (1962). The economic implications of learning by doing. Review of Economic Studies, 29(80), 155–173.

Barro, R.J. (1996). Democracy and growth. Journal of Economic Growth, 1(1): 1–27.

Bertalanffy, L.V. (1973). General system theory: A critical review. General Systems, (07), 1–20.

Chen, H. (2005). An analysis of the effect of the system on China's economic growth. Social Sciences Review, (2), 66–67.

Chen, C. M., (2010). CiteSpace II: detecting and visualizing emerging trends and transient patterns in scientific literature. Journal of the China Society for Scientific & Technical Information, 57 (3), 359–377.

Chen, A.G., & Rao, H.L. (2005). On the development of modern economics from the basic hypothesis of economics. Economic Issues, (1), 6–8.

Compton, R.A., Giedeman, D.C., & Hoover, G.A. (2013). A distributional analysis of the benefits of economic freedom. European Journal of Political Economy, 33(1), 121–133.

Dai, L.L. (2008). Institutional change and economic growth empirical test based on Kaifeng city data. Masteral dissertation: Henan University.

Dawson, J.W. (1998). Institutions, investment, and growth: new cross-country and panel data evidence. Economic Inquiry, 36(4), 603–619.

Deng, P., & Li, Z.X. (2006). Empirical analysis on the economic growth factors including the system factor. Sci-tech information development & economy, (19), 115–116.

Domar, E.D. (1983). Economic growth theory. Beijing: The Commercial Press.

Easton, S.T., & Walker, M.A. (1997). Income, growth, and economic freedom. American Economic Review, 87(2), 328–332.

Gao, P., & Sun, Q.L. (2006). An empirical analysis on the impact of institutional change to the difference of China's regional economic growth. Finance Economics, (11), 53–60.

Gaspar, J., Vasconcelos, P.B., & Afonso, O. (2014). Economic growth and multiple equilibria: a critical note. Economic Modelling, 36(36), 157–160.

Guo, L. (2006). An institutional analysis and empirical research of Chinese economic growth. Economic Survey, (1), 24–27.

Haken, H. (1992). Advanced synergetics. Berlin: Springer.

Han, X.L., & Zuo, L. (2006). An empirical analysis of economic growth model with institutional innovation factors: a case study of Ningxia. Journal of Chongqing Technology and Business University: West Forum, (A01), 39–40.

Harrod, R.F. (1981). Economic Dynamics. Beijing: The Commercial Press.

He, D.W. (2007). Economic growth, factor input and the choice of development strategy - econometrical analysis of long-term mechanism of Chinese economic growth. Journal of Xi'an University of Finance and Economics, (1), 60–64.

Hosoya, K. (2012). Growth and multiple equilibria: a unique local dynamic. Economic Modelling, 29(5), 1662–1665.

Hou, W.M. (2008). China's economic growth under the restriction of dual factors. Doctoral dissertation: Renmin University of China.
Hu, S.S. (2012). Research on the strategy of intellectual property education and culture in China. Doctoral dissertation: Wuhan University of Technology.
Huang, Y.X. (2007). A quantity analysis on factors of China's economic growth. Journal of Anhui University of Technology, (1), 122–126.
Jiang, Z.H. (2000). J-system reconstruct ability: a formalized study. International Journal of General Systems, 29(3), 363–371.
Jiang, Z.H. (2003). Knowledge development, institutional innovation and economic growth. Science of Science and Management of S. &. T., (11), 46–48.
Jiang, Z.H. (2004). Regional economic growth factors of China. Journal of Dalian University, (5), 66–69.
Jiang, Z.H., & Bian, W.J. (2004). An analysis of the influence of institutional change on the economic growth of Shandong province. Productivity Research, (9), 95–97.
Jiang, Z.H., Liu, X.T. (1989). From the general system to J system theory. Seeking, (5), 32–38.
Jin, Y.G. (2001). The contribution of macro institutional change to China's economic growth in transition. Finance and Economics, (2), 24–28.
Jin Wei. (2008). Research of western institution innovation contribution to economic growth - an empirical study of macroeconomic institutional change in the six provinces of western China in the past 1978–2004 years. Doctoral dissertation: Northwest University.
Jones, C.I. (1995). R&D-based models of economic growth. Journal of Political Economy, 103(4), 759–784.
Jones, L.E., & Manuelli, R. (1990). A convex model of equilibrium growth: Theory and policy implications. Journal of Political Economy, 98(5), 1008–1038.
Jones, C.I., & Williams, J.C. (1998). Measuring the social return to R&D. Quarterly Journal of Economics, 113(4), 1119–1135.
Jorgenson, D.W., & Zhong, X.Y. (1989). Productivity in Japan and the United States and economic growth. The Journal of Quantitative & Technical Economics, (4), 74–78.
Jurajda, S., & Mitchel, J. (2001). Markets and Growth. SSRN Electronic Journal.
Knack, S., & Keefer, P. (1995). Institutions and economic performance: cross-country tests using alternative institutional measures. Economics & Politics, 7(3), 207–227.
Kormendi, R.C, & Meguire, P.G. (1985). Macro-economic determinants of growth: cross-country evidence. Journal of Monetary Economics, 16(2), 141–163.
Kwan, Y.Y., & Chiu, C.Y. (2015). Country variations in different innovation outputs: the interactive effect of institutional support and human capital. Journal of Organizational Behavior Special Issue: Contextualizing Creativity and Innovation Across Cultures, 36(7):1050–1070.
Law, S.H., Lim, T.C., & Ismail, N.W. (2013). Institutions and economic development: a Granger causality analysis of panel data evidence. Economic Systems, (37), 610–624.
Li, Z.F. (2005). An empirical analysis on Hubei province economic growth model. Journal of Zhongnan University of Economics and Law, (1), 61–64.
Li, J.S., & Wang, X.J. (2009). Corporate culture reform based on path dependency theory. Journal of Dalian Maritime University (social science edition), (3), 49–52.
Li, H., Jiang, Z.H., & Jiang, Z.N. (2013). The analysis of knowledge graph of the evolution of the economic growth model and the symbiosis theory: the assessment of Japan's model. Journal of Harbin University of Commerce (Social Science Edition), (6), 3–14.
Liu, Z.Y. (1998). Knowledge economics and knowledge values. Forum on Science and Technology in China, (5), 36–39.
Liu, G.Z. (2003). A positive analysis of the efficiency of capital allocation in economic growth of China. Journal of Shandong Finance Institute, (6), 24–28.
Liu, W., & Li, S.R. (2001). The ownership change and the economic growth and upgrading of factors efficiency. Economic Research Journal, (1), 3–9+93.
Lucas, R.E. (1988). On the mechanics of economic development. Journal of Monetary Economics, 22(1), 3–42.

Mankiw, N.G., Romer, D., & Weil, D.N. (1992). A contribution to the empirics of economic growth. The Quarterly Journal of Economics, 107(2), 407–437.

Marx, K.H. (1978). Machines, natural forces and scientific applications. Beijing: Chinese People's Publishing House.

Mauro, P. (1995). Corruption and growth. Quarterly Journal of Economics, 110(3), 681–712.

North D C. Institutional Change and Economic Growth[J]. Journal of Economic History, 1971, 31 (1):118–125.

Pu, X.C. (2007). A study on the institutional factors of regional economic disparity in China. Doctoral Dissertation: Fudan University.

Rodrik, D., Subamanian, A., & Trebbi, F. (2004). Institutions rule: the primacy of institutions over geography and integration in economic development. Journal of Economic Growth, (9), 131–165.

Romer, P.M. (1986). Increasing returns and long-run growth. Journal of Political Economy, 94(5), 1002–1037.

Romer, P.M. (1999). Endogenous technological change. Nber Working Papers, 98(98), 71–102.

Samuelson, P.A. (1992). Economics. Beijing: China Development Press.

Samuelson, P.A. (1992). Factor-price equalization by trade in joint and non-joint production. Review of International Economics, 1(1), 1–9.

Schultz, T.W. (1968). Continuous improvement of the economic value of institutions and people. Journal of Agricultural Economics, https://wenku.baidu.comview/4841ade0524de518964b7d9b.html?from=search, 201 2011-07-02.

Scully, G.W. (1988). The institutional framework and economic development. Journal of Political Economy, 96(3), 652–662.

Seising, R. (2010). Cybernetics, system theory, information theory and fuzzy sets and systems in the 1950s and 1960s. Information Sciences, 180(23), 4459–4476.

Shen, K.R. (2003). New growth theory and China's economic growth. Nanjing: Nanjing University Press.

Sheshinski, E. (1967). Optimal accumulation with learning by doing. Essays on the Theory of Optimal Economic Growth.

Shi, Q.Q., et al. (1988). A model of technological progress based on production function. Soft science research method.

Smith, A. (1972). An inquiry into the nature and causes of the wealth of nations. Beijing: The Commercial Press.

Solow, R.M. (1989). Economic growth proceedings. Beijing: Beijing Economic College Press.

Song, J.D., & Tang, B.Y. (1992). A new method of calculating the effect of scientific and technological progress. Systems Engineering Theory & Practice, (5), 26–31.

Song, D.L, & Zhao, X.Y. (2005). Positive analysis on effects of institutional factors on economy growth. Economic Review, (1), 64–66.

Stokey, N.L. (1988). Learning-by-doing and the introduction of new goods. Journal of Political Economy, 96(4), 701–717.

Uzawa, H. (1965). Optimal technical change in an aggregate model of economic growth. International Economic Review, 6(1), 18–31.

Wang, H.Q., & Zhu, R.L. (2004). An empirical analysis on the contribution of institutional change to the economic growth of Henan province. Productivity Research, (10), 90–91.

Wang, W.G., & Du, X.L. (2005). New growth theory, new institutional economics and economy convergence: an empirical analysis of the economic growth of China. Statistics & Information Forum, (4), 5–9.

Wang, R.Z., & Chen, D.S. (2006). Choices of institutional variable and their agent variable in economic growth model: a literature summary. Shandong Economy, (2), 14–18.

Wang, M.Z. (2008). On endogenous logic of economic growth model and its enlightenment. Thinking, (3), 105–109.

Wang, W.B. (2009). The current situation and prospect of evolutionary game theory. Statistics and Decision, (3), 158–161.

Wang, L.L., & Niu, F.R. (2005). A research report on China's economic development in the period of strategic Opportunities (2005–2020). Beijing: Social Science Academic Press.
Wang, W.B., Chen, C.B., & Xu, H.Y. (2002). An empirical analysis on China's economic growth model containing international factors. Modern Economic Science, (2), 33–37.
Wu, J.G. (2006). Economic growth model of Changsha based on capital - institution - labor. Statistics and Decision, (18), 91–92.
Xu, Z.P. (2006). The research on human capital and economic growth in Dalian. Masteral Dissertation: Dalian University of Technology.
Xu, L. (2009). The analysis of economic growth with endogenous environmental factors in China. Masteral Dissertation: Dalian University of Technology.
Yang, X.P. (2006). The empirical analysis on the factors influencing the economic growth of China. Journal of Inner Mongolia Agricultural University (Social Science Edition), (3), 27–29.
Yang, Y.C. (2015). A model and empirical analysis of institutional changes, path dependence and economic growth - also on China's institutional dividend. Journal of Shandong University (Philosophy and Social Sciences), (4), 141–150.
Ye, F.W. (2004). Factor input and economic growth in China. Beijing: Peking University Press, 2004.
Young, A. (1991). Learning by doing and the dynamic effects of international trade. Quarterly Journal of Economics, 106(2), 369–405.
Yuan, J.X. (1991). Discussion on the contribution of scientific and technological progress in economic growth. China Soft Science, (1), 31–34.
Zhang, A.P. (2005). China's economic growth model and with institutional factors and empirical analysis. Statistics and Decision, (12), 8–11.
Zhao, J., & Liu, L. (2011). Construction of concept granule based on rough set and representation of knowledge-based complex system. Knowledge-Based Systems, 24(6), 809–815.
Zhu, Y. (1999). New growth theory. Beijing: The Commercial Press.
Zhu, B., & Zhang, T.L. (2010). The evolutionary game analysis of knowledge-sharing mechanisms in industrial clusters. Science & Technology and Economy, (2), 48–50.

Chapter 2
The Synergy Theory of Economic Growth

In the Chap. 1, we got to make a detailed analysis on the evolution of economic growth theory from 1957. In terms of assumptions conditions, modeling factors, production functions, and modeling variables, they satisfy the features and mechanism of inclusive evolution through the analysis on the typical economic growth models. The features and mechanism mean that the more elements, the more complex model. The neoclassical economic growth theory puts forward various forms of production function. However, there are numerous excessively strict assumptions on these production function methods which are seriously divorced from reality and affect its applicability. In the Solow-Swan model, it was assumed that there were just two production factors including capital and labor, and the two production factors could replace each other. It also assumed that technological progress was neutral and the returns to scales were persistent. This is not realistic. In fact, science and technology, human capital, and institutions are also important factors determining economic growth. And the new growth theory also has the similar limitation, such as assumptions of Romer's endogenous growth theory that "population and labor supply remains unchanged; the aggregate human capital stock remains unchanged, and its market share also remains unchanged". The new institutional economics represented by North and others opened up a new way for the economic growth theory, but it lacked the quantitative study of the institution in economic growth. At present, domestic research on the contribution of institutional innovation to economic growth in China's reform and opening up is represented by structural analysis method. The main idea is to select agency variables of institutional innovation firstly, and then construct the production function. In the production function, institutional innovation determines the change in the output elasticity of the factor. This method is the original creation of Chinese scholars in the international academia.

In this chapter, synergy theory of economic growth is systematically discussed on the basis of the Chap. 1.

J. H. Liu and Z. H. Jiang, *The Synergy Theory on Economic Growth: Comparative Study Between China and Developed Countries*,
https://doi.org/10.1007/978-981-13-1885-6_2

(1) Research on various determining factors of economic growth based on synergy theory

This section discusses various factors that decision and impact on economic growth, including labor, physical capital stock and investment in physical capital, human capital, science and technology, institutions, and economic environment externalities.

(2) Explanation on concept of synergy and synergy benefits

The meaning of "synergy" presented by this book refers to the interaction and cooperation, and innovation and investment in economic growth are interactive and synergistic. Synergy is built on the flow and sharing of knowledge and the Synergy benefits are the basis of economic organization to exist and develop. The synergy benefits are the benefits shared to some extent by the various actors (investors, employees and other stakeholders) in economic activities through interaction, interdependence, cooperative action and so on. The benefits make various actors mutual support, mutual benefit and common prosperity (Liu and Jiang 2015).

(3) The synergy theory basis of the construction of economic growth model

Synergy theory divides GDP into labor remuneration, capital gains and synergy benefits. The economic growth model is established by establishing a functional relation among labor remuneration, capital gains, synergy benefits, labor, physical capital stock and investment in physical capital, human capital, science and technology (Jiang et al. 2014).

(4) Measurements on the role of institutional innovation and economic externalities in economic growth

Judging from the mechanism, the most fundamental and essential role of institutional innovation to economic growth is to increase the allocation efficiency of production factors. Thus, the DEA method used to measure efficiency is a measure of the contribution of institutional innovation to economic growth. After calculating the contribution of physical capital stock, investment in physical capital, science and technology, human capital, labor, and institution to economic growth, the influence rate of economic externalities is measured by the residual value method.

(5) The synergy theory reveals the limitations of the hypothesis in the previous economic growth theory

Sufficient conditions for the endogenous economic growth are deduced on the basis of the economic growth model of synergy theory, and the basic characteristics of the equilibrium are given. In addition, this chapter reveals the limitations of the three hypotheses of contemporary economic theory from the perspective of co-association.

2.1 The Determining Factors of Economic Growth

2.1.1 Many Determining Factors of Economic Growth

Which factor does determine economic growth? Firstly, people think that capital and labor are the two main factors that determine economic growth, and this thought can be called two-factor theory. Solow summed up the factors that led to economic growth are three elements which are technological progress, capital accumulation, and labor force growth.

According to the data provided by Wu (1988), comparing with Western Europe and Japan, Denison analyze the importance of a variety of factors which promoted economic growth in economic growth, based on the historical data of the U.S. economic growth. In this regard, he put forward in detail and discussed the seven determining factors of economic growth in a series of works such as *Factors of U.S. Economic Growth and the Choice We Face*, *Why Does Japan Grow So Fast* as the following (Denison 1962; Denison and Chung 1987): (1) quantity of employment and age-gender composition (2) hours of work (3) education (4) capital stock (5) knowledge progress (6) resource allocation (the proportion reduction of labor force used inefficiently) (7) scale and save (measured by the expansion of market).

The analysis on proportion of the factors above in economic growth (from 1929 to 1957):

The first factor, Denison estimated that, from 1929 to 1957, the population of employment in U.S. enterprises increased 8.72 million, an increase of 21.2%, and the average annual increase was 0.8%.

The second factor, Denison believed that the shortening of working hours reduced fatigue on the one hand, and caused production losses on the other hand. Because the increase in labor productivity can only compensate 40–50% for the losses caused by the shortening of working hours, and the remaining 60–50% are burdened by capitalists.

For the third factor, Denison thought that the rapidly increasing educational level of the U.S. labor force improved the skills of workers, increased the level of labor technology, and improved the quality of economic growth to increase national income thereby.

In general, with regard to the age-sex composition, the value of output created by men is 2.17 times of the value created by women (the same conditions of working time).

The scale and save is that because of the expansion of production scale and the increase in production, cost is reduced to achieve savings of the raw materials and energy, and thus profits are increased. It is worth clearly pointing out that the scale and save in usual benefits a business at first, and then it will be extended to other enterprises.

About the knowledge progress, Denison believed that it was the most important and fundamental factor which caused the output growth of unit input. The knowledge progress includes the technical knowledge progress, the management

Table 2.1 Distributing of real national income growth rates in U.S. according to growth factors (1929–1957, %)

Variables	Contribution of each factor		
Real national income			2.93
1 The increase in total investment			2.00
1.1 Labor quality adjustment		1.57	
1.1.1 Employment and working hours	0.80		
1.1.2 Education	0.67		
1.1.3 Other	0.10		
1.2 Capital		0.43	
2 The increased output by per unit inputs			0.93
2.1 Knowledge progress		0.58	
2.2 Scale and save		0.34	
2.3 Other		0.01	

knowledge progress and the update of the structure which is generated by the introduction of the new knowledge, and so on. Denison especially emphasized the important position of improving the management in the progress of knowledge, and thought that knowledge progress not only referred to the technological progress, but also the progress of management. He also pointed out that the difference between knowledge progress and other factors was that due to advanced communication technology and information flow, new products, new materials, new technology and new experience which were created by technological innovation of any region or industry, enterprises, would quickly spread to all over the world. The share of these factors in economic growth is shown in Table 2.1.

With the similar analysis of Denison, Hisao (Japan) divided the impact on economic growth into 7 major factors in his book of *Speech of Japan's Economic Growth* (1980): (1) the subjective reasons of economic growth (2) the growth of knowledge (3) the capital accumulation (4) advance in the quality and quantity of labor force (5) economic institution (6) trade (7) natural resources.

The Former Soviet Union scholars Kamaeb's (1983) contribution is dividing the factors which decide the economic growth into direct factors and indirect factors, and shown in Table 2.2. However, his classification needs improvement. On one hand, it is a mistake to put the "scientific research and experimental design" into "indirect factors". On the other hand, there are some indirect factors which are not included, such as the hydrogen of cultural, social situation, political situation, and so on.

This book points out the direct factors that decide and impact on economic growth, in addition to labor, physical-capital (physical capital stock and investment in physical capital), human capital, science and technology and institutional factors, economic environment externalities (including the natural environment, social environment, market environment, policy environment, etc.) is also an important factor. The economic environment externalities in economic growth discussed here include environmental stress costs, resource exploitation pressure costs, social

Table 2.2 Factors of economic growth and basic chart of result structure

Growth factors			Growth results
I	II		
Indirect factors	Direct factors		
Labor resources	All workers labor		Consumer goods (material, cultural, information and other information)
General education and professional education institution		The final product production	For the unproductive accumulation and compensating physical material of non-production fund
Process of population growth			
Scientific research and experimental design research	Productive technology and productive organization		Physical material to meet the social needs
Use of natural resources	Productive fund		Physical material used in the productive accumulation
Surrounding environment	Management of social production		Compensate physical material lost by fixed production fund

stress costs, the unreasonably premium of the backward region's resource-based products and the advanced region's processing products, the flow of mature talent from the backward region to the advanced region (human capital loss of the backward region caused by this condition), the condition where backward regions are away from the regional market center, as well as the environmental policy changes in the backward region and the advanced region (for example during the 1990–2000 period, China's coastal regions enjoyed the benefits of the preferential policies, but the central regions and western regions did not enjoy them) and so on (Liu and Jiang 2015). Among them, environmental stress costs include the economic losses which are brought about by the change of the natural environment, and the increasing costs which are used to restore and manage the natural environment, prevent and control pollution. Resource exploitation pressure costs are caused by changes in natural resource exploitation conditions. The social stress costs are brought about by social security, social relief and other social factors.

We cannot only theoretically deduce, whether capital or technology is the primary impetus of economic growth. In different economic systems, under different environmental conditions, the roles of capital, technology and labor are different in the economic growth. For example, in some conditions, the capital plays a crucial role while in some conditions, science and technology play the decisive role. In the previous stage, the capital is a crucial role while in the latter period, science and technology play a decisive role.

2.1.2 The Role of Institutional Innovation

The institution will help to reduce friction and conflict, so that people can spend the limited time and energy on the production of wealth. The institutional innovation is in a position to improve efficiency, and promotes the economic growth, which is a major discovery in the new institutional economics (Liu 2006).

The new institutional economics are created and developed by Coase. North and Williamson considered the institutions as an important factor in the economic growth (Coase 1998). Institutions is a series of rules (formal rules, informal rules) and its implementation mechanism which is used to controls people's behavior. Institution is not a single rule but system of a variety of rules. There are a variety of complex and non-linear dynamic relationship among the rules. In a sense, on one hand, these rules are consistent and coordinated, but on the other hand, there may also be contradictions, conflicts, antagonisms, and incoordination among certain rules (Jiang 2004). This contradiction movement is the internal driving force for institutional change.

The formal rules are referred to a series of policies and rules made by people consciously. The formal constraint includes political rules, economic rules and contracts, as well as the hierarchical structure constituted by these series of rules. The hierarchical structure is from the constitution to the law of written and unwritten, then the special rules, to the individual contract finally, and they restrict people's behavior together.

The official rules are also called as formal constraints. These rules can be described in the following categories (Samuelson 1992):

(1) The rules define the "responsibility" of the two in the division of labor. It can be illustrated by Adam Smith's famous examples of making a needle. The rules are to define, what work can be done by which people, and all workers complete the production of the needle together. It can also be illustrated by the example of the market. The rules are to agree on who produces which goods. In the words of neoclassical economics, it gives a saying that give people the goal of action.
(2) The rules define what each person can do and what each person cannot do. Because the action that everyone pursues the benefits of the agreement which is exchanged by the minimum effort (or cost) may harm the benefits of others, like making fake products, impersonated products, forged products, or inferior

products. In the words of neoclassical theory, that is to set borders of the "space of choice" (Liu 2005).

(3) The rules of punishment. If one breaks the agreement of the rules, he or she has to pay the cost.

(4) The rules of "Weights and Measures". The parties which exchange each other needs to appoint how to measure each individual's physical inputs and outputs. Only on the basis of this the value of exchange be determined.

Informal rules mainly include the ethical norm, moral idea, customs and habits, ideology and other factors. In the informal rules, ideology is at the core. Because it not only contains values idea, ethical norm, moral idea, and customs and habits, but also can constitute the "prior" mode arranged by a formal institution in the form (Lu 1996).

Institution is a kind of dissipative structure. If there is some kind of positive feedback mechanism, it is possible to enlarge a disturbance factors, so that the institutional changes. From the theory of dissipative structures, the formal rules are formed unconsciously in the long-term communication, with lasting vitality, and constitute a part of the culture from generation to generation. Historically, before the formal rules are set up, the relationship between the people mainly relies on informal rules to maintain. Even in modern society, the formal rules account for only a few parts of the whole rules. Most space where people live is still constrained by informal rules.

Institutional innovation is the process of the order change. Maybe it changes from the disordered to the ordered, or from the ordered to the disordered. From the mechanism of the new institution producing, the institutional innovation can be divided into two types of compulsory and induced (Jiang 2004).

About the impact of the institution on economic growth, Coase Theorem shows that when the cost of the transaction is zero, any institutional arrangements can only affect the distribution of wealth or income, but does not affect the composition of output, namely the resources allocation. The efficient results can be reached by the market negotiations without paying any cost. While the cost of the transaction is greater than zero, the institutional arrangements not only have an influence on the distribution, but also on the allocation of resources, namely the composition of output. Because some institutional arrangements will generate higher transaction cost, so that effective results cannot occur (Jorgenson 2001).

North and Thomas (2009), in the process of analysis of the reasons for the rise of the western world, pointed out that "the efficient economic organization is the key factor for the economic increase. The reason for the rise of the western world is developing an efficient economic organization. Efficient organizations need to establish institutionalized facilities and establish property ownership. They lead the personal economic efforts into a kind of social activity to make the individual return rate close to the social return rate."

Why did the Netherlands and the United Kingdom get the economic growth in the modern sense at first, rather than France and Spain? North and Thomas (2009) replied, "Because at that time, the Netherlands (a province of the former Spanish) and the United Kingdom are the two European countries that walk in the most advanced in the determine institution and the ownership system that can bring individual initiative into play efficiently and ensure that the capital and energy are used for the most beneficial social activities."

Effective institution of ownership is the basic condition that enables personal rate of return close to the social return rate continuously. The concept of "ownership" here means all laws, rules, practices, and regulations which help to make sure the rights that everyone occupies, uses, and transfers the wealth produced (Gong 2005).

Institution of property rights and the corresponding institutional innovation will be conductive to internalization of external revenue, which is an important idea of institutional function in the new institutional economics. In addition, the institution also plays an important role in inhibiting the opportunist motives and actions of people. To sum up (Jiang 2004), we can summarize the process of institutional function and its impact on the person as Fig. 2.1.

Institutional balance, in essence, means that the institution has reached the "Pareto efficiency". Pareto efficiency means that economy examined at this time is no longer possible to increase the utility level of any people (at least one person) by

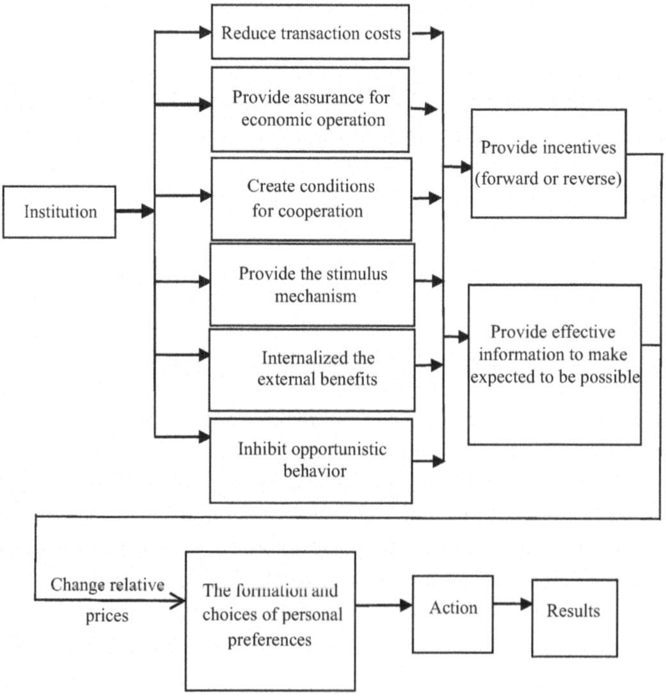

Fig. 2.1 Institutional function and the influence of individual behavior

changing allocation of the products and resources, in the case where the utility level of others (at least one person) does not reduce at least. On the contrary, the so-called "Pareto inefficiency" refers to that it is still possible for economy to make utility level of one or some people improve to some extent through re-allocation of resources, in the case where the utility level of others keeps unchanged. In the presence of economic inefficiency, if re-allocation of resources is carried out, the utility level of some people improve under the condition that others' utility keeps unchanged, that is "re-allocation", known as the "Pareto improvement" (Xu 2005). The institutional change, to some extent, is a process of "Pareto improvement". The existing institutional arrangements and institutional structure have reached an ideal situation, and there is no need to adjust, therefore, institutional balance is similar to the Pareto optimality (Wang et al. 2002).

Efficient institution should make the private return rate constantly close to the social return rate and make the individual efforts really link to their remuneration (Chen 2006). Institutional arrangements have two major goals at least. Firstly, provide a kind of structure so that the members of cooperation can get some additional revenue which cannot be gotten from the outside of the structure. The second is to provide a kind of institution that can influence on laws or property right's changes in order to change the form that individuals (or groups) can compete legally. Institution defines people's space of choice and restricts the people's interrelationship by providing a set of rules, so as to decrease the environmental uncertainty, reduce transaction's cost, protect the property rights, and promote the productive activities.

The roles of institutional innovation in economic growth are as follows: firstly, it can reduce the cost of the institution. In the real world, information is scarce, implementation of property rights needs to cost, and the exchanges in the market have to consume resources. The institutional innovation can reduce all the cost of these institution, so as to create conditions for cooperation; institutional innovation provides incentive mechanism for economic growth by changing the relative price of factor; institutional innovation can inhibit free ride (that is to say enjoy the results of others by paying zero cost) and other external factors. The personal rate of return (single individual or his or her economic organization) is often not equal to the social rate of return (a member of the community's economic activities have a special impact on the other members of society, such as the free-rider), which is the so-called external economic issues. The role of institutional innovation is to internalize the external revenue so that the personal rate of return can be close or even equal to the social rate of return (Jiang 2004).

From the new institutional economics, we can get the following conclusions: the institution defines the people's interrelationship. The institutional innovation could reduce the information cost and uncertainties, decrease transaction cost, minimize factors which hinder continuous cooperation, and improve the allocation efficiency of production factors, so as to increase the returns to scale and promote the economic growth finally.

2.1.3 *Externalities of Economic Environment*

The concept of externality originated by Marshall. The theory is formed after Pigou and Coase researched, and developed constantly. According to some studies of Marshall, Pigou and Coase by Chinese and foreign scholars, this section firstly carding venations of research of externality issues.

2.1.3.1 External Economy of Marshall

Marshall (1981) believed that there was another production factor called "industrial organizations" besides three kinds of production factors raised repeatedly over in the past including land, labor and capital. Marshall said: "We can divide the economy which occurred due to the expansion of production scale of any goods into two categories: the first one is the general developed economy depending on industry; the second one is the economy depending on resources, organization and efficiency of individual companies engaging in this industry." We call the former is an external economy, and the later is an internal economy. External economy can be often obtained because many small businesses with similar properties concentrate in a particular place, known as the regional distribution of industry (Marshall 1981).

2.1.3.2 External Effects of Pigou

Pigou (1999), with the method of modern economics, from the perspective of welfare economics, systematically first studied externality issues and put forward the concept and content of "external diseconomy" based on the concept of "external economy" proposed by Marshall. Pigou illustrated externality by analyzing deviation of the marginal private net output and marginal social net output.

Although concepts of "external economy" and "external diseconomy" endowed by Pigou are borrowed and extended by Marshall, the meanings of those two concepts given by Pigou are different from the meaning gave by Marshall. Marshall mainly put forward the concept of "external economy". It means that when companies expand production scale, unit cost reduces which is caused by various external factors; Pigou referred to the impact of business activities on the outside. These two issues seemed very similar, but in fact, they studied two different problems or the two sides of an issue. Pigou already promoted Marshall's externality theory greatly (Pigou 1999).

2.1.3.3 Transaction Costs and Externality of Coase

Coase theory was formed in the process of criticizing Pigou theory. Coase's critiques on the Pigou tax are concentrated in the following:

Firstly, the external effects are often not one-way problem that one is against the other but a mutual. Secondly, in the case of zero transaction costs, there is no need for Pigou tax. Thirdly, in the case of non-zero transaction costs, to resolve internal issues of externality need to determine through cost-benefits weighed comparison of a variety of policy instruments (Coase 1998).

The view of Zhang (2000) is that to clarify the concept of externalities, we must first clearly define property rights, and secondly, all economic activities can be regarded as a kind of contractual arrangement. Therefore, the contract should be complete and integrate which also has to pay the cost of information.

2.1.3.4 Externality of Political Behavior

Schmid (1999) sees the externality of political behavior as another thing that is different from externality of market, and can also affect externality of market. He exchanged externality into the discussion of "interdependence", and analyzed the externality of political behavior in detail, and made important contributions to the externality of political behavior. He said: "If you do not consider the narrow understanding of externality, externality is a useful term, and can be used in the same sense as 'interdependence effect' or 'interpersonal opportunity costs'." In addition, he examined interdependence or externality from technology, money and politics. The interdependence or externality can be divided into three basic types including externality of technology, externality of money and externality of politics.

Wolf (1994) believed that externality was derived from public policy to try to make up for market failure, whether it is negative or positive. In such precise activities, government intervention may produce "unexpected negative effects" in those areas of "far from operation of public policy".

2.1.3.5 Classification of Economic Environmental Externality

According to the study of new institutional economics, the so-called externality is essentially the issue of the difference between the private return rate and the social return rate. Externality is divided into the positive and negative externality. The positive externality is that the private return rate is lower than the social return rate, and some of the benefits are taken by others; the negative externality is that the private cost is lower than the social cost, and some of the cost are added to society or others. Externality is caused by two main reasons. The first one is whether there is a strict institutional restraint, such as the definition of property rights, the protection of the transfer and so on. The second one is the high or low transaction cost in the economic activity. For example, although the constraint mechanism of property rights institution is sound, if there is a high transaction cost, externality is bound to generate.

From the relationship between private return rate and the social return rate, the private rate of return is the net income that the economic units get from engaging in an activity. The social rate of return is that the society gets the total net income (positive or negative) from the social activities. It is equivalent to the private income pulsing everyone's net income from other social activities. The so-called "free ride", in essence, is to make other people's private rate of return lower than the social rate of return in economic activities, part of which are occupied for free of charge by the people of "free ride" intentionally or unintentionally.

The concept of externality in this book is proposed on the basis of research on externality in the past, which is an important factor to affect economic growth. The impact on economic growth may be positive or negative.

(1) The concept of economic environmental externality

Externality is also known as external costs, externality effect or spillover effect, with regard to the effect of external factors on the economic subject. The externality defined by Samuelson and Nordhaus (1999) was "externality refers to the situation where the production or consumption presses recruitment costs from other groups or the production or consumption gives other groups earning without compensation." Economic entity is represent with A, and the environment of economic entity A is represented by B. The economic externalities B (It appears with respect to economic entity A) refers that the economic environment has an impact on the economic entity, but corresponding to this effect, the economic environment B does not undertake corresponding obligations or get corresponding return.

(2) Classification of externality

The economic externality B is with respect to economic entities A, and can be divided into "positive externality" and "negative externality".

The negative externality is that the economic environment has a positive impact on the economic entities, but corresponding to this effect, the economic environment B does not get corresponding return. At this time, economic environment B is positive to economic entity A.

The positive externality is that the economic environment has a negative impact on the economic entities, but corresponding to this effect, the economic environment B does not undertake corresponding obligations. At this time, economic environment B is negative to economic entity A.

(3) Measurement of externality

In terms of quantitative measurement, corresponding to negative economic externalities, "the effect ratio of economic environmental externalities" is negative.

In terms of quantitative measurement, corresponding to positive economic externalities, "the effect ratio of economic environmental externalities" is positive.

For example, from 1953 to 1976, the externality of China's economic environment was positive. In general, internal and external economic environment were negative to economic growth. From 1977 to 2012, the economic externalities was negative. In general, internal and external economic environment were positive to economic growth.

From 1953 to 1976, the western developed capitalist countries blockaded China's economy, which hindered development of China's economy. Sino-Soviet relations became deteriorated. The Soviet assisted China on economy and technology firstly, and then forced China to pay the debt. Political movements like "Great Leap Forward" and natural conditions like climate in domestic also affected economic development.

After the reform and opening up, western developed capitalist countries have established friendly relations with China one after another. The scale of foreign direct investment becomes larger and economic technological communication is more frequent. China's relations with Russia and other the former Soviet Union Community countries are also getting better. Chinese goods are sold to the world. It has been 40 years since the reform and opening up, and China's economy has been growing rapidly during this period, which is related to good internal and external economic environment.

2.2 The Synergy Theory

Main points of the synergy theory presented in this book can be summed up as follows:

(1) Direct factors that determine economic growth are not only capital (physical capital stock and incremental-investment in physical capital), labor, science and technology, and human capital, but also institutional and economic externalities. This has been discussed in Sect. 2.1 of this book.
(2) Science and technology, human capital and investment in physical capital have a synergistic relationship. This relationship is the basis for synergistic interests in economic system. The foundation of synergy is knowledge flows and knowledge sharing. This will be discussed in Sect. 2.2 of this book.
(3) From the perspective of income decomposition, outputs of economic system include not only compensation of employees, investor's interests, but also synergistic benefits. To some extent, synergistic benefits are common and shared interests of laborers, investors and other stakeholders, but the benefits cannot be clearly allocated to either side. The form of synergistic benefits function depends on synergistic relationship type of science and technology, human capital and investment in physical capital. This will be discussed in Sect. 2.3.

2.2.1 Synergy of Innovation and Investment

This book adopts a generalized concept of "innovation". Generalized concept of "innovation" includes scientific and technological innovation, institutional innovation, innovation in human capital growth of knowledge, intelligence and wisdom in employee's mind, which can be measured by the increment of employee's schooling years in economic growth model (Liu and Jiang 2016).

Science and technology innovation includes technological innovation and transformation. About the concept of "technological innovation", the explanation in "Baidu Encyclopedia" is that technological innovation is a process of the creating and applying new knowledge, new technologies, and new crafts, and adopting new production modes and management models to develop new products, improve product quality, and provide the new service. The connotation of technological innovation includes not only commercialization of new products and new technologies, but also management innovation led by modern science and technology. On the basis of the meaning above, this book dovetails technological transformation into technical innovation. Thus, technological innovation can be divided into four types: product innovation, craft innovation, new knowledge brought about by technological transformation and management innovation led by modern science and technology.

Synergistic benefits come from the interaction of the scientific and technological progress, human capital accumulation and investment in physical capital. As what Chen Baosen and others have commented, Arrow (1962) considered the knowledge progress brought about by technological progress was subjected to the capital accumulation. In his view, the fact was fully proven by the progress brought about by the invention of tools. This era was characterized by learning by doing and learning by testing. In the stimulation of scarcity, people were committed to one work. The more work they did, the more skilled they were. Finally, they found a best approach to it. In Romer model (Romer 1990), technological progress and rising productivity are by-products of capital accumulation, meaning that new investments have spillover effects. Lucas believed that voluntary investment of manufacturers in the education sector brought in technological progress. In the Barro model, technological progress was brought by government investment. While Young (1991) believed that technological progress was the result of both invention and technological diffusion (often accompanied by investment). Chinese scholars have emphasized the combination of investment in physical capital and technology (Song et al. 2011), when do research on the dynamic combination of capital accumulation and technological progress in China's economic growth (Zhao et al. 2007) and the contribution of capital embodied technological progress on economic growth.

New technology spills over by the investment in new equipment. At present, there are many research and analysis concerning technology's spillover. For example, the positive stimulating effects of equipment import on the economic growth rate are emphasized by Jones (1994) and Lee (1995). Why there is this relationship empirically? An important theoretical viewpoint is that a mass of technical progress is hidden in the capital investment.

In the view of Wu (2005), if economy wants the continuous increase, on the one hand, we require capital growth to drive output growth. On the other hand, we require changes in production and interest rates to lead to changes in capital investment. The technical innovation function summarizes the former one and the investment function summarizes the latter one and the investment function could be related to the saving function and the distribution of income. The economic growth is the result of the interaction of the two functions. For example, assuming that the production growth exceeds the capital growth in the period, according to the definition of investment function, the capital growth rate of the next phase would rise under the effects of output and interest rates. Then the higher investment would increase the output according to the technical innovation function. Another cycle of investment adjustment would emerge next. However, this process of adjustment is gradual convergence until the income growth rate equals to the capital growth rate. The productivity growth rate, when capital growth equals to the output growth becomes the productivity equilibrium growth rate which depends only on technology innovation function. Under the condition of balance, the growth rate, the interest rates and capital-production rate keep unchanged with time process (Zeng 2007).

Cohen and Levinthal (1989) undervalued the negative effect of spillover effect on stimulating effect. They thought that the spillover effect of other companies should be that a company should be engaged in its own research and developing investment, and then it would receive the knowledge and related profits created by other companies in reality.

Chuang (1998) assumed that technological study can be caused by import and export. He established an after-model for two countries to indicate that the study and technology spillover could become the engine of economic growth to cause economic convergence among countries. Dan and Loewy (1998) also held similar views. Model presented by Dodzin and Vamvakids (2004) indicated a theoretical mechanism that learns new technique from imported machine and equipment and drives economic growth. They also used cross-country data to prove that the proportion of manufacturing in GDP is positively correlated with the opening degree of trade. In the view of Hendricks (2000), there was a complement relationship between labor skills and technical innovation hidden in capital investment. A main way in which workers raise their skills is using capital goods which stand for new technology level. Differences in equipment prices reflect distorted trade policies. Limiting imports of capital goods and high equipment prices will inhibit technological progress (Zhang 2006). The contribution is that the process of technological innovation is changed from "learning by doing" to "learning by using" (the concretization of learning by trading) (Aghion and Howitt 2004).

Lin et al. (1994, 1999), based on a number of lessons in recent decades of development mode and strategic transformation implemented by developing countries, through induction of a large number of historical evidences, organized systematically the above views, and presented a complete theoretical explanation for the process of China's industrialization, even the practice of industrialization in the whole developing countries by using the analytical framework. According to their research ideas, technology learning costs could be divided into two parts including the cost of the acquisition and the cost of the applications. The cost of technological acquisition is decided by the international market while the cost of application is mainly influenced by endowment structure of their own country.

Technical structure is endogenic from factor input structure. In other words, the achievement of a technology needs corresponding factor input structure (including human capital and physical capital) while the relative price of input is decided by endowment structure within economic system. In their views, in the process of technological diffusion, minimizing application costs was the key to select the appropriate technological structure, and the basic principle was to maintain the consistency of the technical structure and the endowment structure. For economy which follows comparative advantage, because technological progress hides in the introduced capital equipment, in TFP (total factor productivity) empirical analysis, technological progress should not be significant. To some extent, it explains why economic growth of East Asia is rapid, but TFP of East Asia is low (Aghion and Howitt 2004).

Some scholars researched the synergistic relationship between introduction of equipment and independent innovation. Some scholars pointed out that capital accumulation and innovation are complementary and cooperative. Innovation would be irritated by more capital through improving equilibrium profit flow, and just as more innovation would stimulate capital accumulation by increasing productivity growth rate. In the long term, we should not lack either of them. If there is no innovation, new investment will be prevented by diminishing returns. If there is no net investment, innovation will be restrained by increasing capital cost (Li 2005).

2.2.2 *Meaning of Synergy*

According to biological points, synergy refers to the phenomenon that different types of creatures live together, depend on each other, cooperate with each other, and are beneficial to each other. There are also contradictions with each other. Maybe there are competition and destruction. "Synergy" can be mutually beneficial to each other, and also can be harmful to each other, or one side benefits or damages while the other is not affected. In ecology, synergy refers to mutually beneficial cooperation between two different organisms to some extent.

In sociology, synergy refers to interdependence and mutual cooperation among the population units which are different form or nature within social groups. Survival of each unit is inseparable from the continue to live of other units, and each unit's cooperation is the condition where other units develop.

(1) The meaning of "synergy" presented by this book refers to the interaction and cooperation, and innovation and investment in economic growth are interactive and synergy.
(2) Synergy is based on the flow and sharing of knowledge and the synergistic interests are the basis of economic organization to exist and develop.

(3) In a sense, synergy also exists between economic system and its environment. A good external environment will promote economic growth while a poor external environment will curb economic growth.

The synergy theory is different from the neoclassical growth theory about exogenous growth that long-term growth rate will not be affected by capital accumulation. In the Solo-Swan model of neoclassical growth theory, the technological progress is independent of the capital accumulation, and determines the long-term growth rate. Similarly, synergy theory is also different from the endogenous growth theory of Romer (1990), Grossman and Helman (1991) and so on. Endogenous growth theory thinks that the number of product's species and the number of equipment in production determine the long-term growth rate, but have nothing to do with the capital stock (Aghion and Howitt 2004).

2.2.3 Foundation of Synergy

Synergy is based on the flow and sharing of knowledge. Cooperation between workers and investors is built on the basis of flow and sharing of knowledge. The flow of knowledge is the cycle process within endogenous, spillover, internalization, externalization of the knowledge. In the process of internalization, externalization, endogenous and spillover of knowledge, innovation (technological innovation, human capital innovation that the growth of knowledge and wisdom internalized in the mind of the employees, institutional innovation) and investment in physical capital achieve synergy by learning by doing and knowledge sharing. The synergy includes knowledge endogenous (through research and development, new technologies are endogenous from investment goods and so on), as well as technology spillover (materialized knowledge spills from mechanical equipment through reverse engineering, learning by doing and so on). It is also a process of mutual conversion of explicit knowledge and tacit knowledge (Fig. 2.2).

About the explicit knowledge and tacit knowledge, Chandler (2005) discussed the view of Ikujiro and Hiroshi in their writings. They argued that explicit knowledge was systematic and formal. Explicit knowledge could be expressed by use of language or figures, also could be communicated and shared in the form of "hard" data, scientific formulas, written procedures or general principles, etc. Therefore, explicit knowledge was seen as synonyms of computer code, chemical formula or a common set of rules. However, knowledge expressed by words and figures was only the "the tip of the iceberg". Knowledge existed mainly in the form of tacit knowledge (hard to see and express). Tacit knowledge was very personal, and it was difficult to formalize, so that it was difficult to communicate and share with others. Subjective insights, intuitions and hunches were included in tacit knowledge. And tacit knowledge was deeply rooted in the actions, experience, ideas, values and emotions of individuals. To be more precise, tacit knowledge could be divided into two dimensions. The first dimension was the technological dimension including the informal and recorded difficultly technique and skill that were referred to by "knack".

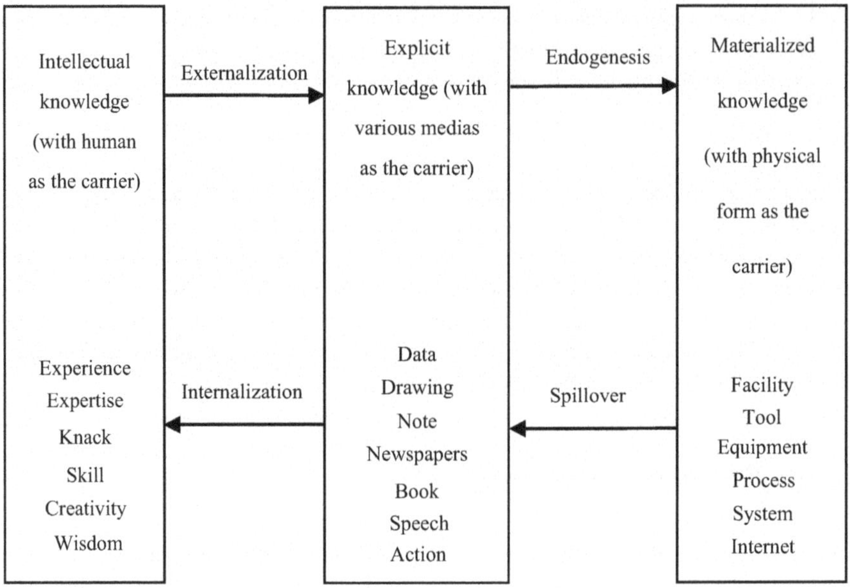

Fig. 2.2 Four processes of knowledge flow

For example, a skilled artisan accumulated a large number of expertise of "present in the fingertips" in long-term practice, but he usually did not speak out scientific or technical principles behind this skill. The second dimension was the cognitive dimension which is more important. It included icons, mental models, beliefs and cognition, etc. which were deep-rooted in people's minds, and were often taken for granted. Cognitive dimension of tacit knowledge reflected the people's impression on reality (what) and people's vision of the future (what should be). Although people cannot easily articulate them out, these tacit modes determined how we understand the world.

Explicit knowledge can be disposed easily by computer and transmitted or stored in the database in the form of electrons. However, tacit knowledge is essentially subjective, intuitive, and it is difficult to dispose or transmit in a systematic and rational way. If organizations need to communicate and share tacit knowledge, they have to convert tacit knowledge to text or figures, etc. which can be understood by all people. The process completes the conversion from explicit knowledge to tacit knowledge.

2.3 The New Model of Economic Growth

2.3.1 Income Decomposition Method

Liu (2004) and others pointed out that the added value (national income) included the property income brought by investment as well as the mixed income of operation income derived from operating and managing these investments. The rapid increase in such mixed income has increased the total amount of capital on the one hand and provided the impetus to China's economic growth on the other. It was an important reason for the expansion of Chinese residents (mainly urban residents) income distribution gap after the reform and opening up. In accordance with this logic, the national income can be decomposed as the following:

$$GDP = laborers' \, income + investments' \, income + mixed \, income \tag{2.1}$$

It is shown that establishing the universal economic growth model which includes the factors of science and technology input and institutional innovation and so on should embark from some kind of basic economic principles. The synergy theory decomposes the gross domestic product into compensation of employees, compensation of investors and synergy benefits, and studies the economic growth by profit value decomposition method.

Using profit decomposition method, GDP can be decomposed into compensation of employees (generalized compensation of employees includes wages, social security, tax revenue, etc.), investors' interests (generalized investors' interests includes depreciation, the profit share of investors, tax revenue, etc.), synergy benefits, and so on. This is the starting point for the synergy theory of economic growth which can be expressed as:

$$GDP = compensation \; of \; employee + investors' \; interests + synergy \; benefits \tag{2.2}$$

Synergy benefits are shared benefits obtained by the various actors (investors, employees and other stakeholders) in economic activities through interaction, interdependence and concerted action. The existence of these benefits makes various actors mutual support, mutual benefit and common prosperity. In formula (2.2), "synergy benefits" in the joint-stock company's account includes "tax", "accumulation fund", "undistributed profit", "loan interest" and so on. It is "the third item" that is independent of compensation of employees and physical capital benefits, and the "surplus" after "compensation of employees" and "investors' interests" are removed from "gross domestic product". The surplus is the source to improve the innovation ability (to expand reproduction and ability to produce new products). The synergy benefits are determined by the knowledge factors which have certain "public product characteristics" of investment in physical capital, science and technology, human capital and so on. At the same time, it is also related to internal and external environmental factors such as pollutant discharge, energy consumption and industrial structure (Jiang et al. 2014).

From the formation mechanism, we can see that synergy benefits are determined by the knowledge factors which have certain "public product characteristics" of investment in physical capital, science and technology, human capital and so on. Thus, the functional form of synergy benefits can be written:

$$G = G(S, H, D, K, L\ldots) \tag{2.3}$$

In (2.3), G represents synergy benefits, L represents labor, H represents human capital (measured by the years of schooling of laborers), S represents science and technology input (measured by R&D expenditure), D represents investment in physical capital, and K represents the physical capital stock of the previous period (If it is the annual data, K is the physical capital stock at the end of last year).

There are many forms of synergy benefits function, such as a common form of

$$\textit{Synergy benefits} = cSHD/(LK) \tag{2.4}$$

We can find that science and technology, human capital, the investment in physical capital are combined in the synergy benefits function, and mathematically they are multiplied together. It is worth noting that the synergy benefits have many forms, so formula (2.3) has various forms. Formula (2.4) is just a relatively simple form of formula (2.3). For example, another form of synergy benefits is $cHD/K + cSD/K$. These different forms represent different types of the synergistic relationship of science and technology input, human capital and investment in physical capital.

Thus, (2.2) is written as a relatively simple quantitative form (there are other quantitative forms, we can see the various forms of functions listed in Table 2.3 as the following:

$$Y = aL^{\alpha}H^{\beta}S^{\gamma}D^{\delta} + bK + cSHD/LK + u \tag{2.5}$$

In the (2.5), Y represents the output of the economic system (GDP), L represents labor, H represents human capital (measured by the years of schooling of laborers), S represents science and technology input (measured by R&D expenditure), D represents investment in physical capital, and K represents the physical capital stock of the previous period. While α, β, γ, δ, a, b, c are parameters, which are determined by the institution and environmental externalities. In the (2.5), $aL^{\alpha}H^{\beta}S^{\gamma}D^{\delta}$ represents compensation of employees, bK represents physical capital benefits, $cSHD/LK$ represents synergy benefits, and u represents "other" of the (2.2).

2.3.1.1 Function of Compensation of Employees

Function of compensation of employees can be written as

$$V = aL^{\alpha}H^{\beta}S^{\gamma}D^{\delta} \tag{2.6}$$

It not only includes the role of labor L, but also the role of knowledge. The role of knowledge consists of three parts: materialized knowledge which is born in investment in physical capital D, new knowledge brought by science and

Table 2.3 Various forms of function of compensation of employees, function of investors' interests, and function of synergy benefits

Country	Period	Function of compensation of employees	Function of investors' interests	Function of synergy benefits
China	1953–1976	$537(HL)^{0.76}(SD/L)^{-0.23}$	$0.33K$	$0.867SD/K - 13.5S$
China	1977–2012	$0.001243(HL)^{0.803}(SD/L)^{0.228}$	$0.19K$	$1334HSD/K^2$
U.S.A	1900–2008	$0.00316(HL)^{0.482} *$ $(SD/L)^{0.001461t-0.0000000488t^3}$	$0.12K$	$0.0007SH/K +$ $0.007HD/K$
Britain	1960–2010	$0.000002(HL)^{0.83}(SD/L)^{0.115}$	$0.12K$	$139SD/K$
South Korea	1960–2010	$0.038(HL)^{1.125}(SD/L)^{0.092}$	$0.14K$	$19.3HSD/LK + 4.5L$
France	1980–2010	$0.013(HL)^{0.57}(SD/L)^{0.08}$	$0.142K$	$74SD/K$
Germany	1980–2010	$0.038(HL)^{0.292}(SD)^{0.15}$	$0.235K$	$0.48SD/K$
Canada	1980–2010	$0.0436H^{1.04}(SDH)^{0.091}$	$0.115K$	$83.7SD/K$
Japan	1955–2009	$0.11788(HL)^{0.4}(SD/L)^{0.36}$	$0.117K$	$99.5SD/K - 332SD/L$
Australia	1980–2010	$0.102(HL)^{0.487}(SD/L)^{0.13}$	$0.14K$	$83SD/K$
Singapore	1980–2009	$0.038(HL)^{0.276}(SD/L)^{0.247}$	$0.27K$	$112.3HSD/K^2 - 8.69S$
New Zealand	1980–2010	$6.6(HL)^{0.32}(SD/L)^{0.14}$	$0.105K$	$84.9SD/K + 1.64L$
Italy	1980–2010	$95.5(HLSD)^{0.12}$	$0.168K$	$0.106SD/K$
Ireland	1980–2010	$7.56(HL)^{0.4}(SD/L)^{0.15}$	$0.316K$	$0.144SDH/K^2$
Sweden	1993–2009	$0.06(HL)^{0.42}(SD/L)^{0.268}$	$0.166K$	$0.36SD/K$
Finland	1980–2010	$1.235(HL)^{0.338}(SD/L)^{0.17}$	$0.154K$	$5SHD/K^2$

technology input S, and human capital H which can be measured by the years of schooling of laborers or the number of professionals. We see that in the function of compensation of employees, science and technology, human capital, physical capital are collaborated together, and mathematically speaking, they are in the form of exponential multiplication together.

2.3.1.2 Function of Investors' Interests

The function of investors' interests is:

$$\text{Return on the physical capital stock} = bK \tag{2.7}$$

In (2.7), K is the physical capital stock, and b is the return coefficient of the physical capital stock in the previous period.

2.3.2 Decomposition of Economic Growth Rate

According to the above model (2.5), the model of economic growth rate can be established through the method of seeking total differential. It can identify the relationship between GDP, labor, human capital, science and technology investment, physical capital stock, investment in physical capital, institutional factors, and the economic externalities in economic growth, thereby integrating the reasonable elements from the new growth theory and the new institutional economics organically (Liu and Jiang 2015).

From the perspective of the production factors, investment in physical capital D and physical capital stock K are the two elements of physical capital, while human capital H and science and technology input S are two elements of knowledge.

According to the model (2.5), the following decomposition model of economic growth rate can be deduced.

$$\begin{aligned} y = & \frac{bK - cSHD/LK}{Y}k + \frac{cSHD/LK + a\delta L^{\alpha}H^{\beta}S^{\gamma}D^{\delta}}{Y}d \\ & + \frac{cSHD/LK + a\gamma L^{\alpha}H^{\beta}S^{\gamma}D^{\delta}}{Y}s + \frac{a\beta L^{\alpha}H^{\beta}S^{\gamma}D^{\delta} + cSHD/LK}{Y}h \\ & + \frac{a\alpha L^{\alpha}H^{\beta}S^{\gamma}D^{\delta} - cSHD/LK}{Y}l + i + q \end{aligned} \tag{2.8}$$

In formula (2.8), y is the rate of change (economic growth rate) of Y(GDP), k is the rate of change of K (physical capital stock), d is the rate of change of D (investment in physical capital), s is the rate of change of S (science and technology input), h is the rate of change of H (human capital), l is the rate of change of L (labor), i is the effect institutional innovation on economic growth and q is the impact of economic environmental externalities on economic growth.

We can easily calculate the contribution of various factors to economic growth by the use of Eq. (2.8). The calculation results are as follows.

$$\begin{aligned} \eta_K &= \frac{bK - cSHD/LK}{Y}\cdot\frac{k}{y};\ \eta_D = \frac{cSHD/LK + a\delta L^{\alpha}H^{\beta}S^{\gamma}D^{\delta}}{Y}\cdot\frac{d}{y}; \\ \eta_S &= \frac{cSHD/LK + a\gamma L^{\alpha}H^{\beta}S^{\gamma}D^{\delta}}{Y}\cdot\frac{s}{y};\ \eta_H = \frac{a\beta L^{\alpha}H^{\beta}S^{\gamma}D^{\delta} + cSHD/LK}{Y}\cdot\frac{h}{y} \\ \eta_L &= \frac{a\alpha L^{\alpha}H^{\beta}S^{\gamma}D^{\delta} - cSHD/LK}{Y}\cdot\frac{l}{y};\ \eta_I = i/y;\ \eta_E = q/y \end{aligned} \tag{2.9}$$

In (2.9), $\eta_K, \eta_D, \eta_S, \eta_H, \eta_L, \eta_I$ and η_E respectively represent the contribution of physical capital stock growth to economic growth, the contribution of investment in physical capital growth to economic growth, the contribution of science and technology input to economic growth, the contribution of human capital growth to economic growth, the contribution of the labor to economic growth, the contribution of institutional innovation to economic growth and the impact rate of economic environmental externalities on economic growth.

The parameters α, β, γ, δ, a, b, c in (2.9) are determined by econometric method, while the calculation of η_I requires Data Envelopment Analysis (DEA). η_E (the impact rate of economic environmental externalities on economic growth) is "surplus after the removal of various factors", and measured by using the residual method.

2.3.3 Steps of Calculating the Contribution of Various Factors to Economic Growth

The calculation process could be divided into the following six steps (Jiang et al. 2014).

Step one is to establish economic growth facts and databases including the sequence data of output Y (GDP), compensation of employees V, investment in physical capital D, physical capital stock K, human capital H, science and technology input S, labor L, and so on[1].

Step two is to establish the model of compensation of employees. Taking log LH and $\log SD/L$ as the independent variables, $\log V$ as the dependent variable, we perform a multiple regression analysis, and obtain model (2.6). Among the above model, $\log L$ is the logarithm of labor (quantity of employment or labor hours), $\log HSD/L$ is the logarithm of investment in physical capital D multiplied by the inputs of science and technology and multiplied by the human capital H and then divided by the labor L, and $\log V$ is the logarithm of the compensation of laborers V.

Step three is to establish investment value model.

If we write the sum of investors' interests and synergy benefits as M, and call M as the investment value function, then the model of investment value function (referred to as the investment value model) is

$$M = bK + cSHD/LK + eS + u \tag{2.10}$$

Thus, model (2.5) can be written as

$$Y = V + M \tag{2.11}$$

Namely,

$$M = Y - V \tag{2.12}$$

[1]Gross domestic product, compensation of employees, investment in physical capital, physical capital stock (previous year), and science and technology input (last two years) are measured at constant prices. Human capital = the quantity of employment * average years of schooling of laborers. The labor force is measured by the quantity of employment or the total labor time.

In Eq. (2.12), V represents compensation of employees, and M is the sum of investors' interests and synergy benefits.

In the empirical calculation, since V is a non-linear function, it is necessary to first calculate each parameter in the model of compensation of employees (2.6), and then calculate each parameter in the formula (2.10). In other words, the empirical model of model (2.5) requires modeling twice.

The method to establish empirical model of the investment value function (2.10) is as follows. Taking physical capital stock, investment in physical capital multiplied by science and technology input and then divided by the physical capital stock as the independent variables, the value of GDP minus compensation of employees as the dependent variable, and then multiple regression of the data.

Step four is that, the models got by the step two and step three are substituted into the model (2.5) to obtain a relationship model of GDP and labor, physical capital stock, science and technology, investment in physical capital and human capital.

Step five is to calculate the contribution of institutional innovation to economic growth by the use of the DEA method.

Step six is that, after calculating the contribution of physical capital stock, investment in physical capital, science and technology, human capital, labor, institution and other factors to economic growth, the impact rate of economic environmental externalities is calculated by using the residual method in accordance with formula (2.9) (Fig. 2.3).

2.4 Three Hypotheses of Economics and the Problems of Endogenous Growth

There are three common hypotheses in modern economics theory as following: output-depletion hypothesis, decomposition hypothesis (decompose all outputs into physical capital benefits and compensation of employees) and marginal revenue hypothesis (under the condition of profit maximization, the price of production factor is equal to its marginal output). These hypotheses are confined to some certain conditions, which mean that they cannot be used universally. These hypotheses have their limitations from the perspective of synergy theory in economic growth.

2.4.1 Three Hypotheses in Modern Economics

2.4.1.1 Output-Depletion Hypothesis

Samuelson (1992) discussed output-depletion hypothesis in the book of *Economics*. In the condition of unchanged returns to scale, if the price is determined by the marginal product of the production factor, the entire output will be just run out and there is no remaining or inadequacy.

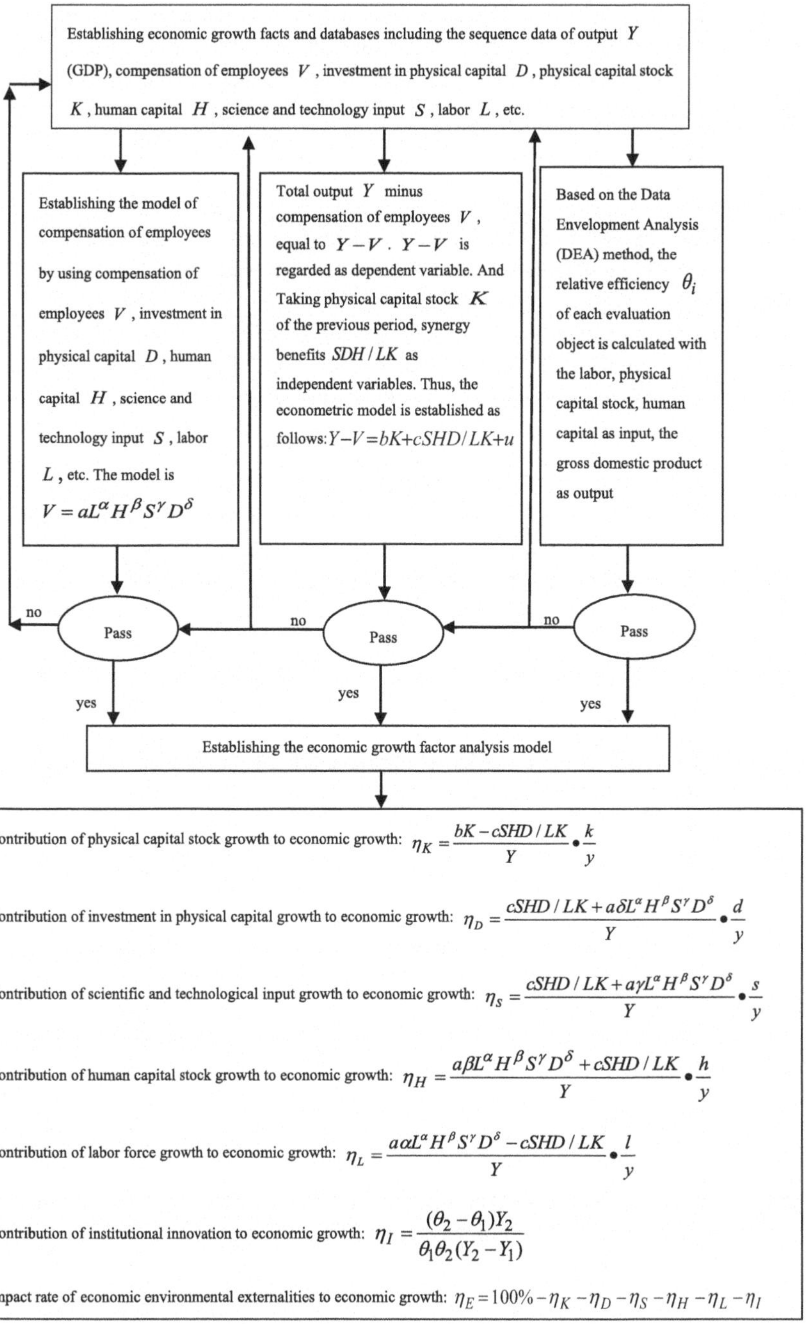

Fig. 2.3 The process of economic growth factor analysis based on synergy theory

According to the output-depletion hypothesis, the compensation of the production factors owner represents the income level, which is determined by the number and price of production factor that owned by the production factor owner. The remuneration of labor is wage, the remuneration of land is rent, interest is the reward of capital, and profit is the reward of entrepreneurial ability.

2.4.1.2 Decomposition Hypothesis: Total Outputs Are Separated into Physical Capital Benefits and Compensation of Employees

Jorgenson (2001) pointed out that outputs were separated into consumption goods and investment goods. Net input is separated into capital and labor service. Identity between input value and output value can be described as:

$$q_C C + q_I I = p_K K + p_L L \tag{2.13}$$

In the equation, C and I respectively refer to quantity of consumer goods and investment good, while K and L respectively refer to quantity of capital and labor input. Their corresponding price are described as q_c, q_I, p_K and p_L.

Many scholars adopted the formula of SNA accounting system in their economic growth accounting:

$$Y = Y_K + Y_L \tag{2.14}$$

In this identity, Y refers to added value (or GDP), Y_K is physical capital benefits and Y_L is compensation of employees.

So,

$$Y_K/Y + Y_L/Y = 1 \tag{2.15}$$

In this equation, Y_K/Y is the share of physical capital benefits in output (expressed by v_K). Y_L/Y is the share of compensation of employees in output (expressed by in v_L).

Namely,

$$v_K + v_L = 1 \tag{2.16}$$

2.4.1.3 Marginal Revenue Hypothesis: The Price of Production Factor Is Equal to It Marginal Output in the Condition of Profit Maximization

Many economics textbook deduced the marginal revenue hypothesis in the behaviors of relevant manufacturers:

Assuming that the manufacturers' output is expressed by the first-order homogeneous function, which the second-order function is continuously differentiable and increasing, and the marginal productivity is decreasing.

$$Y = F(K, L) \tag{2.17}$$

In this equation, K and L respectively are total physical capital stock and labor of input. There is no introduction of technological progress, but if we introduce technological progress into the production, we can draw the same conclusion.

So, manufacturers' profits can be described as

$$F(K, L) - (r + \delta)K - \omega L \tag{2.18}$$

In this equation, δ is the capital depreciation rate, r is the rate of capital return, and ω is salary.

Manufacturers' behavior is to maximize the profit by deciding how much capital and labor to invest, how much goods to product.

$$\max_{K,L} F(K, L) - (r + \delta)K - \omega L \tag{2.19}$$

Then, optimal conditions can be described as:

$$F'(K) = r + \delta; F'(L) = \omega \tag{2.20}$$

Optimal conditions suggest that the marginal productivity of capital equals to the sum of the capital return rate and capital depreciation rate in the market, and the wage rate is equal to the marginal productivity of labor.

2.4.2 *The "Three Hypotheses" of Economics from the Perspective of the Synergy Theory*

2.4.2.1 Externality and Output-Depletion Hypothesis

There are some factors that influence the economic growth. These factors include labor, physical-capital (including human capital stock and investment in physical capital), knowledge (new knowledge brought by human capital, science and technology, etc.), institution, and economic externalities (including the externalities of natural environment, social environment, market environment, policy environment, etc.). The connotation of distribution institution, which is referred to "production factors participate in the distribution in accordance with their contributions", is that production factors (such as labor, capital, technology, and management) in the whole society will obtain corresponding returns according to the share of their performances in the creation of social wealth.

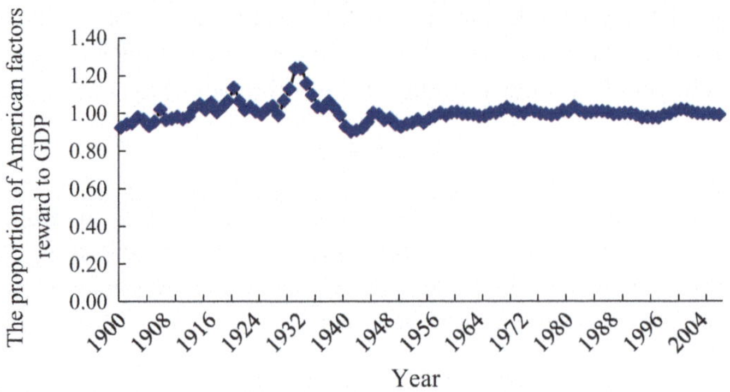

Fig. 2.4 The proportion of American production factors reward to GDP

However, it is impossible that the sum of all distribution rate equal to 100%, due to the objective limitations of the distribution institution and the economic externalities. Taking America as an example, we can see that the sum of all the production factors' remuneration rate[2] approach to 100%, but not 100%, which result from the economic externalities, not the calculation errors (Fig. 2.4).

2.4.2.2 Polynomial of Income and Decomposition Hypothesis

Gross Domestic Product (GDP) could be expressed by three different performance forms, these forms are value form, income form and product form. In the process of actual accounting, the three performance forms correspond to the three calculation methods, including approach of production, approach of income and approach of expenditure. From the view of income performance form, Gross Domestic Product is the sum of the initial distribution income, which is created by all resident units and allocated to resident units and non-resident units over a period of time. Accordingly, from the perspective of factor income, the approach of income believes that GDP is the sum of laborers' incomes, taxes, profits, depreciation of physical capital, and so on (Jiang and Wang 2008).

GDP, according to income approach, is composed of four parts in China Statistical Yearbook (The structure of regional GDP is demonstrated in Table 2.4). Its calculation equation is

[2]In this book, the so-called "the sum of compensation share of the various production factors" = the remuneration of physical capital stock + the remuneration of the investment in physical capital + the remuneration of the science and technology + the compensation of employees + the remuneration of the human capital.

Table 2.4 The structure of gross regional product (2005, some provinces and cities) unit: 100 million yuan

Region	Gross regional product	Compensation of employees	Depreciation of physical capital	Net product tax	Earning surplus
Beijing	6886.31	3114.15	1095.51	1017.05	1659.60
Tianjin	3697.62	1164.82	515.77	727.37	1289.66
Hebei	10096.11	4160.01	1254.97	1316.07	3365.06
Shanxi	4179.52	1496.72	634.89	644.88	1403.03
Inner Mongolia	3895.55	1599.46	544.87	433.21	1318.01

$$\begin{aligned} GDP = {} & compensation\ of\ employee + depreciation\ of\ physical \\ & capital + net\ production\ tax + earning\ surplus \end{aligned} \tag{2.21}$$

According to the synergy theory, from the perspective of earnings decomposition, the output of the economic system includes not only compensation of employees, physical capital benefits, but also the synergy benefits. The synergy benefits are the benefits, which to some extents are shared by laborers, investors and other stakeholders, but cannot be clearly assigned to anyone. Therefore, it is wrong to decompose all the outputs into physical capital benefits and compensation of employees.

2.4.2.3 Returns to Scale and Marginal Revenue Hypothesis

The traditional theory believes that production factors could divide into labor, capital, and land. Every factor's reward is determined by the number of the marginal products of this factor, in other words, it is determined by the number of products produced by the last unit input of this factor. Every factor's service price (the unit income that the owner of this factor) is equal to the marginal product value of this factor. Clark, the American economist, founded the marginal productivity theory. In his opinions, the incomes of various factor owners in distribution are exactly equal to their contributions to production. Specifically, in the static economy, income of labor (wages) is determined by labor's marginal output, and income of capital (interest) is determined by capital's marginal output. Multiply wage by the amount of labor is equal to the total income of the labor factor. Multiply interest by the amount of capital is equal to the total income of capital factor (Jiang and Wang 2008).

According to synergy theory discussed in this book, dating from economics principles of the relationship between GDP and income of production factors, we can draw the conclusion based on the model (2.6):

$$w = \frac{aL^{\alpha}H^{\beta}S^{\gamma}D^{\delta}}{L} = aL^{\alpha-1}H^{\beta}S^{\gamma}D^{\delta} \quad (2.22)$$

Laborers' real wage is $w = aL^{\alpha-1}H^{\beta}S^{\gamma}D^{\delta}$, but workforce's marginal output is $\frac{\partial Y}{\partial L} = \alpha aL^{\alpha-1}H^{\beta}S^{\gamma}D^{\delta}$. α is less than 1 in general. Therefore, real wage (w) is greater than theoretical workforce's marginal output $\left(\frac{\partial Y}{\partial L}\right)$, and the wage rate depends on the following factors, including the number of labor force, investment in physical capital, human capital, science and technology input, and other factors.

Wu (1999) pointed out that the efficiency wage theory of information economics rejected the marginal wages theory to some extent. Assuming that each social member accepts reservation wages, under the condition of reservation wages, each member is willing to accept a certain amount of labor. Assuming that each worker who accepts the reservation wage has different abilities, then the volume of output per worker is different. In this way, if you pay all workers the same wages, workers who have abilities will be lazy. In order to stimulate these workers to work better, you need to pay them extra money which is known as an information rent. This kind of behavior is the inspiration for workers to show their true ability, therefore, the distribution principle that more pays for more work is formed. This is the fundamental view of information economists' efficiency wage theory. An important point of efficiency wage theory is that human capacity is different, and the cost paid to the workers who work more than others is not always large. On the contrary, the new classical economics in fact recognized that the ability of people was homogeneous.[3]

In our view, real wages are compensations paid to workers, and their work includes both the labor force L and the role of knowledge (the role of knowledge is composed by three parts: physical-chemical knowledge which was born within the investment in physical capital D, the new knowledge brought about by science and technology input S, human capital H). Therefore, the compensations paid to workers actually is higher than the marginal output of labor force $\frac{\partial Y}{\partial L} = \alpha aL^{\alpha-1}H^{\beta}S^{\gamma}D^{\delta}$.

Considering all the points discussed above, according to synergy theory, "output-depletion" hypothesis could only be set up on the conditions of the absence of externality; "only under the conditions that the returns to scale remain unchanged, can labor force and capital distributed according to the rules of marginal output"; decomposition hypothesis (all output is decomposed into physical capital benefits and compensations of employees) has its special applicable condition. The condition is that: only considering the two factors of the labor and capital, the returns to scale remain unchanged, and there is no existence of the synergy benefits and externality.

---

[3]Heterogeneity is an important part of information economics. Of course, the efficient wage will lead to certain consequences, such as the unemployment of some workers and the income difference between the workers. Perhaps, the efficient wage is a sub-optimal state.

2.4.3 Endogenous Growth

According to the ideas of the endogenous growth theory (Gong 2005), on the CES utility function and general production function, we can obtain

$$\begin{aligned} \gamma_k &= f(k)/k - c/k - n - \delta \\ \gamma_c &= \frac{1}{\theta}(f'(k) - \rho - \delta) \end{aligned} \tag{2.23}$$

We can know through the condition of transversality

$$\lim_{t \to \infty}(f'(k) - \delta) > \lim_{t \to \infty}(\gamma_k + n) \tag{2.24}$$

If $b - \varphi > \delta + n$, we can know that the growth rate is a positive constant. Therefore, according to (2.22), we can obtain

$$\overset{*}{\gamma_c} = \frac{1}{\theta}(b - \varphi - \delta - \rho) \tag{2.25}$$

The growth rate of the level of per-capita consumption is positive, which means that $b > \varphi + \delta + \rho$, while the condition of transversality requires $\rho > n$, therefore, it is naturally to ensure that $b - \varphi > +\delta + \rho$, then, the per-capita physical capital stock will grow infinitely. $\overset{*}{\gamma_k} = \overset{*}{\gamma_c}$ will be proved in the following paragraph.

First of all, according to the accumulation equation of per-capita physical capital stock, we can get:

$$\overset{*}{\gamma_k} = b - \varphi - \lim_{k \to \infty}(c/k) - n - \delta \tag{2.26}$$

If $\overset{*}{\gamma_k} < \overset{*}{\gamma_c}$, per-capita physical capital stock is growing at a slower rate than per-capita level of consumption, thus $\lim_{k \to \infty} c/k = 0$ and $\overset{*}{\gamma_k} = b - \varphi - n - \delta$. This is inconsistent with condition of transversality $\lim_{t \to \infty}(f'(k) = \overset{*}{\gamma_k} + n + \delta$.

Therefore, according the integrated analysis, we can obtain $\overset{*}{\gamma_k} = \overset{*}{\gamma_c}$.

The above derivation gives the sufficient condition of endogenous economic growth, what means that $\varphi = \lim_{k \to \infty}(cSHD/LK^2)$ is the constant. At the same time, it gives the basic characteristics of equilibrium that the growth rate of per-capita consumption level, per-capita physical capital stock and per-capita output are all equal to a constant.

This constant is

$$\gamma_y = \gamma_k = \gamma_c = (b - \varphi - \delta - \rho)/\theta \tag{2.27}$$

Further, the ratio between the consumption level and the physical capital stock in the equilibrium approaches to the constant is named

$$\lim_{k \to \infty} (c/k) = \zeta \tag{2.28}$$

In this formula, $\zeta = (b - \varphi - \delta)(\theta - 1)/\theta + \rho/\theta - n$ is a constant.

2.5 Summary

This chapter proposes the synergy theory, and holds an idea that science and technology, human capital and investment in physical capital have a synergy relationship. The knowledge flows and knowledge sharing are the basis of cooperation; from the perspective of the profit decomposition, economic system outputs not only include compensation of employees and physical capital benefits, but also synergy benefits. To some extent, synergy benefits are distributed to laborers, investors and other stakeholders, while the benefits cannot be clearly allocated to either side. The form of synergy benefits depends on the type of synergy relationship among science and technology, human capital and investment in physical capital, and from this way we can establish different types of economic growth models. This chapter proposes to measure the contribution of institutional innovation to economic growth by the use of the DEA method, and also derives sufficient conditions for endogenous growth. At the same time, this chapter studies applicable conditions of decomposing hypothesis, output-decomposition hypothesis and marginal revenue hypothesis in modern economic theory, and reveals limitations of these assumptions from the perspective of the synergy theory of economic growth.

References

Aghion, P., & Howitt, P. (2004). Endogenous growth theory. Beijing: Peking University Press.
Arrow, K.J. (1962). The economic implications of learning by doing. Review of Economic Studies, 29(80), 155–173.
Chandler, A.D. (2005). The Dynamic Firm: The Role of Technology, Strategy, Organization, and Regions. Beijing: China Machine Press.
Chen, L.X. (2006). The principle of distributing according to contribution by production elements in primary socialist stage. Commercial Research, (5), 9–11.
Chuang, Y.C. (1998). Learning by doing, the technology gap and growth. International Economic Review, 39(39), 697–721.
Coase, R.H. (1998). The problem of social cost. Shanghai: Shanghai Joint Publishing Press.

Cohen, W.M, & Levinthal, D.A. (1989). Innovation and learning: the two faces of R&D. Economic Journal, 99(397), 569–596.
Dan, B.D., & Loewy, M.B. (1998). Free trade, growth, and convergence. Journal of Economic Growth, 3(2), 143–170.
Denison, E.F. (1962). The sources of economic growth in the United States and the alternatives before us. Washington: Committee for Economic Development.
Denison, E.F., & Chung, W.K. (1987). How Japan's economy grew so fast: the sources of postwar expansion. Pacific Affairs, 51(4), 663.
Dodzin, S., & Vamvakidis, A. (2004). Trade and industrialization in developing agricultural economies. Journal of Development Economics, 75(1), 319–328.
Gong, L.T. (2005). Advanced macroeconomics. Wuhan: Wuhan University Press.
Grossman, G.M., & Helpman, E. (1991). Innovation and growth in the global economy. Boston: The MIT Press.
Hendricks, L. (2000). Equipment investment and growth in developing countries. Journal of Development Economics, 61(2), 335–364.
Hisao, K. (1980). Speech of Japan's economic growth. China Social Sciences Press.
Jiang, Z.H. (2004). Regional economic growth factors of China. Journal of Dalian University, (5), 66–69.
Jiang, Z.H., & Wang, Q.F. (2008). Three hypothesis of distribution theory and economics. Science and Technology Innovation Herald, (2), 115–116.
Jiang, Z.H., Liu, J.H., Liu, S., et al. (2014). The cooperation theoretical analysis of innovation-driven growth model: ZTE, as an example. Science and Technology Management Research, (9), 1–5.
Jones, C.I. (1994). Economic growth and the relative price of capital. Journal of Monetary Economics, 34(3), 359–382.
Jorgenson, D.W. (2001). Productivity Volume 1. Beijing: China Development Press.
Kamaeb, B.D. (1983). The speed and quality of economic growth. Wuhan: Hubei People's Publishing House.
Lee, J.W. (1995). Capital goods imports and long-run growth. Journal of Development Economics, 48(1), 91–110.
Li, B.T. (2005). A review of endogenous innovation growth theory. Masteral Dissertation: Renmin University of China.
Lin, Y.F., Cai, F., & Li, Z. (1994). China 's miracle: development strategy and economic reform. Shanghai: Shanghai Joint Publishing Press.
Lin, Y.F., Cai, F., & Li, Z. (1999). Comparative advantage and development strategy - a reinterpretation of east Asia miracle. Social Sciences in China, (5), 4–20.
Liu, W. (2004). China Economic Growth Report 2004: China's economy entering a new economic growth cycle. Beijing: China Economic Publishing House.
Liu, W.C. (2005). A study on equity and efficiency of public property right change from the perspective of new institutional economics. Doctoral Dissertation: Hunan University.
Liu, G.Z. (2006). The revelation and evolution of western economics distribution of income research normal form. Economic Review, (6), 46–49.
Liu, J.H., & Jiang, Z.H. (2015). Innovation-driven and investment supportive strategies for China's economic transformation based on collaborative theory. Science of Science and Management of S.&.T., (2), 25–33.
Liu, J.H., & Jiang, Z.H. (2016). Innovation drive, transformation and upgrade under the new normal: Henan province as an example. Beijing: Science Press.
Lu, X.X. (1996). Western new institutional economics. Beijing: China Development Press.
Marshall, A. (1981). Principles of economics. Beijing: The Commercial Press.
North, D.C., & Thomas, R.P. (2009). The rise of the western world. Beijing: HuaXia Publishing House.
Pigou, A.C. (1999). The economics of welfare. Beijing: China Social Sciences Press.
Romer, P.M. (1990). Endogenous technological change. Journal of Political Economy, 98(5), 71–102.

Samuelson, P.A. (1992). Economics. Beijing: China Development Press.
Samuelson, P.A., & Nordhaus, W.D. (1999). Economics. Beijing: HuaXia Press.
Schmid, A.A. (1999). Property, Power, and Public Choice: An Inquiry into Law and Economics. Shanghai: Shanghai People's Publishing House.
Song, D.L., Wang, L.H., & Dong, Z.Q. (2011). Technological progress of capital presentation and its contribution to economic growth (1981–2007). Social Sciences in China, (2), 91–106.
Wang, W.B., Chen, C.B., & Xu, H.Y. (2002). An empirical analysis on China's economic growth model containing international factors. Modern Economic Science, (2), 33–37.
Wolf, C.J. (1994). Markets or governments. Beijing: China Development Press.
Wu, R.X. (1988). Economic Growth Theory. Economic Research Reference.
Wu, Y.F. (1999). Western Economics. Beijing: Renmin University Press.
Wu, Y.F. (2005). Schools and trends in contemporary western economics. Beijing: Capital University of Economics and Business press.
Xu, S.W. (2005). Research on real estate tax institution. Doctoral Dissertation: Xiamen University.
Young, A. (1991). Learning by doing and the dynamic effects of international trade. Quarterly Journal of Economics, 106(2), 369–405.
Zeng, Y.Z. (2007). A review of post-Keynesian economic growth theory. Masteral Dissertation: Yunnan University.
Zhang, W.C. (2000). Economic explanation. Beijing: The Commercial Press.
Zhang, X.L. (2006). Research on knowledge agglomeration. Doctoral Dissertation: Tianjin University.
Zhao, Z.Y., Lu, B.Y., & Guo, Q.W. (2007). On the dynamic integration of capital accumulation and technological progress: a stylized fact in China's economic growth. Economic Research Journal, (11), 18–31.

Chapter 3
The Calculation and Empirical Analysis on the Contribution of Institutional Innovation to Economic Growth

Chapter 2 of this book discusses various factors that determine and influence economic growth, including labor, physical capital stock and investment in physical capital, human capital, science and technology, institution, and economic externalities. So, how much do these factors contribute to economic growth? The contribution of labor, physical capital stock, investment in physical capital, human capital, science and technology is calculated according to the economic growth modeling method discussed in the last chapter. According to the theoretical view of new institutional economics that the most fundamental and essential role of institutional innovation to economic growth is to improve the resource allocation efficiency of production factors, the contribution of institutional innovation is measured by using DEA (Data Envelopment Analysis). This chapter discusses the above in detail.

3.1 The Method of DEA

3.1.1 C^2R Model

From the mechanism, the most basic and essential function of institutional innovation in economic growth is to improve the production factors allocation efficiency. Therefore, efficiency analysis can be used to calculate the contribution of institutional innovation in economic growth; Data Envelopment Analysis (Jiang 2004) is such a method. The method uses the total amount of labor force, physical capital stock and human capital stock as input, GDP as output to get relative efficiency of DMU (Decision Making Units). C^2R model is the basic model of analysis of institutional efficiency by DEA.

J. H. Liu and Z. H. Jiang, *The Synergy Theory on Economic Growth: Comparative Study Between China and Developed Countries*,
https://doi.org/10.1007/978-981-13-1885-6_3

One form of C^2R model is

$$D = \begin{cases} \min \theta \\ s.t. \sum_{j=1}^{n} \lambda_j x_j \leq \theta x_0 \\ \sum_{j=1}^{n} \lambda_j y_j \geq y_0 \\ \lambda_j \geq 0, j = 1, \ldots, n \end{cases} \tag{3.1}$$

The above model is used to estimate the validity of DMU_{jo}. Its meaning is to reduce every variable of input (x_0) by the same ratio $\theta(\leq 1)$ in the premise of keeping the output constant in "input possible set". If this can be achieved, it means that output can be kept constant by using fewer inputs than DMU_{jo}, and proves that the current DMU_{jo} must not a valid production activity; conversely, DMU_{jo} is a valid production activity.

The dual model of the above models is

$$D' = \begin{cases} \max \alpha \\ s.t. \sum_{j=1}^{n} \lambda_j x_j \leq x_0 \\ \sum_{j=1}^{n} \lambda_j y_j \geq \alpha y_0 \\ \lambda_j \geq 0, j = 1, \ldots, n \end{cases} \tag{3.2}$$

D' is used to estimate the validity of DMU_{jo}. Its meaning is to expand output in the same ratio of α compared with y_0 in the premise of keeping the input constant in "output possible set". If '$\alpha > 1$', it indicates that the current DMU_{jo} is a valid production activity.

There is a very close relationship between the optimal solution of planning problem D and D'. Generally, if we set up $\lambda^*, s^{*-}, s^{*+}, \theta^*$ as optimal solution of D, $\lambda^{**}, s^{**-}, s^{**+}, \theta^{**}, \alpha^*$ as optimal solution of D', we can draw the conclusion as follows:

$$\lambda^{**} = \frac{\lambda^*}{\theta^*}, s^{**-} = \frac{s^{*-}}{\theta^*}, s^{**+} = \frac{s^{*+}}{\theta^*}, \alpha^* = \frac{1}{\theta^*} \tag{3.3}$$

From two different angles of "constant output, minimal input" and "constant input, maximum output", D and D' construct two linear programming models. In fact, it studies the validity of DMU on the basis of "input possible sets" and "output possible sets".

In the above models, the s refers to waste of input or output compared with the maximum efficiency ($\theta^* = 1$).

When $\theta^* = 1$, we call DMU_0 as C^2R effective, and in accordance with the optimal solution of the above model $\lambda_j^* (j = 1, \ldots, n)$ to judge the returns to scale of DMU_0, that is

If $\sum \lambda_j^* = 1$, DMU_0 is constant to scale;
If $\sum \lambda_j^* < 1$, DMU_0 is increasing return to scale;
If $\sum \lambda_j^* > 1$, DMU_0 is decreasing return to scale.

3.1.2 Calculation Formula for the Contribution of Institutional Innovation to Economic Growth

There are two steps for using DEA to measure the contribution of institutional innovation to economic growth.

The first step is to use model (3.2) to calculate the relative efficiency from the base period to the end period of each year. Using model (3.2) to estimate the validity of DMU_{jo}. Its meaning is to expand output in the same ratio of a compared with y_0 in the premise of keeping the input constant in "output possible set". If $\alpha > 1$, then the current DMU_{jo} is not a valid production activity.

The second step is to set the "output amplification ratio" of the base period as α_1, the relative efficiency of the base period as θ_1, the "output amplification ratio" of the end period as α_2, the relative efficiency of the end period as θ_2.

To use the method of DEA to measure the contribution of institutional innovation to economic growth, we first need to calculate the relative efficiency of the base period θ_1 and the relative efficiency of the end period θ_2.

Institutional innovation can improve efficiency and reduce losses. The reduced loss is $i = Y_2/\theta_1 - Y_2/\theta_2$. Thus, the calculation formula of the contribution of institutional innovation to economic growth is

$$\eta_I = (Y_2/\theta_1 - Y_2/\theta_2)/(Y_2 - Y_1) = \frac{(\theta_2 - \theta_1)Y_2}{\theta_1\theta_2(Y_2 - Y_1)} = \frac{\varphi(1+y)}{\theta y} \tag{3.4}$$

In (3.4), Y_1 and Y_2 are the total production values of the base period and the end period, θ_1 is relative efficiency of base period, θ_2 is relative efficiency of end period, φ is the average annual change in efficiency, θ is the mean of efficiency, y is the average annual economic growth rate.

Table 3.1 shows the calculation results of the contribution of institutional innovation to economic growth of fifteen countries by using the formula (3.4). In different countries, the contribution of institutional innovation to economic growth is quite different. In many countries, the contribution of institutional innovation is zero, or very small. This does not mean that institutional innovation does not work in the economy, but shows that institutional innovation ensures the economic efficiency does not decline; otherwise, if institutional innovation is not carried out, economic efficiency will decline. The contribution of institutional innovation is more than zero, which means that the institutional innovation can not only prevents the decline in economic operation efficiency, but also promotes economic growth rate.

Table 3.1 Analysis of the contribution of institutional innovation in 15 countries (average annual, %)

Country	Period (year)	Economic growth rate	The contribution of institutional innovation	The impact rate of economic externalities
China	1953–1976	5.5	−17	12
China	1977–2000	9.7	31	−15
China	2001–2012	9.8	5	−20
Britain	1961–1980	2.2	−23	14
Britain	1981–2010	2.4	17	−15
Italy	1981–2010	1.5	0	14
New Zealand	1981–2010	2.5	10	−6
Singapore	1981–2009	6.5	0	−10
Sweden	1993–2010	2.2	0	−17
Japan	1955–1973	9.7	−2	6
Japan	1973–1993	3.4	6	−14
Japan	1993–2009	0.75	−5	29
U.S.A	1900–1929	3.1	−1	8.4
U.S.A	1930–1953	3.7	21.7	2.5
U.S.A	1954–1981	3.4	3.1	7.2
U.S.A	1982–2000	3.3	16.7	−3.7
U.S.A	2001–2008	2.2	4.5	13.1
Canada	1980–2010	2.5	1	−2
South Korea	1960–1972	8	4	31
South Korea	1973–1997	7.9	−10	6
South Korea	1998–2010	4	10	−18
Finland	1981–2010	2.3	10	−11
France	1981–2010	1.9	0	3
Germany	1990–2000	1.9	0	−5
Germany	2001–2010	1	0	−5
Australia	1981–2010	4.5	0	−15
Ireland	1981–2010	4.8	9	12
Average		4.0	3.3	−3.8

The calculation shows that institutional innovation is an important reason for the "high growth, high employment, low inflation" of the America's economy from 1982 to 2000. In this period, the contribution of institutional innovation to economic growth reached 16.7%. The American government created a sound institutional environment for enterprises. For example, the American government revised the laws and regulations such as the *Anti-monopoly Law* and the *Communications Law*, which have promoted the expansion of the scale of enterprises and the further globalization of the economy. At the same time, the stock option system and the national innovation system also effectively promoted the American high-tech industry development, as well as overall economic growth (Jiang 2006).

More importantly, the information technology revolution has brought American-style "institutional innovation". Jorgenson (2001) agreed that information and communication technology pricing played a key role in improving the efficiency of resource allocation (institutional innovation) and promoting economic growth after 1990. They pointed out that the continued decline in prices of information technology equipment and software have steadily increased the role of information and communication technology investment. Per-capita communication flow between the United States and other countries increased about 0.7% every year from 1921 to 1970. In comparison, the U.S. real per-capita GDP and foreign trade have increased about 2.7% per year. Per-capita communication flow increased 5.8% per year but real per-capita GDP and foreign trade have increased 1.8% and 4.9% from 1970 to 1994. In short, if we use per-capita flow of international communications to measure America's globalization, we can see it was lagging behind other economic indicators before 1970, while ahead of other indicators after 1970.

Application of new information technologies greatly reduces communication costs and market transaction costs, as well as enterprise operations and management costs.[1] The reduction in communication costs has had a tremendous impact on the economy, as demonstrated by the more coordinated internal business operations in multinational enterprises than ever before and the increased access to information on international trade in goods and services, as well as the significant reduction in the costs of international financial flows. If other conditions remain unchanged in the future, the reduction in communication costs will certainly stimulate trade and investment to achieve greater development. In particular, it is bound to benefit the vertical division of labor (global sourcing) and a wider range of inter industry trade.

3.2 The Role of Institutional Innovation in Promoting Britain's Economic Growth

In 1981–2010, the economic growth rate in Britain averaged 2.4%. Analyzing the cause of economic growth during this period, we find that the contribution of physical capital stock growth is 13% and the contribution of investment in physical capital is 30%. The sum of these two is 43% which is called physical capital contribution; the contribution of human capital growth is 27% and the contribution of scientific and technological progress is 18%. The sum of these two is 45% which

[1]According to the material provided by J. Hering and others, during 1950–1990, the actual cost of 3 min phone call from London to New York declined from $53.20 to $3.32. By the end of the twentieth century, the cost of remote e-mail whose information is the same as the phone content had been almost zero.

is called the contribution of knowledge progress; the contribution of institutional innovation is 17%; and the impact rate of economic environmental externalities is −15% (which shows that the Britain's investment environment is good during this period).[2] The resource allocation efficiency of production factors in the Britain from 1960 to 2001 is shown in Fig. 3.1. The contribution of Broad innovation (technology innovation, human capital promotion, institutional innovation) reached 62%, which shows that Britain's economic growth is driven by innovation.

Institutional innovation is a factor that has a large impact on the growth of the Britain. During almost 40 years since 1979, there were two major institutional changes in British society. The first was the Thatcher reform, and the second was the Labor Party's "third way" reform. These two reforms have had a significant impact on all aspects of British society.

3.2.1 *Thatcher's Reforms*

After Margaret Thatcher came to power in 1979, the British Conservative Government implemented a series of major and radical reform programs. As the reform had a huge range and far-reaching impacts, some scholars even called it the "Thatcher Revolution" (Carter et al. 1992; Massey 1997).

Like other developed countries, the present British government's administrative reforms mainly due to environmental change at home and abroad, financial, management, and confidence crisis that the government faced. In the early 1980s, many countries were facing heavy pressure to reform. Political leaders felt the impact from factors such as technological innovation, re-positioning of the role of government, the emergence of cross-border consultative mechanism, the rapid change in economic environment, as well as other factors (Carter et al. 1992; Peters 2001).

There are three main reasons for promoting this reform.

(1) The economic pressure caused by inflation.

The Middle-East War from 1973 to 1974 doubled the crude oil prices, giving rise to the worldwide energy crisis, and leading the global economy into severe depression. Britain that had a potential economic crisis before, was faced with economic stagnation, high rate of inflation, and unemployment at the same time. Keynesian economics had been powerless. If economic development is simulated in order to reduce unemployment, the inflation rate will reach a higher level. However, controlling inflation would also reduce the effective demand and exacerbate the economic recession, which makes the unemployment rate stay the same or even increased. Figure 3.2 shows the British long-term Phillips curve from 1967 to 2005, we can see that the curve from a donut shape in a clockwise direction and is shifted

[2]During this time, the growth of the British economy was mainly from Thatcher's reform to promote the growth in investment in physical capital, thus driving economic growth.

Fig. 3.1 Resources allocation efficiency of production factors in Britain during 1960–2001

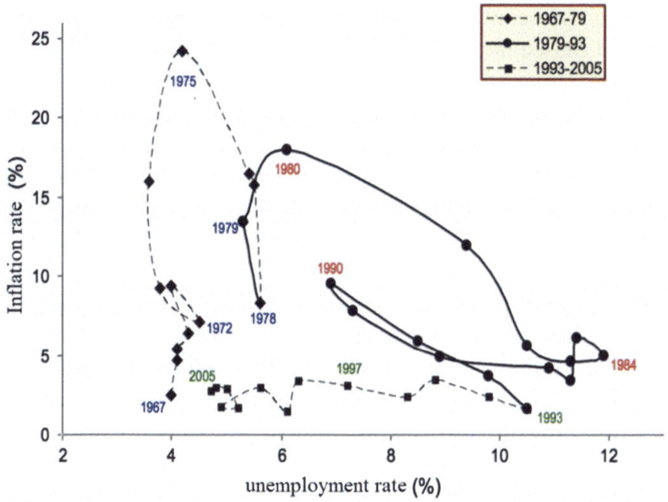

Fig. 3.2 British Phillips curve circle (1967–2005)

to the right. The United Kingdom Phillips curve in 1970s reflected the "stagflation" dilemma in Britain. Moreover, after the mid-1970s, the pound depreciated substantially, and interest rates fluctuated drastically, and the British government's finance worsened. Political consensus which was maintained under the economic stability after the World War II, quickly faced a collapse; with the bankruptcy of Keynesian economic theory, policies of expanding public expenditure and increasing tax which was used to support the state welfare, were suffering severe strike (Carter et al. 1992; Farnham and Horton 1996).

(2) Government agencies were over-bloated, and government spending consumed nearly half of the gross national product.

After the World War II, Britain's general government expenditure (GGE) has been expanding continuously. From 1919 to 1938, the British Government expenditure in public goods and services only on average accounted for 13% of GDP; from 1947 to 1970, the proportion increased to more than 20%. In the mid-1970s, it was as high as 27% (Carter et al. 1992). These figures show the British Government's public expenditure had a huge growth after World War II. The British people are increasingly discontent with the situation that the GGE accounted for a too large a proportion of GDP (Zifcak 1994). The negative consequences were due to too much emphasis on nationalization and social welfare policy which emerged gradually. In 1979, the first White Paper on public spending which was published by the Conservative Party government after they came to power clearly pointed out that: public spending was the core issue of Britain's current economic plight. The huge growth and improper control in public expenditure, was identified as the main factor which had caused the country's economic plight (Thatcher 1998). On the one hand, government spending constituted too much of the GDP which led to a serious shortage of productive investment, very little funding in business technological innovation, scientific and technological progress, and the lack of development potential, which eventually resulted in economic stagnation and high unemployment. On the other hand, the deficit soared, which led to an increasing inflation. The inflation rate was 24.3% in 1975, and upped to 17.9% in 1980 (Fig. 3.3).

(3) The British government was facing the political and administrative plight.

In the late 1960s, there was a "counter-culture" wave in the United Kingdom, that is, the various interest groups no longer followed the traditional political culture, but competed for welfare, high wages, subsidies to enterprises, and other interests. At the same time, the two major parties all promised to provide more interest groups and more benefits which led to counteraction at each other and co-depletion of public resources between the groups and organizations, groups and government, and finally

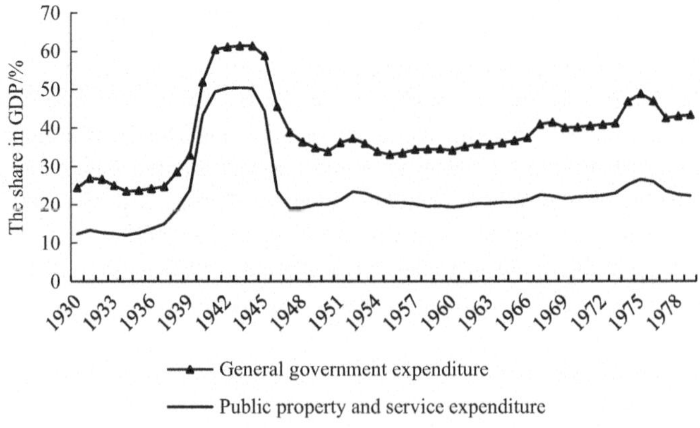

Fig. 3.3 British general government expenditure as a proportion of GDP (1930–1979) (%)

Table 3.2 Several kinds of capitalism system in early 1990s (Pryor 2004)

Degree of coordination	Universal welfare institution	Personalized welfare institution
High level of coordination of production activities above the level of enterprises	Austria, Australia, Belgium, Denmark, Finland, France, Germany, Netherlands, Norway, Sweden	Italy, Japan, Switzerland
Low level of coordination of production activities above the level of enterprises	New Zealand, United Kingdom	Canada, The United States

resulted in "The paralysis of public choice". This phenomenon also indicates that the deliberative corporatism in the United Kingdom constructed during the period of post-war was disorganized, and the government was no longer a powerful arbiter of resource allocation (Carter et al. 1992; Farnham and Horton 1996).

After Margaret Thatcher came to power, a series of reform measures were implemented in response to the above conditions.

(1) Reforming the civil service institution and cutting public spending. Thatcher's government at the beginning of 1979 declared to weaken the political privileges of the civil service, strengthen the cabinet's political control of the civil service system, improve the government departments management, and get rid of the bad habits such as waste and inefficiency by shrinking the size of the civil service system and the introduction of business culture (Thatcher 1998).
(2) Reducing state intervention in the economy and promoting the privatization process. After Margaret Thatcher took office, she began the revolution of sweeping privatization.[3] This reform measure was considered as a political representative of the British Conservative government in the 1980s. The output value of state-owned utilities accounted for 11% of GDP in 1979, while it dropped to only 5.5% of GDP in 1990.
(3) Reconstructing the basis for the normal operation of the market, and launching the "supply economic revolution", namely abolishing government regulation, and promoting enterprises' (supply-side) innovation and development. In addition to tax cuts and privatization, the most important thing in the United Kingdom was the move to scrap the legal privileges of trade unions and liberating the labor market which also provoked widespread controversy in this regard (see Table 3.2). At the same time, the United Kingdom abolished exchange controls, as well as the control of price, income, and dividend (Hu 2005).

The British new public management movement of Margaret Thatcher's cabinet began in 1979, which also can be seen as an important aspect of institutional

[3]These privately-held institutions which have been privileged included the British Aerospace (1981), the British Telecommunications (1984), the British Gas (1986), the British Airways Board (1987), Water Supply and Sewage Treatment (1989), Electricity in England and Wales (1993), and the British Railways (1996).

innovation of the British economic system. The process of British public service career began in the middle of 20th century, and culminated in the 1960s. Keynesian policy and administrative professionalism made the size of the government and scope of activities continue to expand. The resulting economic, social, and political issues were concentrated expressed in the form of a huge budget deficit, and even the financial crisis in oil crisis after the 1970s. This crisis forced Thatcher's cabinet to take the road of specialization and commercialization of public service with a view to improve efficiency and reduce costs. The professionalism and commercialization of public service mean a fundamental change in the internal structure of government and public organizations, the supply of public services. However, Thatcher's ultimate goal was to reduce the size of government, compress the space of government activities, innovate methods of public service supply, and then to achieved public goals with lower costs and higher efficiency. Therefore, it should be said that the most direct and obvious cause of the British new public management movement were the financial and economic needs. Reducing the budget deficit, cutting the public sector, and improving efficiency and quality of public services became the main driving force of British administrative reform (Zhang 2003).

The British new public management movement can be roughly divided into two major stages: the introduction of private sector's management techniques and public services privatization phase (1979–1987), and the stage of public service agents and the public-private sector partnerships after 1988 (Zhang 2003).

Introducing private sector's competition mechanism to the public sector is a major theme of the new public management movement. However, the public sector and private enterprises, after all, are two separate areas. The object, objectives, and nature of management have their own particularities and cannot be simply equated. Taking the mechanism of competition as an example, those internal non-economy departments in the public domain which need to be controlled should not be introduced in market mechanisms. This shows that the introduction of competition mechanism itself has a problem of "degree". Whether economic research methods can fully interpret the political and administrative process or not, it is an issue worth considering. Policy formulation and policy implementation are two stages of the administrative process, and the two have different functions and different steps, but they have continuity in the meantime. So we cannot be biased between policy formulation and policy implementation. Emphasizes policy formulation and weakening executive functions are not conducive to management. Conversely, faced with increasing executive agencies with its own rules, how to strengthen the government's macro-control, and how to coordinate the relationship between the functional organization and the executing agency, are additional topics proposed by the practice. Administrative performance evaluation is an important element of management, and it has three-dimensional uniformity of objective assessment criteria, objective assessment process, and objective assessment results. It is the operative foundation of management mechanism such as contracting and so on. It is the link to establish the responsible institution and implement the internal responsibility institution. However, the administrative performance is both an intangible and tangible, long-term and short-term, indirect and direct complex-formed synthesis. Administrative performance evaluation cannot be simply equated with corporate performance evaluation. Otherwise, new managerialism will be simply equated with the new Taylorism (Deng 2004).

The practice of the British new public management movement has brought a "new public management". This campaign led to the belief of "management" and this belief was called "rarely proven assumption" by Christopher Pilot., namely better management will be proved to be an effective remedy to solve a series of economic and social disease The Blair government implemented the best value plan in 2000, surpassed the one-way pursuit of economic rationality for the compulsory competitive tendering (CCT) of the Conservative government's reform and stressed the harmonious unity of the results-oriented and sustainable improvement. According to OECD analytical database from 1999 to 2000 years, the British government expenditure changes (denoted by proportional accounting for GDP) dropped 3% compared with the previous year. Similarly, the wage of the Government employees (denoted by proportional accounting for GDP) dropped 34.2%. According to the United Kingdom government MORI poll in 2003, the public satisfaction degree on the quality of services was as high as 55%, the recognition degree on government staffs' responsibility was 53%, of which the public satisfaction degree on hospitals was as high as 70%. In addition, through government procurement construction of the information network, up until February in 2006, 540 customers paid fee through the "government procurement card" and made a monthly savings of 800–900 million pounds, which effectively reduced the cost of government procurement and improved the operation of the government efficiency (Zhu 2006).

3.2.2 "The Third Way" Reform of Blair Government

In May 1997 the Labor Party came to power, the British government had inherited objective economic policy from the Conservative Party government. In other words, economic policies did not drastically change with a government change which emerged the first time since World War II, maintaining the stability and continuity of policy. Inflation was under control to some extent, and the economic growth kept at a low speed (Huang 1998).

At the same time, the British government also had "the third way" reforms. The Labor government, mainly reformed the welfare and health care institution, privileges of hereditary nobles in the House of Lords, the education institution, among other things, in order to promote the economic development of the United Kingdom and put forward new initiatives on promoting economic development. Faced with the economy of the era of knowledge, the Labor government which was led by Prime Minister Tony Blair focused on promoting the high-tech development, adjusting the industrial and product structures, and maintaining a sustained economic growth. Major new initiatives were put forward as follows: (1) Transition to a knowledge-based society, and advocating the establishment of the mixed economy model, and forming the so-called "new economy". Britain officially released the White Paper *Our Competitive Future: the Creation of a Knowledge-based Economy* at the end of 1998, taking the promotion of the knowledge-based economy development as a new base to formulate policy on industry, science and technology, and trade (Sheng et al 1996). (2) Enhance vitality and competitiveness of the enterprise, and promote the development of high-tech enterprises. The government uses policies to ensure and encourage equal competition, to encourage greater reproduction, to reduce or exempt taxes for the profit portion of expanded reproduction, to make 100% tax exemption on capital construction of research facilities or construction costs in designated business districts. In order to stimulate investment and encourage the development of enterprises, especially high-tech enterprises, the incentive measures were taken, and the strategy of information industry implemented to help companies adapt to industrial development in the information age. (3) Comprehensively the British government should use fiscal and monetary policies to avoid economic overheating and recession, and ensure a stable and healthy operation of the economy. Gordon Brown, British Chancellor of the Exchequer, named the coordination and cooperation of British fiscal policy and monetary policy to achieve stable economic growth as the "British model", and recommended to other countries as a successful example of economic growth. After Labor Party came to power, they implemented monetary policy reforms. Bank of England could now decide the interest rates independently in order to curb inflation, at the same time the government expanded spending to maintain a loose fiscal policy (Liu 2006).

The effectiveness of the two reforms is obvious. British economy gradually got rid of the image of "sick man of Europe" through the timely reform on the institution and readjustment of the economic structure. British economic indicators became the leader in European countries.

3.3 The Analysis of the Role of Institutional Innovation: China's Reform and Opening Up Policy

Zou (2000) believed that the time was ripe for reform in 1978 for four reasons: first, the "Cultural Revolution" was very unpopular, the party and the government must stay away from the old institution and make changes in order to gain support from the people; second, after years of planned economy, government officials understood the defects of the planning institution and the necessity of reform; third, the successful development of economy in other regions in Asia—including China Taiwan, China Hong Kong, Singapore and South Korea that was called "four tigers"—which showed to Chinese government officials and the Chinese people that the market economy is better than the planned economy. The different speed of economic development between North and South Korea and Eastern and Western Europe highlighted this point; fourth, due to the above reasons, the Chinese people had been ready for the economic reforms and expressed support (He 2006).

On the direction of China's economic reform, Wu and Li (1988) pointed out that modernization of any country in the world could not be achieved out of the world, it had to be open to the outside. Only in this way can we develop comparative advantages, enjoy the benefits of the latter, and achieve an effective growth. To accomplish this, we must adjust the economic operation mechanism to the rest of the world. Specifically, the reform is to establish the roughly same price formation mechanism and price relations with the outside world, as well as the economic regulations and fiscal and tax institutions in line with international norms, and so on.

Since the reform and opening up, China's economy has created almost 40 years of sustaining high-growth miracle. From 1978 to 2012, China's GDP at current prices increased from 364.5 billion yuan to 47.2882 trillion yuan, a 130 folds increased; and the average annual growth rate reached 9.75% at a comparable price, which is the highest growth rates among countries with population of over 50 million in the same period. In the period before the reform and opening up, China's annual growth rate was only 6%, which confirmed the institutional innovation of China's reform and opening up played a positive role in promoting economic growth. Household contract responsibility system led directly to the unconventional development of China's agricultural economy. Guangdong, Fujian and other coastal provinces were the first to implement the faster-than-inland reform of the property right system and market system due to the economic institution restructuring, thus, their economic growth rates were much higher than the inland provinces. This explained the role of institutional innovation from the other hand (Chen Hua 2005).

To sum up, China's reform and opening up as a gradual significant institutional innovation, vigorously promoted economic growth. Furthermore, the empirical results in China have also proved that using DEA to measure the efficiency, and then to calculate the contribution of institutional innovation is scientific.

3.4 Stratification and Types of Institutional Innovations

Institution is a dictate rule that restrains the human behavior. The formation of these rules not only originates from the gambling equilibrium state among divergent interest main body, but also originate from government's rational construction. The order is the realistic condition of institution, it is the structural state in society, economy, politics, among others under given institution conditions.

3.4.1 Stratification of Institutional Innovation

We analyze the institution by dividing it into three levels such as the core institution (or basic institution), behavior order, and implementation mechanism.

Economic policy can be seen as an "action" of the institution which needs to provide the corresponding institutional arrangements throughout the country to have the spontaneously formed institution fixed. The balanced institution of natural evolution itself does not have the validity and may maintain only through the approval of national laws. The institution system which can also implement itself should have the "institutional frame" which is the institutional arrangements provided by the government. By using this, we may discuss the relations between the institution and country's legal framework.

According to the viewpoint of North (1994), the official institution should include regular politics, the economic rule and the contract. They form a rank structure, from the constitution to the written and the common law, then down to the detailed rule, finally down to the individual contract. These rules restrain people's behavior. Ke and Shi (2000) pointed out, the structure level of the official institution is essentially constituted by three different level rules: the top of the constitution, the middle of the statute, and the underlying government regulations. However, we believe that the three levels of the institution are corresponding to the three levels of laws and regulations in this country, see Table 3.3.

The country's constitution, which regulates all the economic rules, corresponds to the basic institution. Take China for instance, our fundamental institution is the socialist institution. This is required by our Constitution: "The People's Republic of China is a socialist state with the people's democratic dictatorship, which is led by the working class, based on the alliance of workers and peasants."

Since the constitution itself generally sets the amendment procedure, the stability of the country's fundamental institution as the constitution has required is strong, and it is not easy to change. In the modern constitutional state, the main body of constitutional amendment, constitutional powers, and constitutional procedures have been strictly limited. Take constitution of the United States for instance, Article 5 of the United States Constitutes states that "the Congress, whenever two thirds of both Houses shall deem it necessary, shall propose amendments to this Constitution, or, on the application of the legislatures of two thirds of the several States, shall call a convention for proposing amendments, which, in either case, shall be valid to all intents and purposes, as part of this constitution, when ratified by the legislatures of three fourths of the several States, or by conventions in three

Table 3.3 The relationship between a country's institution and the legal institution

Institution	Corresponding laws and regulations	Function	Degree of change
The core institution	Constitution	Regulate all economic rules	Difficult to change
Behavior order	Civil and commercial law, economic law, labor law and other departmental law	Provisions of the code of conduct on all sectors of society	Be able to change
Implementation mechanism	Policies and regulations	Standardize the specific implementation of the institution	Easy to change

fourths thereof, as the one or the other mode of ratification may be proposed by the congress" (Liu 2013).

Code of conduct is not decided by the constitution, but decided by different laws of departments, and applies to all sectors of society. Taking China as an example, apart from the constitution, the major legal department of China's legal institution also has: administrative law, civil and commercial law, economic law, labor and social security law, science-education-culture-health law, natural resources and environmental protection law, criminal law, litigation law, and military law.

Compared with the constitution, the restrictions imposed on general legal amendments are relatively low. Thus, the code of conduct regulated by the various branches of the law can be changed, if necessary. For instance, article 64 of the Chinese constitution stipulates that the amendment of the constitution "is proposed by either the Standing Committee of the National People's Congress or by more than one-fifth of the deputies of the National People's Congress and adopted by more than 2/3 of all the representatives in National People's Congress". As for other laws and bills, it is only need to "adopted by more than half of all deputies of the National People's Congress." Obviously, the amendment of the general law is much easier than the constitution.

One country policy and regulations constituted by all levels of governments correspond to the implementation mechanism. These policies and regulations are formulated by the relevant government agencies and changed with the actual situation. Government agencies would deem it appropriate to make amendments to these policies and regulations in order to adapt to the new situation. Therefore, policies and regulations are more prone to change, and there is considerable flexibility.[4]

3.4.2 *Types of Institutional Innovations*

Given the scope and extent of institutional innovation, it can be divided into four types, named institutional change, institutional improvement, institutional perturbation, and institutional sideslip.

3.4.2.1 Institutional Change

Institutional change refers to the fundamental transformation of political and institutional change, for instance, the changes from slave society to feudal society, the transformation from a feudal society to a capitalist society, as well as the system

[4]If the evolution of fundamental institutions determines the long-term period of economic growth while change in behavioral order determines the medium-period of economic growth, then the adjustment of implementation mechanism determines the short-period of economic growth.

change before the establishment of the People's Republic of China, which all belongs to this category.

3.4.2.2 Institutional Improvements

Institutional improvement refers to the continuous growth of production factor resource allocation efficiency over a period of time. In the United States, for instance, from 1982 to 2002, the production factor resource allocation efficiency continued to grow (at the same time, the economy ushered in relatively high-speed growth) (see Fig. 3.4). It belongs to the institutional improvement.

It is generally believed that, the economic growth of the United States is attributed to the 40th president (1981–1989) Ronald Reagan, and the 42nd president (1992–2000) Clinton after the 1980s. At the end of 1980, before and after Reagan entered the White House, Reagan and his economic advisers studied and determined the idea of implementing the "economic recovery plan", later known as tax system reform plan of the *Economic Recovery Tax Act* and "fair, streamlined, and promote economic growth". Details of these plans can be summarized as four basic elements: (1) Reducing overall federal spending growth, the proper way is to remove the activities outside the scope of the federal government and restrict the expenditure growth on other activities. (2) Cutting the tax to a minimum level to enhance stimulation of economic growth on savings, investment, work, and productivity. (3) Abolishing unnecessary intervention that the federal government effectively operated on individual lives, business or state and the work of local governments, and thereby reducing federal regulations. (4) Supporting a stable monetary policy to encourage economic growth and control inflation. The four core content areas mentioned above are designed to increase private savings and investment through tax cut, cutting public spending, reduce government intervention, and mobilize the enthusiasm of local governments to promote economic development (Fu 2004).

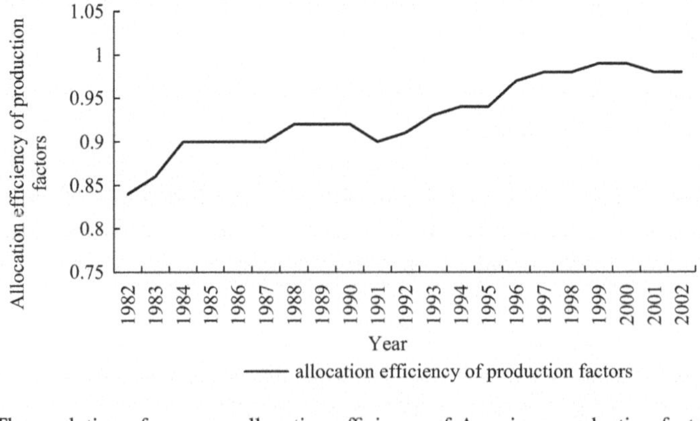

Fig. 3.4 The evolution of resource allocation efficiency of American production factors

It is continuous improvement of these institutions that have also made the U.S. economy succeeded in going out of recession since 1970s. It began to usher in rapid economic growth, this economic growth which reached its peak during the Clinton administration.

3.4.2.3 Institutional Perturbation

Institutional perturbation refers to a period of time, the resource allocation, efficiency of production factors fluctuates within a range so that the institutional innovation is actually limited to stagnation. The institutional innovation in Italian from the year 1961–1993 (see Fig. 3.5) generally fell into this situation.

The biggest characteristic of postwar Italy's political situation was frequent and sudden changes of government. From the end of World War II to the end of 1986, Italian government changed 45 times.

3.4.2.4 Institutional Sideslip

In contrast to the institutional improvement, the institutional sideslip shows that over a period of time, the overall resource allocation efficiency of production factors declines. China, from 1955 to 1977 (Fig. 3.6), generally fell into this situation.

After the completion of socialist transformation in 1956, China finally established a socialist economic institution. Chinese mainland basically formed the traditional socialist economic institution that was characterized by single public ownership and administrative planning management. Government's capacity of administrative mobilization was strong. The officials at all levels were very honest and upright, and very keen to promote industrialization rapidly. Despite of this, due

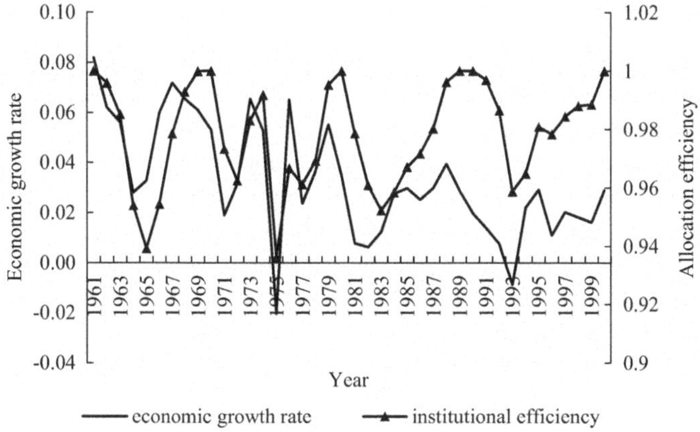

Fig. 3.5 Resource allocation efficiency of production factors and economic growth rate in Italy

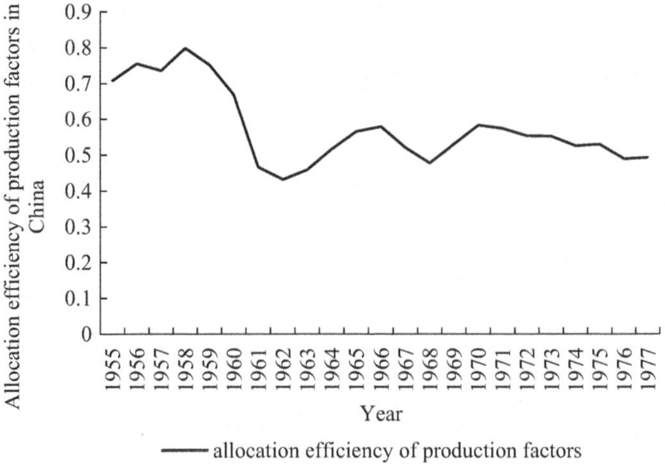

Fig. 3.6 The change of resource allocation efficiency of production factors in China during 1955–1977

to the loss of some wrong policies and environmental conditions at home and abroad, such as the expansion of the "Anti-Rightist" movement, "the Great Leap Forward" in 1958, "Three Years of Natural Disasters", and in particular "the Cultural Revolution" from 1966 to 1976 which sustained a decade, resource allocation efficiency of production factors declined seriously.

3.5 The Relationship Between the Cycle of Resource Allocation, Efficiency of Production Factors and the Business Cycle

Based on the analysis and outline of the traditional business cycle theory, this book analyzed the relationship between the resource allocation, efficiency of production factors and the business cycle, and analyzed the correlative data of Italy, Canada, Japan, Australia, China, and the United States empirically, verified the viewpoint that Snow's institutional innovation was the important reason of the long-term economic growth. This book find that the cycle of resource allocation efficiency of production factors and business cycle are isochronous, and the cycle of resource allocation efficiency of production factors decide the business cycle. Based on this, this book put forward the views of the institutional business cycle.

3.5.1 Overview of the Business Cycle Theory[5]

3.5.1.1 Sunspot Theory

Jevons (1997) put forward the sunspot business cycle theory in his two papers published in 1875 and 1878. He found that sunspot happened once a decade or so, and commercial crisis broke out roughly once a decade. Therefore, he studied a lot of statistical data, trying to figure out the law in order to explain the phenomenon that was described as "perfect consensus", and eventually created the sunspot business cycle theory. In his opinion, the sunspot phenomenon which occurred once a decade would lead to the poor harvest, while agriculture took up an important status in the economy, and then agriculture would affect the industry and other economic activities, which resulted in an economic crisis. The theory got its positive significance in the period when Jevons lived. It promoted the development of research on the business cycle theory. However, this theory seems to be unreasonable now. Because the effects of sunspots on agriculture are limited, and agriculture alone is not enough to cause the business cycle.

3.5.1.2 Psychological Theory

Psychological theory of the business cycle (Hu 2002) thinks that cyclical fluctuations of the economy is mainly due to the interaction between people's pessimistic and optimistic expectations. In 1867, Muller published *The Origin of the Credit Cycle and Commercial Panic* which pioneered the psychological theory of economic cycle. Muller attributed the business cycle to entrepreneurs' mood disorders in the judgment on the business cycle. Pigou, a British economist, is a typical person of psychological theory. In his view, the "psychology" was concretely presented by expectations, and expectations were often uncertain, as it could be optimistic or pessimistic, and even false. "The mistakes of optimistic and pessimistic are ongoing and each of them can be the causes or effects to another". He assumed that in the initial business community, person committed neither optimistic errors nor pessimistic errors. That was, increase or decrease of investment was in line with social needs. When demand maintained growth, as traders could not have been foreseen the consequences of their own and competitors' activity which were based on the reaction of market signals' stimulation, and then they began committing optimistic errors. Pigou thought that investors were interdependent in mentality, so if an investor committed optimism errors, and others would follow step-by-step. As a result, the error would be increased rapidly. Eventually the expected error alternately would lead to cyclical fluctuations.

---

[5]Referred to related information, the authors have wrote this section and cited some scholar's work in this section.

In addition, many economists see the psychological factors which can explain fluctuations as complementary factors in its business cycle theory, only few of economists consider them as single factors.

3.5.1.3 Innovation Theory

Schumpeter (1990), an Austrian economist, used innovation to explain the business cycle. His basic argument was: the implementation of innovation (referring to a new combination of production factors and production conditions) must pay higher costs, and in particular, it must have the support of bank credit. Schumpeterian started with the assumption that the entire economy was in a balanced state and the profit was zero. In such a state, only those innovators who had adventurous spirit and the courage could take the lead in order to put innovative activities into practice, with the help of banks' expand credit, increasing employment, adding new plant and equipment, and ultimately enabling businesses to obtain monopoly profits. This monopoly profits attracted large numbers of competitors to enter, and then quickly stimulated the demand for production and employment to increase, resulting in enterprises scrambling for purchase of raw materials, the overall price rising, and the prosperity picture emerging; subsequently, imitation of large numbers of enterprises would lead to the disappearance of monopoly profits. Entrepreneurs had to reduce the scale of production, employees, investment, and price. As a result, an economic slump produced.

3.5.1.4 Political Business Cycle Theory

Nordhaus (1975) put forward a complete political business cycle model. This model argued that the political business cycle was due to opportunistic manipulation before the election, and the main cause of economic fluctuations was the economic policy which was made by the politicians to win ballot papers. So the business cycle changed with the political cycle. Typical political business cycle was that the current government in order to be re-elected, often used the policy of cutting tax or increasing government spending to stimulate the economy, reduce unemployment, and form a picture of economic prosperity, until the eve of the election. After the election, in order to control inflation brought by this prosperity, it was necessary to adopt constructional fiscal policy, which would lead to an economic slump, and the same thing would happen again in the next election cycle. Nordhaus's theory and the subsequent models of political parties and national parties respectively put forward by Douglass Hibbs (1977) and Alberto Alesina (1988), which analyzed the political impact on the economic operation mainly from the point of the U.S. election cycle. So it could not explain the business cycle changes in China.

3.5.1.5 Underconsumption Theory

Underconsumption theory is one of the original explanations of cyclical instability. Sismondi and Malthus are the early representatives of underconsumption theory, and underconsumption theory can be divided into two types: One is caused by insufficient purchasing power, and the other is a result of excessive savings. Underconsumption theory caused by insufficient purchasing power argues that the economy system is failed to allocate sufficient purchasing power, resulting in lower actual purchasing power than the total value of products, and so all products of society cannot completely sale with a cost price at least, which is the main reason of the economic contraction; while underconsumption theory caused by excessive savings argues that since excessive saving is relatively higher than the poor, and most of the capital is in the hands of the rich. With the development of the production and the growth of social wealth, although consumption of the rich will increase, its growth rate is much less than the rate of society wealth growth, and ultimately results in savings of the community as a whole more than a certain proportion. The proportion of the entire community for the purchase of consumer goods is too small, resulting in inadequate consumption, and causing an economic slump. Obviously underconsumption cannot form prosperity. So in the strict sense, underconsumption theory is not a complete cycle theory.

3.5.1.6 Over-Investment Theory

Over-investment theory (Hu 2002) analyzed the formation of the business cycle on the view of over-investment, and the representative persons were Hayek, Mises, and Robbins of the Austrian School. Its central argument is as follows: the fluctuation of the business cycle is mainly due to the monetary, but it is not a purely monetary reason. The imbalance in the production structure which is caused by monetary factors changes makes the economy from prosperity to collapse. The credit inflation policy of the monetary and financial authorities is the fundamental reason that interferes the equilibrium of the economic system and causes economic expansion, which in turn leads to alternate changes in prosperity and depression. Bank's credit expansion makes the market interest rates lower than the natural rate, and then business enterprise loans investment causes the increase of the need of plants, machinery and equipment. At this time, the increase in demand for investment and means of production caused by the expansion of bank credit can only divert production factors that were originally used to manufacture consumer goods to the manufacture of capital goods. As a result, in the prosperous state of the cycle, capital goods production expands rapidly, while in the depression stage it shrinks quickly. So, "the reason that make the prosperity a trend of collapse is the actual imbalance of the production structure, not only the formation of the lack of funds for the bank's inadequate preparation". The most important contribution of the over-investment theory is the analysis on the imbalances of the production structure during the business cycle fluctuations, especially the imbalance between the productions of capital goods and consumer goods, as well as the supporting role of bank credits for economic changes.

3.5.1.7 Multiplier-Acceleration Theory

Paul Samuelson (1939) issued a paper *Interactions Between the Multiplier Analysis and the Principle of Acceleration* in 1939, which convinced that the main factor affecting economic volatility was the change of investment, only the multiplier principle could not explain the fluctuations in the economy, we must combine the multiplier principle with the principle of acceleration together. Samuelson showed the interaction mechanism between the multiplier and accelerator and the resulting fluctuations in the business cycle through the time-series analysis systematically, which explained that reason why a small perturbation caused a large cycle of volatility in the economic system. The specific process was: first, there was an automatic investment occurring, it would increase spending so that the multiplier could take effect. Accordingly, in order to increase the production of a unit of final goods, we must increase the investment of capital goods a number of times. Thus, in the co-interaction of the multiplier principle and the principle of acceleration, the increasing of production would rapidly reach the edge of social production possibilities. The arising investment due to increasing capital investment had to stop. Stopping new induced investment would also make the multiplier principle and the principle of acceleration effect from the opposite direction, so that there would be a sharp decline in social production into the depression stage. After a recession period, the multiplier principle and the principle of acceleration played a role again to lead to the recovery of the economy, and then to form a continuous loop process. Samuelson's analysis showed that as long as there was the role of the multiplier principle and the principle of acceleration, it produced sufficiently a cyclical fluctuation, and it stressed the role of the endogenous variables, and noted that even without the interference of external factors, the economy would remain in a repeated continuously cycle of movement.

3.5.1.8 Currency Determinism

Hawtrey, the British economist, founded the currency determinism (Xu 2002), and his monetary theory convinced that, business cycle is purely a monetary phenomenon, and the cyclical fluctuations in the economy are mainly due to the instability of monetary credit system. The fluctuations in the number of circulation, money supply, and transaction velocity of money will directly lead to fluctuations in the national income. Lowering interest rates and expanding credit in the banking system will result in increasing investment and expanding production, thus making income increased, which would stimulate the economy to increase and stay at a prosperous stage. However, as the modern monetary system built on the basis of the reserve, the bank credit expansion is limited, and when the banking system is forced to tighten monetary credit, the economy will enter a recession. In accordance with Hawtrey's view, the economic cycle is only a relatively narrow replica of inflation or deflation.

The representative of the new currency determinism is Friedman (1995). Friedman believed that changes in the money supply led to a corresponding national change in nominal income. Due to the higher delay in the adjustment of wages and prices, the higher money supply and lower growth rate led to a corresponding fluctuation of long-term trends in aggregate demand and real economic activity. Economic expansion dated from the continued increase in the money supply; the long-term lower growth rate of the money supply would cause a downturn or recession in the economy, and when the long-term monetary growth rate is negative, it will lead to depression.

3.5.1.9 Cycle Theory of Inventory Investment

The theory believes that the level of production depends not only on sales but also on inventory investment, and inventory investment changes will cause economic fluctuations. In 1923, Kitchin's (1923) research pointed out that when enterprises produce too much, they will form inventory, and then there will be a phenomenon of reducing production. If enterprises raise inventory, it will make enterprises expand production, which leads to the formation of economic prosperity; on the contrary, if companies reduce inventory, it will leads to the formation of economic depression. This change in inventory investment will form its own economic fluctuations with mild depression alternating prosperity, and at the same time, it will increase economic fluctuations of other causes. As a result of these, Kitchin found an economic cycle influenced by the inventory, Kitchin thought that its duration was 10 months in original, but later studies shown that its period lasted from 2 years to 4 years. People referred this short-term adjustment from 2 to 4 years as "inventory" cycle, which also known as "Kitchin-cycle" or "short-cycle".

Lloyd proposed a simple explanation on inventory investment cycle, namely, the entrepreneurs have a certain understanding on the expected inventory-sales ratio. When demand increased in the expansion process, they find that their inventory had reduced. The efforts to restore its inventory levels to a predetermined ratio would result in an increase in new orders. Thereby, it would increase employment and income. The opposite process occurred in the reduced phase: entrepreneurs tries to reduce their inventory levels, while its sales being decreased. Such efforts cause further decline in revenue.

3.5.1.10 Cycle Theory of Rational Expectations

The school of rational expectations (also known as neo-classical macro-economic school) formed in the 1970s, which is an extremely important school to challenge the Keynes doctrine. Lucas (1975) and Barrow (1980) illustrated the emergence of the economic cycle by the use of incompletely price information, which was based on the balanced analysis. The cycle theory of rational expectations suggested that the excessive increase in money supply causes the rise of general price, the economic man, because of incomplete information, wrongly take the general price rise as the relative price changes, and thus expand production as well as increase investment. When they realized that their own judgment was an error, production and investment would be fallen into a lower level. Thus, despite the economic man pursuit of the maximization of profit and utility, the incomplete price information would still cause cyclical fluctuations in macroeconomic. It can be seen that the school of rational expectations hold this view: the impact of random monetary factors lead to fluctuations in the economic cycle, and owing to that its theoretical perspectives and policy perspectives are closely linked with monetary school, it is also called as radical monetarist or new classical macroeconomics.

3.5.1.11 Real Business Cycle Theory

Real business cycle school developed from the result of oil price shock in 1973 and 1980 and food shock in 1972. The principal representatives of this school are Kydland and Prescott (1990) in the United States.[6] The school of real business cycle believed that the impact of actual random factors (rather than the influence of money) led to cyclical fluctuations in the economy. Real business cycle theory seemed the economic cycle as normal fluctuations under the automatic adjustment mechanism, and believed that the cycle is unique. When the money stock maintains continual change at a certain growth rate, the cycle will still be there. The theory assumes that: the original source of economic fluctuations is exogenous, and the source of fluctuations includes shock from the demand, but more importantly, it includes shock from a supply-side, such as advances in technology, and so on. It also assumes that the information of these shocks is not complete, in each case, the economy must select from the noise signal in some way, but precisely they cannot do that, which caused fluctuations in the economic cycle.

3.5.2 The Cycle Theory of Institutional Innovation

Institutional innovation is an important reason for long-term economic growth, the cycle of resource allocation efficiency of production factor and the business cycle are synchronized, and the cycle of resource allocation efficiency of production factor decides the cycle of business.

[6]Based on the real business cycle theory, the theory of dynamic stochastic general equilibrium analysis is developed, and the new Keynesianism is also developed by using this theory.

There are a variety of reasons caused the cyclical economic fluctuations, including the interactions between variables within the economy (endogenous factors in the business cycle), the shock of exogenous variables (exogenous factor in the business cycle). These exogenous variables include terms of trade, personal preference, the demand-side shocks (such as government demand, et al.), the supply-side shocks (such as advances in technology and the supply changes in production factors), and at the same time, also include the changes in the number of currency circulation, currency supply, currency velocity, as well as policies, regulations and natural conditions. Those factors mentioned above, leading to an imbalance between market supply and demand, furthermore, imbalances in market supply and demand will turn triggered a "market order crisis" (market order was caught into chaos and destruction, the actual state of the institution—economic order—distorted, and this chaos and destruction will lead to neither fair nor efficient state), thus reduced the resource allocation efficiency of production factors and affected economic growth.

The economic order is the result of the operation of the institution. Institutional innovation means establishing and continuously improving the good order of conduct. The economic order established under such institutional conditions should promptly respond to the economic changes caused by various factors, and should promptly and effectively prevent or take measures to curb this economic volatility.

For economic fluctuations caused by exogenous variables, institutional innovation is to introduce a negative feedback mechanism through method, for example introducing a policy adjustment. This negative feedback mechanism must react to economic change in time, and adopt measures in time effectively to restrain the influence that aroused the economic fluctuations. For example, if there are impact factors of exogenous which will affect economy, such as the sudden increase in the currency supply, a good institution system is to be able to detect it, analyze its economic impact, and take prompt measures to curb the impact, thus suppressing economic fluctuations.

As for the business cycle caused by endogenous factors, institutional innovation is to establish a comprehensive economic mechanism, in order to avoid economic fluctuations caused by defect of market. For example, referring to the view of the school of inadequate consumption, depression is the result of inadequate consumption brought by uneven distribution of social wealth, "the rich do not want to spend money, the poor cannot afford to cost". A good system is to detect the defects in the economy in time (such as seriously imbalanced distribution of social wealth) and establish an effective mechanism to compensate for these shortcomings, thereby to prevent the occurrence of fluctuations in the economy.

Generally speaking, the institutional innovation is to correct the market order or avoid the crisis through a set of effective mechanisms, thus to reduce the scope of economical fluctuations, and finally promote the adjustment in consumption, production, labor force supply and deposit, and achieve the new balance in economy. If through mechanisms that are brought by the measure of institutional innovations, such as policy adjustment, which can make the market order restore to the good condition, then economical fluctuation will be suppressed; Otherwise, if through mechanisms that are brought by the measure of institutional innovations, such as policy adjustment, which cannot make the market order restore to the good condition, even cause the market order to be more chaotic, then economic cycle's fluctuation must intensify.

3.5.3 The Econometric Test of the Relationship Between the Cycle of Resource Allocation Efficiency of Production Factors and the Business Cycle

From Fig. 3.7 that describes the relationship between the resource allocation efficiency and the economic growth rate, it can be seen that there is a strong correlation between institutional innovation and the business cycle in Finland from 1960 to 2000.

In order to systematically study the impact of institutional innovation in the business cycle, we use the changes in the resource allocation efficiency of production factors to measure institutional innovation, and take the economic growth rate as an indicator of the business cycle. We use Eviews software to analyze the data in more than ten countries, such as Italy, USA, China, Japan, Canada, Australia and so on. Build the model as

$$\Delta y = c + c_1 \Delta\theta + u \qquad (3.5)$$

In formula (3.5), y represents the economic growth rate of a country, Δy represents the change of economic growth rate, θ represents the country's resource allocation efficiency of production factors, $\Delta\theta$ represents the changes in resource allocation efficiency of production factors, u represents the random error term, c and c_1 are the constant.

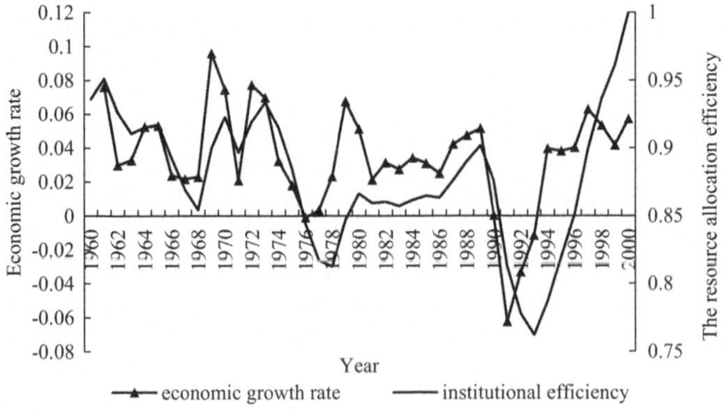

Fig. 3.7 The relationship between resource allocation efficiency and the economic growth rate in Finland in 1960–2000

Table 3.4 Relationship between changes in economic growth rates and changes in the resource allocation efficiency among a number of countries

Countries	Years	Model	R-squared	Lag phase	Probability
Ireland	1983–2010	$y(t+1) = 0.0115 + 0.543y(t) + 1.009\Delta\theta$	0.65	2	0.35
China	1980–2010	$y(t+1) = 0.037 + 0.558y(t) + 0.51\Delta\theta$	0.52	3	0.137
Finland	1983–2010	$y(t+1) = 0.00467 + 0.606y(t) + 1.2\Delta\theta$	0.81	1	0.09
New Zealand	1982–2010	$y(t+1) = 0.015 + 0.358y(t) + 0.4\Delta\theta$	0.33	5	0.338
Australia	1983–2010	$\Delta y = -0.001 + 0.51\Delta\theta$	0.31	2	0.01
Germany	1993–2010	$\Delta y = 0.02 + 1.466\Delta\theta$	0.69	2	0.02
France	1983–2010	$\Delta y = -0.00058 + 1.56\Delta\theta$	0.67	1	0.11
South Korea	1963–2010	$\Delta y = -0.002 + 1.48\Delta\theta$	0.63	1	0.02
Canada	1983–2010	$\Delta y = -0.00025 + 1.3\Delta\theta$	0.38	2	0.1
USA	1903–2008	$\Delta y = -0.001 + 0.387\Delta\theta$	0.23	2	0.015
Japan	1958–2009	$\Delta y = -0.00256 + 0.95\Delta\theta$	0.6	1	0.012
Sweden	1996–2010	$\Delta y = 0.02 + 1.115\Delta\theta$	0.87	2	0
Singapore	1983–2009	$\Delta y = -0.002 + 0.869\Delta\theta$	0.49	1	0.13
Italy	1983–2010	$\Delta y = 0.0009 + 1.33\Delta\theta$	0.62	1	0.016
UK	1962–2010	$\Delta y = 0.00015 + 0.91\Delta\theta$	0.45	2	0.07

Table 3.4 presents the results of data analysis for countries, and the model reflects the relationship between changes in economic growth rates and changes in the resource allocation efficiency of production factors among a number of countries. Table 3.4 is the econometric model, the sample determination coefficient represents the degree that independent variables determine the dependent variable in the model. "Lag phase" and "probability" refer to the lag phase and probability of the Granger causality test. Take Ireland as an example, the probability that $\Delta\theta$ is not the determining cause of $y(t+1)$ is 35%. In other words, the probability that $\Delta\theta$ is the determining cause of $y(t+1)$ is 65%. The lag phase is 2.

We can know that from Table 3.4, there are two types of the relationship between the economic growth rate and the resource allocation efficiency of production. One type is represented by Ireland, China, Finland, and New Zealand. In the models of these countries, the independent variables include not only $\Delta\theta$ but also $y(t)$, while the dependent variable is $y(t+1)$. The other types are represented by Australia, Germany, France, South Korea and other countries. In the model of these countries, the independent variable is only $\Delta\theta$, and the dependent variable is Δy. In these countries, the resource allocation efficiency of production factors is generally stable during the calculation period.[7]

[7]The Granger causality test on the relationship between resource allocation efficiency and economic growth rate shows that institutional innovation has an impact on economic growth and it is an important reason for economic growth. This proves the point of North and others that

According to the above econometric analysis by use of Eviews, there is a rule that the economic growth rate or its change is positively related to the resource allocation efficiency of the production factor in these countries, which indicates that the institutional innovation is influential to the economic growth rate or its changes, and institutional innovation is an important factor in enhancing economic growth rate.

3.6 Summary

From the perspective of the action mechanism, the most basic and essential role of institutional innovation in economic growth is to increase the resource allocation efficiency of production factors. Therefore, efficiency analysis can be used to measure the contribution of institutional innovation in economic growth. Data Envelopment Analysis (DEA) is such a method (Jiang 2004). This book uses this method to establish the formula to measure the contribution of institutional innovation to economic growth. The calculation results in the United Kingdom, the United States, China and other countries show that this method is reasonable. The econometric study on the relationship between resource allocation efficiency and economic growth rate shows that the cyclical change in resource allocation efficiency of production factors is an important cause of the business cycle.

References

Alesina, A. (1988). Credibility and policy convergence in a two-party system with rational voters. American Economic Review, 78(4), 796–805.

Barro, R.J. (1980). A capital market in an equilibrium business cycle model. Econometric Society, 48(6), 1393–1417.

Carter, N., Klein, R., & Day, P. (1992). How organizations measure success: the use of performance indicators in government. London: Routledge.

Chen, H. (2005). An analysis of the effect of the system on China's economic growth. Social Sciences Review, (2), 66–67.

Deng, S.L. (2004). An analysis of the characteristics and effects of British new public management movement. Journal of Fujian School of Administration and Fujian Institute of Economics and Management, (1), 15–16.

Farnham, D., & Horton, S. (1996). Managing the new public services. London: Macmillan.

Friedman, M. (1995). A monetary and fiscal framework for economic stability. American Economic Review, 38(3), 245–264.

Fu, Z. (2004). Tax reduction - former US president reagan's great performance. International Taxation in China, (8), 78–79.

He, H.Y. (2006). The political and economic logic of the regional disparity in the transitional period – from the perspective of new political economics. Doctoral dissertation: Nankai University.

---

institutional innovation is an important reason for long-term economic growth. To some extent, it can be considered that the cyclical change of resource allocation efficiency of production factors is an important cause of the business cycle.

Hibbs, D.A. (1977). Political parties and macroeconomic policy. American Political Science Review, 71(71), 1467–1487.
Hu, Y.G. (2002). Contemporary western economic cycle theory. Shanghai: Shanghai University of Finance and Economics Press.
Hu, X.Y. (2005). On Blair government's third way. Journal of Henan Institute of Education: Philosophy and Social Sciences, (4), 101–104.
Huang, R.Z. (1998). Analysis and enlightenment of British economy. Masteral dissertation: Renmin University of China.
Jevons, W. S., Black, R. D. C. (1991). Theory of Political Economy. London: Macmillan.
Jiang, Z.H. (2004). Regional economic growth factors of China. Journal of Dalian University, (5), 66–69.
Jiang, Z.H. (2006). The distributive analysis theory of S&T progress and economic growth - a test of fifteen countries. Science of Science and Management of S. &. T., (9), 113–118.
Jorgenson, D.W. (2001). Productivity Volume 2. Beijing: China Development Press.
Ke, W.G., & Shi, M.F. (2000). Institutional economics: social order and public policy. Beijing: The Commercial Press.
Kitchin, J. (1923). Cycles and trends in economic factors. Review of Economics & Statistics, 5(1), 10–16.
Kydland, F.E., & Prescott, E.C. (1990). Business cycles: real facts and a monetary myth. Quarterly Review, 3–18.
Liu, G.Z. (2006). The revelation and evolution of western economics distribution of income research normal form. Economic Review, (6), 46–49.
Liu, H. (2013). Amendments to the constitution and the amendment to the constitution: a study of American constitutional change. Tsinghua Journal of Rule of Law, (2), 200–214.
Lucas, R.E. (1975). An equilibrium model of the business cycle. Journal of Political Economy, 83 (6), 1113–1144.
Massey, A. (1997). Globalization and marketization of government services: comparing contemporary public sector developments. New York: St. Martin's Press.
Nordhaus, W.D. (1975). The political business cycle. Review of Economic Studies, 42(2), 169–190.
North, D.C. (1994). Institutions, institutional change and economic performance. Shanghai: Shanghai Joint Publishing Press.
Peters, B.G. (2001). The future of governing: four emerging models (2ND). Kansas: University Press of Kansas.
Pryor, F.L. (2004). The Future of U. S. Capitalism. Beijing: China social sciences press.
Samuelson, P.A. (1939). Interactions between the multiplier analysis and the principle of acceleration. Review of Economics and Statistics, 21(2), 75–78.
Schumpeter, J.A. (1990). Theory of economic development. Beijing: The Commercial Press.
Sheng, Z.H., Zhu, Q., &Wu, G.M. (1996). DEA theory, method and application. Beijing: Science Press.
Thatcher, M. (1998). Road to power - autobiography of Mrs. Thatcher. Beijing: Contemporary World Press.
Wu, J.L., &Li, J.G. (1988). The goal and strategy of economic system reform. Study and Research, (8), 3–6.
Xu, Z. (2002). Economic growth from the perspective of institutional transition. Inquiry into Economic Problems, (8), 8–11.
Zhang, G. (2003). New public management movement and the paradigm transformation in the field of public Public Sector Studies in UK. Journal of Dialectics of Nature, (1), 44–50.
Zhuo, Y. (2006). The theory and practice of new public management movement in U. K. expanding horizons, (6), 72–74.
Zifcak, S. (1994). New managerialism: administrative reform in Whitehall and Canberra. Buckingham: Open University Press.
Zou, Z.Z. (2000). China's economic reform and policies at the beginning of the 21st century. Foreign Investment in China, (11), 12–14.

Chapter 4
The Calculation of the Contribution of Science and Technology Progress and Human Capital to Economic Growth

Chapter 2 of this book discussed various factors that determine and impact on economic growth, including labor, physical capital stock, investment in physical capital, human capital, science and technology, institution, and economic environment externalities, and expounded the modeling method of economic growth based on synergy theory. On this basis, this book calculates the contribution of labor, physical capital stock, investment in physical capital, human capital, science and technology, and other factors to economic growth. Taking South Korea as the sample of empirical analysis, this chapter discusses the calculation of the contribution of science and technology progress and human capital to economic growth.

4.1 The Calculation of the Contribution of the Science and Technology Progress: The Case Study of South Korea

Calculating the contribution of science and technology progress to economic growth needs to establish relevant economic growth model. The following mainly introduces the function model of compensation of employees and the function model of investment value.

4.1.1 The Function Model of Compensation of Employees

Taking $\log HL$ and $\log SD/L$ as the independent variables, $\log V$ as the dependent variable, we make multiple regression analysis on the South Korea's data from 1960 to 2010. Among the above, $\log HL$ is the logarithm of human capital H (the average years of schooling of laborers multiplied by the number of workers)

J. H. Liu and Z. H. Jiang, *The Synergy Theory on Economic Growth: Comparative Study Between China and Developed Countries*,
https://doi.org/10.1007/978-981-13-1885-6_4

multiplied by the labor L (number of employment, hours of work), $\log SD/L$ is the logarithm of investment in physical capital D multiplied by the inputs of science and technology S and then divided by the labor force L, $\log V$ is the logarithm of the compensation of employees V. And then, the following model (4.1) is obtained.

$$V = 1.16(HL)^{0.53}(SD/L)^{0.18} \tag{4.1}$$

The following is a simple explanation of the inspection result of the econometric regression model (4.1). In Table 4.1, the R-squared is 0.998, which indicates that all independent variables and the dependent variable have strong linear correlation generally. The adjusted R-squared is 0.998, which indicates that the explanatory power of the independent variables is very strong, and the sample regression equation is well fitted to the sample. The S.E. of regression is 0.023. Regression equation passed the F-test shows that the effect of the linear regression is obvious. Similarly, the two independent variables passed the T-test. Table 4.2 shows that there is a co-integration relationship between the variables. Model (4.1) is a long-term stable law, while Table 4.3 shows that $\log HL$, and $\log V$ are mutually influential and have a causal relationship.

Table 4.1 Regression model of compensation of employees $\log V$ in South Korea and its testing

Dependent variable: $\log V$				
Method: Least squares				
Sample (adjusted): 1963–2010				
Included observations: 48 after adjusting endpoints				
Convergence achieved after 52 iterations				
Variable	Coefficient	Std. Error	T-Statistic	Prob.
C	0.062808	0.680	0.09	0.9267
$\log HL$	0.532579	0.090	5.99	0
$\log SD/L$	0.180383	0.030	6.22	0
AR(3)	0.733073	0.120	6.19	0
R-squared	0.997938	Mean dependent var	6.082917	
Adjusted R-squared	0.997797	S.D. dependent var	0.485114	
S.E. of regression	0.022768	Akaike info criterion	−4.647251	
Sum squared resid	0.022809	Schwarz criterion	−4.491317	
Durbin-Watson stat	0.8	F-statistic	7098	

Table 4.2 Co-integration test of regression models of compensation of employees $\log V$ in South Korea

Eigenvalue	Likelihood ratio	5% Critical value	1% Critical value	Hypothesized No. of CE (s)
0.380068	37.40161	29.68	35.65	None
0.162638	13.97252	15.41	20.04	At most 1
0.102063	5.275102	3.76	6.65	At most 2

Table 4.3 Granger causality test of regression models of compensation of employees $\log V$ in South Korea

Pairwise Granger Causality Tests			
Sample: 1960–2010			
Lags: 1			
Null hypothesis:	Observations	F-Statistic	Probability
$\log HL$ is not a Granger Cause of $\log V$	50	4.40019	0.04134
$\log V$ is not a Granger Cause of $\log HL$		1.05663	0.30925
$\log SD/L$ is not a Granger Cause of $\log V$	50	1.39604	0.24333
$\log V$ is not a Granger Cause of $\log SD/L$		26.7102	4.8E-06
$\log SD/L$ is not a Granger Cause of $\log HL$	50	1.02057	0.31756
$\log HL$ is not a Granger Cause of $\log SD/L$		12.2825	0.00102

4.1.2 The Function Model of Investment Value

The function of investment value is defined as the gross domestic product (Y) minus the compensation of employees (V), that is

$$M = Y - V \tag{4.2}$$

Taking the physical capital stock K (the previous year) and the SD/K (investment in physical capital D multiplied by the science and technology input S and then divided by physical capital stock K) as the independent variables, the investment value M as the dependent variable, we run multiple regression analysis on the South Korea's data from 1960 to 2010. And then, the following model is obtained.

$$Y = 1.16(HL)^{0.53}(SD/L)^{0.18} + 0.189K + 19SD/K + 11.5LD/K + 1810 \tag{4.3}$$

According to the inspection summary of the econometric regression model (4.3), we give some simple instructions. From Table 4.4 we can see that the multiple correlation coefficient R^2 is 0.998, which indicates that all dependent variables and independent variable are in general have strong linear correlation. Revised determination coefficient of sample is 0.998, which indicates that the dependent variable has a strong explanatory power, the sample regression equation matches the sample preparation well. Regression equation shows that the ρ-value of the F-test is significant, which shows that the results of the linear regression are obvious. Similarly, for the two variables the ρ-values of t-test is also significant.

4.1.3 Overall Model

Putting the model (4.1) and model (4.3) into the Eq. (4.2), the quantitative relationship model (4.4) among gross domestic product, labor, physical capital stock,

Table 4.4 *M* function regression models of South Korea and its test

Explained variable: $Y - V$				
Method: Least squares				
Sample (adjusted): 1963–2006				
Included observations: 44 after adjusting endpoints				
Convergence achieved after 8 iterations				
	Coefficient	Std. Error	T-Statistic	
C	1810	8034.452	2.25486	0.03
K	0.189112	0.013328	14.18877	0
hSD/K	19	86.84337	2.211049	0.0331
L	11.4759	3.120802	3.677228	0.0007
AR(1)	1.089222	0.099214	10.97853	0
AR(3)	−0.324086	0.100674	−3.219166	0.0026
R-squared	0.998	Mean dependent var	160714	
Adjusted R-squared	0.998	S.D. dependent var	120498	
S.E. of regression	5224	Akaike info criterion(AIC)	20.1	
Sum squared resid	1.04E + 09	Schwarz criterion(SC)	20.3	
F-statistic	2.18	Durbin-Watson stat	4567	

investment in physical capital, investment in science and technology, and human capital are obtained.

$$Y = 1.16(HL)^{0.53}(SD/L)^{0.18} + 0.189K + 19SD/K + 11.5LD/K + 1810 \quad (4.4)$$

4.1.4 *The Calculation Formula for Contribution of Science and Technological Progress to Economic Growth*

According to the derivation method in Chap. 2, the contribution of science and technological progress to economic growth in South Korea is measured as follow by using model (4.5).

$$\eta_S = \frac{a\gamma L^{\alpha} H^{\beta} S^{\gamma} D^{\delta} + cSD/K}{Y} \cdot \frac{s}{y} \quad (4.5)$$

In Eq. (4.5), η_S denotes contribution of science and technological progress to economic growth, while s is the change rate (economic growth rate) of Y (gross domestic product). s is the change rate of S (investment in science and technology). K is the physical capital stock, D is investment in physical capital, h is the change rate of human capital, and L is the labor force. While a, c are coefficients. It is worth noting that Eq. (4.5) is derived from Eq. (4.4). Therefore, it is only applicable to the calculation of the contribution of science and technological progress to economic growth in South Korea. When it comes to the other countries, the form of calculation formula depends on the overall model.

4.1.5 Calculation Result and Analysis

Like the measurement of the contribution of science and technological progress in other regions, the academic community also has a completely different view on the contribution of science and technological progress to the economic growth in East Asia. The World Bank's report showed that from the early 1960s to 1990s, the average growth rate of labor input account for about 18% of the output growth among Taiwan, South Korea, Singapore, and Hong Kong. During this period, the capital accumulation accounted for about 48% of output growth in Hong Kong, accounted for about 72% in Taiwan, and the proportion was 67% in South Korea. The contribution of science and technological progress to economic growth varied from 14% in South Korea to 35% in Hong Kong. However, as we can see, the contribution of science and technological progress to economic growth is smaller than the contribution of the capital accumulation in East Asia (Zhang 2007).

In T*otal Factor Productivity Growth: Survey Report*, Lee (2004) put forward that, after the Asian financial crisis, the growth of total factor productivity (TFP) had played an increasingly important role in South Korea's economic growth, while the investment in R&D had played an active role in enhancing the contribution of TFP growth of South Korea's economic growth. This article introduced the economic value-added, input of labor and capital under the growth accounting framework, and provided an estimate of changes in TFP. In 1972–1999, the average annual TFP growth rate was 1.92%, the average contribution of investment in physical capital to the GDP growth rate was 60.1%, and the average contribution of labor and non-adjusted TFP growth to GDP respectively were 15.4 and 24.4%. The crisis in South Korea reflects the weakness of its economic structure. In order to improve TFP growth, South Korea government was committed to economic restructuring, thus enhanced the quality of education and training, and attracted foreign direct investment and the fund of R&D to promote economic development. As a result, the increment in imports and exports resulted in TFP growth. The companies which operate in the international market can master the knowledge and technology spillovers from their global contacts, and gain access to more markets so that they can obtain the economy of scale. From this viewpoint, the innovation of economic policy will further promote the South Korea economy in the global markets and may lead to rapid growth of total factor productivity.

The analysis of the determining factors to economic growth in South Korea can be seen in the Table 4.5.

Table 4.5 The calculation results of the economic growth factors in South Korea, 1960–2000, (%)

Period	The contribution of physical capital stock growth to economic growth	The contribution of investment in physical capital growth to economic growth	The contribution of science and technology progress to economic growth	The contribution of human capital growth to economic growth	The contribution of labor growth to economic growth	The contribution of institutional innovation to economic growth	The impact rate of economic externalities to economic growth
1960–1972	21	14	7	17	6	4	31
1973–1997	24	35	20	18	7	−10	6
1998–2010	48	7	25	22	6	10	−18

4.2 The Calculation Results of the Contribution of Human Capital Innovation to Economic Growth

4.2.1 Calculation Methods for the Contribution of Human Capital Innovation to Economic Growth

On the issue of the rate of return in educational investment, Schurz used the salary difference between graduates with different educational levels as a base for calculating the rate of return in educational investment (Qin and Wu 1999). In the process of calculating, the first step is to calculate the balance of average incomes of adjacent educational levels of graduates, and then express the rate of return by the ratio of this balance to average educational costs in some educational stages. According to Schurz's calculation, the return rates of different educational levels in the USA respectively are 35% in elementary education, 10% in secondary education, and 11% in higher education. The second step is to calculate the average rate of return. According to the ratio of the investment in different educational levels, the average rate of return is calculated to be 17.3%. On this basis, the economic profits of education are calculated to be $49.5 billion in the increased educational investment of $186 billion. The economic profits of education account for 32.6% of the extra national income. In other words, the educational investment makes a contribution of 32.6% to the extra national income.

Professor Denison not only analyzed the effects of education, but also studied the economic growth factors. For example, through the growth accounting in American during 1929–1982, he pointed that the profit of education makes up 0.4% of the 2.92%, which is the average annual growth rate of national income. In other words, the contribution of profit of education to the growth rate of national income was 13.7% (Qin and Wu 1999). The effects of education on economic growth are calculated by the growth factor analysis method which is shown in Table 4.6.

Consulting the method used by professor Schurz, Japanese scholars analyzed the effect of education in Japan during 1930–1955, and pointed out that educational investment in Japan increased from 1864. 9 billion yen in 1930 to 5380 billion yen in 1955. In Japan, the educational rate of return is fixed at 30% of elementary education, 20% of secondary education, and 10% of higher education, and at average the educational rate of return is 23%. Hence, the profit of educational investment was 808.4 billion yen, and accounts for 25.8% in the newly-gained national incomes.

Depending on the method mentioned above, C. T. Ctpymnjinh analyzed the development of national economy during 1940–1960 in the Soviet Union. According to his results of these calculations, the raise of education levels of laborers had caused an addition to the national income by 30%.

Table 4.6 International comparison of national income growth rate and educational function

Country (region)	Period (year)	National income growth rate (%)	Growth rate of education (%)	Contribution of education to national income growth rate (%)
America	1973–1982	1.55	0.47	30.32
Canada	1950–1967	4.95	0.36	7.27
Belgium	1950–1962	3.03	0.43	14.19
Denmark	1950–1962	3.63	0.14	3.86
France	1950–1962	4.70	0.29	6.17
West Germany	1950–1962	6.27	0.11	1.75
Italy	1950–1962	5.60	0.40	7.14
Netherlands	1950–1962	4.07	0.24	5.90
Norway	1950–1962	3.43	0.24	7.00
Britain	1950–1962	2.38	0.29	12.18
South Korea	1963–1976	9.28	0.36	3.90
Japan	1953–1971	8.81	0.34	3.86
Argentina	1950–1962	3.19	0.53	16.61
Brazil	1950–1962	5.49	0.18	3.28
Chile	1950–1962	4.20	0.20	4.76
Columbia	1950–1962	4.79	0.20	4.18
Ecuador	1950–1962	4.72	0.23	4.87
Honduras	1950–1962	4.52	0.29	6.42
Mexico	1950–1962	5.97	0.05	1.11
Peru	1950–1962	5.63	0.14	2.49
Venezuela	1950–1962	7.74	0.19	2.45

Source Denison E F, Chung W K. 1976. How Japan's Economy Grew So Fast.1976. Oxford: Oxford University Press; Jin G X, Pu J Q. 1981. South Korea's economic growth factors. Beijing: Xinhua Press; CohnE L. 1989. The Economics of Education. Shanghai: East China Normal University Press

4.2.2 Calculation Formula for the Contribution of Human Capital Innovation to Economic Growth

According to the derivation methods in Chap. 2 of this book, the contribution of human capital to economic growth in South Korea can be easily estimated by formula (4.4):

$$\eta_H = \frac{a\beta L^{\alpha} H^{\beta} S^{\gamma} D^{\delta}}{Y} \cdot \frac{h}{y} \tag{4.6}$$

In the formula (4.6), η_H denotes the contribution of human capital growth to economic growth, y is the rate of change (economic growth) of Y (GDP), h is the growth rate of H (human capital), D is the investment in physical capital, L is the labor, S is investment in science and technology, and a is a coefficient. While α, β,

γ, and δ are elastic coefficients. It is worth to mention that the formula (4.6) is based on the formula (4.4), so it is only available for the calculation of the contribution of human capital to economic growth in South Korea. When it comes to the other countries, the form of measurement formula depends on the overall model.

4.3 Dynamic Stochastic General Equilibrium Model for South Korea's Economic Growth

With the growth rate of China's economy decreased from 10% to about 7%, the driving force structure for economic growth needs to be adjusted and changed in time to achieve the goal of medium-high economic growth in the new normal. Can we realize the medium-high economic growth under the new driving force structure that, is innovation-driven is the first driving force? More and more economists pay attention to the research. However, South Korea had rapid growth from 1960 to 1985 with an economic growth rate of over 8%. From 1986 to 2002, South Korean economy achieved medium-high growth (without repeating Japan's mistakes) with an average growth rate of 7%. Therefore, this section uses DSGE method to study the relationship among medium-to-high-end industrial development, innovation driven and medium-high economic growth from 1986 to 2002 in order to provide lesson for China.

In this section, we set up a multi-sector model group for economic growth in South Korea based on the synergy theory on economic growth. We will further study the impacts of urbanization, industrialization, informatization, agricultural modernization, foreign debt, population, debt capitalization ratio, industrial capacity utilization, medium-to-high-end industries, R&D personnel at universities, funds from abroad, basic research funding, R&D personnel of private enterprises, technology trade, exports, FDI, environmental protection expenditures/GDP, environment-related taxes, the proportion of high energy-consuming industry, and physical capital stock on economic growth, fiscal revenue, interest rate, exchange rate, non-performing loans, employment, investment in physical capital, human capital, science and technology, energy consumption, carbon emissions, and pollutant emissions, establish a relationship model among them and build the DSGE equation set. We use MATLAB software to solve and simulate the model.[1]

4.3.1 Model Group of South Korea's Economic Growth

The DSGE model for South Korea is constituted by the resident sector, business sector, science and technology sector, foreign trade sector, monetary sector, financial sector, environment sector and other sectors.

[1]This section is completed in collaboration with the Harbin University of Science and Technology.

4.3.1.1 Resident Sector Model

Resident sector model includes informatization model, relationship model among four modernizations (urbanization, informatization, industrialization, agricultural modernization) and investment in physical capital, science and technology, average years of schooling, employment and unemployment or others.

(1) Informatization model

This part cooperates with Harbin University of Science and Technology.

According to the available measurement data for South Korea, the informatization model is

$$INF_{t-2} = a_1 TE_{t-2} + a_2 EL_{t-2} + a_3 ICT_{t-2} \tag{4.7}$$

Among them, $INF_{t-2}, TE_{t-2}, EL_{t-2}$ and ICT_{t-2} represent informatization index, the proportion of communications and computer services in service exports, the proportion of the electronic information industrial added value in industrial added value, and ICT investment. While a_1, a_2, a_3 represent the contribution of the three indicators to informatization, which are the weight coefficient. We use principal component analysis to solve the coefficient.

(2) Model of four modernizations and investment in physical capital

Urbanization increases investment demand for urban infrastructure and housing, and every step of urbanization has spurred the development of related industries and increased investment demand. Suppose South Korea's model of four modernizations and the investment is:

$$D_t = a_4 + a_5 URB_{t-2} + a_6 HI_{t-2} \tag{4.8}$$

where D_t represents investment in physical capital, and URB_{t-2} represents urbanization, HI_{t-2} represents the added value of high-end industries.

(3) Model of four modernizations and science and technology investment

According to the cluster theory, the city, as a center of knowledge, information, and skill, keeps gathering forces of science and technology, so that the level of science and technology continues to increase.

$$S_{t-2} = a_7 + a_8 INF_{t-2} * HI_{t-2} + a_9 URB_{t-2} \tag{4.9}$$

(4) Model of four modernizations and average years of schooling

According to the cluster theory, cities and towns generally have better environmental conditions and educational conditions such as cultural, medical and health care. The level of education received by urban citizens is usually higher than that in rural residents. Therefore, the model of four modernizations and average years of schooling is:

$$E_t = a_{10} + a_{11} URB_{t-2} + a_{12} INF_{t-2} \tag{4.10}$$

(5) Model of four modernizations and employment

The four modernizations (urbanization, industrialization, informatization and agricultural modernization) promote employment, while the number of jobs depends mainly on the number of urban residents. We assume that the model of four modernizations and the employment in South Korea is:

$$L_t = a_{13} + a_{14}[URB_{t-2} * IND_{t-2} * (1 + INF_{t-2}) * AGR_{t-2}] + a_{15} PO_t \tag{4.11}$$

In model (4.11), L_t represents the added value of high-end industries. PO_t represents the population, IND_{t-2} represents industrialization (the proportion of tertiary industry in GDP), and AGR_{t-2} represents agricultural modernization (agricultural labor productivity).

(6) Employment rate model

When the economy enters the stage where efficiency and productivity utilization rate are high, or when the economy is in the rising period of the business cycle, the employment rate is high. On the contrary, employment is low, so the employment rate model is:

$$EE_t = a_{16} + a_{17} EFF_t + a_{18} CU_t \tag{4.12}$$

EFF_t represents economic operating efficiency (resource allocation efficiency of production factors), CU_t represents productivity utilization rate, and EE_t represents employment rate.

4.3.1.2 Business Sector Model

(1) Economic growth model

According to the synergy theory established in this book, the economic growth model for South Korea during the period from 1990 to 2013 is:

$$Y_t = (E_t * L_t * L_t)^{\alpha_3} (S_{t-2} * D_t / L_t)^{\alpha_4} + a_{19} K_{t-1} + a_{20} S_{t-2} D_t E_t L_t / K_{t-1}^2 \tag{4.13}$$

where Y_t represents GDP, L_t represents labor, K_{t-1} represents fixed capital stock in the previous period (in the case of annual data, the fixed capital stock at the end of the year), D_t represents fixed assets investment, S_{t-2} represents technology investment (ahead of two phases), E_t represents years of per capita education.

$(E_t * L_t * L_t)^{\alpha_3}(S_{t-2} * D_t/L_t)^{\alpha_4}$ represents compensation of employees, $a_{19}K_{t-1}$ represents investors' interests, $a_{20}S_{t-2}D_tE_tL_t/K_{t-1}^2$represents synergy benefits.

(2) Efficiency decomposition model

We assume that South Korea's efficiency decomposition model is:

$$EFF_t = a_{21} + a_{22}INF_{t-2} * CU_t + a_{23}DRT_t * CH_t/(IND_{t-2}) \tag{4.14}$$

In model (4.14), CU_t represents productivity utilization rate, DRT_t represents debt capitalization ratio, and CH_t represents exchange rate.

(3) Investment in physical capital model

In accordance with the leading role of real estate and medium-to-high-end industry, the following model is established:

$$D_t = a_{24} + a_{25}FE_t * HI_{t-2}/ES_t + a_{26}ES_t \tag{4.15}$$

In model (4.15), ES_t represents the number of new housing permits.

4.3.1.3 Science and Technology Sector Model

(1) International paper model:

$$GP_t = a_{27} + a_{28}N_t + a_{29}YJ_t + a_{30}FC_t \tag{4.16}$$

Among them, GP_t presents S&E articles in all fields combined, N_t represents university researchers, YJ_t represents foreign research and development funding, and FC_t represents basic research funding.

(2) Licensed patent and PCT patent model in the United States Patent Office.

$$USP_t = a_{31} + a_{32}(GP_t + PN_t) + a_{33}TR_t \tag{4.17}$$

where USP_t represents the United States Patent Office authorized patents and PCT patents, PN_t represents R&D personnel in private enterprise, and TR_t represents the scale of technology trade.

4.3.1.4 Foreign Trade Sector's Import and Export Model

Export model is:

$$Y_t - C_t = a_{34} + a_{35}D_t + a_{36}EX_t \tag{4.18}$$

where EX_t represents the export value.

4.3.1.5 Monetary Sector Model

(1) M_2 model is

$$M_{2t} = a_{37}((E_t * L_t * L_t)^{\alpha_3}(S_{t-2} * D_t/L_t)^{\alpha 4} + a_{38}K_{t-1} - C_t) + a_{39}ED_t \quad (4.19)$$

where ED_t is external debt.

(2) The non-performing loan model is:

$$NPL_t = a_{40} + a_{41}DRT_t * (1 - EE_t) * CH_t \quad (4.20)$$

The NPL (called weighted non-performing loan increment) is calculated as

$$NPL_t = NP_t - 0.52NP_{t-1} \quad (4.21)$$

where NP_t is non-performing loans, DRT_t is debt capitalization ratio, EE_t is the employment rate, and CH_t is the South Korea's gained in exchange rate against the U.S. dollar.

(3) Exchange rate model

According to the exchange rate formation mechanism, the exchange rate model is

$$CH_t = a_{42} + a_{43}ED_t/Y_t + a_{44}FDI_t/Y_t \quad (4.22)$$

where CH_t is exchange rate, and ED_t is external debt.

(4) Interest rate model

According to the interest rate adjustment rules, the interest rate model is

$$R_t * 100 = a_{45}Y_t * P_t/YP + a_{46}M2_t/M2 \quad (4.23)$$

where R_t represents the interest rate, Y_t is on behalf of the gross domestic product, Y is the trend value of GDP, P_t is the price, P is the trend value of the price, and $M2$ is the trend value of $M2_t$.

(5) Loan model

$$LO_t = a_{47}HI_t/R_t + a_{48}R_t^2 + a_{49}FE_t \quad (4.24)$$

where FE_t is financial expenses.

4.3.1.6 Financial Sector Model

The financial model is:

$$FB_t = a_{50} + a_{51} FE_t + a_{52} ED_t * (1 - EE_t) \quad (4.25)$$

where FB_t represents the financial income, FE_t represents the financial expenditure, and ED_t represents the total of external debt.

4.3.1.7 Environment Sector Model

(1) Energy consumption model

$$EC_t = a_{53} + a_{54} INF_{t-2} * HI_{t-2} + a_{55} IND_{t-2} * S_{t-2}/(Y_t * EDI_t) \quad (4.26)$$

where EC_t is energy consumption, RE_t is the proportion of the total expenditure on research and development accounted for GDP, and EDI_t is added value of high energy-consuming industry in GDP.

(2) Carbon emissions model

$$CE_t = a_{56} + a_{57} EC_t + a_{58}[IND_{t-2} * (1 + INF_{t-2}) * S_{t-2}]/(Y_t * EDI_t) \quad (4.27)$$

where CE_t represents carbon emission, and EDI_t represents the ratio of added value of high energy-consuming industry to GDP.

(3) Pollutant emissions model

$$PE_t = a_{59} + a_{60} EF_t + a_{61} EC_t/(ER_t * IND_{t-2} * INF_{t-2} * S_{t-2} * HI_{t-2}/Y_t) \quad (4.28)$$

where PE_t represents pollutant emission, EF_t represents the ratio of environmental protection expenditure to GDP, EC_t represents energy consumption, ER_t represents environment-related tax revenue (millions USD 2005 PPP), S_{t-2} represents total expenditure on research and development, Y_t represents GDP, and HI_{t-2} represents the added value of high-end industries.

4.3.1.8 The Objective Function

The objective function of the entire economy system is shown as (4.29).

$$E_0\left[\sum_{t=0}^{\infty}\beta^t U(C_t, M_{2t}/P_t, L_t)\right] \tag{4.29}$$

where U is utility function, E_0 is anticipation, and β^t is discount factor.

Now, the above models form the basic framework of the DSGE model of the South Korea's economy, where $[P_t]$ is state variables, $[NPL_t, EFF_t, R_t, M2_t, Y_t, INF_{t-2}, D_t, S_{t-2}, L_t, E_t, ES_t, EC_t, CE_t, PE_t, GP_t, USP_t, EE_t, C_t, CH_t, GR_t, LO_t]$ are the control variables, while $[ED_t, EL_{t-2}, ICT_{t-2}, TE_{t-2}, URB_{t-2}, IND_{t-2}, AGR_{t-2}, PO_t, DRT_t, CU_t, FE_t, HI_{t-2}, EF_t, ER_t, EDI_t, FDI_t, YJ_t, N_t, FC_t, PN_t, TR_t, EX_t, K_{t-1}]$ are random variables.

4.3.2 *Logarithm Linearization and Parameter Solving of Model*

In order to transform the nonlinear model into a sufficiently good linear model, we should use a relatively simple logarithmic linearization method proposed by Harald Uhlig. Considering the general variable X_t, it is defined as $X_t = X(1+x_t)$. The capital letter X without the subscript indicates the trend value of X_t, and x_t indicates the deviation of the trend component X from the fluctuation component of the variable. Since x_t is close to 0, $e^{x_t} = 1 + x_t$. Thus, using Bayesian econometric methods to estimate parameters based on South Korea's data from 1990 to 2013, above models can be linearized into the following model systems:

(1) $0 = c_t + p_t - 7.5E_t p_{t+1} - 0.3m_t$
(2) $0 = -eff_t + 0.066\inf_{t-2} - 0.001dr_t - 0.001ch_t + 0.001ind_{t-2} + 0.067cu_t$
(3) $0 = -npl_t + 0.1dr_t + 0.03ee_t + 0.094ch_t - 0.037lo_t$
(4) $0 = -r_t + 10.1y_t - 0.16p_t + 2.4m2_t$
(5) $0 = -m2_t + 0.9d_t - 0.45c_t + 0.586ed_t$
(6) $0 = -y_t + 0.6842e_t + 0.45215l_t + 0.22d_t + 0.20286k_{t-1} + 0.22s_{t-2}$
(7) $0 = -\inf_{t-2} + 0.4012te_{t-2} + 0.2854el_{t-2} + 0.3149ict_{t-2}$
(8) $0 = -d_t + 0.6urb_{t-2} + 0.4hi_{t-2}$
(9) $0 = -l + 0.18urb_{t-2} + 0.18ind_{t-2} + 0.07\inf_{t-2} + 0.18agr_{t-2} + 0.62po_t$
(10) $0 = -s_{t-2} + 0.6\inf_{t-2} + 0.47urb_{t-2} + 0.6hi_{t-2}$
(11) $0 = -e_t + 0.22\inf_{t-2} + 2.11urb_{t-2}$
(12) $0 = -es_t + 4.1d_t - 1.14fe_t - 1.14hi_{t-2} - agr_{t-2}$
(13) $0 = -pe_t - 0.831ef_t + 0.08ec_t - 0.084er_t - 0.084ind_{t-2} - 0.084\inf_{t-2} - 0.084s_{t-2} + 0.084y_{t-2} - 0.084hi_{t-2}$

(14) $0 = -ce_t + 1.205ec_t - 0.224ind_{t-2} - 0.224s_{t-2} + 0.224y_t + 0.224edi_t - 0.09\inf_{t-2}$
(15) $0 = -ec_t - 0.1323\inf_{t-2} - 0.1323hi_{t-2} - 0.03ind_{t-2} - 0.03s_{t-2} + 0.03y_t + 0.03edi_t$
(16) $0 = -gp_t + 1.72n_t + 0.21yj_t + 0.54fc_t$
(17) $0 = -usp_t + 0.09gp_t + 1.37pn_t + 1.23tr_t$
(18) $0 = -c_t + y_t - 0.91d_t - 0.375ex_t$
(19) $0 = -ee_t + 0.038eff_t + 0.064cu_t$
(20) $0 = -ch_t + 0.235ed_t + 0.152fdi_t - 0.387y_t$
(21) $0 = -lo_t + 0.267hi_{t-2} - 0.7r_t + 0.99fe_t$
(22) $0 = -gr_t + 1.22fe_t - 2.48ed_t - 2.4ee_t$

The random variable models are

(1) $0 = ed_t - 0.89ed_{t-1} + \varepsilon_{1t}$
(2) $0 = -te_{t-2} + 0.91te_{t-3} + \varepsilon_{2t}$
(3) $0 = el_{t-2} - 0.82el_{t-3} + \varepsilon_{3t}$
(4) $0 = ict_{t-2} - 0.95ict_{t-3} + \varepsilon_{4t}$
(5) $0 = urb_{t-2} - 0.92urb_{t-3} + \varepsilon_{5t}$
(6) $0 = ind_{t-2} - 0.87ind_{t-3} + \varepsilon_{6t}$
(7) $0 = agr_{t-2} - 0.76agr_{t-3} + \varepsilon_{6t}$
(8) $0 = po_t - 0.95po_{t-1} + \varepsilon_{7t}$
(9) $0 = drt_t - 0.92drt_{t-1} + \varepsilon_{8t}$
(10) $0 = cu_t - 0.34cu_{t-1} + \varepsilon_{9t}$
(11) $0 = fe_t - 0.98fe_{t-1} + \varepsilon_{10t}$
(12) $0 = hi_{t-2} - 0.97hi_{t-3} + \varepsilon_{11t}$
(13) $0 = pn_t - 0.94pn_{t-1} + \varepsilon_{12t}$
(14) $0 = er_t - 0.87er_{t-1} + \varepsilon_{13t}$
(15) $0 = edi_t - 0.55edi_{t-1} + \varepsilon_{14t}$
(16) $0 = pn_t - 0.98pn_{t-1} + \varepsilon_{15t}$
(17) $0 = yj_t - 0.49yj_{t-1} + \varepsilon_{16t}$
(18) $0 = fc_t - 1.02fc_{t-1} + \varepsilon_{17t}$
(19) $0 = ef_t - 0.94ef_{t-1} + \varepsilon_{18t}$
(20) $0 = tr_t - 1.03tr_{t-1} + \varepsilon_{19t}$
(21) $0 = ex_t - 0.89ex_{t-1} + \varepsilon_{20t}$
(22) $0 = fdi_t - 0.88fdi_{t-1} + \varepsilon_{21t}$
(23) $0 = k_{t-1} - 0.936k_{t-2} + \varepsilon_{22t}$

4.3.3 Simulation Analysis

Since the 1990s, the standard deviation of fluctuations in China's GDP has been 3.10%, while the standard deviation of actual GDP in South Korea has been 2.26%, and the degree of volatility of its economic growth is stable. The rate of urbanization in South Korea reached 73.8% in 1990 and reached 83.7% in 2013. The added value of the machinery and transportation equipment industry, the chemical products industry, the telecommunications and computer industry has a high degree of volatility among these macroeconomic indicators and is also above the fluctuations of the GDP. This shows that the volatility of these three indicators will have a greater impact on the gross domestic product. Therefore, reducing the volatility of the three indicators has a certain effect on the steady growth of the economy.

The standard deviation of non-performing loans, technology import, FDI, technology trade and so on are the larger of the selected macroeconomic indicators, followed by the scale of technology trade, which are 15.05 and 14.34% respectively and has a significant impact on the fluctuation of the GDP. We can see Table 4.7 for details. The simulated standard deviation of DSGE is also given in the table. Overall accuracy of DSGE simulation is above 60%.

Table 4.7 Simulated standard deviation and actual standard deviation of variables

The standard deviation of the state variables and control variables			Standard deviation of random variables	
State variables and control variables	Actual standard deviation	Simulated standard deviation	Random variables	Standard deviation
eff	0.012	0.004	ed	0.257
npl	0.7	0.013	te	0.39
r	0.167	0.35	el	0.107
y	0.023	0.03	Ict	0.125
inf	0.051	0.051	urb	0.0033
d	0.08	0.041	ind	0.036
l	0.0158	0.0158	agr	0.085
s	0.065	0.0684	po	0.002
e	0.005	0.0129	drt	0.058
es	0.17	0.1128	cu	0.034
pe	0.072	0.067	fe	0.059
ce	0.076	0.043	hi	0.113
ec	0.03	0.017	ef	0.086
gp	0.33	0.14	er	0.081
usp	0.13	0.19	edi	0.11
c	0.031	0.04	n	0.052
ee	0.244	0.002	yj	0.51
ch	0.12	0.08	fc	0.083
lo	0.1	0.277	pn	0.083
fb	0.048	0.07	tr	0.143
p	0.012	0.0102	ex	0.176
m2	0.051	0.144	fdi	0.384
			k	0.026

For the linear model system which estimated the parameters, the DYNARE software based on MATLAB is used to carry out the variance decomposition, and the influence degree of the fluctuation values of the state variables and the control variables on the deviation of the trend values is analyzed according to each random impact, as shown in Tables 4.8 and 4.9 (The variables omitted subscripts).

The different research shows that the instrumentation industry, computer and electronic products and equipment manufacturing, medical equipment and supplies (including pharmaceuticals), chemical industry, machinery manufacturing, electrical equipment, transportation equipment manufacturing, appliance and component manufacturing, e-commerce, real estate and leasing, financial services, professional services, science and technology services, information service and education and cultural industries are all the mid-to-high-end industries. These industries are more innovative and have relatively good economic returns. The density of scientific and technological personnel, research and development funding density, patent intensity is relatively high.

The statistics on the added value of the electronic information industry, machinery transportation equipment industry and chemical product industry in the mid-to-high-end industries in South Korea, shows that the total added value of the

Table 4.8 Variance decomposition (in percent) (HP filter, lambda = 100)

	ed	te	el	ict	urb	ind	agr	po	drt	cu	fe
p	78	0	0	0	0	0	0	0	0	0	0
eff	1	16	21	34	0	0	0	0	0	28	0
npl	33	0	0	0	0	0	0	0	27	0	0
r	74	0	0	0	0	0	0	0	0	0	0
m2	88	0	0	0	0	0	0	0	0	0	0
y	0	7	9	14	3	1	5	0	0	0	0
inf	0	22	30	48	0	0	0	0	0	0	0
d	0	0	0	0	0	0	0	0	0	0	0
l	0	1	2	2	0	14	80	1	0	0	0
s	0	4	6	10	0	0	0	0	0	0	0
e	0	17	22	36	25	0	0	0	0	0	0
es	0	0	0	0	0	0	49	0	0	0	30
pe	0	0	0	0	0	0	0	0	0	0	0
ce	0	4	5	8	0	4	0	0	0	0	0
ec	0	4	6	9	0	0	0	0	0	0	0
gp	0	0	0	0	0	0	0	0	0	0	0
usp	0	0	0	0	0	0	0	0	0	0	0
c	0	2	2	3	0	0	1	0	0	0	0
ee	0	0	0	0	0	0	0	0	0	100	0
ch	51	0	0	0	0	0	0	0	0	0	0
lo	4	0	0	0	0	0	0	0	0	0	0
gr	9	0	0	0	0	0	0	0	0	0	91

Table 4.9 Variance decomposition (in percent) (HP filter, lambda = 100)

	hi	ef	er	edi	n	yj	fc	pn	tr	ex	fdi	k
p	19	0	0	2	0	0	0	0	0	1	0	0
eff	0	0	0	0	0	0	0	0	0	0	0	0
npl	16	0	0	0	0	0	0	0	0	0	24	0
r	22	0	0	0	0	0	0	0	0	3	0	0
m2	8	0	0	0	0	0	0	0	0	3	0	0
y	58	0	0	0	0	0	0	0	0	0	0	3
inf	0	0	0	0	0	0	0	0	0	0	0	0
d	100	0	0	0	0	0	0	0	0	0	0	0
l	0	0	0	0	0	0	0	0	0	0	0	0
s	80	0	0	0	0	0	0	0	0	0	0	0
e	0	0	0	0	0	0	0	0	0	0	0	0
es	20	0	0	0	0	0	0	0	0	0	0	0
pe	2	96	1	0	0	0	0	0	0	0	0	0
ce	40	0	0	40	0	0	0	0	0	0	0	0
ec	78	0	0	3	0	0	0	0	0	0	0	0
gp	0	0	0	0	37	53	9	0	0	0	0	0
usp	0	0	0	0	0	0	0	29	70	0	0	0
c	6	0	0	0	0	0	0	0	0	85	0	1
ee	0	0	0	0	0	0	0	0	0	0	0	0
ch	1	0	0	0	0	0	0	0	0	0	47	0
lo	95	0	0	0	0	0	0	0	0	0	0	0
gr	0	0	0	0	0	0	0	0	0	0	0	0

Table 4.10 The investment in science and technology industry of the mid-to-high-end industries in South Korea

Year	Chemical products (million won)	Computer industry (million won)	Machinery transportation equipment industry (million won)	Electronic information industry (million won)	The proportion of total investment in science and technology (%)
2009	1376218.797	13885549.6	14698.1	1285551.104	44
2010	1668544.609	17221061.4	64520.47	1590572.39	47
2013	2544165.734	23251176.1	48989.29	1869517.584	47

three industries accounted for more than half of the industrial added value of South Korea, and it's the main driver of economic growth (Table 4.10).

The investment in science and technology in these four industries has reached 47% of the total investment in science and technology, which has played an important stimulating role in innovation and also contributing more than 3.5% of GDP to research and development in South Korea (Fig. 4.1).

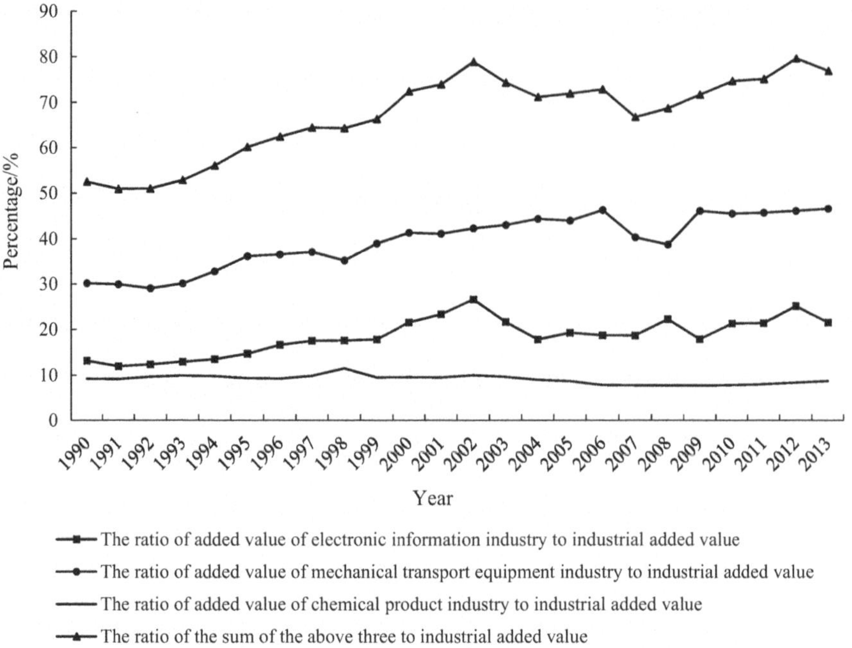

Fig. 4.1 The proportion of high-end industries in industry in South Korea

In the actual economic growth, the GDP volatility, the technology volatility, the employment volatility, and others, we can observe the result of the combined impact of all random variables impact such as foreign debt, internet, urbanization, industrialization, agricultural labor productivity, fiscal revenue, exports, FDI, physical capital stock. In the previous studies, it is quite difficult to analyze the impact of combined impact on the state variables and the control variables in the national innovation system. However, by establishing a DSGE model with random shock, we can use the simulation method to analyze the combined impact on state variables and control variables (Table 4.11).

Simulating the combined impact on state variables and control variables. The impact values of foreign debt, Internet, information technology and so on are shown in Table 4.5. In such a combined impact scenario, South Korea is authorized in the United States with state variables and control variables such as patents, research and development funds. All variable show positive volatility responses at the beginning of the period, especially the positive response in 2–3 years, and it's also followed by a gradual steady state. Among them, South Korea's interest rate was the largest in response to the combined impact, reaching 5%, followed by GDP and science and technology, at 1.7 and 1% respectively, while the energy consumption rate was negative to the reaction, see Fig. 4.2 for details (Liu 2016).

Table 4.11 Combined shocks of random variable

Random variables	Shock value
External debt	−0.005
The Internet	0.005
Information service	0.005
ICT industry	0.005
Urbanization	0.005
Industrialization	0.005
Farming modernization	0.005
Population	0.005
Capital and liabilities	0.005
Industrial production capacity utilization	0.005
Financial expenses	0.005
High-end industries	0.01
Environmental funding/GDP	0.005
Environmental related taxes	0.005
The proportion of high-energy-consuming industries	−0.005
R&D staff at university	0.005
Funds from abroad	0.005
Basic research funding	0.005
Private enterprise R&D personnel	0.005
Technical trade	0.005
Export	0.005
FDI	0.005
Physical capital stock	0.01

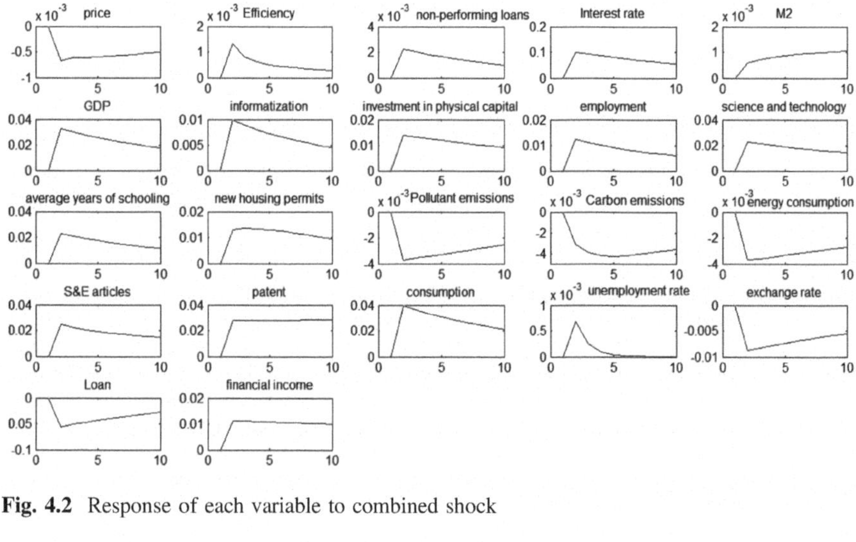

Fig. 4.2 Response of each variable to combined shock

4.4 Summary

This chapter, taking South Korea etc. as the empirical analysis objects, discusses the calculation of the contributions of science and technological progress and human capital innovation to economic growth and other issues.

Analysis of the South Korea's economic growth factors in this chapter shows that labor force growth was the main factor in South Korean rapid economic growth (average annual growth rate of 8s%) from 1960 to 1972 (the contribution of labor force growth was as high as 6%, and the contribution of human capital growth to economic growth was 17%; the contribution of physical capital growth to the economic growth was 35%; the contribution of science and technological progress was 7%). Therefore, South Korea's economic growth from 1960 to 1972 adopted dual growth model that physical capital was as the first power and the workers quantity and quality were as the secondary power. During the period of 1973–1997, the contribution of labor force growth was 7%, the contribution of human capital growth to economic growth was 18%, and the contribution of physical capital growth in economic growth was 59%. At the same time, the contribution of science and technology progress to economic growth was 20%, and the contribution of institutional innovation was –10%. Therefore, from 1973 to 1997, South Korea's economic growth was based on the dual growth model that is, physical capital was the first driving force and innovation was the secondary driving force.[2] After the financial crisis of 1998, the model of South Korea's economic growth had changed to innovation-capital dual growth model, and the contribution of physical capital growth to the economic growth decreased to 55%. At the same time, the contribution of science and technological progress to economic growth improved to 25%, the contribution of human capital growth to economic growth was 22%, the contribution of institutional innovation was 10%. The sum of the three together was 57%. Therefore, the economic growth of South Korea from 1998 to 2010 was a dual-drive growth model of innovation and capital.

(1) Based on the synergy theory of economic growth and the theory of reform of supply-side structure, this paper sets up a DSGE model group which includes residents, enterprises, science and technology, foreign trade, currency, finance and environment. And the unified optimization objective function is adopted,

[2]On the basis of the controversy over the causes of sustained high growth in the 1998 financial crisis, including South Korea, Singapore and China Taiwan and Hong Kong, Krugman's research on Young and Lau, In 1997, pointed out that "East Asia miracle" more originated in the sweat (labor) and investment, rather than wisdom, because science and technology progress did not play important role in this miracle, and thus there may be a great financial crisis? In fact, the financial crisis broke out in Southeast Asia in 1998, confirming Krugman's prediction. From the results of this book, the contribution of innovation (technological innovation, human capital promotion, institutional innovation) in South Korea was low (total of 28%) during 1973–1997, but also played an important role.

instead of each main body being optimized separately. In these models, the structure variables such as urbanization, informatization and industrialization are fully adopted, which expands the field of research and realizes the synthesis of structural reform, innovation-driven, financial stability, opening-up, energy saving and emission reduction and economic growth.

(2) The supply side industrial structure reform is the main driving factor of the rapid growth in South Korea. According to the simulation, the proportion of knowledge-intensive industries, such as computer and electronic products and equipment manufacturing, has gradually increased with GDP. The stochastic impact of value-added in knowledge-intensive industries has an important effect on the variance decomposition of state variables and most control variables. For example, the impact on GDP is 58%, the impact on fixed asset investment is 100%, the impact on loans is 95%, and the impact on technology investment is 80%.

(3) Correctly revealed the causes of the South Korean financial crisis. December 1997, the South Korean outbreak of a serious financial crisis, marked by a significant devaluation of the won, from January 1997 won against the dollar 844:1 fell to the end of December 2,060:1, the fuse is the external debt repayment crisis: December 24, 1997, South Korea's total external debt of up to 200 billion U.S. dollars. The short-term external debt of $66 billion trillion, and 200 ~ 300 billion of billions of dollars in debt to be repaid at the end of 1997, when the central Bank of Korea can be used to repay foreign exchange reserves of only 30 billion U.S. dollars, the debt repayment crisis immediately erupted, and caused a currency crisis (Wang 2005). The variance decomposition of Table 2 shows that the stochastic impact of external debt on Korean M2 fluctuation is 88%, the decision effect on interest rate fluctuation is 74%, the decision function of exchange rate fluctuation is 51%, the decision effect on price fluctuation is 78%, and the decisive effect on the fluctuation of non-performing assets is 33%.

(4) The adjustment of industrial structure and the investment of environmental protection funds are the main reasons for South Korea's energy saving and emission reduction and pollution prevention. The impact of knowledge-intensive industry on the fluctuation of energy consumption in South Korea is 40%, the decisive effect on the fluctuation of carbon emission is 78%. The impact of pollution control funds on the fluctuation of pollutant emissions is 96%, and the impact of high energy consuming industry on energy consumption fluctuation has a decisive effect of 40%.

References

Lee, B. (2004). Measuring total factor productivity growth: survey report. Tokyo: Asian Productivity Organization.

Liu, S. (2016). The Research on rapid economic growth of South Korea driven by innovation based on DSGE. Dalian University of Technology, Dalian, Liaoning.

Qin, B.T., & Wu, J.C. (1999). Knowledge and economic growth. Beijing: Scientific and Technical Documentation Press.
Zhang, L. (2007). Factors analysis of S&T and education in Kaoea's economic growth. Masteral Dissertation: Dalian University of Technology.
Wang, Y. (2005). Korean currency crisis triggered by foreign debt dependency and pegged exchange rate system. China Finance, (16): 60–62.

Chapter 5
The Analysis on the Factors of Economic Growth in the United States and Other Developed Countries

5.1 Research on the USA Economic Growth and Transformation Since 1900

This sector briefly reviews the researches of Jones, Jorgensen, and the Bureau of Labor Statistics, as well as domestic research on America's economic growth. Furthermore, from the perspective of the synergy theory, we establish the economic growth model for America's economy in recent 100 years from 1900 to 2008, and then calculate the contribution of science and technological progress[1], human capital, labor force, physical capital stock, investment in physical capital, institution and the economic externalities to America's economic growth. At last, it analyzes and explains the calculation results. And the transformation of America's economic growth mode is further studied, which can provide an important reference for China to build an innovation-oriented country and promote the transformation of economic development mode.

[1]With regard to the research and development input of the United States since 1900, according to the collection of Machlup in the book *The Production and Distribution of Knowledge in the United States*, the ratio of American R&D input to gross domestic product (GDP) was 0. 09% in 1920, 0.147% in 1930, 1.37% in 1940 and 1.47% in 1950. The estimated value of American R&D input during 1900–1930 in this book is slightly higher than Machlup's, but the gap is not significant.

J. H. Liu and Z. H. Jiang, *The Synergy Theory on Economic Growth: Comparative Study Between China and Developed Countries*,
https://doi.org/10.1007/978-981-13-1885-6_5

5.1.1 Researches Related to the Analysis on Economic Growth Factors

5.1.1.1 Jones' Research

The first generation of R&D endogenous economic growth model derived from the endogenous technological transition model put forward by Romer in 1990, who claimed that the increase in intermediate input could boost the productivity of R&D sectors. Jones (1995) studied the effect of R&D on productivity growth in OECD countries after World War II, but found no substantive effect on productivity growth despite their R&D input was sharply increased. Therefore, he constructed an endogenous growth model for R&D. This model reserved the two-sector model framework of the endogenous growth theory, which included final output sector and knowledge production sector, thus it retained the substitutive characteristic of knowledge that it was diffused cross time. While the model abandoned the presumed condition that endogenous cumulative factors had constant return to scale, thereby it reached the conclusion that there was no scale effect. This presumption implied that the contribution of population or knowledge stock to their own accumulation was far less than what was assumed by R&D endogenous growth model (Eicher and Turnovsky 1999).

5.1.1.2 Jorgenson's Research

Another influential research was carried out by Jorgenson, an economics professor from University of California, Berkeley, who studied the economic growth of Japan and America from 1960 to 1979, and separated their output growth into three sources, which were the contribution of capital input, the contribution of labor input, and the technical progress rate. Through calculation, Jorgenson drew the conclusion that in the economic growth of the two countries, the capital input had played a decisive role, while the labor input had made significant contributions (Jorgenson and Zhong 1989). Through modeling about the labor supply and demand of the USA in the next 25 years, Jorgenson et al. (2008) arrived at the following conclusion: despite the scheduled arrival of the aging problem, the appropriate population increase still had provided sufficient supply for the labor market in the 21st century. The improvement of the labor force was due to the recognition and emphasis on education. This pattern would last for a certain period of time, but it bounded to disappear eventually. The year-to-year variation of economic activities was mainly the result of the capital accumulation; however, for a long period to come, the driving force of economic growth would transfer to the labor force and technology.

5.1.1.3 Bureau of Labor Statistics (BLS)' Research

In May 2001, Bureau of Labor Statistics (BLS) published a research report *Multifactor Productivity*, which analyzed the factors of US labor productivity growth during more than 50 years from 1948 to 1999, and then put forward the concept of multifactor productivity.

According to the report, the multifactor productivity resulted from the interactions of multiple factors, including R&D, new technology, scale economy, organization and management technology and etc., and actually it was the science and technological progress in a general sense. The significance of this report was that it directly combined labor productivity and science and technology progress, and analyzed the latter in diverse aspects, which had greatly carried out researches on the USA productivity. Previous studies, such as the Solow residual method and so forth, simply defined science and technological progress as: gross output—(labor force + capital).

5.1.1.4 Chinese Scholars' Research

Since the reform and opening up, China's economic strength has undergone enormous changes. At this time, Romer, Lucas, and a number of well-known foreign economists on the economic growth theory had a new exploration, so many domestic scholars had a strong interest in this field. However, the exploration of economic growth theory in China was still in the stage of absorbing and re-innovating foreign theories, and there were few researches on breakthrough progress. Hu and Sun (2000) argued that technological innovation was the fundamental driving force of economic growth, but China's technological innovation was still at a low level. And from this point of view, the "new economy" phenomenon in the United States gave us a good revelation. Sun and Wu (2004) argued that there were two types of economic growth: extensive and intensive, and pointed out that science and technological progress was the most active factor in economic growth and the driving force for the transformation from extensive growth to intensive growth. Hu (2002a) believed that China's "high savings-high investment-high growth" mode to stimulate economic growth would inevitably lead to the results of low-quality growth. Through analysis, she concluded that only taking the road of technological innovation could promote high-quality growth of China's economy (Wang and Du 2005).

5.1.2 The Measurement of America's Economic Growth in Recent Century

5.1.2.1 Economic Growth Model of America

Firstly, establish the logarithmic model of compensation of employees $\log V$, and then establish the M model. Thus the economic growth accounting model of America built in this book is as follows:

$$Y = 0.00324(HL)^{0.48} * (SD/L)^{0.001434t-0.0000000455t^3} + 0.12K + 0.007HD/K + 0.0007SH/K + 11.72 \quad (5.1)$$

In the model (5.1), t represents time, the year 1900 = 1, the year 1978 = 79 … the year 2008 = 109. Y represents GDP, K represents the physical capital stock, D represents the investment in physical capital, S represents science and technology input, H represents human capital, and L represents the labor force (Tables 5.1 and 5.2).

The model (5.1) is used to analyze and estimate the America's economic growth factors from 1900 to 2008. The results[2] obtained are shown in Table 5.3.

5.1.2.2 Measurement on the Contribution of Institutional Innovation to Economic Growth

According to the view of the new institutional economics, the basic and essential effect of institutional innovation on economic growth is to improve the resource allocation efficiency of production factors. Therefore, the contribution of institutional innovation to economic growth can be calculated through efficiency analysis, and the Data Envelopment Analysis (DEA) is just that kind of approach. Through this approach, taking the total quantity of labor force, physical capital stock, and human capital stock as the input, and GDP as the output, the relative efficiency of different DMU (Decision Making Units) can be obtained.

The relative efficiency of each period in the USA is shown in Fig. 5.1.

5.1.2.3 Analysis and Interpretation

(1) Characteristics of America's economic growth in recent century.

This book, combining the new growth theory with ideas and methods of new institutional economics, based on the analysis on the relationship of GDP and knowledge, labor force, physical capital and other factors, from the perspective of synergy theory of economic growth, establishes new model of America's economic growth. This book uses the model to measure the contribution of the various factors to the economic growth of the United States over the past 100 years, and proves the correctness of the theory from the empirical point of view.

According to the results of the above calculation, this book has analyzed the characteristics of economic growth in the United States since 1900:

[2]Table 5.3 shows that science and technological progress plays an increasingly important role in the development of America's economy in the 20th century. Especially in recent decades, innovation has become the primary driving force for America's economic growth. The contribution of technological innovation, human capital promotion, and institutional innovation exceeds the contribution of material capital (stock and increment) growth.

Table 5.1 Test of American compensation of employees model

Dependent variable: log *V*				
Method: least squares				
Sample (adjusted): 1902–2002				
Included observations: 101 after adjusting endpoints				
Convergence achieved after 5 iterations				
Variable	Coefficient	Std. error	T-Statistic	Prob.
C	−2.490222	0.643256	−3.87127	0.0002
log *HL*	0.481456	0.06472	7.439013	0
logSD/*L*	−4.88E-08	8.93E-09	−5.46037	0
logSD/*L*	0.001461	0.00018	8.110894	0
AR(1)	0.789106	0.064115	12.30758	0
R-squared	0.998978	Mean dependent var	3.012006	
Adjusted R-squared	0.998935	S.D. dependent var	0.46807	
S.E. of regression	0.015275	Akaike info criterion (AIC)	−5.47691	
Sum squared resid	0.0224	Schwarz criterion (SC)	−5.34745	
Log likelihood ratio	281.5839	F-statistic	23449.42	
Durbin-Watson stat	1.283108	Prob. (F-statistic)	0	
Inverted AR roots	0.79			

Table 5.2 Test of American investment value model

Dependent variable: *M*				
Method: least squares				
Date: 03/22/10 time: 08:24				
Sample range: 1900–1945				
Number of observations: 46				
Variable	Coefficient	Std. error	T-Statistic	Prob.
C	11.72797	11.03289	1.063001	0.2939
K	0.115745	0.00644	17.97427	0
SH/*K*	0.000696	0.000117	5.963635	0
HD/*K*	0.006999	0.000431	16.24785	0
R-squared	0.991766	Mean dependent var	366.9098	
Adjusted R-squared	0.991178	S.D. dependent var	161.7081	
S.E. of regression	15.18876	Akaike info criterion (AIC)	8.36193	
Sum squared resid	9689.334	Schwarz criterion (SC)	8.520942	
Log likelihood ratio	−188.324	F-statistic	1686.24	
Durbin-Watson stat	1.043807	Prob. (F-statistic)	0	

Over the past 100 years, America's economic growth rate averaged 3.14%, and amplitude of fluctuation was in a tight range substantially (the exception of a few larger crisis in 1929–1931). For the nearly 20 years, the period from 1990 to 2000 was the new economic period of high growth, low inflation, and low unemployment

Table 5.3 The result of the America's economic growth accounting in this book (%)

	1900–1929	1930–1947	1948–1981	1982–2000	2001–2008
Economic growth rate	3.1	3.7	3.4	3.3	2.2
Contribution of the physical capital stock growth	55.7	31.7	31.4	20.6	27.6
Contribution of the investment in physical capital growth	1.4	4.4	10.5	19.3	2.2
Contribution of science and technology progress	2.6	12.8	17.4	16.3	29.6
Contribution of the human capital growth	20	17.5	18.7	21.1	16.9
Contribution of the labor force growth	12.9	9.4	11.7	9.7	6.1
Contribution of institutional innovation	−1	21.7	3.1	16.7	4.5
Contribution of the economic externalities	8.4	2.5	7.2	−3.7	13.1

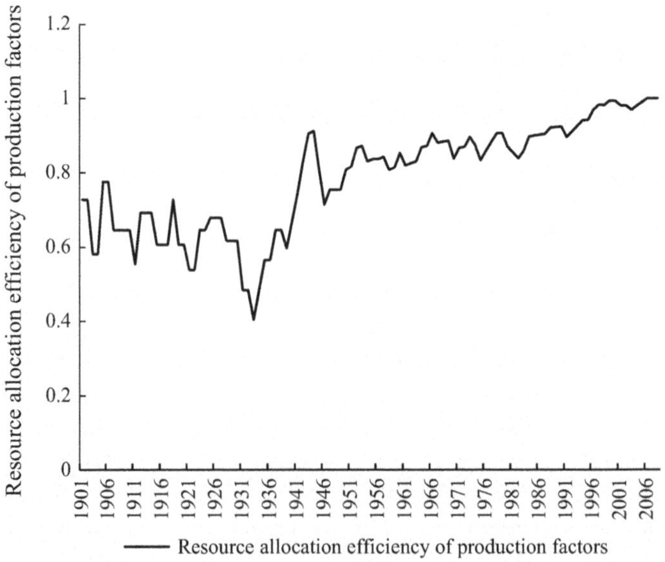

Fig. 5.1 The resource allocation efficiency of production factors in 1900–2008 in America

driven by the information technology revolution; but after 2001, financial volatility and depth adjustment took place (especially financial crisis began in 2008).

The contribution of science and technological progress is not linear with the economic growth rate. It often happens that low economic growth rate corresponds to the high contribution of science and technological progress. However, the contribution of investment in physical capital is linear with the economic growth rate substantially, which shows the growth rate of investment in physical capital is the first factor to determine the economic growth rate.

The reason why resource allocation efficiency of production factor increased rapidly from 1933 to 1945, was that the government adopted economic policies of Keynesian, and strengthened market intervention. The resource allocation efficiency of production factor increased rapidly from 1983 to 2000 due to information technology revolution, which greatly reduced transaction costs, and "Moore's Law" reduced investment costs.

(2) The prominent role of human capital growth.

The average years of schooling of laborers in the United States increased from 6.91 years in 1900 to 13.78 years in 2008. In the above calculation, the sum of the contribution of the labor force growth and the human capital growth to economic growth in 1990–1929, 1939–1947, 1948–1981, 1982–2000, 2001–2008 respectively are 32.9, 26.9, 30.4, 30.8 and 23%.

(3) Immigrant promoted continued growth in population and labor force.

The American population in 1900 was 76 million, increased to 300 million in 2002, and keep growing continuously. At the same time, American urbanization rate increased from 40 to 80%. However, population aging in the United States was serious. The proportion of elderly (65 years old) was three times of the last century, while the proportion of young people dropped by a third. In fact, the proportion of children whose age was from zero to five years old decreased from 12.1 to 7%. Aging population of 65-year-old increased year by year from 1900 to 2000, while the young population of zero to 24-year-old decreased in general.

Immigration is an important reason why the American population and labor force increase. In 1900, there were less than 50 million immigrants in the United States. It increased in a fluctuating tendency from 1900 to 2000. In the 1980s, the number of immigrants accounted for 1/3 of American increasing population and increased in the 1990 s again. The migrants accounted for 40% of American increased population from 2000 to 2001.

(4) The leading role of science and technology.

Over the past 100 years, the United States had gone through a complex technological structure change. In the 20th century, several major technological changes appeared: power, internal combustion engines, automobiles, aircraft, chemical, atomic energy, aerospace, especially electronic information technology revolution, which effectively promoted the long-term sustained economic growth.

(5) The promoting role of institutional innovation.

Institutional innovation provides a good institutional guarantee for the United States to mobilize favorable factors to promote stable economic growth. It is mainly reflected in the three changes in the American corporate system and promoting of the information technology revolution since the 1980s (Table 5.4).

Table 5.4 Three changes of American corporate system

Stage	Content	Organizational form of enterprise	Characteristic
The first corporate transformation (1897–1940)	Corporate mergers and acquisitions. Large enterprises had set up their own personnel organization, and conducted internal integration of administration management. Many large companies had been expanded through vertical integration to build their own business chain	Organizational form of company	The first wave of mergers was that large enterprises annexed small enterprises in the same industry sector; The feature of the second mergers was shown in the process that was from controlling production to controlling the supply and processing of raw materials, and finally to controlling the sales market
The second corporate transformation (1940–1970)	Centralized enterprise (U-company) transformed to Multi-sectoral company (M-company). The general trend was towards decentralized management structures	Multi-sector form of decentralization	The third wave of mergers appeared after World War II, characterized by mixed merger, that these enterprises which had no relationship between each other in production and sales began to merger, and finally formed a mixed alliance company
The third corporate reform (1970 to the present)	Companies in each industry were looking for an approach that cut costs and improve quality of their products and services while re-design the function of their products and services, make vertical decomposition, and outsource some verticals to form an innovative network. The company implemented new financing instruments and leveraged buyouts, management buyouts, and improved innovation capacity hardly	Transnational corporations	American big companies have become modern multinational corporations. Companies in the United States, many of which are service sector firms, have undergone restructuring, and take appropriate strategies to cope with the international economy with fierce competition and innovation as the basic characteristics

5.1.3 Transformation of Development Mode in the Innovation-Oriented Country and the United States

The so-called innovation-oriented country refers to those countries whose contribution of innovation (the contribution of science and technological progress, the contribution of human capital, the contribution of institutional innovation) is above 50%, R&D expenditures account for more than 2.5% of GDP, and technology ownership rate exceeds 50%. According to these three criteria, the United States has become an innovation-oriented country since 1982: the contribution of innovation was 54% in 1982–2000, and 51% in 2001–2008; the average ratio of R&D expenditure to GDP was 2.7%; the average proportion of proprietary technology in effective technology was 53%.

Under the innovative national environment, as the economic growth is more dependent on innovation than investment, America's economy has entered a new stage in which water consumption, energy intensity and major pollutant emissions continue to decrease, and the efficiency of resource allocation continues to increase (Wu 1999).

The rapid increase and continuous innovation in environmental regulations, technological innovation and other measures promote emissions to decrease persistently. The American Commonwealth enacted the *Antiquities Act* in 1906. After 1960, relevant pollution regulation of the United States was formally put on the agenda, which began with *the National Environmental Policy Act (1969)* (NEPA). In 1970, many epoch-making environmental laws and regulations were formulated under the leadership of the American President and parliament. The USA became the world leader in environmental protection, and the number of environmental protection laws and regulation increased rapidly. Thus, the 1970s is called "10 years of environment". According to *Trend of American Environmental Law* compiled by Qu, the number of environmental law enacted by The American Commonwealth reached more than 100 in 1990.

According to the statistics of United States Environmental Protection Agency (EPA), before 1970, the growth trend of total volatile organic compounds and nitrogen oxide emissions in the United States was obvious, while the sulfur dioxide emissions increased in the state of wavy. The emissions of all three peaked in around 1970 and gradually declined steadily.

Decline in per capita water consumption. According to Gleick (2008), saving and efficient water use can reduce water use while promoting economic growth over the past 23 years. American per-capita water consumption decreased from 1950 gallons per person per day in 1977 down to 1480 gallons per person per day in 2000.

This section establishes economic growth model of America for more than 100 years (1900–2008), calculates the contribution of science and technological progress, human capital, physical capital stock, investment in physical capital, institutions and the economic externalities to economic growth in the United States, and explains and analyzes the results of the calculation. Analysis pointed that human capital and labor were important factors in America's economic growth. Total contribution of human capital and labor for 1900–1929, 1939–1947, 1948–1981, 1982–2000, 2001–2008 are 32.9, 26.9, 30.4, 30.8 and 23%, which effectively promoted the long-term growth of America's economy. The calculation results show that from the perspective of the driving factors of economic growth, the United States has entered the development state of an innovative country since 1982, and the sum of contribution of science and technology progress, human capital, and institutional innovation to economic growth has exceeded 50%. Under the innovative national environment, the America's economy has entered a new stage in which water consumption and major pollutant emissions continue to decrease, and the efficiency of resource allocation continues to increase.

5.2 The Calculation and Analysis of Japanese Economic Growth

With regard to the miracle of growth created by East Asia (Japan, Singapore, South Korea, etc.) in the 1960s and 1980s, and the long-term stagnation of the Japanese economy in the last 20 years, there had been much debate in the international academic community (Lau 2003). This book intends to establish a model of Japan's economic growth from the perspective of the synergy theory, calculate the economic growth factors from 1955 to 2009, and analyze the reasons for the long-term stagnation of the Japanese economy.

5.2.1 Japanese Economic Growth Model

5.2.1.1 Japanese Economic Growth Over the Past 50 Years

Looking back at the course of Japanese economic growth for over 50 years, Japan's economy grew rapidly from 1955 to 1972, and the average annual economic growth rate reached 9.65%. In 1973–1980, after two global oil crises, there was an obvious fluctuation in Japan's economy, even some recessions. From 1981 to 1993, a series of economic policies were formulated and implemented, and the domestic economy experienced rapid growth. When it came to 1993 to 2000, due to the burst of economic bubbles and the severe impact of the Asian Financial Crisis in 1997, a severe recession hit Japan again. After 2000, with the economy re-booming all over the world and the rapid economic growth in China, Japan's international economic environment improved and the economy began to recover. However, by 2005, the economic growth rate declined once again (Fig. 5.2).

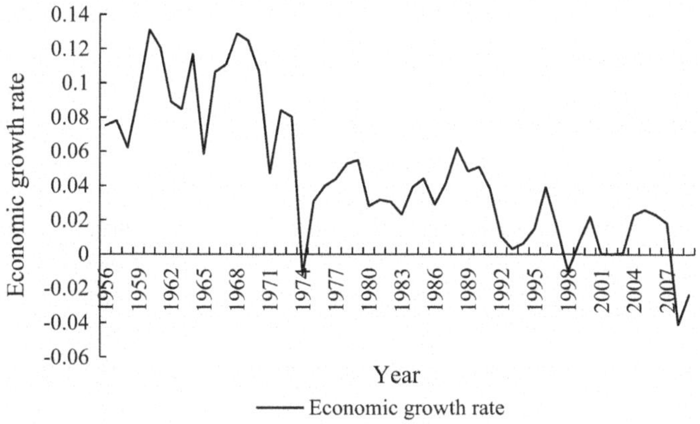

Fig. 5.2 The economic growth rate in Japan in 1955–2005

5.2.1.2 The Economic Growth Model in Japan

Based on the synergy theory of economic growth and the Japanese economic growth data in the Appendix H of this book, this book establishes the following economic growth model in Japan:

$$Y = 0.11788(HL)^{0.4}(SD/L)^{0.36} + 0.117K + 95.5SD/K - 332SD/L + 19.95 \tag{5.2}$$

In the model (5.2), Y represents GDP, L represents the amount of labor, D represents investment in physical capital, H represents human capital, S represents science and technology input, K represents physical capital stock. In the above model, the function of compensation of employees is $V = 0.11788(HL)^{0.4}(SD/L)^{0.36}$, and Table 5.5 is the result of the econometric test after taking the logarithm of compensation of employees.

In the above model, the investment value function is $M = 0.111K + 120SD/K - 391SD/L$, and the results of the model test are shown in Table 5.6.

5.2.1.3 Analysis of Contribution of Institutional Innovation to Economic Growth

Data Envelopment Analysis (DEA) was utilized to analyze the allocation efficiency of Japan's economic growth factors in 1955-2009. It can be seen from Fig. 5.3, after 1990, the allocation efficiency of factors was declining from 1991 to 1999. Allocation efficiency decreased from 100% in 1990 to 94% in 1999, and then increased from 96% in 2000 to 100% in 2005, and then began to decline to 95.5% in 2009.

Table 5.5 The results of econometric tests of function model of compensation of employees

Dependent variable: logV				
Method: least squares				
Sample (adjusted): 1958–2009				
Included observations: 52 after adjusting endpoints				
Convergence achieved after 24 iterations				
Variable	Coefficient	Std. error	T-Statistic	Prob.
C	−0.9289	1.991792	−0.46636	0.6431
logHL	0.404921	0.226382	1.788662	0.0801
logSD/L	0.3627	0.058007	6.252709	0
AR(2)	0.824307	0.177945	4.632365	0
AR(3)	−0.22271	0.176883	−1.25908	0.2142
R-squared	0.992958	Mean dependent var	2.136302	
Adjusted R-squared	0.992358	S.D. dependent var	0.320654	
S.E. of regression	0.028031	Akaike info criterion	−4.21983	
Sum squared resid	0.036928	Schwarz criterion	−4.03221	
Log likelihood	114.7156	F-statistic	1656.724	
Durbin-Watson stat	1.159227	Prob. (F-statistic)	0	
Inverted AR roots	0.72	0.3	−1.02	
Estimated AR process is nonstationary				

Table 5.6 Japanese investment value model

Dependent variable: M				
Method: least squares				
Sample (adjusted): 1957–2009				
Included observations: 53 after adjusting endpoints				
Convergence achieved after 25 iterations				
Variable	Coefficient	Std. error	T-Statistic	Prob.
C	19.95185	38.06488	0.524154	0.6025
K	0.116835	0.033885	3.447958	0.0012
SD/K	99.4963	40.69508	2.444922	0.0181
SD/L	−332.158	193.7689	−1.7142	0.0928
AR(1)	0.925468	0.058853	15.72516	0
R-squared	0.992961	Mean dependent var	148.7911	
Adjusted R-squared	0.992387	S.D. dependent var	74.35621	
S.E. of regression	6.487816	Akaike info criterion	6.665751	
Sum squared resid	2062.496	Schwarz criterion	6.849916	
Log likelihood	−174.975	F-statistic	1728.167	
Durbin-Watson stat	1.756441	Prob. (F-statistic)	0	
Inverted AR roots	0.93			

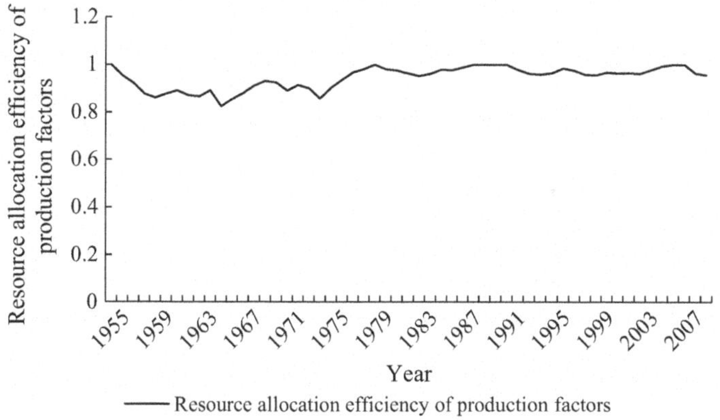

Fig. 5.3 The resource allocation efficiency of production factors in 1956–2009 in Japan

5.2.1.4 The Calculation Results

Table 5.7 shows the results of the contribution of science and technological progress, human capital innovation, physical capital stock growth, the increase of investment in physical capital growth, labor force growth, institutional innovation, and the economic externalities to Japan's economic growth.

The analysis demonstrates that the physical capital accounted 52% of the growth for Japan's economy from 1955 to 1973. Then the direct cause of Japan's economic stagnation after 1993 can be considered as the decline in investment in physical capital. The underlying reason is the incompatibility of the economic system.

During 1955–1973, Japan's economic growth rate averaged at 9.65%, of which, the contribution of physical capital stock growth was 12%, the contribution of investment in physical capital was 40%, and the sum of this two is the contribution of physical capital (52%); the contribution of human capital growth was 4%, the contribution of science and technology progress was 39%, the contribution of institutional innovation was −2%, and the sum of these three is the contribution of innovation (41%), while the impact rate of the economic externalities was 6%. This shows that the externalities of Japan's economic environment has little effect on economic growth. This period is a typical phrase of high speed growth driven by "capital-innovation".

During 1974–1993, Japan's economic growth rate averaged at 3.4%, of which, the contribution of physical capital stock growth was 4%, the contribution of investment in physical capital was 27%, and the sum of the two is the contribution of physical capital (31%); the contribution of human capital growth was 12%, the contribution of science and technological progress was 63%, the contribution of institutional innovation was 6%, and the sum of the three reached 81%. Therefore, the economic growth of this period was driven by innovation. The contribution of the economic externalities was −14%, which indicated that the economic

Table 5.7 The analysis of the contribution of different factors to Japanese economic growth (%)

Year	1955–1973	1973–1993	1993–2009
Contribution of the increase of physical capital stock	12	4	10
Contribution of the increase of investment in physical capital	40	27	−36
Contribution of science and technology progress	39	63	86
Contribution of the increase of human capital	4	12	17
Contribution of the increase of labor force	1	2	−1
Contribution of institutional innovation	−2	6	−5
Impact rate of the economic externalities	6	−14	28

environment during this period was conducive to human capital growth, science and technological progress and institutional innovation.

After 1993, the Japanese economy stagnated. From the growth factor analysis, the main reason is that the investment rate declines, and the contribution of investment in physical capital has fallen significantly, which is a type of investment inactivity.

5.2.2 *Analysis of Reasons for Japanese Economic Recession Since 1990s*

Japanese economic growth rate averaged 9.65% during 1955–1973, while it averaged at 3.4% during 1973–1993. After 1993, the Japanese economy stagnated. From the above analysis of growth factors, the main reason is that the contribution of investment in physical capital has dropped drastically, the investment in physical capital showed a downward trend in 1993–2009 (see Appendix H of this book), and the contribution of physical capital to economic growth was negative −36%). The decline of investment in physical capital is mainly due to the impact of the real estate bubble burst, the change of industrial structure, the weakening of financial system function, the deterioration of international economic and trade environment (Cororaton 2002), the continue declining of the ability of government regulation and promotion of economy, the mismatching between government-oriented export-oriented economic system and its economic environment.

5.2.2.1 The Impact of the Bursting of Real Estate Bubble

After World War II, the Japanese economy developed at a high speed. As the rapid rise of the heavy chemical industry and the acceleration of urbanization, the land appeared in short supply. At the same time, due to the huge profits, large-scale real estate speculation occurred. As a result, land prices in Japan continued to rise before the 1990s (Smitka 2005).

In the early 1990s, Japanese real estate bubble burst, the domestic enterprises and the banking sector suffered heavy losses, and the domestic consumption market was greatly impacted. It was not until 2003 that the Japanese real estate market began to show signs of improvement (Yang and Jiang 2006). The statistics of Japan Real Estate Institute showed that the average price of the apartment house in Tokyo in 2013 was 545,000 Yen/m^2, which was only one-fifth of the peak of Tokyo's real estate in 1988. The serious consequences of the bursting of the Japanese real estate bubble still affected the Japanese economic development and until now the problem of insufficient domestic market demand still exists.

5.2.2.2 Industrial Structure Changes

Heavy chemical industry has always been an important driving force for Japanese economic development. It has attracted a lot of investment and played an important supporting role in Japanese economic growth (Ma and Chen 2000). After 1980, Japan adjusted the ways of economic growth and then the industrial structure presented sweeping changes. With the change of industrial structure in the past 20 years after 1980, the proportion of the original heavy chemical industry decreased significantly and capital investment was reduced. Meanwhile, due to the deterioration of the financial situation after the economic bubble burst, the research and development of heavy chemical industry technology lagged behind. As a result, under the circumstances that the development of high-tech industries is still immature, major products that have dominated the world market such as heavy chemical industry, manufacturing industry, and household appliances, which have dominated the Japanese industrial structure, have experienced industrial decline.

5.2.2.3 Weakening of the Financial System Function

In the 1990s, Japan's international financial policy followed the Mundell-Fleming paradox. That is to say, under the conditions of free capital flow and the floating exchange rates, there is a conflict among maintaining the stability of the exchange rate, maintaining the convertibility of the domestic currency, and the policy goal of promoting domestic economic growth. The policy of appreciating the Yen is the manifestation of the Japan falls into the paradox in mid-1990s. The appreciation of the Yen has not eased the economic downturn that emerged in the country. Instead, Japan's expansionary fiscal policy has almost failed and domestic policy goals have not been realized. At the same time, the appreciation of the yen has reduced the competitiveness of Japanese products in the international market, leading to a decrease in demand (Cui 2005).

5.2.2.4 Deterioration of International Economic and Trade Environment

Before the 1980s, Japan has always implemented the "trading nation" strategy, and continued to expand international economic relations. It created a favorable international environment for rapid economic growth and formed pillar industries such as automobiles, steel and household appliances, and the international market competitiveness of related products increased significantly. However, according to the global economic competitive power report of Swiss International Institute for Management Development (IMD), the Japanese international competitiveness dropped from the No. 1 consecutive during 1989–1993 to the 30th in 2002.

This is a great correlation with the deterioration of Japanese international economic relations, especially the deterioration of the US-Japan economic and trade relations. The economic friction between the United States and Japan has expanded from industrial products such as semiconductors and automobiles to agriculture, construction, and insurance (Ahn 2003). In the Asian and European markets, Japan has also encountered varying degrees of deterioration in economic and trade relations.

5.2.2.5 The Government's Regulation and Promotion Capacity of the Economy Continues to Decline

Before 1990, the Japanese government investment occupied a higher proportion in total physical capital investment from 26.5% in 1970 to 32.0% in 1980. Since 1990, the proportion of Japanese government investment in total physical capital investment has declined year by year (Mitsubishi Research Institute 2001), which shows that the ability of Japanese government to regulate and promote the economy is declining (Fig. 5.4).

After the Second World War, Japan established a government-oriented export-oriented economic growth model, and the government has played an important role in promoting the development of pillar industries and adjusting the economic order. Before the 1980s, Japanese economy had achieved rapid growth, driven by the continued large-scale investment in physical capital by domestic enterprises. In the 1990s, real estate bubbles burst, exports blocked, and many industries were facing serious overcapacity, therefore, the investment in physical capital had become an obstacle to economic development. Excess equipment and productivity became the idle resources of the Japanese economy, which brought the Japanese enterprises the great difficulties of digesting the excess productivity and adjusting the production structure. Moreover, the dilemma and the low operating efficiency of the bank-enterprise bundle in financial system had also reduced the efficiency of the Japanese economy. Therefore, the Japanese government had repeatedly performed fiscal stimulus, which resulted in Japanese huge fiscal deficit for a long time, overall, the ability of Japan government to intervene in the economy is very limited (Li et al. 2013).

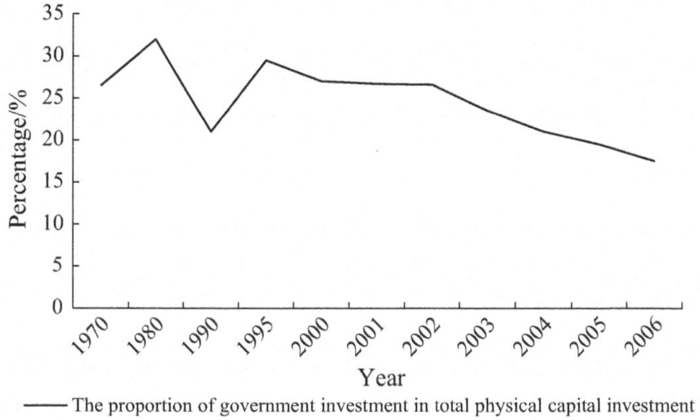

Fig. 5.4 The proportion of government investment in total physical capital investment in Japan during 1970–2007

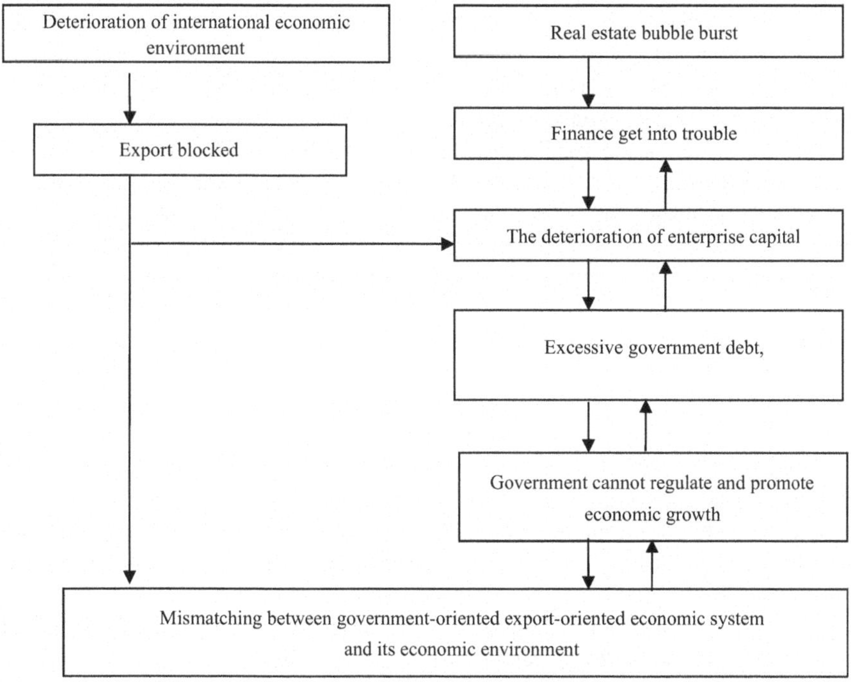

Fig. 5.5 Comprehensive reasons for the decline in the physical capital investment in Japan after 1990

After 1993, the Japanese economy had stagnated, from the view of the growth factor, the main reason was that the investment rate and the contribution of investment in physical capital declined significantly. Although the contribution of science and technological progress and human capital innovation was very high, the case of Japanese stagnant economy belonged to the type of inefficient investment (Fig. 5.5).

5.3 The Analysis of the Factors Affecting Germany's Economic Growth

5.3.1 Correlation Study on Germany's Economic Growth

Andreas (2006), from German IFO Institute for Economic Research at the University of Munich, in his paper *German Productivity–A Reassessment* via *the New IFO Productivity Database*, used a unique database named IFO to analyze the sources of Germany's economic and productivity growth since 1970, and then predicted the growth rate of the Germany's economy over the next decade, finally drew the conclusion that the productivity growth will be at 1.67% per year (variable range is of ±1.25%). Furthermore, average labor productivity will grow at an annual rate of 1.72% (variable range is of ±1.00%).

Andreas decomposed output growth into contribution of labor input, capital input and total factor productivity (TFP). The growth accounting model is based on the production theory of micro-economics and on the following assumptions: the production technology is represented by the production function of labor L and capital service K is the main input, which has the characteristic of constant returns to scale. Moreover, production market and factor market are in the condition of perfect competition.

The methodology used by Andreas is based on the concept of production possibility frontier introduced by Jorgenson (1996). This concept holds that capital and labor inputs have a substitute relationship between each other, and divides capital into information technology capital (IT capital) and non-information technology capital (non-IT capital).

In the concept of production possibility frontier, output can be decomposed into investment and consumption while investment consists of capital service (K) and labor input (L). Capital service can be decomposed into capital flows of computer hardware (K_c), computer software (K_s), communications equipment (K_m) and non-information technology capital services (K_n). The input function (X) is amplified by total factor productivity (A). The production possibility frontier can be represented as:

$$Y = (I_t, C_t) = AX(K_n, K_c, K_s, K_m, L) \tag{5.3}$$

Under the assumptions of competitive relationship between product market and factor market, and constant returns to the scale, Eq. (5.3) can be transformed into an Eq. (5.4) that accounts for the economic growth:

$$\begin{aligned}\Delta \ln y = \bar{v}_{K_n} \Delta \ln k_n + \bar{v}_{K_c} \Delta \ln k_c + \bar{v}_{K_S} \Delta \ln k_s \\ + \bar{v}_{K_m} \Delta \ln k_m + \bar{v}_l \Delta \ln L + \Delta \ln A\end{aligned} \tag{5.4}$$

where $\bar{v}$ denotes the average input shares, and $\bar{v}_{K_n} + \bar{v}_{K_c} + \bar{v}_{K_s} + \bar{v}_{K_m} + \bar{v}_l = 1$.

The output is calculated by using the Eq. (5.4), and the results are shown in Table 5.8. During the period 1970–1990, the average annual growth rate of output was 2.5%, and the contribution of capital input to output growth was 26.6% (or it contributed output growth rate of 0.67%). The main contribution of output growth during this period was not caused by the labor and capital input, but by total factor productivity which contributed 70.2%, while labor input contributed only 3.2%. The reason of low contribution of labor input mainly caused by the change of working time, which was dramatic reduction (−0.78%) in 1970s and small increased (0.18%) in 1980s.

5.3.2 German "Economic Miracle" and the Recession

Before the German reunification in 1990, Germany's economic development could be divided into three phases: the first phase was the reconstruction in the 1950s. With the aid of the United States, Germany returned to the ranks of the Western industrial powers. The second phase, in the 1960s, was marked by rapid economic expansion and modernization, and low interest rates led to the growth of exports. Although Germany's economy was better than other European countries, the third phase, under the influence of the two oil crises in 1973 and 1979, was still at a low growth.

After the reunification of Germany in October 1990, compared with most developed countries, the Germany's economy was more sluggish, and trapped in a

Table 5.8 German GDP growth rate and its source during 1970–2001

Sources of growth	1970–1980	1981–1990	1991–2001
Growth in GDP (Y)	2.73	2.27	1.49
Capital (K)	0.43	0.90	1.09
Others	0.38	0.72	0.94
Computer	0.03	0.12	0.07
Software	0.01	0.03	0.05
Communication	0.01	0.03	0.04
IT contribution	0.05	0.18	0.15
Labor (L)	−0.28	0.44	−0.31
Total factor productivity (TFP)	2.58	0.94	0.71

predicament of low growth and high unemployment. The reunification quickly brought improvement in the level of wages and welfare in Eastern Germany. At the beginning, the reunification produced a huge domestic demand, but then caused fierce competition losses among the Eastern German business owners, and a sharp rise in unemployment, resulting in the worst economic crisis since the second world war. Initially, the reunification of Germany promoted the prosperity of western Germany since the end of the 80s. However, it led to the excessive expansion of the economy. Germany turned production from exports to the extended domestic market which had regularly resulted in the current account change from surplus to deficit and over 5% of inflation. A serious economic recession occurred between 1992 and 1993, prompting the central bank to implement contractional monetary policy. It can be argued that before 2004, the Germany's economy had not fully recovered from the shock of the reunification of Germany, of course, Germany's rigid labor market and a series of unfavorable factors were also responsible for the sluggishness of the Germany's economy.

In 1999 and 2000, Germany's economy momentary improved. However, in the late 2000s, the decline in domestic demand caused by the shrinking exports and construction industry, had led to the decline in commercial confident again. With the temporary high inflation and low wage growth rate, these resulted in the shrinking of real incomes of resident. German GDP growth rate was only 0.8% in 2001 which was the result of both weak domestic demand and the plummeting export growth. Furthermore, the stock market slump also worsened the economic situation. In addition, as a result of the deterioration of the labor market, foreign demand stayed at the situation of stagnation and the domestic demand had not been improved. As a result, the German GDP growth rate further fell to 0.1% and −0.1% in 2002 and in 2003 (Table 5.9).

After the world war II, the Germany's economy made remarkable achievements. The "economic miracle" also made German economy the third-largest economy in the world[3], only after the United States and Japan. The important factors in the success of the Germany's economy are the support of the external "Marshall Plan" assistance, the careful fiscal and monetary policies, and the efforts of the post-World War II reconstruction. An important element of economic policy is the concept of the social market economy which was originally proposed by the Conservative Party, and later supported by the Leftist. This concept requires the economy to be governed by market forces, while the state only plays a role in adjusting social equity and correcting market deficiencies. From the 1950s to the 1980s, the concept of market economy played an important role in the harmonious labor relations.

However, over the past 20 years, the shortcomings of social market model were gradually exposed. Extensive social security system and high personal income taxes reduced the enthusiasm of the workers. And the high labor cost, rigid employment

[3]Compared with other developed countries, manufacturing and related services remained at the center in the Germany's economy, and German manufacturing mainly included industrial machinery, automotive and chemical industries. In 1992–2002, although the share of total industrial output (excluding construction) in GDP fell from 26.9 to 22.3%, it rose to 23% in 2004.

Table 5.9 Germany's economic indicators, 2000–2004

Year	2000	2001	2002	2003	2004
Total GDP (calculated at current prices) (Billion dollars)	1876	1858	1991	2410	2708
Total GDP (calculated at current prices) (Billion mark)	2030	2074	2107	2128	2177
Calculated at 1995 price (Billion mark)	1970	1986	1988	1985	2016
GDP growth rate (%)	2.9	0.8	0.1	−0.1	1.6
Labor (Million)	41.7	42.0	42.1	42.1	42.3
Unemployment (Million)	3.9	3.9	4.1	4.4	4.4
Employment (Million)	39.1	39.3	39.1	38.7	38.9
Unemployment rate (%)	9.6	9.4	9.8	10.5	10.6
OECD national unemployment rate (%)	7.2	7.4	8.2	9.1	9.6

protection, and sustained weakness in domestic demand weakened enterprise demand for labor.

In 1980s, these problems affected the Germany's economic growth, and seriously undermined the government's ability to cope with the economic problems brought by the reunification. In 1995–2004, the Germany's economy was the worst performing among European Union countries. In particular, in 2001–2003, the Germany's economy was continued to decline, and the people demand for more government intervention to take out the economy from the hurdle. Under this condition, in March 2003, Prime Minister Schrader, announced his reform plan called the 2010 agenda, which tried to solve the structural problems of the economic growth. The agenda included the following measures: raising standards for unemployment insurance and reducing unemployment insurance; reforming the social welfare system, especially the public health insurance; and relaxing restrictions on individual entrepreneurship.

5.3.3 *Slow Economic Growth and the Decline of Investment in Physical Capital in Germany*

According to the synergy theory of economic growth and the Germany's economic growth data which was shown in the appendix of this book, this book established Germany's economic growth model as follows:

$$Y = 0.038(HL)^{0.292}(SD)^{0.15} + 0.235K + 0.48SD/K - 2326 \quad (5.5)$$

In this model (5.5), Y stands for gross domestic product; L represents the number of labor, H is human capital, S means scientific and technological input, D is on behalf of investment in physical capital and K represents the physical capital stock. In this model, the function of compensation of employees is

$V = 0.038(HL)^{0.292} * (SD/L)^{0.15}$, and Tables 5.10 and 5.11 is the result of the econometric test after taking the logarithm of compensation of employees.

In 2001–2010, the Germany's economic growth rate was only 0.985% on average. From the analysis for the Germany's economic growth in mentioned period, we obtain the following conclusions. The contribution of physical capital stock growth to economic growth was 41%, the contribution of investment in physical capital was −6%, and the sum of the two is the contribution of physical

Table 5.10 German model for the compensation of employees

Dependent variable: log *V*				
Method: least squares				
Sample (adjusted): 1991–2010				
Included observations: 20 after adjusting endpoints				
Convergence achieved after 9 iterations				
Variable	Coefficient	Std. error	T-Statistic	Prob.
C	0.808033	1.29516	0.623887	0.5415
log *HL*	0.291655	0.135362	2.154622	0.0468
log *SD*	0.144784	0.06956	2.081424	0.0538
AR(1)	0.581123	0.17059	3.406545	0.0036
R-squared	0.945822	Mean dependent var	4.049502	
Adjusted R-squared	0.935664	S.D. dependent var	0.023937	
S.E. of regression	0.006072	Akaike info criterion	−7.19355	
Sum squared resid	0.00059	Schwarz criterion	-6.9944	
Log likelihood	75.93548	F-statistic	93.10759	
Durbin-Watson stat	2.13404	Prob. (F-statistic)	0	
Inverted AR roots	0.58			

Table 5.11 German investment value model

Dependent variable: *M*				
Method: least squares				
Sample: 1990–2010				
Included observations: 21				
Variable	Coefficient	Std. error	T-Statistic	Prob.
C	−2325.69	563.2719	−4.12889	0.0006
K	0.23538	0.016766	14.03913	0
SD/K	0.479968	0.138263	3.471427	0.0027
R-squared	0.965623	Mean dependent var	9996.099	
Adjusted R-squared	0.961803	S.D. dependent var	1198.594	
S.E. of regression	234.2544	Akaike info criterion	13.88226	
Sum squared resid	987752.1	Schwarz criterion	14.03147	
Log likelihood	−142.764	F-statistic	252.7993	
Durbin-Watson stat	1.059194	Prob. (F-statistic)	0	

capital (35%). The contribution of human capital growth was 19%, the contribution of technical change was 49%, and the sum of the two is the contribution of knowledge progress (68%); the contribution of institutional innovation was 0, and the impact rate of economic externalities was −5% (see Table 5.12).

5.3.4 Analysis for the Reasons of the Slow Growth of Germany's Domestic Investment

For the analysis by taking 2005 price as the base price, German investment in physical capital in 2010 was 414.8 billion Euros, less than the 427.2 billion Euros in 2000, resulting in a reduction in investment in physical capital. Therefore, the contribution of investment in physical capital to economic growth was −6% during 2000–2010.

In 1990s, German company investment in abroad increased significantly. Especially since 1995, foreign capital stock of the German companies increased significantly from 10% of GDP in 1995 to 28% in 2000. In 2000, the total foreign capital of German companies was 570 billion Euros. By contrast, the capital of invested in foreign by American companies accounted for only 13.2% of GDP in 2000. The data shows that in the manufacturing sector, foreign investment of German companies was less than half the total amount of foreign investment, and in 2000, foreign capital was approximately 220 billion Euros. The main areas of foreign investment were in banking, insurance, real estate and housing industry. In 2000, the total foreign investment capital stock of German companies was 320 billion Euros.

At the same time, we should observed that not only German companies invested in abroad but foreign companies also invested in Germany. From 1995 to 2000, foreign enterprises invested more in Germany, even though at a low level. The foreign enterprises investment accounted 7% of the GDP in 1995, while it accounted 14% in 2000 (about 280 billion Euros, in 2000). Among them, banking, insurance and real estate industry accounted for about 50% (about 140 billion

Table 5.12 Analysis of economic growth factors in Germany (%)

Period	1990–2000	2001–2010
Economic growth rate	1.9	0.98
Contribution of physical capital stock	49	41
Contribution of investment in physical capital	23	−6
Contribution of science and technology progress	24	49
Contribution of human capital	7	19
Contribution of labor	2	2
Contribution of institutional innovation	0	0
Impact rate of economic externalities	−5	−5

Euros), while manufacturing accounted for roughly a third. This shows that for foreign enterprises, Germany is still a certain attraction. However, in any case, the foreign investment of German companies is about twice as much as the investment that foreign investors invested in Germany.

Countries who invested in Germany are primarily some EU countries, followed by the United States. Major areas of investment in Germany by the United States and the European Union are in the financial sector and real estate services followed by manufacturing. The main area of investment in Germany by central and eastern European countries is in Wholesale and Retail Trade (Geishecker and Rg 2004).

Germany's capital stock doubled from 1970s to 1990s. However, in 1990s, German capital slowed down from 3.4% in 1980s to 2.9% in 1990s. In terms of the contribution of the capital stock, the market service sector still maintained a leading position. The manufacturing sector, which was second in the 1980s, however, has given way to the non-market services sector (Thomas and Oliver 2005).

5.3.4.1 A Relatively High Tax Rate

After entering the new century, Germany's attractiveness to foreign investment is still in the doldrums. In an annual report given by the United Nations, in 2004, Germany ranked 118th in the performance index of foreign direct investment, only higher than Japan in developed countries. This is mainly caused by the tax. Due to the fact that the corporate income tax rate has a significant impact on foreign direct investment, foreign investment is sensitive to the tax rate, when they choose investment country. UNCTAD found that in 2004, about 20 countries reduced corporate income tax, in which nine countries were developed countries. In the developed countries as a whole, the tax rate decreased significantly from 29.7 to 26.5%. By contrast, Germany is one of three countries which raised the tax rate, from 38.29 to 38.31% (Barnard and Cantwell 2007).

5.3.4.2 Poor Mobility of Labor and Lack of Motivation to Hire Employees in Enterprises

Germany's rising unemployment problem has also been attributed to the imbalance of the sector. Compared with other OECD countries, the employment in German industrial sector has shrunk faster, while the employment in the service sector has not increased accordingly. The employment of the traditional industrial sector with higher productivity still has a huge attraction. This is because the rigorous organized trade unions in the industrial sector, and employment in the industrial sector can get a higher salary than in the service sector. In Germany, industrial unemployed were reluctant to work in the service department, particularly young men and they were willing to become an apprentice in the industrial sector. This unreasonable phenomenon was more prominent in the mining industry sector, because the mining sector can get higher salaries than other industrial sectors. And the background was that the mining industry in Germany was not a for-profit sector, and the mining industry was able to exist due to various government subsidies (Berthold and Fehn 2003). The rigidity of the labor market is mainly caused by the following reasons.

Firstly, German trade unions were powerful. Even in the western European countries, the probability of German wages determined by collective bargaining is also very high. As a result of the German wage agreement by the two sides through their own organization, that is, the Union and the employer of the federation of free negotiations. In the negotiations, German trade unions took the enterprises whose benefits were higher in the industry as criteria, but they did not consider differences in region, enterprise scale, technical level, etc., which made enterprises have to pay a higher wage costs, and was not conducive to labor factor mobility as well. Since the reunification of Germany, the wage level in the east of Germany has been growing by leaps and bounds, which has lost its competitiveness compared with the Eastern European countries (Table 5.13).

Moreover, the trade unions used their power to negotiate on the national, regional, industry and enterprise levels. And finally reached a number of collective agreements in favor of workers and a wide range of employment protection measures, such as strict dismissal procedures, high severance pay, statutory minimum wage and working time limit, which inhibited the enthusiasm of enterprises to hire workers, resulting in enterprises are very cautious when they hire employees (Zhang and Hou 2005).

The average operation time of German workers fell quickly. Taking western Germany as an example, the average operation time of workers fell from 1467 h in 1991 down to 1347 h in 2001 (a reduction of 120 h or 8% decline). In 2001, the total working hours of German workers were 47.7 billion hours, decreased 7% from 1991 (Spitznagel 2003).

Secondly, protection for employees hindered enthusiasm of companies in hiring staff (Table 5.14). German employees are protected by the *Labor Law* and other regulations, and therefore, the cost of hiring and firing is high. Rigid labor markets made enterprises afraid to hire new employees, resulting in a big increase in unemployment (Dai 2005). From the end of 1960s, the cost of firing employees in Germany rose sharply, and then remained at this high level. The cost of dismissing employees in European countries is higher than that of the United States (Berthold and Fehn 2003).

Thirdly, the German high-welfare social security system stifled the work enthusiasm of the workers. The comprehensive social security system has played an important role in the social stability and economic development after the World War II. However, excessive welfare weakened the enthusiasm of the workers. Like

Table 5.13 Comparison of collective bargaining in European countries (Wang and Li 2005)

Country	Britain	Germany	Netherlands
Collective bargaining rate (%)	47	90	71

Table 5.14 Strictness indicators for employee legal protection

Country	Late 1980s	Late 1990s
Germany	2.7	2.8
Britain	0.8	0.8
America	0.2	0.2
Switzerland	1.2	1.2
Italy	2.8	2.8
Denmark	1.6	1.6
Australia	1.0	1.0
Japan	2.7	2.7

other northern European countries, in terms of the protection of workers from unemployment, Germany mainly relies on generous unemployment benefits and social welfare. In some cases, the income of the work is even lower than the income from the relief, so many people prefer to receive unemployment benefits and do not want to engage in lower income work.

Fourthly, the spirit of hard work of German declined. With the development of the economy, especially Germany's unique social welfare system, which bring residents the superior material life, affected the Germans' work habits and work attitude to a certain extent as well. The meticulous and hard-working spirit of German were increasingly rare, while the thought that get without any labor and Sit idle and enjoy the fruits of others' work were breeding. Most of the Germans, especially those young people, do not want to work in the poor environment, and tend to work in a comfortable environment with high pay (Wang 2005).

5.3.4.3 Heavy Burden on Enterprises

Compared with other developed countries, the burden of German companies was heavier, which was an important reason for the domestic enterprises invested in the doldrums in Germany in recent years. Overweight burden of enterprises mainly manifested in two aspects: high labor costs and high taxes.

Firstly, the high labor costs. Compared to other major industrialized countries, the German labor costs were too high. Taking a worker income per hour in 1996 for example, calculated at the then-current exchange rate between US dollar and Mark, it was \$31.87 in Germany, \$31.87 in Japan, \$17.70 in US, and only \$5.82 in Taiwan (Fang 2001).

High wage in Germany was also reflected in its high additional wage costs. According to statistics, in 1996 the German manufacturing industry average annual labor cost was 86,200 Mark, the direct salary is 47,400 Mark, accounting for the total cost of 55%. And the additional wage is 38,800 Mark, accounted for 45% of the total cost, about 2.5 times that of the United States and Japan (Yin 2001).

Another fact that cannot be ignored is that the actual wages of German workers have grown too fast in the 1980s and 1990s compared to other developed countries. Taking manufacturing as an example, in two decades, real wages of German workers increased by about 40%, while the American wages remained essentially unchanged over the same period (Berthold and Fehn 2003).

German workers actually did not have such a high income, even though Germany's high taxes and high welfare policies were considered. However, if we consider the fact that the shortening of the working hours of German workers, especially when compared with other developed countries, the situation can be imagined. In addition, the German workers retire early, have the longest sick leave and have a high rate of absenteeism, resulting in the German industrial equipment utilization rate is the lowest in Western countries. As some German entrepreneurs complain, high hourly wages and ultra-short week working hours, making German companies look like they are carrying two handcuffs when competing with rivals.

In the intensification of international economic integration, especially the internationalization of capital flows of today, enterprises must choose the countries and regions where they can maximize profits and where their investment are more fruitful. The high cost of labor will adversely affect the enterprise competition, forcing companies to reckon very carefully in hiring, and to use fewer of labors to reduce labor costs as much as possible. Today, many German unions keep high level of pay and benefits, which made Germany an expensive place to invest. In such a situation where there is high cost of labor, domestic investment in Germany is not vibration. It is not surprising that the international competitiveness of German companies is declining (Wang 2005).

Secondly, a factor that burdens on German enterprises too heavy is that the enterprises need to bear a high tax. High taxes inevitably lead to low investment. Due to the profit driven of capital, especially in the capital flow internationalization of today, the capital will avoid the higher tax state. High tax policy forces companies to transfer capital, and with the help of multinational corporations to easily transfer capital to countries with low cost, thereby obtaining a greater profit. And for the welfare states, they lost an important source of revenue that supports the national economy.

In 1999, the German corporate income tax rate was 57%, higher than other industrialized countries. Due to the German tax reform, this situation has changed. Through reform, the highest corporate income tax rates fell from 57% in 1999 to 38.9% in 2005. The purpose of the German government's tax reform is to increase the investment of enterprises, to strengthen the competitiveness of the Germany's economy, and to expand the government's financial resources through reduce the tax rate.

Germany, however, is not the only country to implement tax reform. Similar reforms have also occurred in other European countries. As a result, tax reform did not significantly change the status of the German tax in the international. Therefore, it is uncertain whether Germany will attract more business investment to expand the tax source as wished or not (Hagen and Strauch 2001). A report released by the United Nations in 2005 showed that Germany was one of three countries that increased tax rates, while other developed countries generally lowered tax rates.

Germany's high tax policy is linked to its fiscal policy. In the Eurozone, the euro exchange rate is unified under the control of the European Central Bank. Germany also lost the exchange rate, an important macroeconomic control tool, and is more dependent on the role of finance. Since the German government is not maintaining its expenditure on the debt of the central bank (because this will lead to inflation) when it is in deficit, it is maintained through the issuance of national debt. The interest payment on the government's huge debt become another burden on finance, so the importance of finance is even more significant.

Meanwhile, in order to pay high welfare costs, the German government has to raise the tax rate repeatedly. However, the high tax rate would be further discouraged the investment initiative of enterprises and individual. For individuals, high tax policy led to its low consumption, high wage expectations and high labor costs. For enterprises, high tax policy made enterprises profit reduce, leading investors to transfer the capital to other countries and regions whose tax costs was relatively low (Dai 2005).

5.3.4.4 More Complicated Market Regulation

Excessive management rules and over-protection of certain industries suffocate the venture capital activities and the entrepreneurial spirit of innovation, making the innovation of enterprises insufficient vitality and eventually leading to a lack of labor productivity growth. Too complicated laws and regulations in Germany affected the competitiveness of German companies. When German companies and businessmen invested and set up factories in foreign countries, they are less bound by the law. However, in their country, they had to deal with strict rules of the network. The mire of rules made German entrepreneurs have so few new ideas (Fang 2001).

In terms of the density of rules and regulations, in 1980s, Germany in all aspects was in the third from the bottom in Western Europe. In 1990s, the rank of Germany advanced. This is only the result of the relaxation of the management of temporary employment rules and regulations, and the index fell from 3.8 to 2.3. However, there was no change in other factors, although the composite index also fell by 0.7 points. Germany has only improved one in terms of the sort because other European countries to take the same action.

As a whole, management rules and regulations of the German labor market were much more rigorous than more than half of the European countries observed. In the world, Germany was one of the countries that had the most stringent rules and regulations, while the Anglo Saxon countries (United States, Britain, Canada, Australia and New Zealand) were the countries with less regulations density (Camille and Zhang 2005) (see Table 5.15).

In terms of trade barriers, the German index of 2.1 was higher than most OECD countries, while the US was 1.3, and the UK was only 0.5. Therefore, the entry of German new firms was limited, which was mainly reflected in the high costs of entry and dull bureaucracy. In the efficiency of government, in Germany, obtaining government approval needed an average of about 90 days, only less than Italy, higher than other countries. These factors led to the monopoly of some German companies, thus affecting the quality of outputs (Table 5.16).

Table 5.15 International comparison of the regulation of labor market in Germany

Indicator	Late 1980s			Late 1990s		
	Index	Sorted in the observed OECD countries	Sorted in 16 OECD countries	Index	Sorted in the observed OECD countries	Sorted in 16 OECD countries
Composite index	3.2	14(19)	11	2.5	18(26)	10
Protection of general employment	2.7	13(20)	10	2.8	21(27)	12
General procedure inconvenience	3.5	18(22)	12	3.5	24(27)	13
General procedure inconvenience	3.5	14(20)	12	3.5	20(27)	12

Note (1) The index ranges from 0 (no regulation) to 6 (strict regulations); (2) Figures in brackets is the number of the OECD countries observed

Table 5.16 OECD countries business barrier index

Country	Required program steps	Approved days	Per capita GDP cost	Entrepreneurial innovation mental disorders
Germany	7	90	0.0851	2.1
Australia	3	3	0.2090	1.1
Canada	2	2	0.0140	0.8
France	16	66	0.1970	2.7
America	4	7	0.0096	1.3
Britain	7	11	0.0056	0.5
Italy	11	121	0.2474	2.7
Japan	11	50	0.1144	2.3
Sweden	4	17	0.0254	1.8

In terms of product market regulation, in the 1990s, the German index of 1.5 was higher than the US (1.0), the UK (0.5) and other countries, lower than Italy (2.3), France (2.1) and other countries. All in all, the German product market regulation was more serious than Anglo-Saxon product market regulation, but lower than France and Italy market regulation, and in the middle position in the entire OECD (Berthold and Fehn 2003).

5.4 The Analysis of the Factors Affecting Singapore's Economic Growth

5.4.1 The Relative Study on the Economic Growth of Singapore

5.4.1.1 Lau's Research

Kim and Lau (1994a, b) applied the production function method to analyze the economic growth of East Asian "Four Asian Tigers"–Hong Kong, South Korea, Singapore and Taiwan and developed G5 countries–France, Germany, Japan, Britain and the United States, and established models with two inputs (tangible capital and labor). Through a series of hypotheses, the calculation results showed that: first, the assumptions of no science and technological progress cannot be rejected by the East Asian NIEs, but can be firmly rejected by G5; second, tangible capital expansion is the most important source of economic growth in East Asia, including Japanese postwar economic growth. However, science and technological progress is the most important source of growth in G5 (except Japan) which meets Lau and Boskin's (1990) early findings.

Kim and Lau (1995) introduced human capital into the production function, measuring added human capital by the average years of schooling of the working-age population, and does not change the basic findings of Kim and Lau (1994b). Tangible capital is the most important source of post-war economic growth of East Asian "Four Asian Tigers", accounting for 65–85% growth, followed by the labor force. Human capital accounted for 6% in the economic growth of postwar East Asia "Four Asian Tigers". Recently, the proportion of R&D expenditure in East Asia "Four Asian Tigers" to GDP has increased rapidly, which has been synchronized or surpassed that of some G7 countries. In the next long period of time, due to the accumulation of tangible and intangible capital, East Asian's development in economy still has the potential to continue to grow strong,.

The importance of productivity growth is more important in Singapore's long-term growth, because it structurally adjust higher value-added of economy (Lau 2003). The key component of Singapore's long-term economic growth is the quality of education of the workforce. The government is to increase education, training and expenditure for the retraining of workers to meet the challenges of the knowledge economy (Lee 2004).

5.4.1.2 Crafts and Others' Study on the Economic Growth of Singapore

Crafts' (1996) study on economic growth of Singapore shows that capital investment has positive contribution to the growth of actual GDP. The share of capital investment in real GDP growth was particularly high in the first half of the 1980s, and the vast majority of them were the result of large-scale investment in the construction industry. The economic recession in Singapore in 1985 marked a significant decline in the contribution capital input in the second half of the 1980s. In 1990s, it has been restored to 56% per year of actual GDP. This recovery is due to the strong growth of construction and investment in most of the decade.

In the entire period of 1973–1996, capital investment is the main factor of real GDP growth. For the real GDP of 7.4% growth, the capital investment accounted for 67%. In the first half of the 1980s, the allocation of capital investment in the real GDP growth is especially significant, it can account for an average of 99%. Investment in buildings is the most obvious manifestation in that period. However, during the latter half of the 1980s, it can be seen that the effect of capital investment on the output growth is obviously degraded. And in the period from 1990 to 1996, its contribution rebound to 51% a year (Wong and Benson 1997). During the period of 1973–1996, the contribution of labor to the actual GDP growth was 20%. In the 1980–1985, the contribution of labor change dropped to 12%, and then it has been gradually increasing in the rest of period.

During the entire period of 1973–1996, the growth of multi-factor productivity contributed 14% per year to the growth of real GDP. However, unlike the contribution of labor, the contribution of multi-factor productivity growth is more unstable. At the beginning of the two periods, the contribution of the multi-factor productivity growth is negative. However, the growth of multi-factor productivity has been significantly restored, in 1985–1990, and 1990–1996, respectively, the contribution of real GDP growth was 47 and 23%. This will promote more technology diploma holders and university graduates to join the labor force, at the same time it will make the existing workforce skills concentrated. From a qualitative point of view, the performance of the multi-factor productivity in the two mid-terms is similar to the conclusions drawn by Young in Singapore in 1992.

Multi-factor productivity performed well in the mid 1980 s, and its growth has eased in recent years. However, since reached the highest point of 4.3% in 1993, the increase of multi-factor productivity has been reduced to 0.8% in 1996. (Department of Statistics Singapore 1997).

5.4.2 Analysis on the Motive Force of Singapore's Economic Growth

According to the synergy theory of economic growth and the growth data of Singapore's economy in the appendix of this book, the model of economic growth of Singapore is established as follows:

$$Y = 0.038(HL)^{0.276}(SD/L)^{0.247} + 0.27K + 112.3HSD/K^2 - 8.69S - 0.84 \quad (5.6)$$

In above model (5.6), Y represents the gross domestic product, L represents the number of labor, D represents the investment in physical capital, H represents

Table 5.17 Singapore model of compensation of employees

Dependent variable: log V				
Method: least squares				
Date: 06/22/13 Time: 06:36				
Sample: 1981–2005				
Included observations: 25				
Variable	Coefficient	Std. error	T-statistic	Prob.
C	0.843274	0.46382	1.818105	0.0827
$\log HL$	0.275616	0.093325	2.953283	0.0073
$\log SD/L$	0.247201	0.037129	6.657927	0
R-squared	0.982575	Mean dependent var	2.593506	
Adjusted R-squared	0.980991	S.D. dependent var	0.224872	
S.E. of regression	0.031003	Akaike info criterion	−3.99727	
Sum squared resid	0.021147	Schwarz criterion	−3.85101	
Log likelihood	52.96592	F-statistic	620.2948	
Durbin-Watson stat	0.687342	Prob. (F-statistic)	0	

human capital, S represents the scientific and technological investment, K represents the stock of physical capital. In above model, the function of compensation of employees is $V = 0.038(HL)^{0.276} * (SD/L)^{0.247}$, and Tables 5.17 and 5.18 are the results of the econometric test after the logarithm of compensation of employees and investment value.

In 1981–2010, the average rate of economic growth in Singapore reached 6.5%. The reasons for its economic growth were analyzed. The contribution of physical capital stock growth was 37%, the contribution of investment in physical capital was 19%, and the sum of the two is the contribution of physical capital (56%). The contribution of human capital growth was 18%, the contribution of science and technology progress was 35%, and the contribution of institutional innovation was 0, and the sum of these three is the contribution of innovation (53%). However, the impact rate of the economic externalities is −10%, which demonstrates that the economic environment is very conducive to economic growth. In this period, the high growth of Singapore's economy was driven by the growth of physical capital and the promotion of innovation, which belonging to the capital-innovation dual drive type of economic growth.

5.4.3 *Double Driven Capital-Innovation Mode of Singapore's Economic Growth*

5.4.3.1 The Role of Investment and Capital

Singapore has a huge financial system, which provides an important source of funding for the rapid economic development. Investment and financing system is perfect, and the government industry financing plan in conjunction with the

Table 5.18 Singapore's investment value model

Dependent variable: M				
Method: least squares				
Sample (adjusted): 1985–2005				
Included observations: 21 after adjusting endpoints				
Convergence achieved after 17 iterations				
Variable	Coefficient	Std. error	T-statistic	Prob.
C	−0.83908	60.48565	−0.01387	0.9891
K	0.271161	0.049336	5.496187	0
SHD/K^2	112.3432	56.98123	1.971583	0.0627
S	−8.69051	4.602327	−1.88829	0.0736
AR(1)	0.874405	0.187679	4.659033	0.0002
AR(3)	−0.46458	0.16666	−2.78759	0.0114
R-squared	0.991823	Mean dependent var	676.7143	
Adjusted R-squared	0.989779	S.D. dependent var	0.9891	
S.E. of regression	34.84135	Akaike info criterion	0	
Sum squared resid	24278.4	Schwarz criterion	0.0627	
Log likelihood	−125.803	F-statistic	0.0736	
Durbin-Watson stat	2.369576	Prob. (F-statistic)	0.0002	
Inverted AR roots	0.72 − 0.55i	0.72 + 0.55i	0.57	

commercial banking system is better. On the one hand, the government directly uses the financing assistance program to promote the development of the government's selected strategic industries and investment projects. On the other hand, the government also uses state controlled or holds banks to raise funds to support industrial development. In order to establish the status of international financial center, the government has been encouraging the development of overseas financial securities to Singapore in addition to its strong support for the development of its own financial institutions (Yu 2003).

Crafts (1996) pointed out that some of the failure of the nation's financial system would endanger the capital expansion. Developing countries are often faced with capital and technology shortages. The only resource is that they have adequate supply of unskilled labor. For the economy of capital shortage and labor adequate, giving workers more capital to work will increase productivity rapidly and dramatically. We must also take the relationship between physical capital and human capital into consideration, which is most likely to be complementary than alternative. Tangible or physical capital and intangible capital are complementary, which imply that there is more tangible capital, more productive is invisible capital. And it is also implies that if there is very little tangible capital, intangible capital investment cannot be prolific. We need to look at capital levels, rather than its growth (Bayhaqi 2000). Singapore has tried to make joint investments by public venture capital, and to stimulate private investment through tax incentives (Charles River Associates Ltd. 2003).

The Singapore government encourages the free development of enterprises to attract domestic private capital and foreign investment in Singapore by formulating unique investment policies. Because Singapore's domestic private capital is weak, the government adopts a policy to actively support and encourage private capital. Since 1970s, the "capital funding scheme" and "small industry financing plan" have been implemented on private capital. As a result, the scope of private capital business has expanded from the original commercial and financial fields to investment, real estate, mining tourism and other field. Singapore government not only to encourage domestic private investment, but also to develop positive policies to encourage foreign investment (Li 2004).

5.4.3.2 The Role of Education

Lim (1996) pointed out that there are 6 ways in which education can contribute to economic growth: (1) it gradually improves the quality of labor by giving technology and working knowledge; (2) increase the labor mobility, and stimulate labor allocation; (3) make new knowledge accepted more quickly, and make the unfamiliar inputs and new knowledge more effectively applied; (4) improve the management skills of leading more efficient resources allocation; (5) remove many social and institutional obstacles to economic growth; (6) encourage the spirit of entrepreneurs for a long time by improving the personal sense of responsibility, and ability of organization (Bayhaqi 2000).

Singapore has developed an educational system that is competitive in the management of the elite, established and maintained a cohesive society, to promote the rapid development of economy and industry. Education has a very high status in Singapore, which has a high level of social and political consensus. Singapore's education system is shaped according to the British education system. In particular, people who own the academic qualifications of advanced education have a high status. Singapore and the United Kingdom have many connections in production training and attach great importance to the education of leisure activities, sports and natural sciences (Council 1998).

The alternative categories of vocational and technical education to Singapore nationals are mainly the full-time training for secondary school graduates, the continuing education and training for in-service workers, the basic education of reading, writing, arithmetic that provided for the less educated workers, the training of adjust skill that established specifically for those who wish to upgrade or acquire new technology and so on (Hu 2002b).

Education has always been Singapore's strengths. And government investment in primary, secondary and university education, funding for employee training programs are relatively abundant (Charles River Associates Ltd. 2003).

5.4.3.3 The Role of Technology

Singapore R&D policy includes the public financial support for public research institutions and the stimulation for private R&D sector (for example, through the tax system); and publicly fund that help scientists and engineers seconded from the institute to local companies.

Since the 1980s, the new government proposed "economic restructuring" strategy to speed up the development of high-tech, promote the upgrading of products, and enhance the international competitiveness of their products. To this end, from 1979 to 1981 the government sharply raised salary, forcing the enterprises to develop high-tech and save labor. At the same time, measures taken include: give rewards to the research and development of high-tech enterprises; selectively strengthen the high-tech field of research and development; encourage foreign companies to invest in biotechnology, electronics, high tech, high value-added projects, and all of foreign investment in high-tech and high value-added can be duty-free for 5–10 years; encourage "advanced technology" company (that promising enterprise), and the approved as "advanced technology" of the enterprise can enjoy 5 to 10 years preferential corporate tax relief etc. Information technology is one of the fastest developing industries in Singapore. By the 1990s, Singapore was second only to Japan, becoming the highest concentration degree of computer information technology in Asia and one of the largest manufacturers of computer-related products in the world. To a great extent, Singapore is becoming Southeast Asia's "Silicon Valley". The development of high-tech industry, not only overcame the weakness of small territory and poor resource, but also made full use of the higher quality of human resources and excellent geographical location and other favorable conditions. It will undoubtedly become an important factor of Singapore in tracking the world trend and promoting economic progress continuously (Mao 2002).

Singapore's innovation policy aims to improve the development of local technology through the development of technology-centric small and medium enterprises (SMES). The key to doing so is the generation of skilled workers and innovative entrepreneurs. Meanwhile, the state encourages positive spillover from foreign companies operating in the country through variety of means. Although Singapore is one small city-state which is only over 400 million people and do not have natural resources, but it shows a spectacular economic performance. These economic performances should be attributed to the non-interference government and the business of many foreign owned companies that are encouraged by the state. This may be true, and the government is increasingly relying on intervention, especially in the competition of technological development (Mani 2000).

5.4.4 Policies to Promote Innovation and Transformation

At the turn of the century, the Singapore's economy appeared sharp fluctuations that it transferred from rapid recovery to suddenly worsened, and then plunged into a severe recession. In 1997, a serious financial crisis broke out in Southeast Asia. In 1998, Singapore's economy fell into a severe recession, while there was a rapid recovery and a strong rebound in 1999 and 2000, and by 2001 the Singapore's economy had worsened, or even negative growth. According to Singapore's official statistics, it shows that from 1996 to 2000, Singapore's economic growth rate was 7.7, 8.5, −0.9, 6.4, 9.4% (Wang 2001).

Singapore's economic recession in 1998 was mainly due to the following points. (1) Singapore is highly dependent on the world market. Like Japan, Singapore is poor in natural resources, and it implements the "both in the overseas" of the export-oriented economy, its two-thirds of economic activity is dependent on foreign trade, and therefore the Singapore economy is vulnerable to external economic fluctuations. (2) The lack of technological innovation capability. Singapore mainly to introduces, imitates and transforms the existing technological achievements of the west, the development of their own technology is not much. (3) Strong dependence on foreign investment. Singapore's domestic private capital is fragile, although the government participated in the enterprise investment, and encourages private capital to invest in manufacturing, but private capital tends to invest in smaller, less capital recovery period of fiber textile, light industry and other enterprises. Therefore, Singapore's economy is mainly dependents on international capital, especially from the United States, Japan and the European Union's capital (Li 2004).

The government has taken measures to deal with this economic situation. First of all, increase the intensity of the implementation of expansionary macroeconomic policies to get rid of the domestic economic downturn. Second, continue to promote the adjustment and upgrading of industrial structure to promote the transformation of the domestic economy. Third, speed up the pace of foreign investment, and expand economic development space. Fourth, launch the "China strategy", attach importance to developing economic and trade cooperation with China (Wang 2001). Fifth, vigorously develop the entrepot trade, dig human resources, and it is necessary to realize the industrialized countries to dig this treasure of human resources. Sixth, turn the focus of economic development from labor-intensive industries to capital-intensive industries, and actively introduce foreign investment, give foreign investors with various benefits. Seventh, by using the unique geographical position, vigorously develop the "no-smoke industry". It has generated a lot of foreign exchange for Singapore. This is also an important reason for Singapore's economic take-off (Wang and Yao 2001).

Due to the openness of the economy in Singapore and its stable macroeconomic policies, coupled with the continuous improvement of the external environment, it is expected that the economy will continue to develop rapidly. But at the same time, opportunities and challenges coexisted, the long-term challenges that Singapore faced are as followed: (1) technical change, human capital improvement, and institutional innovation are weak; (2) the increasingly fierce competition from manufacturers in low cost areas, which will lead to structural changes in the Singapore economy and rising unemployment, especially in the manufacturing sector; (3) because of the high degree of openness, it is vulnerable to be affected by the international economic crisis. This requires the government to take reform measures to enhance Singapore's economic competitiveness and efficiency, and strengthen themselves in front of opportunities.

References

Ahn, K. (2003). Are east Asian economies dynamically efficient? Journal of Economic Development, 28(1), 101–110.

Andreas, K. (2006). German Productivity – a reassessment via the new IFO productivity database. IFO Working Paper.

Barnard, H., &Cantwell, J. (2007). World investment report 2005: transnational corporations and the internationalization of R&D. United Nations Conference on Trade and Development United Nations, New York and Geneva (2005). Research Policy, 36(8), 1288–1291.

Bayhaqi, A. (2000). Education and macroeconomic performance in Indonesia: a comparison with other ASEAN economies.

Berthold, N., & Fehn, R. (2003). Unemployment in Germany: reasons and remedies. Cesifo Working Paper, (2).

Boskin, M.J., & Lau, L.J. (1990). Post-war economic growth in the group-of-Five countries: a new analysis. Cambridge: National Bureau of Economic Research.

Camille, L., &Zhang, N. (2005). The latest research on the labor market system and unemployment. Journal of Translation from Foreign Literatures of Economics, (1), 75–82.

Charles River Associates Ltd. (2003). Innovation policies in Singapore, and applicability to New Zealand. Wellington: Ministry of Economic Development Wellington.

Cororaton, C.B. (2002). Technological innovations in Japan and S&T experiences in the Philippines: drawing policy lessons for the Philippines. Philippine Institute for Development Studies Discussion Paper Series. 125–132.

Council, F.E.F. (1998). Post-school education and training in Singapore: international report from the Inspectorate September 1998. Further Education Funding Council.

Crafts, N., & Toniolo, G. (1996). Economic growth in Europe since 1945. London: Cambridge University Press.

Cui, J. (2005). On the institutional causes of Japan's economic recession and its enlightenment. Academic Journal of Shanxi Provincial Committee Party School of C. P. C., 28(4), 70–72.

Dai, Q.X. (2005). On the predicament of German reform from the angle of general election. Deutschland-studien, (4), 35–38 + 79.

Eicher, T.S., &Turnovsky, S.J. (1999). Non-scale models of economic growth. Economic Journal, 109(457), 394–415.

Fang, Z.Q. (2001). Influences of globalization on competitive forces of German science technology and economy. Science and Technology Review, (8), 62–64.

Geishecker, I., & Rg, G.H. (2004). Investment by German firms abroad—unpatriotic? Economic Bulletin, 41(11), 407–410.

Gleick, P.H. (2008). Water conflict chronology. http://www.Worldwater.org/Conflictchronology.html.

Hagen, J.V., & Strauch, R.R. (2001). German public finances: Recent experiences and future challenges. Zei Working Papers.

Hu, S.L. (2002a). Reflections on technological innovation and China 's economic growth. China Economist, (4), 14–15.

Hu, C.W. (2002b). Singapore's rapid economic growth in vocational and technical education cannot be wiped out. Continuing Education and Personnel, (11), 13–15.

Hu, N.Y., & Sun, J.X. (2000). Technological innovation and economic growth. Journal of Shandong Institute of Trade Unions' Administration Cadres, (6), 89–92.

Jones, C.I. (1995). Time series test of endogenous growth models. Quarterly Journal of Economics, 110(2), 495–525.

Jorgenson, D.W. (1996). Technology in growth theory. Conference Series – Federal Reserve Bank of Boston, 45–89.

Jorgenson, D.W., & Zhong, X.Y. (1989). Productivity in Japan and the United States and economic growth. The Journal of Quantitative & Technical Economics, (4), 74–78.

Jorgenson, D.W., Goettle, R.J., Ho, M.S., et al. (2008). US labor supply and demand in the long run. Journal of Policy Modeling, 30(4), 603–618.

Kim, J.I., & Lau, L.J. (1994a). The sources of economic growth of the east Asian newly industrialized countries. Journal of the Japanese & International Economies, 8(3), 235–271.

Kim, J.I., & Lau, L.J. (1994b). The sources of economic growth of the newly industrialized countries on the pacific rim. Economic Development of Roc and the Pacific Rim in the 1990s and Beyond, 61–103.

Kim, J.I., & Lau, L.J. (1995). Sources of economic growth of the newly industrialized countries of the pacific rim, Economic Development of Roc and the Pacific Rim in the 1990s and Beyond, 61–103.

Lau, L.J. (2003). The sources of east Asian economic growth revisited. Cornell University, 6–7.

Lee, B. (2004). Measuring total factor productivity growth: survey report. Tokyo: Asian Productivity Organization.

Li, X.D. (2004). Reasons and inspirations of economic advancement and economic recession in Singapore. Contemporary Finance & Economics, (9), 87–90.

Li, H., Jiang, Z.H., & Jiang, Z.N. (2013). The analysis of knowledge graph of the evolution of the economic growth model and the symbiosis theory: the assessment of Japan's model. Journal of Harbin University of Commerce (Social Science Edition), (6), 3–14.

Lim, D. (1996). Explaining Economic Growth: A New Analytical Framework. Cheltenham: Edward Elgar Publishing.

Ma, W.X., &Chen, W.H. (2000). Japan's economic growth and adjustment of industrial structure. Japanese Research, (4), 9–13.

Mani, S. (2000). Policy instrument for stimulation R&D in the enterprise sector. UNU-INTECH Discussion Paper Series 1, United Nations University – INTECH.

Mao, Y. (2002). Causes of rapidly economic development in Singapore since self-government. Around Southeast Asia, (6), 10–13.

Mitsubishi Research Institute. (2001). Outlook for Japan's Economy 2000. Japan: Mitsubishi Research Institute.

Smitka, M. (2005). Japanese macroeconomic dilemmas: the implications of demographics for growth and stability. The Journal of Japanese Studies, 31(2), 5–9.

Spitznagel, E. (2003). Hours and Volume of Work in Germany. Paris group meeting.

Sun, M.G., & Wu, Y.H. (2004). The value of scientific and technological progress during the process of social progress and economic growth. Scientific Management Research, (5), 76–78.

Thomas, F., Oliver, R. (2005). Leaders and laggards of German productivity growth from 1970–2001: did globalization change the picture?

Wang, Q. (2001). Singapore's economic recession and its government's countermeasures. Southeast Asia, (4), 21–25.

Wang, Q.Z. (2005). Review of the social welfare security in Germany. Inner Mongolia Finance and Economics College, (2), 82–84.

Wang, X.A., & Yao, S.R. (2001). A brief discussion on the rapid development of Singapore's economy. Development of Small Cities & Towns, (10), 54–55.

Wang, W.G., & Du, X.L. (2005). New growth theory, new institutional economics and economy convergence: an empirical analysis of the economic growth of China. Statistics & Information Forum, (4), 5–9.

Wang, S.J., & Li, W. (2005). Social harmony and economic growth: logic of the rise of great powers. Forum of World Economics and Politics, (3), 8–13.

Yang, M., & Jiang, Z.H. (2006). Cause analysis and prospect of Japanese-style economic growth trajectory. Research on Economics and Management, (03): 82–85.

Yin, T.S. (2001). German economy and "German disease". International Forum, (2), 66–69.
Yu, G,A. (2003). The successful experience of Singapore's economic development and further reflections on related issues. Review of Economic Research, (70), 31–41.
Zhang, Y., & Hou, T. (2005). A comparative study of labor employment in western developed countries and its enlightenment. Contemporary Finance & Economics, (03): 22–27.
Wong, S.T., & Benson, S. (1997). Total Factor Productivity Growth in Singapore Methodology and Trends. Capital Stock Conference, 1–8.
Wu, W. (1999). Analysis on American economic growth patterns. World Economy, (12), 69–74.

Chapter 6
The Calculation of China's Economic Growth Factor

According to the synergy theory described above, this chapter establishes a new model of economic growth in China. Furthermore, this chapter also makes a calculation of China's economic growth factors from 1953 to 2012, and further forecasts some of the key indicators of China's economic transformation[1] until 2020.

6.1 The Studies on China's Economic Growth

6.1.1 Estimate of Different Scholars

The method that is proposed by Jorgenson et al. (1987), Young (2003) found that the growth of human capital in non-agricultural sectors kept on 1.1% per year in China during 1978–1998. Based on the rebuilding data, Young found that the TFP growth rate in the China's economy was 1.4% per year during this phrase.

Wang and Yao (2001) recognized the improvement of labor quality in China. However, they stated that they were skeptical about Young's (2000) data on labor income in special types. They used the data that can be represented by the average years of schooling in accordance with the methods of Barro and Lee (1997), and found that the quality of China's labor increased significantly. Wang and Yao found that even taking the improvement of the labor quality into account, the contribution of TFP to economic growth was still great. To this end, Wang and Yao put forward the idea about a selective share of labor. For example, before the reform period during 1953–1977, they assumed that the share of labor was 0.40 and found that output, physical capital, labor quality, human capital stock, and TFP respectively were at annual growth rate of 6.46, 6.11, 2.63, 5.30, and −0.57%, and the contribution of

[1]An important indicator of economic transformation is that the contribution of the innovation to economic growth is more than 50%.

J. H. Liu and Z. H. Jiang, *The Synergy Theory on Economic Growth: Comparative Study Between China and Developed Countries*,
https://doi.org/10.1007/978-981-13-1885-6_6

physical capital, labor, human capital, and TFP to output was 56.8, 16.3, 32.8, and 5.9% respectively. For the reform period (1978–1999), they assumed that the share of labor was 0.50 and found that output, physical capital, labor quality, human capital stock, and TFP respectively were at annual growth rate of 9.72, 9.39, 2.73, 2.69, and 2.32%, and the contribution of physical capital, labor, human capital, and TFP to output was 8.3, 14.0, 13.8, and 23.9% respectively. Thus, TFP growth rate was −0.57% before the reform, while in the reform period, it was 2.32%.

Li and Gao (2009) used structural equation model to look for exogenous variables that measured human capital, physical capital and technological level, and calculated the contribution of each latent variable to economic growth. By measuring the contribution of human capital, physical capital, and science and technological progress to China's economic growth, it is proved that the promotion of technological growth in economic growth is very significant in China over the past few decades, which reflects the importance of the technique level to a certain extent. They proved that Krugman's view is falsification, which said that China's economic progress and development relied on sweat rather than inspiration, and was driven by working more hard rather than working smarter. They measured that the contribution of the science and technological progress to economic growth reached at 43%. To this end, on the basis of the reform and development, and with the aim of improving the ability of independent innovation, we need to accelerate to establish a national technological innovation system which not only plays the role of the market, but also plays the role of government that mobilizes and organizes innovation resources effectively. This system also stimulate technological innovation vitality, and achieve the effective integration of the various parts of the system, and has the Chinese characteristics, giving full play to the important role of science and technology in economic growth.

According to the fact since China's reform and opening up, Chen (2008) used the standard measurement method for empirical testing and measured the contribution of factor inputs and TFP to China's economic growth. The results showed that China's economic growth was the result of combined effects of factor inputs and total factor productivity (TFP, including human capital, institutional changes, science and technology progress) in which the contribution of TFP to economic growth was 1/3. Therefore, since the reform and opening up, China's economic growth do not belong to the type of investment-driven.

Yu et al. (2007) used C-D production function to measure the quality of China's economic growth, and thus to judge the economic growth mode. The results showed that the average value of China's economic growth quality index was 0.36 during the 1981–2004. In other words, 36% of China's economic growth depend on increased productivity, while 64% depend on resource investment. According to the quantitative index, China's economic growth mode was extensive. The elasticity coefficient of physical capital investment to economic output was 0.718. That is to say if physical capital investment increased by 1%, then the economic output increased by 0.718%. Physical capital had a significant impetus to the Chinese economy, which showed that China's physical capital was relatively scarce and the capital marginal product was great. Therefore, the expansion of physical capital investment is meaningful for promoting China's economic development. The elasticity coefficient of labor input to economic output was 0.894 in China. That is, labor input increased by 1%, while the economic output increased by 0.894%. Although China has rich labor resources, the quality of workers is low. Therefore, we should improve the quality of workers in China.

Liu and Zhang (2008) decomposed the science and technological progress and industrial structure changes from TFP, empirically measured the contribution of the industrial structure change to China's economic growth, and compared the result with the contribution of science and technological progress. Empirical studies showed that in the three decades since the reform and opening up (till 2008), the contribution of the industrial structure change to China's economic growth was very significant, but with improvement in marketization degree, the contribution of the industrial structure change to economic growth showed a decreasing trend and gradually gave way to science and technological progress. That is to say, the market power represented by the industrial structure change gradually gave way to the power of science and technological progress. In addition, the study also found that the weakening of structural change effect did not mean that the benefits of market-oriented reforms would disappear, and some factors of development and institution still hindered the further improvement in resource allocation efficiency. From this point of view, improving the market mechanism is still a long way to go in China.

Lin and Liu (2003) introduced the assumption "different economies face different technological frontier at the same moment", and they also improved the existing Data Envelopment Analysis method. They used this method to decompose the per-labor GDP growth of 29 provinces in China during 1978–2000 into three factors' contribution, including technical efficiency changes, science and technological progress and per-labor physical capital accumulation. After that, on the basis of Barro regression, by controlling characters of development strategy, they tested the two hypotheses that capital accumulation and science and technological progress were influenced by development strategy summarized by Lin (2002).Test results showed that the empirical facts in China and assumptions were compatible.

6.1.2 Research on the Contribution of Institutional Innovation to China's Economic Growth

From 1978 to 2007, China's economic growth rate was more than 9.5%, the reform and opening up achieved a great success and institutional innovation played a significant role. In this regard, some scholars made a thorough study. Liu (2006) believed that China's economic system reform and institutional innovation since 1978 had made great achievements. Firstly, after years of reform, market system had been the basic mechanism of resource allocation in China instead of planning system, and price signal had been the main signal that guided resource allocation instead of quantity signal. Secondly, in all the economic system transition countries, China can be seen as the faster one, especially compared with the Russian economic transition. It was generally believed that China's marketization index or economic liberalization index was higher than that of Russia. In the international trade practice, there were about 50 countries recognizing China's market economy status (Liu and Zhang 2008). Thirdly, China's economic system reform had promoted China's economic development unprecedentedly. Whether the changes in economic growth indicators and in economic structure indicators, economic development level and social development level, or the progress of absolute indicators and the increase of relative indicators, there are significant changes.

Lin et al. (1993) analyzed the three characteristics of China's gradual reform. The first one was the incremental reforms. China's economic reform was not carried out in accordance with an ideal mode and scheduled timetable, and the new efficient resources allocation and incentive mechanisms were unlikely to work in all sectors of economy at once, but it works in those sectors, where the reforms were carried out firstly and those developed after the reform. The second one is test and promotion. Most of China's economic reforms were not carried out nationwide at the same time. On the contrary, every reform started from the trials in a smaller area. Based on the test results, related people gave summaries, and then the reform was promoted in local areas. Furthermore, the promotion of economic reform was from point to surface, continuous summary and observation, then expanded its scope of implementation. Therefore, this way also meant that the characteristic of China's reform was locality. The third one was non-radical reform. With the implementation of non-radical progressive reform, we can make full use of existing organizational resources firstly, and maintained the relatively stability and effective convergence of the institution in the process of institutional innovation.

In the *China Regional Market Relative Progress Report* published by Fan and Wang (2003) built a set of "marketization process" index system constituted of 25 indicators and sub-indicators in five areas. They pointed out that after 20 years of marketization reform, China's economy had basically transferred from the planned economy to the market economy.

The study of Li (1992) found that the contribution of productivity growth was negative in the 26 years before the reform and opening up. In the 12 years before the reform and opening up, the contribution of productivity growth to economic growth had risen from negative to 30.3% and productivity growth had become the primary factor in economic growth. The sharp contrast before and after the reform and opening up proved that the reform and opening up policy had effectively promoted the science and technological progress in China's production field. It showed that the reform and opening up promoted the economic growth, accelerated the science and technological progress, improved the reasonable use of resources, and improved the quality of economic growth. Zou and Liu (1995) estimated the aggregate economy and the production functions of the five sectors (agriculture, industry, construction, transportation, and commerce) by studying the China's economic data from 1952 to 1980. They also measured the impact of major institutional changes such as economic reforms after 1978 on economic growth, which confirmed the impact of institutional change on the economic growth. In another article, he pointed out that since China began economic reforms in 1978, GDP had grown at an average annual rate of 9.5%. He believed that this phenomenon can only be explained by the Chinese government's adoption of new institutions and policies (Zou 2000).

Zhang argued that the government transformation, political administration were closely related to economic growth. For the former, the Chinese government had accelerated the update speed of the human capital in the party and the cadre team, so that China had better realized the transformation of the government, especially the local government; for the latter, under the premise of keeping the political system unchanged, through the use of a flexible and plastic political administration mode, the situation where the market institution, the legal system and other institutions were imperfect had been made up (Zhang 2006). Both of them promoted China's economic growth in different levels.

Ma (2010) said that the long-term effects of institution on economic growth were not the same at different stages of development. Combined to China's development history since the Founding of the People's Republic of China, first of all, he measured the main institutional variables that affected the economic growth in different periods by using the Gray System Correlation Analysis. Converting to 1990 constant price by GDP deflator index, system factor sequence was the five types of factors: property rights index (CQ), openness index (DWKF), national effectiveness index (YXGJ), industrialization index (GYH), dual economic transformation index (EYDB). Select the data of 57 years from 1952 to 2008 as the macroeconomic data to calculate. On this basis, synthesize new institutional agent variables according to different periods of time by using Principal Component Analysis. Finally, based on the econometric regression method, recalculate the contribution of the institution to China's economic growth after the reform and opening up. According to the regression analysis of data from 1978 to 2008, it could be seen that since the reform and opening up, the institution played an important role in economic growth. The fitting coefficient of the institution in the regression model was 0.544. This showed that the institution was highly resilient to economic growth, only second to capital. On the contrary, the contributions of science and technology progress and labor to economic growth were far less than the institution's, which was consistent with China's actual economic growth and reflected that China should change the economic growth mode and transform the extensive economic growth to intensive economic growth. Finally, the following conclusion was drawn: property rights, openness, and dual economy transformation were important factors that affected the long-term economic growth of China.

From the calculation result of this book, the resources allocation efficiency of production factors in China have been maintained at a relatively high level after 1994. This shows that it is necessary to deepen the reform in order to further improve the China's resources allocation efficiency of production factors. Then, on how to deepen the reform, Liu etc. held that: (1) the center of reform or the key to success was to shift the focus of reform from enterprises reform, especially state-owned ones reform, to the government reform, especially the transformation of the central government's function; (2) the basic content of reform was to shift the focus on perfecting the market economic order rather than constructing a socialism market economic system; (3) the historical process of reform focused on the product marketization rather than factor marketization; (4) The value judgments standard for the reform performance was changing from a set of single and clear standard to a set of more comprehensive and overall one. At the beginning of the reform, the contradictions of social development that need to be solved were relatively explicit, and the requirements for the productivity development were relatively clear. Thus, the development, especially the economic development, and the emancipation of the productivity and the improvement of people's living standard brought correspondingly by economic development, becoming the most direct and the most convincing basic standards that evaluate reform. But after 20 years of reform and development, the socio-economic situation has been transferred from poverty to the situation where people have only adequate food and clothing, and finally to well off. At this time, the contradictions of social development are more complex, the social problems brought by the uneven development are more acute, how to understand and deal with the relationship between fairness and efficiency is more uncertain, and the divergence about the requirement of social reform between different social interest groups becomes more serious. As a result, the evaluation standard of reform that society has is increasingly integrated, and the requirements for deepening the objectives of reform are increasingly diversified. How to deepen the reform in this historical changes of evaluation standard integration and the objectives requirements diversification is a new historical proposition we are facing with (Liu 2006).

Figure 6.1 shows the trend of China's resource allocation efficiency of production factors from 1953 to 2007 that is calculated by the use of DEA model. Since the reform and opening up, China's economy has created a miracle that economic high growth lasts for nearly 40 years. The institutional innovation has played a positive role in promoting economic growth after China's reform and opening up. China's economic institutional innovation is carried out basically by four aspects. First, the changes in property right of the economic subject. The diversification reform of China's ownership makes non-state-owned components expend, township enterprises and private enterprises develop rapidly, and diversified property rights institution become an efficient institutional arrangement and the source of vitality of China's economic growth by developing the private economy and the collective economy, expending the non-state-owned economy, and "grasp the large and neglect the small" for state-owned enterprise. The second one refers to the change in resource allocation mode. Through China's marketization reform, the allocation mechanism of resources elements transforms. The progressive institutional innovation of turning the planned economy into the market economy continually playing a positive role, in the process of market distribution. Third, comprehensive adjustment of development strategy. Through comprehensive reform of foreign trade system and other appropriate institutional measures, import-oriented development mode is replaced by the export-oriented development mode. The fourth one is the reform of the distribution institution (Ye 2005).

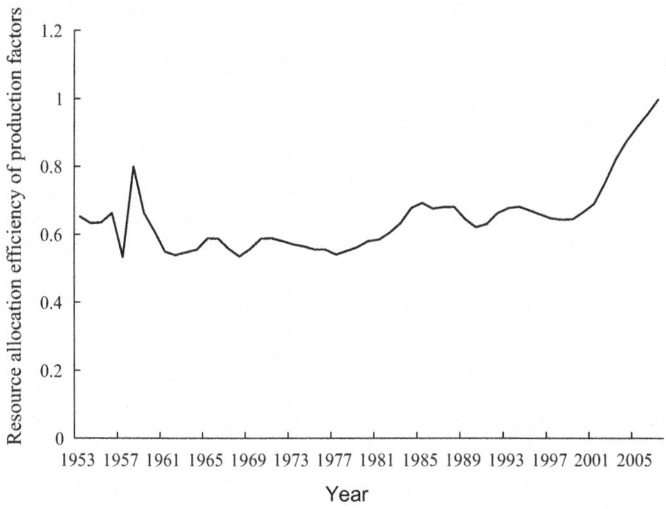

Fig. 6.1 China's resource allocation efficiency of production factor in 1953–2007 (based on analysis results of DEA)

6.2 China's Economic Growth Model and the Analysis of Factors Affecting Economic Growth from 1953 to 1976

6.2.1 China's Economic Growth Model

(1) The economic growth accounting model of China during 1953–1976

At first, establishing the compensation of employees function model, by taking log HL and log SD/L as the independent variables, log V as the dependent variable, we perform a multiple regression analysis of China's data from 1953 to 1976. Among the above model, log HL is the logarithm of labor L (number of employment hours of work) multiplied by the human capital H(the average years of schooling of laborers multiplied by the number of workers), log SD/L is the logarithm of investment in physical capital D multiplied by the inputs of science and technology S and then divided by the labor force L, and log V is the logarithm of the compensation of laborers V. Finally obtain Table 6.1.

Then, establishing $Y - V$ function model. The dependent variable is the output Y minus the compensation of labors V, with the physical capital stock K, innovation ability SD/K, and technical input S as the independent variables. Then through a multiple regression analysis of the China's data from 1953 to 1976, we obtain Table 6.2.

Table 6.1 Compensation of employees model and the test during 1953–1976

Dependent variable: log V				
Variable	Coefficient	Std. Error	T-Statistic	Prob.
C	2.730231	0.169864	16.07307	0.0000
log HL	0.757707	0.133338	5.682596	0.0000
log SD/L	−0.233484	0.120964	−1.930186	0.0704
AR(1)	0.767804	0.225318	3.407653	0.0034
AR(2)	−0.431496	0.209817	−2.056530	0.0554
R-squared	0.915817	Mean dependent var		2.893723
Adjusted R-squared	0.896009	S.D. dependent var		0.139747
S.E. of regression	0.045065	Akaike info criterion		−3.164699
Sum squared resid	0.034525	Schwarz criterion		−2.916735
Log likelihood	39.81169	F-statistic		46.23497
Durbin-Watson stat	1.844689	Prob(F-statistic)		0.000000

Table 6.2 $Y - V$ Model and test of the 1953–1976 periods

Dependent Variable: $Y - V$				
Variable	Coefficient	Std. Error	T-Statistic	Prob.
C	152.1957	42.64249	3.569109	0.0028
K	0.3261324	10.35525	3.149440	0.0066
SD/K	0.866791	0.162929	5.320061	0.0001
S	−13.50080	3.511089	−3.845188	0.0016
R-squared	0.983734	Mean dependent var		723.8269
Adjusted R-squared	0.980480	S.D. dependent var		338.5944
S.E. of regression	47.30601	Akaike info criterion		10.73582
Sum squared resid	33567.87	Schwarz criterion		10.93464
Log likelihood	−97.99025	F-statistic		302.3818
Durbin-Watson stat	1.378476	Prob(F-statistic)		0.000000

According to Tables 6.1 and 6.2, we obtain the economic growth accounting model of China during 1953–1976:

$$\begin{aligned} Y = {} & 537.3163(HL)^{0.757707} * (SD/L)^{-0.233484} \\ & + 0.3261324K + 0.866791SD/K - 13.5S + 152.2 \end{aligned} \tag{6.1}$$

6.2.2 *Analysis of China's Economic Growth Factors*

China's economic growth accounting results of this book is shown as follows. During 1953–1976, the contribution of human capital and labor growth to economic growth has reached 42 and 23%. It was understandable that, because of the relative lack of physical capital before 1976, it relies mainly on labor force and human capital for economic development. China has succeeded in rapidly improving the quality of its population and making human capital the first driver of economic growth. The contribution of physical capital stock growth was 28%, the contribution of investment in physical capital was 20%. While the contribution of science and technology progress was −8% (mainly because the technology investment focuses on the military industry, such as research and development of "two bombs and one satellite", science and technology investment growth affects the growth of investment in physical capital, etc., thus affecting the economic growth), the contribution of institutional innovation was −17% (mainly due to the impact of the Great Leap Forward after 1985, etc.), and the impact rate of the economic environment externalities was 12% (China was faced a very poor internal and external economic environment).

6.3 China's Economic Growth Model and Accounting from 1977 to 2012

As for the data sources, investment in physical capital, the number of employed people, science and technology investment use the data from *China Statistical Yearbook*, while the physical capital stock and average years of schooling of laborers use the data from the article *Capital Deepening, Human Capital Accumulation and China's Economic Sustained Growth* written by Tang.

6.3.1 Construction of China's Economic Growth Model

This book firstly established the logarithmic model of compensation of laborers in China in 1977–2012, which is the log V model, and the test results are shown in Table 6.3. Then the M model is established ($M = Y - V$, in value), and the test results are shown in Table 6.4. Thus, the empirical model of China's economic growth factor analysis in 1977–2012 is:

$$Y = 0.001243(HL)^{0.803}(SD/L)^{0.228} + 0.19K + 1334HSD/K^2 - 16.95 \tag{6.2}$$

In the model (6.2), according to the Granger test, the data of S(science and technology input) adapt the data value of two years advanced. For example, the gross domestic product (Y) in 2003 corresponds to science and technology input in 2001. It is assumed that, it takes an average of 2 years for science and technology to have an effect on economic growth started from input. The data of physical capital

Table 6.3 Labor compensation logarithmic model (log *V*) and test in China from 1977 to 2012

Dependent Variable: log *V*				
Method: Least Squares				
Sample(adjusted): 1981–2012				
Included observations: 32 after adjusting endpoints				
Convergence achieved after 9 iterations				
Variable	Coefficient	Std. Error	T-Statistic	Prob.
C	−2.90546	0.447708	−6.48963	0
log *HL*	0.803157	0.068434	11.73617	0
log SD/L	0.22755	0.017545	12.96943	0
AR(3)	−0.36579	0.231261	−1.58173	0.1254
AR(4)	0.890066	0.235719	3.775962	0.0008
R-squared	0.996792	Mean dependent var	2.228862	
Adjusted R-squared	0.996317	S.D. dependent var	0.373678	
S.E. of regression	0.022678	Akaike info criterion	−4.59227	
Sum squared resid	0.013885	Schwarz criterion	−4.36325	
Log likelihood	78.47635	F-statistic	2097.511	
Durbin-Watson stat	1.106366	Prob(F-statistic)	0	
Inverted AR Roots	.55 − .16i	.55 + .16i	−1.11	
	Estimated AR process is nonstationary			

stock (*K*) adapt the data value of the beginning of the year. For example, physical capital stock in 2000 adapt the data value of the beginning of 2000.

As it is shown in Tables 6.3 and 6.4, in the two regression models, all the independent variables are highly linear correlation with the dependent variable on the whole. The modified sample decision coefficient (R^2) is very high, which indicates strong explanatory power of the independent variables and high fitting of regression equation; the regression equation that passed F-test shows that the linear regression effect is significant. Similarly, independent variables and constant term passed the T-test as well.

6.3.2 China's Economic Growth Factors

China's economic growth calculation in this book in 1977–2012 is shown in Table 6.5. Since 40 years of reform and opening up, the faster pace of physical capital formation, transformed the surplus labor into practical productivity, and effectively promoted the economic growth. From 1977 to 1992, the contribution of physical capital stock growth was 39%, the contribution of the increase of investment in physical capital growth was 14%, the contribution of human capital

Table 6.4 *M* model and test from 1977 to 2012

Dependent Variable: *M*				
Method: Least Squares				
Sample(adjusted): 1980–2012				
Included observations: 31 after adjusting endpoints				
Convergence achieved after 9 iterations				
Variable	Coefficient	Std. Error	T-Statistic	Prob.
C	−16.9506	10.47311	−1.61849	0.116
K	0.189535	0.018582	10.20018	0
HSD/K^2	1334.287	225.6204	5.913861	0
AR(2)	0.457366	0.323686	1.412994	0.1679
R-squared	0.996045	Mean dependent var		248.367
Adjusted R-squared	0.995649	S.D. dependent var		227.3159
S.E. of regression	14.994	Akaike info criterion		8.363308
Sum squared resid	6744.602	Schwarz criterion		8.54288
Log likelihood	−138.176	F-statistic		2518.234
Durbin-Watson stat	1.126434	Prob(F-statistic)		0
Inverted AR Roots	0.68	−0.68		

Table 6.5 China's economic growth accounting results obtained in this book and the forecast for 2020 (%)

Year	1953–1976	1977–2000	2001–2012	2013–2020
Contribution of the increase of physical capital stock	28	39	57	32
Contribution of the increase of investment in physical capital	20	14	21	20
Contribution of science and technology progress	−8	9	29	27
Contribution of the increase of human capital	42	17	7	20
Contribution of the increase of labor force	23	5	1	2
Contribution of institutional innovation	−17	31	5	5
Impact rate of the externality of economic environment	12	−15	−20	−6

was 17%, the contribution of labor force growth to economic growth reached 5%, the contribution of science and technology progress was 9%, the contribution of institutional innovation was 31%, and the impact rate of economic environment externalities was −15%. While from 2001 to 2012, the contribution of physical capital stock growth was 57%, the contribution of investment in physical capital growth was 21%, the contribution of human capital was 7%, the contribution of labor force growth to economic growth was 1%, the contribution of technical change reached 29%, the contribution of institutional innovation was 5%, the impact rate of economic environment externalities was −20%.

6.3.3 Discussion About Calculation Results

As it is shown in Table 6.5, various factors play different roles in the China's economic growth.

(1) Institutional innovation promotes strongly the economic growth. Since the reforms and opening up, the China's economy has created a miracle of 40 years of rapid growth. The contribution of institutional innovation to China's economic growth is 8% on average, which confirms that institutional innovation has played a positive role in promoting China's economic growth after reform and opening up.
(2) The growth of investment in physical capital and capital stock are the decisive factors of economic growth. Capital formation is an important factor in ensuring economic viability for any economy. China's rapid development over the past 40 years is closely related to the rapid formation of capital. The main manifestation includes the contribution of investment in physical capital growth and capital stock growth reached 53% in 1977–2000 and 78% in 2001–2012.
(3) Science and technology progress play an increasingly important role. In 2001–2012, the contribution of the science and technology progress to economic growth reached 29%. Science and technology progress mainly came from international technology transfer and "learning by doing" in the process of the reform and opening up policy. China introduced the foreign advanced technology directly by the purchase of technology and the introduction of advanced equipment. Meanwhile, through the channel of direct foreign investment and other channels as well, China has also indirectly introduced foreign advanced technology and combined it with independent innovations.
(4) Human capital and labor growth play a very important role in economic growth. Massive rural-urban migration transformed surplus labor into real productivity, boosting the economic growth strongly. The model of "urbanization + institutional reform + emerging-industry orientation" developed by labor resources in China and its comparative advantage translated the population burden successfully into the demographic dividend, and promoted economic growth strongly. The sum of the contribution of human capital and labor

force to economic growth was 22% in 1977–2000, while it decreased to 8% in 2001–2012.

(5) Economic environment externalities is beneficial to economic growth as a whole. The impact rate of economic environmental externalities shows the influence of internal and external economic environment for economic growth. If the value of contribution is negative, it indicates that the economic environment promotes economic growth. The impact rate of economic environmental externalities has been −15% in 1977–2000, while it was −20% in 2001–2012. For the past 40 years, the economic environment has been beneficial to economic growth as a whole.

6.4 The Selection of Time-Series Data for R&D Expenditure

6.4.1 Considerations on Data Selection

In the establishment of economic growth accounting model, this book argues that the following principles can be used to select time-series data for research and R&D expenditure.

(1) In the process of establishing the economic growth accounting model, both the previous (the previous period or previous periods) and current period time-series data of R&D expenditure can be selected for modeling. Selecting the previous data or the current data mainly depends on the actual issue at hand. If the previous data can be better tested by econometrics, and more in line with economic reality, then select the previous data; otherwise, select the current data.

(2) If we select the previous data, the initial period needs to be determined scientifically. In addition, the R&D expenditure has two implications: on the one hand, R&D expenditure represents the thrust of science and technology for the economy; on the other hand, R&D expenditure (as a kind of market consumption or demand) represents the pulling force of science and technology on the economy.

(3) From the perspective of econometrics view, if it had been proved by the Granger test that current R&D expenditure was the cause of the current economic aggregate (in other words, the probability that current R&D expenditure is not the cause of the current economic aggregate is less than 10%), then the current R&D expenditure data can be used in the economic growth accounting model; if the R&D expenditure of two periods advanced is the cause of the current economic aggregate, the R&D expenditure data of two periods advanced can be used in the economic growth accounting model.

6.4.2 *The Autocorrelation of Time-Series Data for R&D Expenditure*

The current year R&D expenditure $S(t)$ is often directly related to the R&D expenditure of the last year $S(t-1)$ or the past few years, which is the function of the previous R&D expenditure. For example, both of the United States and China have shown this kind of functional relationship, see Tables 6.6, 6.7 and 6.8.

Table 6.6 Chinese R&D expenditure data

Period (year)	Current year	Last year	The year before last	Three years ago
1980	0.99216	1.06395	0.9888	0.76713
1990	1.48384	1.42952	1.3732	1.5422
1991	1.62032	1.48384	1.42952	1.3732
1992	1.6191	1.62032	1.48384	1.42952
1993	1.845774	1.6191	1.62032	1.48384
1994	2.08757	1.845774	1.6191	1.62032
1995	1.984385	2.08757	1.845774	1.6191
1996	2.182823	1.984385	2.08757	1.845774
1997	2.703936	2.182823	1.984385	2.08757
1998	3.000574	2.703936	2.182823	1.984385
1999	3.828218	3.000574	2.703936	2.182823
2000	4.999744	3.828218	3.000574	2.703936
2001	5.902048	4.999744	3.828218	3.000574
2002	7.266179	5.902048	4.999744	3.828218

Table 6.7 Relationship between R&D expenditure of current year and previous period, China

Dependent Variable: R&D expenditure in current year				
Sample range (adjusted): 1982–2002				
Variable	Coefficient	Std. Error	T-Statistic	Prob.
C	−0.787568	0.403104	−1.953758	0.0684
R&D expenditure of the year before last	0.651481	0.193132	3.373248	0.0039
R&D expenditure of three years ago	1.126455	0.222089	5.072085	0.0001
AR(1)	1.299617	0.236966	5.484406	0.0000
AR(2)	−0.632889	0.229278	−2.760360	0.0139
R-squared	0.983957	Mean dependent var		2.488358
Adjusted R-squared	0.979947	S.D. dependent var		1.657460
S.E. of regression	0.234712	Akaike info criterion		0.143343
Sum squared resid	0.881437	Schwarz criterion		0.392039
Log likelihood	3.494899	F-statistic		245.3361
Durbin-Watson stat	1.737398	Prob(F-statistic)		0.000000

Table 6.8 Relationship between R&D expenditure of current year and previous period, U.S

Dependent Variable: R&D expenditure in current year				
Sample range: 1958–2002				
Variable	Coefficient	Std. Error	T-Statistic	Prob.
C	87.56738	1260.010	0.069497	0.9449
R&D expenditure of last year	1.678990	0.117811	14.25153	0.0000
R&D expenditure of the year before last	−0.666015	0.123553	−5.390534	0.0000
R-squared	0.996967	Mean dependent var		133736.2
Adjusted R-squared	0.996822	S.D. dependent var		59197.94
S.E. of regression	3337.051	Akaike info criterion		19.12790
Sum squared resid	4.68E + 08	Schwarz criterion		19.24835
Log likelihood	−427.3778	F-statistic		6902.253
Durbin-Watson stat	1.658523	Prob(F-statistic)		0.000000

$$S(t) = F(S(t-1), S(t-2), \ldots, S(t-n)) \tag{6.3}$$

6.5 The Test of Economic Growth Model

To establish a good economic growth econometric model requires the following five tests.

(1) Theoretical test. The established econometric model of economic growth should conform to certain theories. For example, the theoretical basis of model (5.1) is the synergy theory of economic growth.
(2) Routine test of econometric. The routine test of Econometrics includes the T-Statistic, the sample determination coefficient R^2, the DW statistic, and the F-test statistic. Tables 5.1 and 5.2 are econometric test results of the model of America's economic growth model (log V model and M model). T-Statistic and other statistics in these test results have passed the test.
(3) Test of constant term. For example, the constant term of model M in the model of South Korea's economic growth is 1810, and the minimum value of the dependent variable of this model (GDP minuses the compensation of employees) is 22,223. Therefore, the ratio of the constant term of the M model to the minimum value of the dependent variable of the model is 0.08, and the constant term is reasonable.
(4) Kalman filter test. Kalman filter method is used to estimate the evolutionary trend of the parameters in the model of the varying parameter. Using this method, it can be verified that whether the parameters estimated by econometric method are basically consistent and stable.

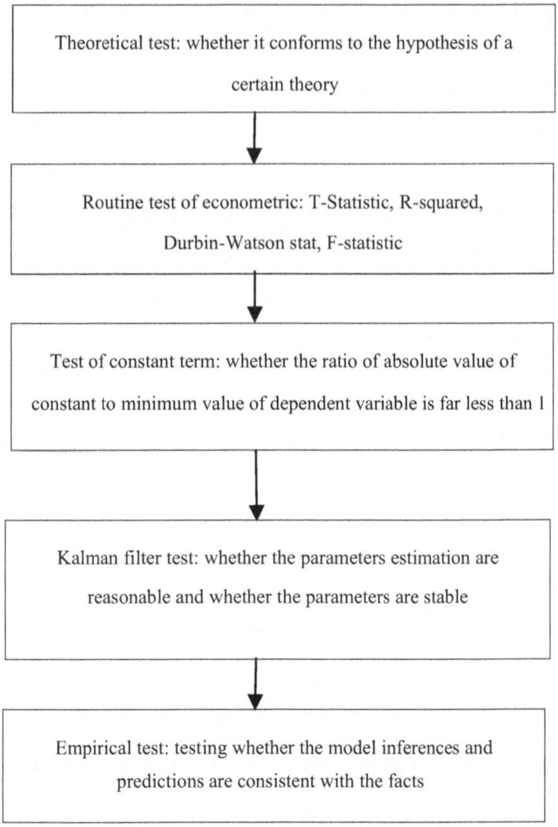

Fig. 6.2 5 tests of econometric models of economic

(5) Empirical test. It is to test whether the inferences and predictions of the model are consistent with the facts. If it is seriously inconsistent with the facts, the model needs to rebuild (Fig. 6.2).

6.6 Summary

The model established in this chapter has not only passed the econometric test, but also consistent with the fact of China's economic growth. For example, this chapter has estimated the marginal revenue rate of physical capital was 33% in 1953–1976, and 21.5% in 1977–2012, which are in line with the fact.

(1) The transformation of China's economy

During 1953–1976, China's economic growth mode was the type of relying on the labor and accumulating physical capital. The contribution of human capital and labor force to the economic growth rate reached 42 and 23%. The total of these two is 65%. The growth of labor became the first driven force. The contribution of physical capital stock was 28%, the contribution of investment in physical capital was 20%, while the contribution of science and technology progress and institutional innovation were negative (Liu and Jiang 2015).

During 1977–2000, the contribution of physical capital stock was 39%, the contribution of investment in physical capital was 14%. The total of these two is 53%. The growth of capital become the first driven force. The contribution of human capital was 17%, the contribution of labor force was 5%, the contribution of science and technology progress was 9%, the contribution of institutional innovation was 31%, while the impact rate of economic environmental externality is −15%.

During 2001–2012, the contribution of physical capital and investment in physical capital was 78%, which was a type of investment driven.

(2) The new transformation of China's economy

Based on relevant research from domestic and foreign scholars, this chapter predicts China's economic growth rate is 6–7% from 2013 to 2020 by using the method of general equilibrium analysis. The contribution of science and technology progress and human capital are 27 and 20% respectively, the contribution of institutional innovation is 5%. The total of these three is 52%. The contribution of physical capital stock and investment in physical capital are 32 and 20% respectively. The total of these two is also 52%. Therefore, China's economy will begin to turn to innovation-investment dual driven growth model.

From the perspective of synergy theory, this chapter studies the theoretical basis and modeling method of the calculation of China's economic growth factors and the calculation method of contribution of each factor in economic growth, and obtains the relative practical results. From the view of calculation results and the logical structure of the whole theory, the synergy theory of economic growth absorbs the rational thoughts and methods of New Growth Theory and New Institutional Economics. It has a solid theoretical basis and has been tested empirically, can be applied to the calculation of economic growth factors in other countries or regions as well as industries and enterprises.

References

Barro, R.J., & Lee, J.W. (1997). International measures of schooling years and schooling quality. American Economic Review, Papers and Proceedings, 86(2), 218–223.

Chen, L. (2008). Analysis and estimation of factors contributing to China's economic growth since the reform. Economic Survey, (3), 24–27.

Fan, G., & Wang, X.L. (2003). Marketization index for China's provinces. Economic Studies, (3), 9–18.

Jorgenson, D.W., Gollop, F.M., & Fraumeni, B.M. (1987). Productivity and US economic growth. Boston: Harvard University Press.

Li, J.W. (1992). Productivity and China's economic growth (1953–1990). The Journal of Quantitative & Technical Economics, (1), 66–70.

Lin, Y.F. (2002). Development strategies, viability and economic convergence. China Economic Quarterly, (1), 269–300.

Li, P., & Gao, N. (2009). An analysis of the mystery of China's economic growth: technological progress and its contribution—Estimation based on structural equation. Tianfu New Idea, (4), 54–57.

Lin, Y.F., & Liu, P.L. (2003). The impact of economic development strategy on labor capital accumulation and technological progress: an empirical study based on China's experience. Social Sciences in China, (4), 18–32.

Lin, Y.F., Cai, F., & Li, Z. (1993). On the gradual way of China's economic reform. Economic Research Journal, (9), 3–11.

Liu, W. (2006). The turn of economic development and reform. Economic Research Journal, (1), 4–10.

Liu, J.H, & Jiang, Z.H. (2015). Innovation-driven and investment supportive strategies for China's economic transformation based on collaborative theory. Science of Science and Management of S.&.T., (2), 25–33.

Liu, W., & Zhang, H. (2008). Structural change and technical advance in China's economic growth. Economic Research Journal, (11), 4–15.

Ma, L.J. (2010). Recalculation of long-term economic growth affecting institution—Based on China's empirical study. Contemporary Economics, (13), 140–143.

Wang, Y., & Yao, Y. (2001). Sources of China's economic growth, 1952–1999: incorporating human capital accumulation. China Economic Review, 14(1), 32–52.

Ye, F.W. (2005). A study on the long path of China's economy. Investment Research, (5), 21–26.

Young, A. (2000). Gold into base metals: productivity growth in the People's republic of China during the reform period. NBER working papers 7856.

Young, A. (2003). Gold into base metals: productivity growth in the People's republic of China during the reform period. Journal of Political Economy, 111(6), 1220–1261.

Yu, A.J., Han, S.Z., & Zhang, S.C. (2007). Using C-D function to measure the quality and mode of China's economic growth. Statistics and Decision, (24), 48–49.

Zhang, J. (2006). The government transformation, political administration and economic growth: China's experience. Journal of Yunnan University (Social Sciences Edition), (4), 325–325.

Zou, Z.Z. (2000). China's economic reform and policies at the beginning of the 21st century. Foreign Investment in China, (11), 12–14.

Zou, Z.Z, & Liu, M.Q. (1995). Capital formation and economic growth in China. The Journal of Quantitative & Technical Economics, (3), 35–43.

Chapter 7
Urbanization and Structural Changes in China's Economic Growth

7.1 The Role of Urbanization in Economic Growth

How many percentage points of economic growth increased while the urbanization rate increased by one percentage point? This is an important issue that urgent need to be answered theoretically while the economy maintains a medium-high-speed growth under the new normal in China. Based on the synergy theory of economic growth, from the intermediary theory of that urbanization's pulling function on direct factors (supply-side elements) of China's economic growth and the agglomeration theory of new economic geography, this book analyzes the influence of urbanization on employment, human capital, investment in physical capital, science and technological progress and other factors, and then sets up the corresponding model. What is more, this book builds a model group based on the new economic growth model and calculates the pulling function of urbanization on innovation-driven and economic growth. Calculation results show that an average increase of one percent point in the urbanization ratio of permanent residents during 1991–2012 has resulted in an average 2.2-percent-point increase in the GDP growth. From 2016 to 2020, urbanization ratio of permanent residents will increases averagely one percent point, there are 2.2 percentage points increased in the GDP growth. The pulling function of urbanization on the GDP growth remains at a high level of 34%. Therefore, continuing to promote urbanization is one of the most important strategies in stabilizing the GDP growth.

7.1.1 Urbanization Has Become the Driving Force of Economic Growth

In 2015, The Central Cities Work Conference pointed out that cities are the most concentrated areas for various kinds of resources, economic and social activities in

J. H. Liu and Z. H. Jiang, *The Synergy Theory on Economic Growth: Comparative Study Between China and Developed Countries*,
https://doi.org/10.1007/978-981-13-1885-6_7

China, and for comprehensive constructing a well-off society and speeding up the realization of modernization, China must promote the new-type urbanization centering on person and reach the greatest potential of enlarging domestic demand. According to the historical experience of economic and social development in various countries, the urbanization ratio between 30 and 70% belongs to the acceleration phrase. The advancement of new-type industrialization, informatization, urbanization, agricultural modernization, greenization and so on (Liu 2016), will achieve a leaping development in China's total economic output, per capita GDP, and income of urban and rural residents.

At present, there is much progress made in the research on urbanization and economic growth at home and abroad. The new economic geography represented by Krugman argued that the agglomeration effect of urbanization could promote economic growth (Krugman 1991). Vernon Henderson (Henderson 2003) argued that urbanization plays an important role in promoting industrial and economic development in Japan and France, that is why cities have become the fundamental factor in the process of industrialization. Jonathan Eatona and Zvi Eckstein (1997) studied the important role of urbanization in economic growth. Increasing urbanization rate has a significant impact on economic growth, meanwhile, urbanization is affected and limited by national policies and institutions. Berry (1981) analyzed the principal components among 43 variables in 95 countries to explain the relationship between urbanization level and economy, technology, population, education and other factors, finally confirmed that there is a positive correlation between urbanization and economic growth.

Chinese scholars believe that urbanization primarily through enhancing consumption and investment demand, and influencing relevant determinants to promote economic growth. Labor clustered formed by urbanization saves economic cost, increases the utilization of shared facilities, reduces transaction cost, and promotes economic growth through cluster and diffusing effects. Ren (2014) assumed that China's economic growth has the characteristic of Cobb-Douglas production function, and also considered the impact of urbanization on economic growth, they drew the conclusion that the urbanization level increase one percent point while the per capita output will increase 7.6%. Xiang's (2013) research showed that there is a stable long-term co-integration relationship between urbanization and economic growth, and that one percentage point increase of urbanization rate led to an average increase of 2.33 percentage points in the economic growth rate. Li (2013) held that the two major driving forces for promoting China's economic growth in the future are urbanization and innovation. Urbanization promotes economic growth primarily by improving the resource allocation efficiency of production factors, raising savings rates and investment rates, improving household consumption levels and structure, increasing human capital, and other ways. In the next 20 years, an average annual increase of 0.2 percentage points in the urbanization level will promote an average annual growth rate of GDP by 0.13 percentage points.

The above research and other previous studies have yielded many important results. However, most of these research directly introduced the urbanization level variables into the production function to establish the economic growth measurement model. From the perspective of analysis of economic growth factor, the direct factor (first level factor) that determines economic growth is physical capital, labor, science and technology progress, and human capital. Therefore, the urbanization variables (second levels factor) cannot directly enter the production function like the variables of capital, employment and other variables. Additionally, the existing research fails to analyze the impact of urbanization on these direct factors. In this regard, this book first analyzes the pulling function of urbanization on employment, investment in physical capital, science and technology progress, and other factors, and then combines with economic growth model, furthermore, calculates the role of urbanization in the process of economic growth.[1]

7.1.2 Analysis of the Pulling Function of Urbanization on the Direct Factors (Supply-Side Factors) of China's Economic Growth: Intermediary Theory

7.1.2.1 Intermediary Theory

There are mainly three methods for studying economic growth: the "Troika" method, the "three industries" method and the "multiple direct factors" (employment, human capital, investment in physical capital, physical capital stock, science and technology progress, and institutional innovation) method. From the perspective of studying the pulling function of urbanization on economic growth, the research method of "troika" is too simple, and the "three industries" research method is attributed to the four direct factors of employment, human capital, investment in physical capital, and science and technological progress ultimately. Therefore, we must study the relationship between urbanization and the direct factors of economic growth firstly if we study the role of urbanization in stimulating China's economic growth. Most scholars also studied from the perspective of the relationship between urbanization and the direct factors of economic growth. For example, Shen and Jiang (2007) used provincial panel data to point out that urbanization promotes economic growth by accelerating the accumulation of physical capital and human capital. Wu and Liu (2008) took 16 cities in the Yangtze River Delta as the research sample and found that urbanization promoted the regional economic growth through two mechanisms: increasing R&D efficiency and investment in physical capital. Cheng (2009) pointed out the advantages of urbanization in the fields of specialization and diversity, accumulation of human capital, formation of an information exchange network, improvement of transaction efficiency and infrastructure, so that it is beneficial to the emergence and spread of technology innovation. Then, we can say urbanization promotes economic growth through innovation.

[1]Part of this section is collaborated with other university.

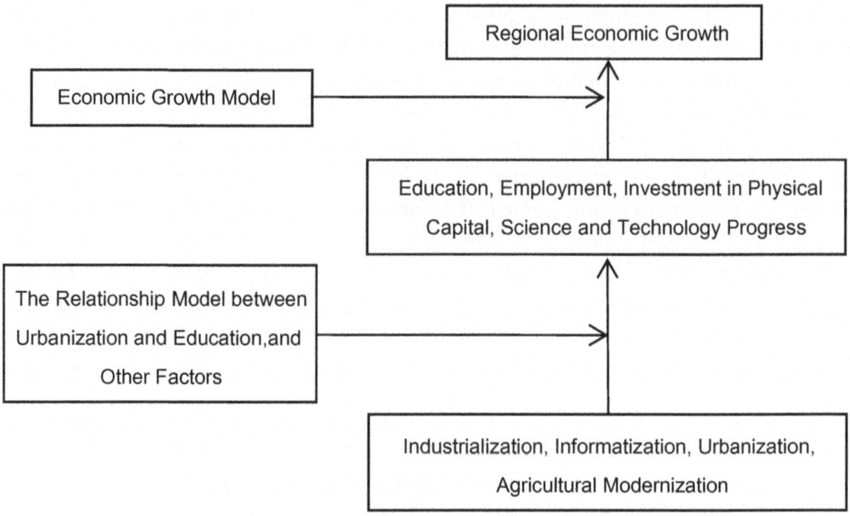

Fig. 7.1 The relationship between urbanization and direct factors of economic growth

According to intermediary theory of Cheng, urbanization can promote economic growth through those intermediary factors, such as science and technology progress, investment in physical capital and promotion of human capital. From the perspective of the mechanism of urbanization on economic growth, labor, investment in physical capital, science and technology progress, and human capital are the direct factors determining economic growth. Therefore, the pulling function of urbanization on economic growth mainly reflects in such aspects as increasing employment, raising the average years of schooling of laborers, increasing the scale of investment in physical capital, and promoting science and technological progress.

As shown in Fig. 7.1, this book firstly analyzes the intermediary role of education, employment, investment in physical capital, and science and technology progress. Furthermore, this book establishes the relationship model between urbanization, industrialization, informatization, agricultural modernization and the average years of schooling of laborers, employment, investment in physical capital, science and technology progress, and then combines with economic growth model to analyze the pulling function of urbanization on GDP growth.

7.1.2.2 The Promotion of Urbanization in Increasing Human Capital

According to the agglomeration theory, urbanization refers to the process of gathering population and economic elements from rural areas to urban areas in the process of economic development. At the same time, urban production and life style, urban culture and urban values radiate to the surrounding areas. The concentration of crowds has also brought about the development of market activities, commercial management and service industries, which have increased employment opportunities. What mentioned above makes a simultaneous progress in industrialization, marketization, urbanization and modernization (Liu and Cai 2005).

According to the study by Ma (2009), the impact of urbanization on human capital is mainly manifested in that cities generally have better environmental conditions (such as cultural, medical and health care), and especially because of the better general education conditions in urban areas, the level of general public education in urban areas is usually obviously higher than that in rural areas. Urbanization is also conducive to provide the convenience and opportunity of obtaining vocational and technical training for laborers. According to the study by Cheng (2007), metropolis is a place where talents can get together. Under the spillover effect of human capital, the rate of human capital accumulation is much faster in city than in rural areas. The presence of a large number of manufacturers in big cities enables the urban labor market to compete sufficiently, and sufficient competition is more conducive to ensure that the level of people's skills is obviously positively correlated with the level of wages. In this way, people are willing to invest in human capital to improve their skills and obtain higher wages. In addition, urban environment of dynamic and economic diversification offers a broader market for everyone's talent which contributes to people's further professional development, and it is good for people to improve their own skills, and then promotes the formation and accumulation of human capital (Xu and Yuan 2013). Bertinelli and Black (2004) studied the urban agglomeration, and pointed out that cities continue to grow and expand with the spillover of knowledge and information until formed the final urban agglomeration. The spillover of knowledge and information can generate the agglomeration of labor and human capital, which can promote economic growth. Those studies showed that permanent residents urbanization, informatization and industrialization are important factors that determine the average years of schooling of laborers.

Based on the average years of schooling of Chinese laborers (h), urbanization rate for permanent residents (URB), informatization index (INF) and industrialization (IND) data in 2001–2013, we build the model (7.1) of the effect of urbanization on increasing the average years of schooling of laborers (human capital) through regression analysis, and the results of econometric test are shown in Table 7.1.

$$h = 5.03URB * (1 + INF) * IND + 7.34 \tag{7.1}$$

7.1.2.3 The Effect of Urbanization on Increasing Employment

The transfer of population from rural areas to urban areas will inevitably increase the number of labor force in secondary and tertiary industries and make a part of the original labor force in rural areas obtain employment in urban areas, thus increasing

Table 7.1 The econometric tests of the effect of urbanization on increasing the average years of schooling of laborers

Method: least Squares				
Sample (adjusted): 1994–2012				
Included observations: 19 after adjusting endpoints				
Convergence achieved after 7 iterations				
Variable	Coefficient	Std. error	t-Statistic	Prob.
C	7.341337	0.067994	107.9702	0
$URB * (1 + INF) * IND$	5.025309	0.307323	16.3519	0
AR(1)	1.138115	0.142987	7.95959	0
AR(3)	−0.51046	0.137608	−3.7095	0.0023
R-squared	0.993824	Mean dependent var	8.436726	
Adjusted R-squared	0.992501	S.D. dependent var	0.484872	
S.E. of regression	0.041989	Akaike info criterion	−3.30969	
Sum squared resid	0.024683	Schwarz criterion	−3.11183	
Log likelihood	33.78718	F-statistic	750.9653	
Durbin-Watson stat	2.793534	Prob(F-statistic)	0	
Inverted AR Roots	0.84–0.46i			

the overall number of labor force (Ma and Peng 2012). Hu et al. (2012) pointed out that after 2010, China has entered a decline period of demographic dividend, and the working-age population (aged 16–64) in the total population decreased from 74.5 to 73.4% in 2014. At the same time, the proportion of the population with a college education or above in the total population increased from 8.75 to 11.01%. Among them, a considerable workforce has obtained job opportunities through the urbanization route from rural areas to urban areas. Data show that the number of floating migrants in China exceeded 100 million in 2000 and reached 147 million in 2005, of which 84.4% were migrated from rural areas to cities and towns. The main reason for the migration was carrying on business. In 2010, migrant population in China further increased to 220 million, accounting for 16.53% of the total population. According to the statistics of the migrant population division from the National Health and Family Planning Commission, migrant population reached 253 million at the end of 2014. The migrant population in China, including those planning to settle down in urban areas, will gradually increase to 291 million with an average annual increase of 6 million by 2020. Among them, the agricultural transfer population is about 220 million and the migrant population between cities is about 70 million. The number of migrant population with a college degree or above has continuously increased from 7.6% in 2010 to 12.1% in 2014. Since the reform and opening up, China has gradually relaxed its restrictions on the transfer of rural surplus workforce to urban employment, which has led to the process of migration of urbanization being the process of obtaining employment opportunities for the rural surplus workforce, and provided policy protection for turning the structure of the population age advantage into an economic growth advantage,

Table 7.2 The econometric test of the pulling function of urbanization on employment

Dependent variable: *L*				
Method: least squares				
Sample: 1992–2012				
Included observations: 21				
Variable	Coefficient	Std. error	t-Statistic	Prob.
L	110.7311	12.15579	9.109325	0
AGR	−32.82671	7.533408	−4.35748	0.0004
P	54.09543	0.217145	249.121	0
R-squared	0.998269	Mean dependent var	721.3013	
Adjusted R-squared	0.998076	S.D. dependent var	35.32693	
S.E. of regression	1.549503	Akaike info criterion	3.845309	
Sum squared resid	43.21725	Schwarz criterion	3.994526	
Log likelihood	−37.37574	Durbin-Watson stat	1.056993	

which makes migrant population and migration of urbanization an important way for China's economic growth to obtain more demographic dividend. Those studies show that urbanization of permanent residents, agricultural labor production, resident population are important determinants of the quantity of employment.

Using the data of employment from 2001 to 2003 in China (*L*), urbanization rate of resident population (*URB*), agricultural labor productivity (*AGR*) and resident population (*P*), we build the following model (7.2), and the results of econometric test are shown in Table 7.2.

$$L = 110.7 * URB - 32.8 * AGR + 54.1 * P \tag{7.2}$$

7.1.2.4 The Effect of Urbanization on Increasing Investment in Physical Capital

According to Ma's study, urbanization has a significant effect on raising people's income, and urbanization can generate income-increasing effects to promote investment growth. With the marginal propensity to consume keeps unchanged, incomes will increase and domestic savings will inevitably increase accordingly. Urbanization not only generate an investment need in urban infrastructure and housing, but also stimulate the development of related industries. Therefore, from the perspective of investment demand, the process of population urbanization will encourage countries and investors to increase investment, thus to stimulate economic growth. From a supply-side perspective, these studies show that urbanization of permanent population, the value of foreign loans, per capita living space and some other factors are important factors to determine investment value of physical capital.

Urbanization, on the basis of investment in physical capital (such as infrastructure, real estate and industrial equipment), brings the agglomeration of

Table 7.3 The econometric test of the pulling function of urbanization on increasing investment in physical capital

Dependent variable: log D				
Method: least squares				
Date: 05/15/16 Time: 13:10				
Sample(adjusted): 1994–2012				
Included observations: 19 after adjusting endpoints				
Convergence achieved after 6 iterations				
Variable	Coefficient	Std. error	t-Statistic	Prob.
$\log URB * V/IND * (1 + INF)$	0.853493	0.053029	16.09488	0
$\log(URB * HS)$	1.000507	0.221775	4.511369	0.0004
AR(2)	0.300626	0.192565	1.56117	0.138
R-squared	0.950233	Mean dependent var	10.33822	
Adjusted R-squared	0.944012	S.D. dependent var	0.762333	
S.E. of regression	0.180381	Akaike info criterion	−0.44355	
Sum squared resid	0.520599	Schwarz criterion	−0.29443	
Log likelihood	7.213694	Durbin-Watson stat	1.317845	
Inverted AR Roots	0.55	−0.55		

population and industry. Through regression analysis, we establish a relationship model (7.3) between urbanization and investment in physical capital:

$$D = (URB * V/IND * (1 + INF))^{0.854} * URB * HS \tag{7.3}$$

where D is investment in physical capital, URB is the permanent population urbanization rate, V is the sum of the actual value of foreign capital and the added loan balance of financial institutions, HS is per capita housing space, and the results of econometric test are shown in Table 7.3.

7.1.2.5 The Promotion of Urbanization to Science and Technology Progress

The study by Henderson (2003) shows that the optimal degree of urban concentration can maximize productivity growth and science and technology progress, while the optimal degree of urban concentration change with the development level and country size. Over-dispersion or over-concentration can have a big impact on productivity and science and technology progress. According to the study by Fang, technological innovation is a process of interaction and learning. Innovation requires frequent exchange of information and contacts among various actors. As a center of knowledge, information and skills, cities have obvious advantages in forming a regional innovation network, thus their science and technology are improving constantly. Through spatial aggregation of production factors, urbanization not only enable manufacturers to share infrastructure, save production costs and gain scale economy, but also gain faster access to technology and market information, improves transaction efficiency and reduces transaction costs, so that it can promote division of labor and specialization and gain the benefits of "Scope Economy" or "Specialization Economy". Under the effect of benefits of agglomeration economic, R&D investment is continuously promoted and innovation-driven capacity is continuously enhanced. Cities are the product of human settlements, and thousands of people gather in the cities, who are different in the interest, ability and, demand and wealth. Therefore, cities need as much diversity as possible to fulfill the demand of humans. And with the division and specialization of urban industries and talents, the formation of a diverse urban environment is further promoted. Therefore, as Jane Jacobs pointed out: "diversity is the nature of big cities". The diversity of cities creates opportunities for communication among people in different industries and disciplines, thus contributing to the emergence of new knowledge, new technology and new industries.

According to the study of Cheng, urbanization can promote economic growth through the intermediary of technological innovation. Cities have advantages in the specialization and diversity of technology, the accumulation of human capital, the formation of information exchange network, the improvement of transaction efficiency, and infrastructure, which is beneficial to the emergence and spread of technological innovation. Urbanization promotes economic growth through the intermediary effect of technological innovation. The analysis of time series and cross-sectional data shows that there is a high degree of positive correlation between urbanization level and technological innovation in China. The input-output model confirms that urbanization is good for technological innovation. Based on the multi-model estimates of provincial panel data, scholars found that urbanization and science and technology progress play a positive role in promoting economic growth; the high population density of cities is conducive to the interaction and the circulation of information; the diversity of urban activities makes it easy for one department to adopt the technologies used by another department; cities bring educational activities together to provide the environment for originality and innovation. From the perspective of innovation and ecological conditions, these studies show that the permanent population urbanization, informatization, industrialization, the added value of mid-to-high-end industries and loan increment are the important determining factors of science and technology progress.

Based on the data of the R&D inputs *S* from 2001 to 2013 in China and the urbanization rate of permanent population *URB*, informatization *INF*, industrialization *IND*, the added value of mid-to-high-end industries *HI* and loan increment *LO*, the following model (7.4) was established through regression analysis, and the results of econometric test are shown in Table 7.4.

$$S = 0.0766URB * IND * HI * (1 + INF) + 0.0068LO + 106.8 \tag{7.4}$$

Table 7.4 The econometric tests of the pulling function of urbanization on increasing investment in science and technology

Dependent variable: *S*				
Method: least squares				
Sample: 1990–2012				
Included observations: 23				
Variable	Coefficient	Std. error	t-Statistic	Prob.
C	106.8257	51.32755	2.081255	0.0505
$URB * IND * (1 + INF) * HI$	0.076563	0.007101	10.78185	0
LO	0.006786	0.003852	1.761477	0.0934
R-squared	0.985855	Mean dependent var	853.081	
Adjusted R-squared	0.984441	S.D. dependent var	751.5225	
S.E. of regression	93.7429	Akaike info criterion	12.0401	
Sum squared resid	175,754.6	Schwarz criterion		
Log likelihood	−135.461	F-statistic	696.9683	
Durbin-Watson stat	0.780692	Prob(F-statistic)	0	

7.1.3 *The Overall Analysis of the Pulling Function of Urbanization on China's GDP*

Based on the model of the pulling function of urbanization on the direct factor of China's economic growth (supply-side elements), combining with economic growth model, a complete model group is formed to measure the pulling function of urbanization.

7.1.3.1 Economic Growth Model

The synergy theory of economic growth (Liu and Jiang 2015; Liu and Jiang 2016) divides GDP into compensation of employees, physical capital benefits and synergy benefits. However, by using the method of value decomposition, GDP can be decomposed into compensation of employees, physical capital benefits and synergy benefits. This can be written in a quantitative form as (7.5):

$$Y = aL^{\alpha}H^{\beta}S^{\gamma}D^{\delta} + bK + cSHD/K^2 + u \tag{7.5}$$

In Formula (7.5), Y represents GDP, L represents labor, D represents investment in physical capital, S represents investment in science and technology, H represents human capital, and K represents physical capital stock in the previous period (if the data is annual data, K represents physical capital stock in the end of last year). From the point of view of production factors, the stock of physical capital in the previous period and the current investment in physical capital both are capital factors, and these two factors together represent the current physical capital stock; $\alpha, \beta, \gamma, \delta, a, b, c$ are parameters, and they are determined by the institution (Liu and Li 2001) and environmental externalities. The significance of the theory that "the institution determines the output elasticity of the production factors" lies in that it is not enough to increase the scale of the factors of production for innovation-driven and economic growth, the key lies in improving the output elasticity of factors of production (including research and development) through the institutional innovation (such as reform and opening up).

In Formula (7.5), $aL^{\alpha}H^{\beta}S^{\gamma}D^{\delta}$ represents the compensation of employees, bK represents physical capital benefits, $cSHD/K^2 + u$ represents synergy benefits. Based on the above theoretical model, the empirical analysis model of China's economic growth factor in 1978–2012 is:

$$Y = 0.001243(HL)^{0.803}(SD/L)^{0.228} + 0.229K + 1186HSD/K^2 - 2983 \tag{7.6}$$

In model (7.6), according to Granger's test, the value of S (investment in science and technology) adopts the data of two years advanced. For example, the investment in science and technology in 2001 is corresponding to Y (GDP) in 2003. In other words, we assume that the time that transfer investment into productivity is about two years; H represents for human capital, which is defined numerically as the product of average years of schooling of laborers and the number of labor force.

7.1.3.2 Model Group

The following model groups are composed of models (7.1)–(7.6)

$$Y = 0.001243(HL)^{0.803}(SD/L)^{0.228} + 0.229K + 1186HSD/K^2 - 2983 \tag{7.7}$$

$$h = 5.03URB * (1 + INF) * IND + 7.34 \tag{7.8}$$

$$L = 110.7 * URB - 32.8 * AGR + 54.1 * P \tag{7.9}$$

$$D = (URB * V/IND * (1 + INF))^{0.854} * URB * HS \tag{7.10}$$

$$S = 0.0766URB * IND * HI * (1 + INF) + 0.0068LO + 106.8 \tag{7.11}$$

$$K_{t-1} = (1 - \delta)K_{t-2} + D_{t-1} \tag{7.12}$$

Take the relations (7.8)–(7.12) of h, L, S, D, K_{t-1} and URB into (7.7) to get the relations between Y and URB.

7.1.3.3 Calculation of Marginal Revenue of Urbanization

Calculating the derivative of *Y* to *URB* and we get the marginal revenue of urbanization to economic growth, that is, the pulling function on economic growth carried by increasing one unit of urbanization, see more detail in column 6 of Table 7.5.

In Table 7.5, column 2, "marginal revenue of labor driven by urbanization" is obtained by taking Eq. (7.9) into Eq. (7.7) and calculating the derivative of *Y* to *URB*; in column 3, the "marginal revenue of human capital driven by urbanization" is obtained by taking Eq. (7.8) into Eq. (7.7) and calculating the derivative of *Y* to *URB*; in column 4, "marginal revenue of investment in physical capital driven by urbanization" is obtained by taking Eq. (7.10) into Eq. (7.7) and calculating the derivative of *Y* to *URB*; in column 5, "marginal revenue of science and technology progress driven by urbanization" is obtained by taking Eq. (7.11) into Eq. (7.7) and calculating the derivative of *Y* to *URB*.

Multiplying "the total urbanization marginal revenue" by "the actual increased value of urbanization rate" (the urbanization rate of permanent population at current year minus the urbanization rate of permanent population in the previous year), and then, dividing by the gross domestic product of the previous year, thus, we get the calculation results of "the GDP growth rate driven by the urbanization". See Tables 7.5, 7.6 and Fig. 7.2 for details.

Table 7.5 Marginal revenue of economic growth driven by urbanization (100 million yuan)

Years	The marginal revenue of labor force driven by an increase of 1 percentage point in the urbanization rate	The marginal revenue of human capital driven by an increase of 1 percentage point in the urbanization rate	The marginal revenue of science and technology progress driven by an increase of 1 percentage point in the urbanization rate	The marginal revenue of investment in physical capital driven by an increase of 1 percentage point in the urbanization rate	The total urbanization marginal revenue driven by an increase of 1 percentage point in the urbanization rate
1990	10	15	12	309	360
1995	16	26	46	511	654
2000	23	42	71	638	824
2005	33	68	116	862	1177
2010	53	100	250	1252	1878
2015	137	137	464	2106	3116
2016	148	140	489	2197	3261
2017	156	144	523	2270	3395
2018	165	148	550	2346	3527
2019	175	153	579	2430	3673
2020	185	155	615	2512	3821

Table 7.6 The pulling function of urbanization on China's GDP growth

Years	Permanent population urbanization rate (%)	The pulling function on the GDP growth rate when the urbanization rate is increased by 1% (%)	The pulling function of the increase of urbanization rate on the GDP growth rate at current year (%)	The ratio of urban-driven GDP growth to total GDP growth (%)
1991	26.37	1.3	0.7	7.2
1995	29.04	2.6	1.4	12.6
2000	36.22	1.7	2.5	29.3
2005	42.99	2.0	2.4	23.5
2010	47.5	2.5	4.0	38.2
2015	56.07	2.1	2.5	36.6
2016	57.27	2.1	2.5	37.0
2017	58.47	2.0	2.4	37.1
2018	59.67	2.0	2.4	36.5
2019	60.87	2.0	2.0	30.1
2020	62.07	2.0	2.0	30.1

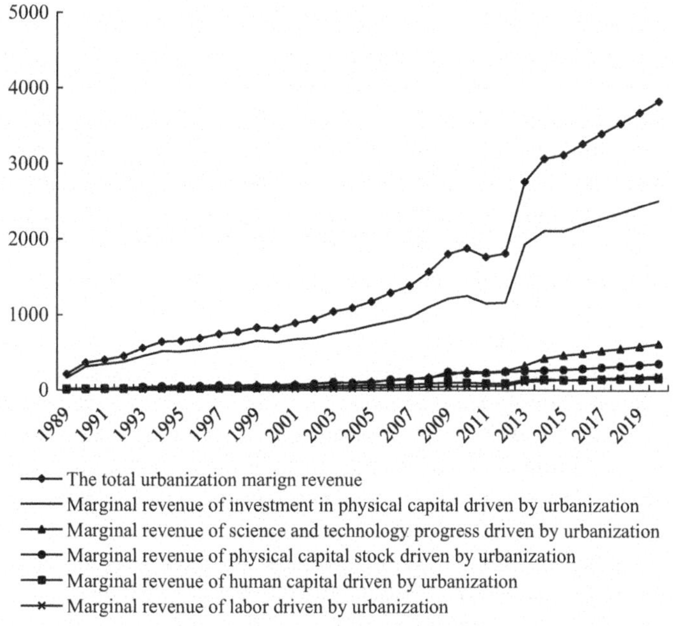

Fig. 7.2 Marginal revenue of economic growth driven by urbanization

7.1.3.4 Calculation Results and Analysis

As can be seen in Table 7.6, an average increase of 1 percent point of urbanization rate of permanent population in 1991–2012, results in an increased in the growth rate of GDP nearly by 2.2 percent points on average. In fact, during this period, the average annual urbanization rate of China's permanent population increased by 1.2 percent points (the urbanization rate of permanent population increased from 26.4% in 1991 to 52.5% in 2012), and correspondingly, the average annual growth rate of the GDP increased by 2.7 percent points. Judging from the calculation results of various indicators, as the increase of GDP has been growing in recent years and the influence of complicated economic conditions at home and abroad, the growth rate of GDP has shown a downward trend. However, the improvement of urbanization rate will still have a strong stimulating effect on economic growth.

7.1.3.5 Forecast by 2020

Under the new normal and new concept, from the perspective of supply-side structural reform, the center of industrial structure will change from low-to-mid-end to mid-to-high-end; the solution of the problem of overcapacity (which mainly depends on the combination of macro-interval plan control and micro-market regulation) and the promotion of the development of mid-to-high-end industries will be combined together; the tertiary industry will grow faster than the secondary industry; correcting the distortions in the resource allocation; expanding the effective supply; and the economic growth will shift from capital and investment as the primary driving force to innovation (technological innovation, human capital innovation and institutional innovation) as the primary driving force; innovation-driven and investment structure will be combined better; China's economic growth rate will shift from high-speed to medium-high-speed growth. From the perspective of demand-side, consumption growth will grow faster than investment growth; adopting the combination of active fiscal and monetary policies (increasing the proportion of real economy loans in M2, reducing the proportion of fictitious economy in M2, and preventing financial risks) and differentiated industrial policy; promoting the mergers and acquisitions of non-state-owned enterprises and their growth and development; reducing the debt rate and the cost; and enhancing the ability to allocate the global resources through a further step to reform and opening up. In this way, the average economic growth rate during the 13th Five-Year Plan period would reach at 6.5% or above, which requires making full use of the effect of urbanization and informatization.

As can be seen from Fig. 7.3, from 2016 to 2020, the effect of increasing urbanization rate on the growth rate of GDP is 2.2 percent points, when the urbanization rate of resident population increases by 1% on average each year (Zhang et al. 2011; Liu et al. 2014), and urbanization drives GDP growth rate at a high level of 34%, which means that urbanization has become an important factor in stabilizing GDP growth.

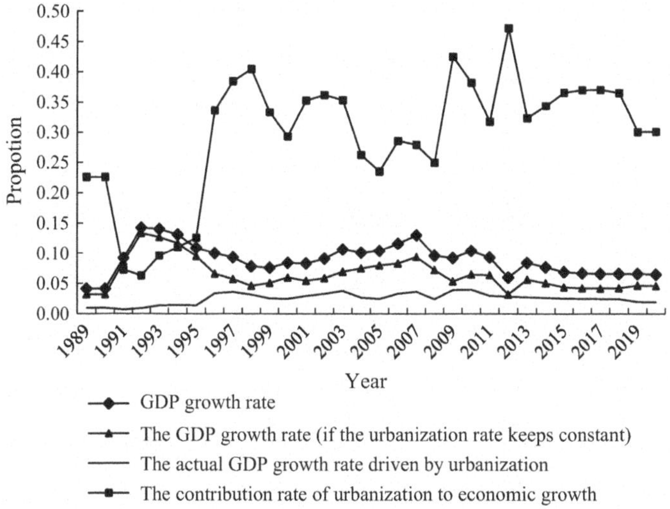

Fig. 7.3 The pulling function of urbanization on China's GDP growth rate

7.1.4 Related Verification

The above results also can be calculated from the growth of urban population and output per capita, and we compared this method with the above method to illustrate the reliability of the growth factor analysis results.

7.1.4.1 The Verification Based on the Data of Urban Population Growth and Output Per Capita

Assuming that the GDP per capita of the newly increased urban population is 1.15 times as big as the GDP per capita of urban permanent residents, and then, the increase in GDP driven by the newly increased urban population can be calculated. For example, the urban population increased from 341.69 million in 1994 to 351.74 million in 1995, and the increase in GDP carried by newly increased urban population was 109.7 billion yuan, as a result, the pulling function of newly increased urban population to GDP growth was 9%. Here, the ratio of GDP per capita of urban population to GDP per capita of rural population is estimated based on the ratio of urban-rural income (Table 7.7).

7.1.4.2 The Basic Consistency of the Two Results

From the comparison between the economic growth accounting and the urban population growth accounting in Fig. 7.4, the results of these two accounting

Table 7.7 Rough accounting from the perspective of output per capita (selected representative years)

Year	Urban population (million)	Rural population (million)	GDP (100 million yuan)	Income gap between urban and rural areas	The pulling effect on the growth rate of GDP
1990	30,195	84,138	18,548	0.45	0.23
1995	35,174	85,947	33,073	0.37	0.13
2000	45,906	80,837	49,997	0.36	0.29
2005	56,212	74,544	79,444	0.31	0.24
2006	58,288	73,160	88,659	0.31	0.29
2007	60,633	71,496	100,185	0.30	0.28
2008	62,403	70,399	109,802	0.30	0.25
2009	64,512	68,938	119,904	0.30	0.43
2010	66,978	67,113	132,374	0.31	0.38
2011	69,079	65,656	144,685	0.32	0.32
2012	71,182	64,222	153,366	0.32	0.47
2013	73,111	62,961	166,249	0.33	0.32

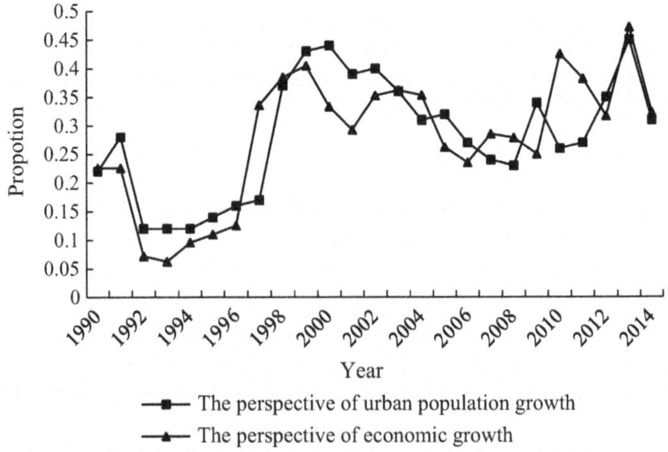

Fig. 7.4 The result comparison of economic growth accounting and urban population growth accounting

methods are generally achieved at an agreement. From 1989 to 2013, the average value of these two accounting methods was 28%—the pulling function of the urbanization rate on the GDP growth rate was averagely 2.8 percentage points per year.

7.1.5 Conclusion

(1) Intermediary theory and agglomeration theory of urbanization and economic growth hold the view that urbanization, informatization, industrialization and agricultural modernization promote the growth of employment and human capital through agglomeration, and then economic growth is stimulated by promoting science and technological progress and the growth of investment in physical capital. Employment, human capital, science and technological progress and investment in physical capital are the direct factors that determine economic growth, as well as the intermediary factor for economic growth driven by urbanization. This book builds a model group of urbanization along the "modeling path" mentioned above.

(2) Urbanization, informatization, industrialization and agricultural modernization are important innovation ecological conditions for promoting innovation capability and innovation-driven. On the one hand, these factors promotes the growth of employment, human capital, science and technological progress, and investment in physical capital through the following aspects, such as agglomeration effects, diversification effects and association effects. On the other hand, these factors also promote the growth in employment, human capital, science and technology, and investment in physical capital by reducing costs, boosting financing and increasing household incomes and consumption.

(3) Every 1% increase in the urbanization rate of the resident population from 1991 to 2012 resulted in an average increase of 2.2% in the growth rate of the GDP. In fact, during this period, the average annual urbanization rate of China's resident population increased by 1.2% (the urbanization rate of resident population increased from 26.4% in 1991 to 52.5% in 2012), and correspondingly, the growth rate of the GDP annually increased 2.7% on average. From 2016 to 2020, the urbanization rate of resident population will increase by 1% on average each year, that is to say, the pulling function of the urbanization rate on the growth rate of GDP will be 2.2 percentage points, which will play a very important role in stabilizing the GDP growth rate.

7.2 Supply-Side Structural Reform and the Analysis of Economic Growth Based on DSGE Model

7.2.1 Introduction

The DSGE model stems from the real business cycle (RBC) model put forward by Kydland and Prescott (1982). Ireland (2004) combined the DSGE model with the VAR (multi-variable auto-regressive time series model), and through the maximum likelihood estimation method, he explained the fluctuation in gross output and employment of the post-war America's economy. Smets and Wouters (2005) used the DSGE model to study on the state of shocks and frictions between America and the European Economic Community during 1974 and 2002. Walque et al. (2005) and Rabanal and Tuesta (2006) applied the DSGE model to predict the macroeconomic policies of several countries. Smets and Wouters (2007) used the new Keynesian DSGE model as an extension of labor-enhanced science and technological progress to discuss the volatility sources of the economic cycle in U.S. and the impact of science and technological progress on working hours. On the choice of optimal monetary policy and fiscal policy, Lorenzo Forni et al. (2009) used the DSGE model to study on the effect of European fiscal policy, and the result shows that the variables of fiscal policy have little contribution to the cyclical influence of major macroeconomic variables. At present, the research on the macroeconomic issues have become a trend by using the DSGE method, and on this basis, the Keynesianism has also developed rapidly. The current DSGE researches have made great progress, but the analysis of economic growth and its related problems are not ideal because of that the entire DSGE model system has deviated from the economic reality on the basis of the old economic growth model.

At present, the studies of DSGE are mostly based on classical economics (Cobb-Douglass production function theory), thus, the accuracy of the model is not high, and the complete market competition hypothesis is not in conformity with the actual. Additionally, the method of determining the steady state value and the logarithm linearization error problem also needs to be solved.

The correct model of economic growth is the foundation of research of economic and sustainable development. In this section, we combine the synergy theory of economic growth with the theory of supply-side structural reform that put forward by Chinese scholars, and apply it to the study of DSGE analysis of China's economic growth and sustainable development.

According to the theory of supply-side structural reform, the main methods of demand management are monetary policy and fiscal expenditure policy; and supply management involved with more methods, such as the tax policy, administrative management and legal system management (Liu 2010). Supply-side reform pays more attention to structural problems, including further adjustment of industrial structure, especially under the support of innovation, easing overcapacity, allowing overcapacity to gradually be reduced to the normal level of less than 20% and increasing technical threshold in duplication of investment based on technological innovation, so as to improve the market mechanism and improve competitiveness in order to form a phase-out mechanism. We must improve the level of technological and institutional innovation, and create new points of investment growth through technological innovation, and then form an effective investment mechanism through institutional innovation, so as to avoid serious duplication of investment in technical systems.

In the short run, the supply-side structural reforms should focus on the five major tactical tasks, such as eliminating production capacity, removing inventory, removing leverage, lowering costs and making up for shortcomings (Hu 2016). In the long run, the supply-side reform must take changing the mode of economic growth as the goal, in particular, we must change the concept of development and implement the five major development concepts of "innovation, coordination, greenness, openness and sharing". We should further promote the development of high-end manufacturing based mainly on science and technological progress and innovation, give full play to the dual advantages of capital accumulation and talent accumulation, and eliminate backward production capacity. We should promote the service industry, especially the highly-oriented service industry represented by the financial service industry and manufacturing service industry. We should also cultivate a batch of high-end manufacturing and service industries, which makes our economic structure keep on a more reasonable platform and maintains the sustainability of economic growth (Liu 2014a).

By using some key structural indicators, such as industrialization, the added value of mid-to-high-end industries, the proportion of high energy consumption industries, real estate investment, infrastructure investment and other industrial structural indicators, urbanization (structure indicators of regional population), industry concentration and other market structure indicators, this book builds model group of China's economic growth and sustainable development.

7.2.2 A Model Group of DSGE Based on the Synergy Theory and Supply-Side Structural Reform

The synergy theory, supply-side structural reform theory and theoretical analysis of the promoting role of urbanization, industrialization, informatization and agricultural modernization to economic growth and sustainable development are combined to build (Dynamic Stochastic General Equilibrium) DSGE model group, and construct the expected utility function and Lagrange function, then construct the DSGE model system for China's economic growth and sustainable development. Furthermore, using Bayesian method and econometric methods to estimate the parameters and carry out simulation and policy experiments to analyze the effect of the fluctuation of structural variables (such as urbanization, industrialization and informatization) on the state variables and control variables of China's economic growth. The correctness of the model is verified by comparison with the fluctuation characteristics of the main variables of China's economic growth analyzed by H-P filtering, which provides the basis for promoting the policy formulation of regional economic growth and sustainable development.

7.2.2.1 Economic Growth Model

According to the synergy theory established in this book, China's economic growth model is:

$$Y_t = a_1(E_t * L_t * L_t)^{\alpha_1}(S_{t-2} * D_t/L_t)^{\alpha_2} + a_2K_{t-1} + a_3S_{t-2}D_tE_tL_t/K_{t-1}^2 + a_4 \quad (7.13)$$

where E_t is the average years of schooling of laborers.

7.2.2.2 The Relationship Module Among Urbanization, Informatization, Industrialization, Agricultural Modernization and Direct Elements

(1) Informatization model

This book measures information index by using three variables, such as the number of internet users, the total volume of postal services/GDP, the proportion of electronic information industry added value in industrial added value. Assuming $INF_{t-2}, TE_{t-2}, EL_{t-2}, XL_{t-2}$ is the information index, the number of internet users per ten thousands people, the total volume of postal services (100 million yuan)/GDP, the proportion of electronic information industry added value in industrial added value respectively. The following information model is:

$$INF_{t-2} = a_5 TE_{t-2} + a_6 EL_{t-2} + a_7 XL_{t-2} \tag{7.14}$$

(2) Urbanization and employment model

According to the agglomeration theory, population and labor elements transfer from rural areas to cities and towns, which increases the employment opportunities. The $URB_{t-2}, INF_{t-2}, IND_{t-2}, AGR_{t-2}, PO_{t-2}$, and L_{t-2} represent urbanization, informatization, industrialization, agricultural modernization, population and employment. The following employment model is:

$$L_t = a_8 URB_{t-2} + a_9 IN_{t-2} + a_{10} AGR_{t-2} + a_{11} PO_t + a_{12} \tag{7.15}$$

(3) Urbanization and physical capital investment model

Urbanization not only generate the investment demand in the urban infrastructure and housing, but also stimulate the development of related industries and increase investment demand. The $URB_{t-2}, INF_{t-2}, IND_{t-2}, LO_{t-2}, PO_{t-2}, JC_t$ and D_t represent the urbanization, informatization, industrialization and built-up area and the investment in physical capital. The following physical capital model investment is:

$$\log D_t = \alpha_3 \log[URB_{t-2} * (1 + INF_{t-2}) * LO_{t-2}/IND_{t-2}] + \alpha_4 \log(JC_t) \tag{7.16}$$

(4) Urbanization and R&D model

According to the agglomeration theory, as the center of knowledge, information and skills, cities have obvious advantages in forming a regional innovation network, that is why the level of science and technology is constantly improving. The $S_{t-2}, URB_{t-2}, INF_{t-2}, HI_{t-2}, IND_{t-2}$ and LO_{t-2} represent R&D investment, urbanization, informatization, added value of mid-to-high-end industries, industrialization, loans. The following R&D model is:

$$S_{t-2} = a_{13} + a_{14} URB_{t-2} * (1 + INF_{t-2}) * HI_{t-2} * IND_{t-2} + a_{15} LO_{t-2} \quad (7.17)$$

(5) Urbanization and schooling years model

According to the agglomeration theory, cities and towns generally have better environmental conditions and better education conditions such as cultural, medical and health care. The level of education received by urban citizens is usually higher than that in rural areas. The $E_t, D_t, URB_{t-2}, INF_{t-2}$ and IND_{t-2} represent the average years of schooling of laborers, urbanization, informatization and industrialization, the following schooling years models is:

$$E_t = a_{16} + a_{17} URB_{t-2} * (1 + IND_{t-2}) * IND_{t-2} \quad (7.18)$$

(6) Built-up area model

According to the agglomeration theory, the advantage of cities, such as specialization and diversity, accumulation of human capital, formation of information exchange networks, transaction efficiency improvement and infrastructure, is benefit to save land and increase output per unit area. With the output grows, built-up area also grows. The $JC_t, Y_t, S_{t-2}, IND_t, INF_{t-2}, PU_t$, and URB_{t-2} represent built-up area, GDP, R&D investment, industrialization, informatization, urbanization. The following built-up area model is:

$$JC_t = a_{18} + a_{19} Y_t - a_{20} S_{t-2} * IND_{t-2} * INF_{t-2} * PU_t \quad (7.19)$$

7.2.2.3 Finance and Banking Module

(1) Financial budget revenue model

According to the relationship between fiscal revenue and expenditure, FB_t represents fiscal revenue, FE_t represents fiscal expenditure, and CZ_t represents fiscal deficit. The government budget constraint behavior model is as follows:

$$FB_t = a_{21} FE_t + a_{22} CZ_t \quad (7.20)$$

(2) Interest rates model

According to the rules of monetary policy, the IR_t represents the interest rates, $GDPT$ represents the trend of GDP_t at time t, $CPIT$ represents the trend of CPI_t and M_2T represents the trend of M_{2t}. The following interest rates model is:

$$IR_t = a_{23} + a_{24}(GDP_t/GDPT) * (CPI_t/CPIT) + a_{25}M_{2t}/M_2T \tag{7.21}$$

(3) Non-performing loan model

The number of non-performing loans depends on the number of liabilities and profits, NPL_t represents non-performing loans, DR_t represents asset-liability, and ROA_t represents returns of assets. The following non-performing loan model is:

$$NPL_t = a_{26}DR_t * IR_t + a_{27}ROA_t \tag{7.22}$$

7.2.2.4 The Modules of Export and Three Major Demands

(1) Export model

EX_t represents exports, IO_t represents overseas investment, HEX_t represents mid-to-high-end exports and CH_t represents exchange rates. The following export model is:

$$EX_t = a_{28} + a_{29}IO_t * CH + a_{30}HEX_t * CH_t * FDI_t/IO_t \tag{7.23}$$

(2) Three major demands model

C_t represents consumption, GDP_t represents the GDP, D_t represents investment, EX_t represents exports, CH_t represents exchange rates. The following export model is:

$$GDP_t = a_{31} + a_{32}CH_t + a_{33}D_t * EX_t/C_t + a_{34}EX_t * ADD_t + a_{35}D_t \tag{7.24}$$

7.2.2.5 Enterprise Reform Module

According to the structure-behavior-performance theory in industrial economics, ADD_t represents added value (performance theory), OI_t represents the ratio of ex-factory price index to purchase price index in industrial enterprises (competitive behavior), IC_t represents industry concentration (industry structure), the following export model is:

$$\log ADD_t = \alpha_5 \log OI_t + \alpha_6 \log IC_t \tag{7.25}$$

7.2.2.6 Transport and Other Infrastructure Investment Module

From the view of industrial structure, the investment in physical capital mainly depends on the state of infrastructures, real estate investment as well as the development of mid-to-high-end industries. $D_t, IF_t, ES_t, HI_{t-2}$ represent investment in physical capital, infrastructure investment, real estate investment, the added value of mid-to-high-end industries respectively. The following investment in physical capital model is:

$$D_t = a_{36}(IF_t + ES_t^2/HI_{t-2} + a_{37}HI_{t-2}) \tag{7.26}$$

7.2.2.7 National Innovation System Module

S_{t-2} represents the research and development expenditure, PA_{t-2} represents the number of patents at time $t-2$, N_{t-2} represents the number of research and development personnel and SY_{t-2} represents the innovation system (measuring by the proportion of the research and development expenditure in enterprises in the total R&D expenditure). The relationship among R&D expenditure, the number of patents and the number of existing research and development personnel is a typical C-D production function, thus, the following model is:

$$S_{t-2} = SY_{t-2}^{\alpha_7} PA_{t-2}^{\alpha_8} N_{t-2}^{\alpha_9} \tag{7.27}$$

7.2.2.8 Energy-Saving Emission Reduction Module

(1) Energy consumption rate model

We can introduce informatization factors, and technological factors, and structural factors (such as high energy-consuming industries and tertiary industries) into the model. The high energy-consuming industries make the energy consumption rate rise faster, while the ratio of R&D investment to GDP, industrialization and informatization are the factors to reduce the energy consumption rate. EC_t, EDI_t, S_{t-2}/Y_t, IND_{t-2}, and INF_{t-2} represent the energy consumption rate, the proportion of 6 major energy-consuming industries, the ratio of R&D investment to GDP, and industrialization and informatization. Then, the following model of energy consumption rate is:

$$EC_t = a_{38} + a_{39}EDI_t/(S_{t-2} * IND_{t-2} * INF_{t-2}/Y_t) + a_{40}S_{t-2} * IND_{t-2} * INF_{t-2}/Y_t \tag{7.28}$$

(2) Carbon emission model

High energy-consuming industries are the mainly source of carbon emissions, and the ratio of R&D investment to GDP, industrialization and information technology is the factors that can reduce carbon emissions. EC_t, S_{t-2}/Y_t, EDI_t, IND_{t-2}, and INF_{t-2} represent energy consumption rate, the proportion of 6 major energy-consuming industries, the ratio of R&D investment to GDP, industrialization, informatization. The following model is:

$$CE_t = a_{41} + a_{42}S_{t-2} * EDI_t * IND_{t-2} * INF_{t-2} + a_{43}EC_t * Y_t \tag{7.29}$$

(3) Pollutant discharge model

High energy-consuming industries are the mainly source of emissions of pollutants, and the ratio of energy-saving emission reduction funds to GDP, the ratio of R&D investment to GDP, industrialization, informatization are used to reduce carbon emissions. PE_t, GF_t, S_{t-2}, IND, INF_{t-2}, EC_t, Y_t represent pollutant emissions (equivalent), the ratio of energy-saving emission reduction funds to GDP, the ratio of R&D investment to GDP, industrialization, the ratio of energy consumption to GDP, and GDP. The following model is:

$$PE_t = a_{44} + a_{45}GF_t * S_{t-2} * IND_t * INF_{t-2} + a_{46}EC_t * Y_t \tag{7.30}$$

7.2.2.9 Objective Function and Resident Module

The objective function of the entire economy is shown in (7.31).

$$E_0[\sum_{t=0}^{\infty} \beta^t U(C_t, M_{2t}, L_t)] \tag{7.31}$$

where U is utility function, E means the anticipation value, β^t is discount factor.

Now, Eqs. (7.13)–(7.31) together formed the DSGE model framework for the China's economy, where [CPI_t] is state variables, [PA_t, FR_t, L_t, D_t, S_{t-2}, E_t, EX_{t-2}, C_t, ES_t, PA_t, IR_t, NP_t, JC_t, EC_{t-2}, CE_t, PE_t, INF_t, ADD_t, Y_t] are the control variables, while [M_2, FE_t,CZ_t, URB_{t-2},IND_{t-2}, AGR_{t-2},PO_t, LO_{t-2},HI_t, CH_t,IO_t, FDI_{t-2},IF_{t-2}, N_{t-2},SY_t, DR_{t-2},BI_t, ES_t,XS_t, PU_t,HEC_t, GF_t,TE_{t-2}, EL_t,XI_t, OI_t,IC_t, K_{t-1},HS_t] are random variables.

7.2.3 *Model Solution and Parameter Estimation*

The DSGE model framework of China's economic growth and sustainable development is formed by (7.13) and (7.31), and it is a nonlinear model group that is not convenient for direct solution. The question now is how to transform a nonlinear model into a linear model, Harald Uhlig proposed a relatively simple logarithmic linearization method. This method takes the general variable X_t into consideration, and also define that $X_t = X(1 + x_t)$, where X without the subscript indicates the trend value of X_t, and x_t indicates the deviation of the fluctuation value from the trend value X. Since x_t is close to 0, $e^{x_t} = 1 + x_t$. The convenience of the Uhlig method is that it does not require to find a clear derivative, and it can directly do the variable substitution, and the substitution of such variables is easy to mechanize. The results obtained with this method can characterize the deviation of the fluctuation value from the trend value. Thus, using Bayesian and econometric methods to estimate parameters, on the basis of 1990–2013 data, Eqs. (7.13) and (7.31) can be linearized into the following model system:

(1) $0 = c_t + p_t - 7.5E_t p_{t+1} - 0.3m2_t$

Among them, fr_t, fe_t, cz_t respectively represent the volatility of consumption, price and M2 to their respective trend values;

(2) $0 = -fr_t + 1.08fe_t - 0.087cz_t$

Among them, $c_t, p_t, m2_t$ respectively represent the volatility of fiscal revenue, fiscal expenditure and fiscal deficits to their respective trend values;

(3) $0 = -l_t + 0.055urb_{t-2} - 0.012agr_{t-2} + 0.956po_{t-2}$

Among them, $l_t, urb_{t-2}, agr_{t-2}, po_{t-2}$ respectively represent the volatility of employment, urbanization, agricultural modernization and population to their respective trend values;

(4) $0 = -d_t + 1.79(urb_{t-2} + \inf_{t-2} - hs_t) + 1.68jc_t$

Among them, $d_t, urb_{t-2}, \inf_{t-2}, hs_t, jc_t$ respectively represent the volatility of investment in physical capital, urbanization, informatization, resident per capita housing area and built-up area to their respective trend values;

(5) $0 = -s_{t-2} + 0.43(urb_{t-2} + hi_{t-2} + ind_{t-2}) + 0.16\inf_{t-2} + 0.259lo_{t-2}$

Among them, $s_{t-2}, urb_{t-2}, hi_{t-2}, ind_{t-2}, \inf_{t-2}, lo_{t-2}$ respectively represent the volatility of R&D expenditure, urbanization, the added value of mid-to-high-end industries, industrialization, and informatization, the sum of loans and FDI to their respective trend values;

(6) $0 = -e_t + 0.12(urb_{t-2} + \inf_{t-2} + ind_{t-2})$

Among them, $e_t, urb_{t-2}, \inf_{t-2}, ind_{t-2})$ respectively represent the volatility of the average years of schooling of laborers, urbanization, informatization, industrialization to their respective trend values;

(7) $0 = -ex_t + 0.20(io_t + ch_t) + 0.07(hex_t + ch_t + fdi_t - io_t) + 0.51(hex_t + ch_t)$

Among them, $ex_t, io_t, ch_t, hex_t, fdi_t$ respectively represent the volatility of export, overseas investment, exchange rates, mid-to-high-end exports, FDI to their respective trend values;

(8) $0 = -y_t + c_t + 0.233ch_t + 0.143(d_t + ex_t - c_t) + 0.12(ex_t + add_t) + 0.179d_t$

Among them, $y_t, c_t, ch_t, d_t, ex_t, add_t$ respectively represent the volatility of GDP, consumption, exchange rates, investment in physical capital, export and the rate of added value to their respective trend values;

(9) $0 = -d_t + 0.64(if_t + es_t) + 0.468hi_t$

Among them, d_t, if_t, es_t, hi_t respectively represent the volatility of investment in physical capital, infrastructure investment, real estate investment and the added value of high-end industries to their respective trend values;

(10) $0 = -s_{t-2} + 0.6sy_{t-2} + 0.6pa_{t-2} - 0.004n_{t-2}$

Among them, $s_{t-2}, sy_{t-2}, pa_{t-2}, n_{t-2}$ respectively represent the volatility of R&D expenditure, the proportion of R&D expenditure in enterprises to total R&D expenditure, the number of patents that granted to domestic applicants, the number of R&D personnel to their respective trend values;

(11) $0 = -ir_t + 0.92(y_t + p_t) + 0.56m_{2t}$

Among them, ir_t, y_t, p_t, m_{2t} respectively represent the volatility of interest rates, GDP, prices and M2 to their respective trend values;

(12) $0 = -np_t + 0.425dr_t - 0.32bi_t - 0.32\theta_t$

Among them, $np_t, dr_t, bi_t, \theta_t$ respectively represent the volatility of non-performing loans rate, the asset-liability rate, the rate of return to assets and the resource allocation efficiency of production factors to their respective trend values;

(13) $0 = jc_t + 0.89y_t - 0.116(s_{t-2} + ind_{t-2} + \inf_{t-2} + pu_t + urb_{t-2})$

Among them, $jc_t, y_t, s_{t-2}, ind_{t-2}, \inf_{t-2}, pu_t, urb_{t-2}$ respectively represent the volatility of built-up area, GDP, R&D expenditure, industrialization, informatization, urban population and urbanization to their respective trend values;

(14) $0 = -ec_t + 0.068(edi_t - s_{t-2} - ind_{t-2} - \inf_{t-2}) - 0.088(s_{t-2} + ind_{t-2} + \inf_{t-2})$

Among them, $ec_t, edi_t, s_{t-2}, ind_{t-2}, \inf_{t-2}$ respectively represent the volatility of energy consumption, the added value of the six high energy-consuming industries, R&D expenditure, industrialization and informatization to their respective trend values;

(15) $0 = -ce_t - 0.052(s_{t-2} + ind_{t-2} + \inf_{t-2}) + 1.16 * ec_t + 1.21y_t$

Among them, $ce_t, s_{t-2}, ind_{t-2}, \inf_{t-2}, ec_t, y_t$ respectively represent the volatility of carbon emissions, R&D expenditure, industrialization, informatization, energy consumption and GDP to their respective trend values;

(16) $0 = -pe_t - 0.350(gf_t + s_{t-2} + ind_{t-2} + \inf_{t-2}) + 0.855ec_t + 1.2y_t$

Among them, $pe_t, gf_t, s_{t-2}, ind_{t-2}, \inf_{t-2}, ec_t, y_t$ respectively represent the volatility of pollutant discharge (equivalent), pollution control funding, research and development expenditure, industrialization, informatization, energy consumption and GDP to their respective trend values;

(17) $0 = -in_t + 0.06te_t + 0.072el_t + 0.14xi_t$

Among them, in_t, te_t, el_t, xi_t respectively represent the volatility of informatization, internet users per 10,000 people, total volume of posts and telecommunications services and the added value of electronic information industry to their respective trend values;

(18) $0 = -add_t + 0.515oi_t + 0.94ic_t$

Among them, add_t, oi_t, ic_t respectively represent the volatility of the added value rate, the ratio of ex-factory prices to purchase prices and industries concentration to their respective trend values;

(19) $0 = -y_t + 0.823e_t + 0.35l_t + 0.203s_{t-2} + 0.203d_t + 0.244k_{t-1}$

Among them, $y_t, e_t, l_t, s_{t-2}, d_t, k_{t-1}$ respectively represent the volatility of GDP, average years of schooling of laborers, the number of employees, research and development expenditure, investment in physical capital and physical capital stock to their respective trend values;

7.2.4 Variance Decomposition and Simulation

7.2.4.1 Variance Decomposition

For the linearized model system which estimated the parameters, the DYNARE software based on MATLAB is used to carry out the variance decomposition, and analyzes the deviation of the fluctuation values of the state variables and the control variables from the trend values, as shown in Table 7.8 (these variables omitted superscript).

7.2.4.2 Simulation Analysis

Simulating the impact of random variables on status variables and control variables. The change of each random variable is: epm2 = [0.01 zeros(1,50)]; fe = [0.015 zeros(1,50)]; cz = [−0.015 zeros(1,50)]; urb = [0.015 zeros(1,50)]; ind = [0.015 zeros(1,50)]; agr = [0.015 zeros(1,50)]; po = [0.003 zeros(1,50)]; lo = [0.015 zeros (1,50)]; hi = [0.02 zeros(1,50)]; hex = [0.005 zeros(1,50)]; ch = [0.01 zeros(1,50)]; io = [0.03 zeros(1,50)]; fdi = [0.01 zeros(1,50)]; if = [0.005 zeros(1,50)]; pn = [0.03 zeros(1,50)]; sy = [0.01 zeros(1,50)]; dr = [0.01 zeros(1,50)]; bi = [0.01 zeros(1,50)]; es = [0.01 zeros(1,50)]; pu = [0.02 zeros(1,50)]; hec = [−0.01 zeros (1,50)]; gf = [0.015 zeros(1,50)]; te = [0.01 zeros(1,50)]; el = [0.01 zeros(1,50)]; xi = [0.01 zeros(1,50)]; oi = [0.01 zeros(1,50)]; ic = [0.01 zeros(1,50)]; k = [0.01 zeros(1,50)]; hs = [0.01 zeros(1,50)];

In this combination of impact scenarios, state variables and control variables, such as CPI, fiscal revenue, employment, investment and GDP produced positive volatility responses at the beginning of the period, especially within two or three years, these variables responses fairly to the extent in time, and then gradually keep at a steady state, as shown in the Fig. 7.5.

Table 7.8 Variance decomposition (in percent) (HP filter, lambda = 100)

	cpi	fr	l	d	s	e	ex	c	es	pa
m2	12	0	0	0	0	0	0	0	0	0
fe	0	87	0	0	0	0	0	0	0	0
cz	0	13	0	0	0	0	0	0	0	0
urb	0	0	1	52	13	40	0	0	7	12
ind	3	0	0	0	11	35	0	1	0	10
agr	0	0	0	0	0	0	0	0	0	0
po	2	0	83	0	0	0	0	1	0	0
lo	0	0	0	38	17	0	0	0	5	15
hi	1	0	16	0	58	0	0	3	2	52
hex	11	0	0	0	0	0	64	43	0	0
ch	66	0	0	0	0	0	27	42	0	0
io	1	0	0	0	0	0	8	2	0	0
fdi	0	0	0	0	0	0	2	1	0	0
if	0	0	0	0	0	0	0	0	84	0
n	0	0	0	0	0	0	0	0	0	0
sy	0	0	0	0	0	0	0	0	0	10
dr	0	0	0	0	0	0	0	0	0	0
bi	0	0	0	0	0	0	0	0	0	0
st	0	0	0	0	0	0	0	0	0	0
pu	0	0	0	0	0	0	0	0	0	0
hec	0	0	0	0	0	0	0	0	0	0
gf	0	0	0	0	0	0	0	0	0	0
te	3	0	0	1	0	2	0	0	0	0
el	0	0	0	3	1	12	0	1	0	1
xi	0	0	0	3	0	11	0	1	0	0
oi	0	0	0	0	0	0	0	0	0	0
icd	0	0	0	0	0	0	0	0	0	0
k	1	0	0	0	0	0	0	4	0	0
hs	0	0	0	3	0	0	0	0	0	0

	ir	np	jc	ec	Ce	pe	in	add	y
m2	71	0	0	0	0	0	0	0	0
fe	0	0	0	0	0	0	0	0	0
cz	0	0	0	0	0	0	0	0	0
urb	6	0	23	4	34	10	0	0	41
ind	2	0	0	34	4	12	0	0	4
agr	0	0	0	0	0	0	0	0	0
po	1	0	10	0	4	2	0	0	3
lo	3	0	18	5	14	3	0	0	22

(continued)

Table 7.8 (continued)

	ir	np	jc	ec	Ce	pe	in	add	y
hi	2	0	3	16	0	1	0	0	8
hex	6	0	12	0	13	6	0	0	11
ch	7	0	0	0	0	0	0	0	0
io	0	0	0	0	0	0	0	0	0
fdi	0	0	0	0	0	0	0	0	0
if	0	0	0	0	0	0	0	0	0
n	0	0	0	0	0	0	0	0	0
sy	0	0	0	0	0	0	0	0	0
dr	0	80	0	0	0	0	0	0	0
bi	0	19	0	0	0	0	0	0	0
st	0	1	0	0	0	0	0	0	0
pu	0	0	19	0	0	0	0	0	0
hec	0	0	0	25	8	2	0	0	0
gf	0	0	0	0	0	44	0	0	0
te	0	0	0	1	1	1	8	0	0
el	0	0	1	8	5	7	49	0	0
xi	0	0	1	7	4	6	43	0	0
oi	0	0	0	0	0	0	0	3	0
icd	0	0	0	0	0	0	0	97	0
k	2	0	10	0	11	5	0	0	9
hs	0	0	1	0	1	1	0	0	1

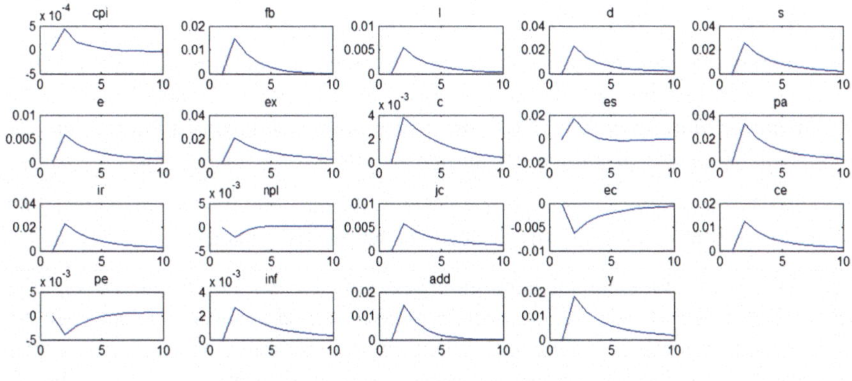

Fig. 7.5 Corresponding response to control variables for each random shock

7.3 China's Economic Structural Change and Long-Term Sustainable Development

7.3.1 The Main Problems Existing in China's Economic Growth

At present, there are some urgent problems needed to be solved in China's economic growth:

(1) The risk of further declining or large fluctuations in economic growth is greater

currently, with many domestic and international influence factors and the complex and changeful situation, China's economic and social transformation (Cui and Jiang 2011) is likely to impacted by multiple inflection points. Now, many inflection points start to appear, including the income gap inflection point between urban and rural (Lewis turning point: labor shortage, labor-force shortage, rising labor costs), the regional economic inflection point (advanced regional economic growth is relatively declining), pollutant emissions inflection point (Kuznets turning point: pollution emissions is declining), the savings rates inflection point (the savings rates begins to decline), the industrial structure inflection point (the proportion of secondary industry begins to decline), economic growth inflection point (economic growth rate begins to decline), and then the population quantity inflection point is coming (the peak of China's population is not far off). In this case, the importance of improving the combination of human capital and investment and the combination of independent innovation and investment would be increasing. However, as the economy cannot possibly operate in the path of rapid growth as before, it has entered the track of medium growth since 2013. Moreover, the rate of economic growth declines further and the economic growth is facing greater risks of volatility.

(2) The typical investment-driven extensive growth mode

By analyzing the contribution of several factors to economic growth in 2001–2012, it can be seen that the contribution of investment in physical capital and capital stock increase more than 70%, while the contribution of human capital is relatively small. This is typical of an investment-driven extensive growth mode.

(3) The efficiency of economic performance in recent years has not improved, and the quality of economic growth needs to be greatly enhanced

Since 2007, the efficiency of economic performance has not improved rapidly, which shows that if we are to further improve the allocation efficiency of the production resources in China and adapt to the economic restructuring under increasingly diversified conditions, we must deepen the reform in an all-round way. This is a new historical proposition faced to us.

(4) The combination degree among human capital, investment in physical capital and independent innovation is relatively low

Through the above calculation, we can see that innovation (broad innovation, including the innovation in technical change, human capital growth and institutions) plays an important role in economic growth on average. In 2000–2012, the average annual contribution of innovation to growth was 41%, while the contribution of human capital to economic growth in China showed a decreasing trend. The contribution of human capital decreased from an average of 22% in 1978–2000 to an average of 8% in 2001–2012, which required a further analysis.

Meanwhile, due to the distribution system and the incentive mechanism for talent growth and promotion, human capital is not fully utilized. For example, in recent years, due to the pulling function of real estate, marginal revenue of physical capital investment grows much faster than marginal revenue of human capital investment, which reduced the allocation efficiency of human capital and affected the full play of human capital.

Improving the combination of human capital, investment and independent innovations are an important channel for China's economic growth, which is an investment-innovation dual-driven growth method that relies on low-cost high-quality workforce and advanced technology. Therefore, improving the combination of human capital, investment in physical capital, and independent innovation is the theme of the transformation of China's economic development pattern. The national innovation system and its international development are important ways to promote this combination.

We should attach great importance to improving the combination of human capital and investment, and independent innovation, and give full play to the role of this combination in economic and social transformation.

Given the above analysis, the suggestion of this book about the problem to improve the contribution of human capital to China's economic growth is as follows: under the condition that the employment growth rate inevitable decline, improving the growth rate of average years of schooling of labors to compensate the decline of employment growth rate. Meanwhile, it is necessary to vigorous reform the talent system, the education system, the employment system and the science and technology system, similar to the financial system reform in the past few years. This reformation may need to take some program control methods, such as government provide some of the jobs with high capital intensity to some college students; government relief tax for the enterprises that received university students, and provide public rental house for college students, increase government venture capital fund, promote industry-university-research cooperative and so on.

(5) The problem of overcapacity still remains unresolved

In China, the problem of overcapacity in some industries has existed for a long time. The most representative one is the steel industry. If overcapacity cannot be effectively controlled, it will lead to a series of negative effects, such as a large amount of idle production equipment, excess inventory, falling prices and inefficiencies in the steel industry. In addition, the rapidly changing economic environment at home and abroad may exacerbate the overcapacity in the steel industry. Therefore, overcapacity has become a pressing issue.

(6) The risk of the financial crisis is still large

At present, the ratio of newly added M2 to GDP, the ratio of new loans to GDP is all in the normal range, while the actual difference of deposit-loan interest rates may be larger. The model only has a poor benchmark interest rates, but has a high capital adequacy ratio. Take above factors into account, the current fiscal and financial conditions are sound and in good condition. However, the risk of crisis lies in the rising rate of non-performing loans that may result from overcapacity. Therefore, overcapacity, such as steel industry, is the most important issue now.

(7) Industrial organization structure is scatter and low-concentration

Increasing industrial concentration by mergers and reorganizations, and reducing the prices of raw materials and basic industries are two key tasks of structural reform. In order to increase export competitiveness, low-cost competition is also a strategy. However, relevant enterprises should learn from Huawei that selling high-end products at the high price.

(8) China's growing economy is still at the expense of high energy consumption and environmental degradation

At present, China's economic growth is still at the expense of high energy consumption and environmental quality, which also gives us a warning that we must turn to an intensive development mode that is resource-saving, environmental-friendly and balanced population (Omri 2013).

(9) There still has a long way to go for structural reform.

In terms of the promotion effect of consumption, investment and export, the key task of structural reform is to shift from investment-oriented to driven by consumption, investment and export.

Increasing the impetus of exports to GDP growth lies not in the increase of the number of export products, but in brand, intellectual property, technology, and profitability—the increase of added value rate, especially the rapid growth of the mid-to-high-end industry and the cooperation among overseas investment and FDI and capacity of internationalization through the improvement of brand, intellectual property rights, technology and standards, should depend on the high-tech industries and mid-to-high-end industries instead of the low-end links (such as import processing, material processing and assembly), in this way can we solve the problem: China's total international trade is large, but its contribution to GDP is relatively small. The emphasis of solving this problem is on increasing the value-added rate of exports.

7.3.2 Optimal Design Methods of China's Sustained Economic Growth and Transformation from 2015 to 2020

The sustained growth and transformation of China's economic should change from the current economic growth pattern that mainly depend on capital-driven, high energy consumption intensity, high pollution level to a new economic growth pattern of investment-consumption balance, innovation-investment dual-drive, low-energy consumption intensity, low pollution level, low-carbon (Jiang 2012). The design of this new growth pattern (Liu 2013), in economics, first needs to build an optimization function by using the general equilibrium analysis method (Shen and Zhou 2013). The optimization function is as follows:

$$\max E\left[\sum_{t=0}^{\infty}\beta^t(\frac{(C_t)^{1-\eta}}{1-\eta}+\frac{(M_t/CPI_t)^{1-\xi}}{1-\xi}-\frac{L_t^{1+\zeta}}{1+\zeta})\right] \tag{7.32}$$

The relationship between investment and consumption can be described by the following equation:

$$Y = C + D + C_1 \tag{7.33}$$

Among it, C represents the consumption, D represents investment in physical capital and C_1 represents the volume of import and export. The relationship between investment in physical capital D and physical capital stock K is

$$\dot{K} = D - \delta K \tag{7.34}$$

That is $D = \dot{K} + \delta K$, and we obtain the following constraint condition:

$$\dot{K} = a(HL)^{\alpha}(SD/L)^{\beta} + bK + cHSD/K^2 + u - C - \delta K - C_1 \tag{7.35}$$

Now, according to Eq. (7.32), (7.34) and (7.35) to construct Hamiltonian function

$$H = \frac{C^{1-\eta}}{1-\eta} + \lambda_1(a(HL)^{\alpha}(SD/L)^{\beta} + bK + cHSD/K^2 + u - C - \delta K + C_1) \tag{7.36}$$

For the control variable C

$$\frac{\partial H}{\partial C} = 0 \tag{7.37}$$

Obtain that

$$\lambda_1 = c^{-\eta} \tag{7.38}$$

And according to the Euler's theorem, we obtain that

$$\dot{\lambda}_1 = \rho\lambda_1 - \frac{\partial H}{\partial K} \tag{7.39}$$

Obtain that

$$-\theta C^{-\eta}\frac{dC}{C} = \rho C^{-\eta} - C^{-\eta}(b - \delta - 2cHSD/K^3) \tag{7.40}$$

That is

$$\theta\frac{dC}{C} = b - \delta - \rho - 2cHSD/K^2 \tag{7.41}$$

$$\frac{dC}{C} = \frac{b - \delta - \rho - 2cHSD/K^2}{\eta} \tag{7.42}$$

If

$$cHSD/K^3 = \gamma = \text{constant} \tag{7.43}$$

Then

$$\frac{dS}{S} + \frac{dD}{D} + \frac{dH}{H} = 3\frac{dK}{K} \tag{7.44}$$

Under the above conditions, $\frac{dC}{C}$ is a steady-state constant, and if $\frac{dD}{D}$ is a constant, then $\frac{dY}{Y}$ would be a constant. Under the general equilibrium situation that economic structure is reasonable, one of the best choices is

$$\frac{dY}{Y} = \frac{dC}{C} = \frac{dD}{D} = \frac{dS}{S} = \frac{dK}{K} = \frac{b - \delta - \rho - \gamma}{\eta} \tag{7.45}$$

That is, output growth rate, consumption growth rate, investment growth rate, technology investment growth rate and physical capital growth rate are equal.

In the case of economic structure restructuring, an optimization option is

$$\frac{dS}{S} > \frac{dC}{C} > \frac{dY}{Y} > \frac{dD}{D} \tag{7.46}$$

And

$$\frac{dK}{K} > \frac{dD}{D} \tag{7.47}$$

7.3.3 Optimized Design for China in 2020

(1) The forecast of consumption growth rate

Use the following model to predict China's economic growth in 2020

$$Y = 0.00135(HL)^{0.803}(SD/L)^{0.228} + 0.176K + 1151HSD/K^2 - 10.4 \tag{7.48}$$

Model (7.48) is the same as the model (7.31). According to the model (7.48), $b = 0.176$, and the estimation of the average value of $1151HSD/K^3$ from 2013 to 2020 is 0.04; the depreciation rate $\delta = 0.09$; while ρ, θ, according to the estimation of Chen and Ruan (2009), $\rho = 0.03, \theta = 0.2$. Thus, we determine the value of various parameters of optical consumption growth rate:

$$b = 0.176, \delta = 0.09, \rho = 0.03, \theta = 0.2, 1151HSD/K^3 = 0.04$$

Then

$$\frac{dC}{C} = \frac{0.176 - 0.09 - 0.03 - 0.04}{0.2} = 8\% \tag{7.49}$$

Considering

$$\frac{dS}{S} = 10\% = \frac{dC}{C} = 10\% > \frac{dY}{Y} = 7.5\% > \frac{dD}{D} = 7.4\% \tag{7.50}$$

The changing trends of the elasticity coefficient of labor force to GDP from 1978 to 1981 showed a rapid rising. In subsequent years, it showed a rapid declining and then stable at around 0.2, and stabilized at about 0.1 from 1991 to 2012 (see Fig. 7.6).

Based on the changing trends of the elasticity coefficient of labor force from 1978 to 2012 (see Fig. 7.6), we can see that the coefficient has been stable at around 0.1 in recent years. Therefore, the next few years the coefficient is identified as 0.1, then the growth rate of labor force would be 0.8%.

The forecast of human capital growth rate in 2020 is 2.6%, then

$$\frac{dH}{H} = 2.6\% > \frac{dL}{L} = 0.8\% \tag{7.51}$$

In our design of China's economic growth in 2020, there are some basic assumptions as follows: first, the average annual growth rate of investment in

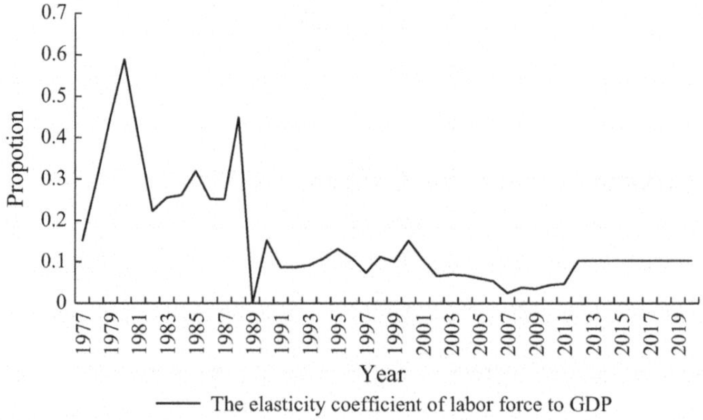

Fig. 7.6 The changing trends of the elasticity coefficients of labor force to GDP

research and development during the period 2013–2020 is 10%; second, the average years of schooling growth rate is 1.8%; while investment growth rate is 7.7%.

Under the above conditions, the simulation results of this book are: from 2013 to 2020, China's economic growth is 6–7%. Among them, the contribution of physical capital stock and investment in physical capital are 32 and 20% respectively; the contribution of science and technological progress and human capital are 27% and 20% respectively; the contribution of labor force is 2%; the contribution of institutional innovation is 5%, the impact rate of the economic externalities is −6%.

(2) The forecast of the ratio of research and development investment to GDP

In the competition of globalization, more and more examples had proven that technology would be a key factor for the success of international competition in the future. According to relevant statistics, the proportion of research and development funds in developed countries accounted for more than 2.5% of the GDP on average. In 2012, China's research and development (R&D) expenditures were 1024 billion yuan, rising up 17.9% over last year, accounting for 1.97% of GDP in 2012. And then, the proportion of China's research and development funds to GDP is steadily increasing year by year (see Fig. 7.7), and it is expected to reach about 2.5% by 2020.

(3) The evolution trends of investment rate

The investment rate improved rapidly during 1977–2002, and reached a high level of 43% in 1993. And then through a process of falling first and then rising, it was to reach at 65% by 2010. With the deepening of construction of innovative country, the investment rate in the period 2013-2020 would show a slight downward trend (Fig. 7.8).

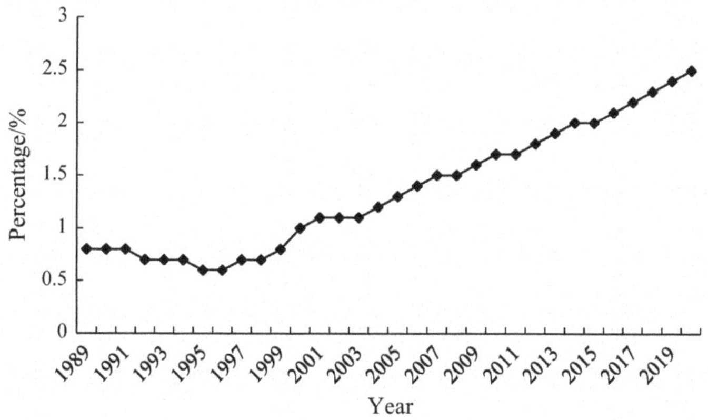

Fig. 7.7 The changing trends of the ratio of research and development funds to GDP (%)

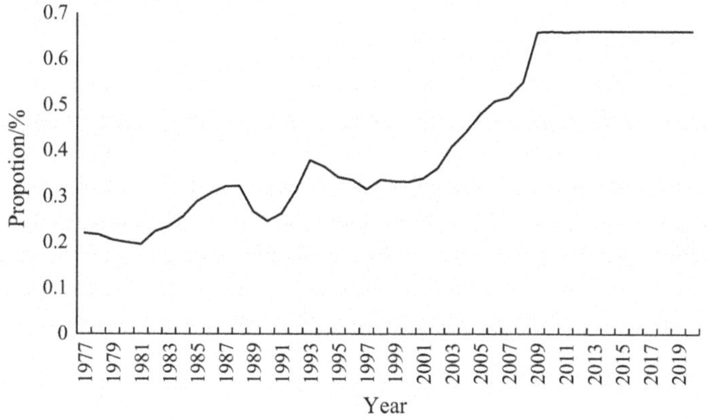

Fig. 7.8 The evolutionary trends of the rate of investment in physical capital from 1978 to 2020 in China (%)

(4) The evolution trends of the average years of schooling of laborers

China's the average years of schooling of laborers and labor productivity are always maintained at a steady growth. This shows that Chinese policies in recent years that prior to develop education and construct strong human resources initiatives play a significant role in it. As long as maintains a growth rate of 1.8%, China's the average years of schooling of laborers will be nearly 12 years by 2020 (see Fig. 7.9). Then, China will accelerate the transition of completing from a populous quantity country to a strong human resource country.

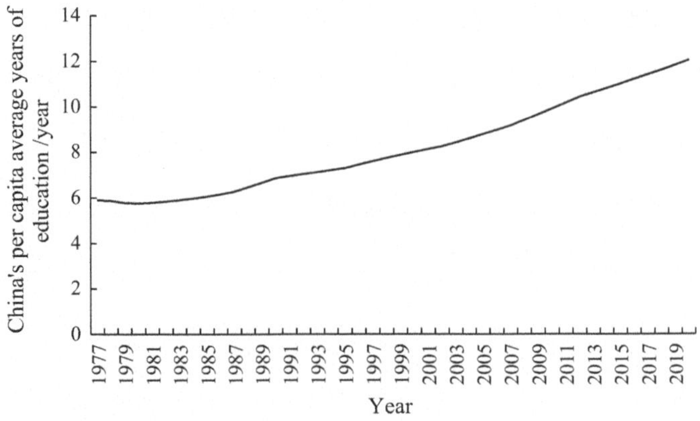

Fig. 7.9 The evolution trends of the average years of schooling of laborers in China from 1977 to 2020

(5) The proportion of the tertiary industry

In many countries, the proportion added value of the tertiary industry in GDP and the proportion of the number of employment in total labor force are in an arising trend. And the tertiary industry of the United States in 2020 is expected to account for 86.9% of GNP (Jing and Wang 2006). Compared with the production structure and employment structure of the three industries in the developed countries, the proportion of the tertiary industry in the production and employment structure in China is obviously low. According to the good trend of economic development in recent years in China and the change trend of the proportion of the three industry, it can be speculated that the proportion of the tertiary industry added value in China will be close to 60% of GDP in 2020 (see Fig. 7.10).

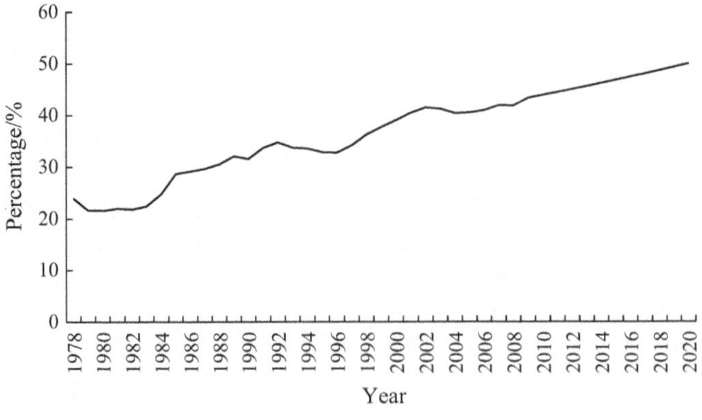

Fig. 7.10 The trend of the proportion of tertiary industrial added value accounted for GDP (%)

7.3.4 Forecast and Analysis of Energy Consumption and Pollutant Emission

7.3.4.1 The Prediction of Energy Consumption of China in 2020

This book predicts that China's energy consumption in 2020 will be 5.5 billion tons of standard coal. Since the reform and opening up, China has made remarkable achievements in economic development with the rising problems of resource consumption and increased carbon emissions. The total carbon dioxide in the first phase increased from 1.883 billion tons in 1978 to 3.281 billion tons in 1995, and the carbon dioxide emissions at this stage kept at a steady annual growth rate 4.9%. The second stage was from 1997 to 2002, carbon dioxide emissions were basically stable, and the total carbon dioxide emissions in 2002 was 3.65 billion tons, the average annual growth rate during this stage were 0.9%; The third stage was from 2003 to 2008, the carbon dioxide emissions had a rapid growth, and it reached at 6.897 billion tons in 2008 with an average annual growth rate of 11.3%. China's carbon dioxide emissions are keeping increasing in recent years which accused by other countries, especially the developed countries. However, as a new industrialized country, China's substantial increase in carbon emissions is based on rapid economic development as the background, China is now aware of the relationship between economic development and energy consumption, and now is along with the road of sustainable development. At the same time, China has made a positive contribution in increasing energy efficiency and reducing carbon dioxide emissions and other aspects. In 2015, the carbon dioxide emissions were 8.713 billion tons. In 2020, the carbon dioxide emissions are expected to 10.261 billion tons (see Fig. 7.11).

7.3.4.2 The Kuznets Curve in China

As for the prediction of the proportion of China's pollution control funding in GDP, the result of 2020 will be more than 1.9% (see Fig. 7.12). Thus, in order to achieving the set goals, reducing pollutant emissions, we must further increase the pollution control funding.

According to the relationship among pollution control funding, the proportion of research and development expenditure to GDP and the ratio of third industrial structure to GDP derived by the above model, we predict the volume of the pollution emissions by 2020.

According to the predicted changing trend of energy consumption and pollutant control funding, the pollutant emission as shown in Fig. 7.13, the discharge of pollutants reached the maximum emission value of 131.5 million tons in 2006, and then began to decline. In 2020, it will decrease to 115 million tons. China's pollution emissions show a typical Kuznets curve trend, which means that with the

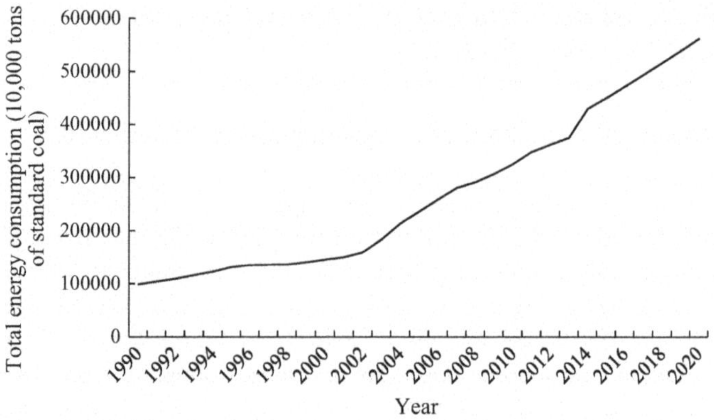

Fig. 7.11 Total energy consumption (10,000 tons of standard coal)

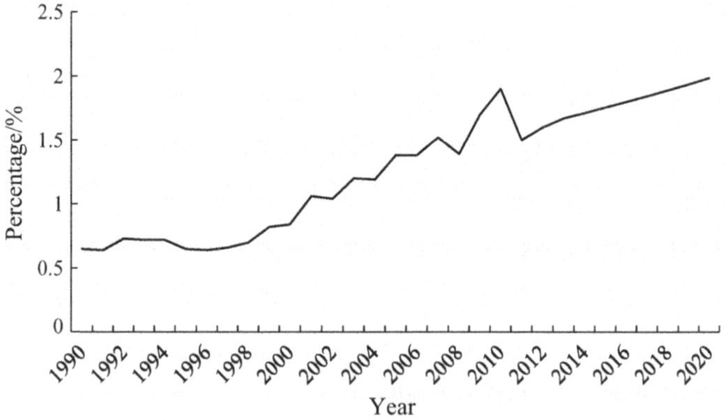

Fig. 7.12 The ratio of pollution control funding to GDP

economic development, the environment gradually deteriorates and then has an improvement. The Kuznets curve is of great significance to the development countries, especially the social economy in the transition period. In the early stage of economic development, resources and environment have enough affordability for the economic development, and the government's pollution control funding keep at a low level, that is why the pollutant emissions increased. With the further development of the economy, the awareness of prevention and control of pollution has been strengthened, then the environment will be a certain improvement. Kuznets curve has a very large reference value for China.

Fig. 7.13 The changing trends of pollutant emissions (10,000 tons)

7.4 Structural Reform and the Innovation-Driven Strategy

7.4.1 The Analytical Framework of Gradual System Reform of Dual Track

The analytical framework of this book is divided into five levels. The first level is "the overall design of the reform". The second level is "the four dimensions of the dual track reform". The third level is "driven by multiple motives", the fourth level is "the reform of all kinds of subjects", and the fifth level is "the political and social foundation of the reform", as shown in Fig. 7.14.

(1) The overall design of the reform

On the basis of accurately distinguishing the internal and external environmental conditions, emancipate the mind and seek truth from facts to develop a progressive dual-track reform program, and this way is leading by the strategic planning. The overall design of the reform is mainly reflected in the plenary sessions of the Central Committee, the National People's Congress and the Central Economic Work Conference of all previous years, in which the reports of the general secretary and the premier have all constantly revised and improved the program of reform and opening up. These programs have been implemented, deepened, substantiated and perfected through the "Five-year Plan for National Economic and Social Development" and various development plans, regional plans, and industrial revitalization plans. Through the promotion of scientific procedures which is obtained by Chinese-style economic reform experiment to lead the development of business, universities and other types.

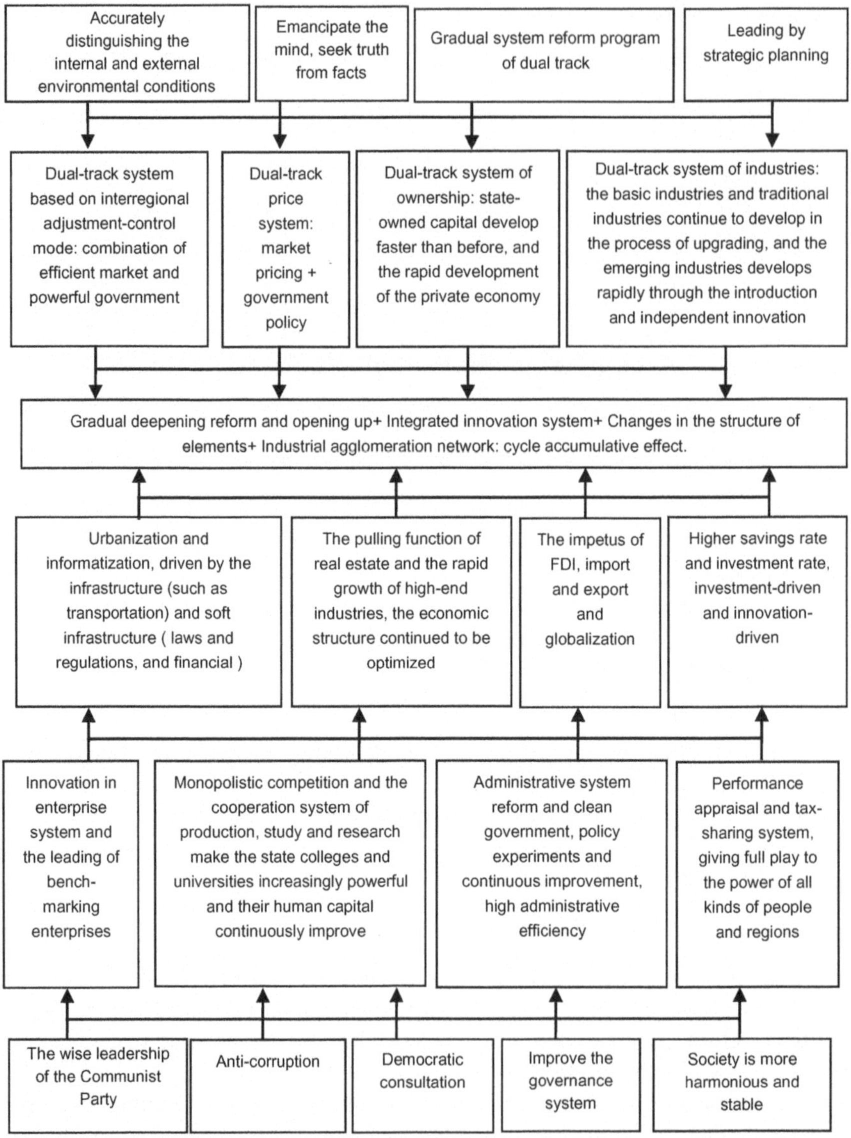

Fig. 7.14 The analysis framework of China's dual-track system of progressive institutional reform

(2) The four dimensions of a gradual, dual-track reform

The general feature of China's reform and opening up is a gradual dual-track reform, which is mainly reflected in the following four aspects: dual track system based on interregional adjustment and control mode: combination of efficient market and prominent government; dual-track price system: market pricing + government policy; dual-track system of ownership: state-owned capital develop faster than before and the private economy also develop rapidly; dual-track system of industries: the basic industries and traditional industries continue to develop in the process of upgrade, and the emerging industries develop rapidly through the introduction and independent innovation.

Gradual dual track reform is in line with China's national conditions, in particular, the price-based dual-track reform, as an innovative institutional arrangement in China's economic reform, it realizes the transition of the price formation mechanism of production materials from planning to markets. In the process of China's reform and opening up in the past 40 years, it has promoted the gradual establishment and formation of the socialist market mechanism, greatly reduced the cost of system reform, and it also maintained economic and social stability, and achieved rapid economic growth in China. At the same time, it also narrowed the gap with developed countries (Zhang 2014).

The policy of dual-track price system embodies the interaction among the spontaneous power of folk, the exploration of academic knowledge, high-level political decision-making and the impact on the reform. It can be seen that the smooth progress of the reform needs some conditions. First, we should respect the spontaneous creation of the people and dare to deny the current ideology and laws and regulations. Second, we should believe in the power of knowledge and use mature theories to analyze social problems. Third, considering the complexity of reality, we need to pay attention to tactics and pace, when implementing the reform. The success and failure in the process of the reform of the dual-track price system illustrate both of these positive and negative aspects (Yu 2008).

(3) The reform of various types of subjects

The establishment of a modern enterprise system is the main task of enterprise reform and innovation. More than 100 state-owned enterprises have rapidly developed into top 500 companies. The rapid rise of Huawei and other well-known private enterprises also played an important leading role. In the monopoly competition and under the institutional cooperation of industry, education and research, the reform has been deepened and the strength of scientific research has been rapidly improved. Universities, such as Tsinghua University and Peking University, have been successively ranked among the top 100 universities in the world, and the total human capital in the whole society has been constantly upgraded. Administrative reform has also been promoted, the government is relatively clean. Through continuous policy experiment and policy improvement, administrative efficiency has been continuously improved. The performance appraisal and the implementation of the tax-sharing system have fully mobilized the enthusiasm of various officials and the full development of the economic power in various regions.

The tax-sharing reform established the border between the central and local governments on the basic of border between the government and the market, and by structuring a shareholding system based on the principal taxes, it creates the framework of incentives that is necessary for the governance of a great nation. The strengthening of tax collection and management brings steady growth of fiscal revenue, which provides the necessary financial resources for public finance and market economy development. The affirmation of local interests by the tax-sharing system has promoted investment attraction and economic growth, and it has also shown a propensity for fiscal expenditure (Fu 2016). Regional competition among local governments has driven China's rapid economic growth. The centralized fiscal power brought by the tax-sharing system has gradually led local governments to a development mode dominated by land acquisition, development and transfer, thus forming land finance. Compared with the fiscal package system, the tax-sharing system is a rational system reform (Sun 2013), which established a stable and interactive framework for the relationship between the central and local governments. The land-centered urban expansion model is an important achievement of this reform.

(4) The driving force of sustained high growth

Investment in transportation and other infrastructure facilities has led to the development of real estate investment. With the promotion of urbanization and informatization driven by continuously adjustment of laws, regulations and the soft infrastructure, the economic growth has been greatly stimulated. At the same time, high-end industries, FDI, import and export are the driving forces for rapid growth.

The unbalanced development of the regional economy and the preferential development of the coastal areas with good conditions have played a leading role. In order to narrow the regional economic disparity and promote the coordinated economic development in the eastern, central and western regions, China started implementing the strategy of western development, revitalizing the northeast and the strategy of central China's rise from 1999. However, the gap between regional economic development has not been significantly narrowed. The analysis shows that the gap between regional economic development and the development of private economy shows a strong positive correlation (Hu 2006).

However, the research in this book shows that the dual-drive of investment and innovation (technological innovation and human capital innovation) is the main driving force of China's sustained and rapid economic growth from the perspective of economic growth factor analysis.

(5) Irreversible cycle cumulative effect

In the era of economic transition into a new normal, with the changes in international and domestic market conditions, the rise in factor costs and the enhancement of environmental constraints, the shift from factor-driven to innovation-driven is the direction for China's economic development, the transformation and upgrading of China's economy, and also is the inevitable choice of rejuvenation and development. Innovation-driven have the following four basic characteristics: (1) a continuously growing and innovative group and innovation base; (2) four types of catalytic elements: institutional mechanisms, policy guidance, innovative culture, young entrepreneurs; (3) five strong innovation and entrepreneurship abilities:

innovation input ability, talent pooling ability, achievement output and application ability, open network connection ability, external influence and radiation force; (4) with three relatively good environment for innovation and entrepreneurship: active investment and financing environment, the dissemination of innovative achievements, exchange and trading platform environment, efficient innovation and entrepreneurship public service system environment.

The strategy of "Gradual and deepening reform and opening up + integrated innovation system + structural transformation of elements + industrial agglomeration network" has formed an irreversible cycle of cumulative effects. The so-called hyper-cyclical agglomeration effect, according to the hypercycle theory proposed by Nobel laureate German physicist Manifoldgen (M. Eigen) in 1971, constitute the cycle which includes the interaction of various factors in the entire national economic system and the causal transformation. Hypercycle is a complex reaction cycle composed of multiple reaction cycles combined with each other. In the hypercycle system, each factor can not only copy itself (accumulation and accumulation), but also catalyze the development of other factors. Ultra-cycle can make all kinds of organizations more closely together, so that the system can continue to gather advantages (Cui and Shi 2011).

7.4.2 Structural Reform and the Improvement of Allocation Efficiency of Production Factors

In recent years, China has proposed a supply-side structural reform to improve the allocation efficiency of the elements (physical capital, labor force and human capital) from the perspective of economic structure. As shown in Table 7.9, the forward indicators include the urbanization rate of resident, informatization index, industrialization indicators (the proportion of tertiary industry), the export value/GDP, the proportion of equipment, fiscal budget revenue/GDP, fiscal expenditure/GDP, Gini coefficient of residents income, the proportion of corporate disposable income, R&D expenditure/GDP.

As shown in Table 7.10 the negative indicators include the employment rate of the primary industry, the ratio of the ex-factory price index to the purchase price index, the income gap between urban and rural areas, the asset-liability ratio, per capita income of the most backward five provinces/per capita income of the most advanced five provinces.

As shown in Table 7.11, as for the enterprise structure indicators that promote the resources allocation efficient of production factors, they include the export value/GDP, industry concentration, the size of each non-state-owned enterprise/the size of each state-owned enterprise.

Table 7.12 shows the weight of each index obtained by principal component analysis, in which the weight of negative structure index is negative, and the weight of corporate structure indicators and forward indicator is positive.

Table 7.9 Forward indicators (2020 and 2035 for the forecast value)

Year	The permanent residents urbanization rate	Information index	Industrialization index (the proportion of tertiary industry)	The proportion of equipment	Fiscal budget revenue/ GDP	Fiscal expenditure/ GDP	Resident income Gini coefficient	The ratio of enterprise disposable income	R&D expenditure/ GDP
1991	0.26	0.03	0.32	0.19	0.16	0.17	0.45	0.12	0.01
1995	0.29	0.17	0.33	0.19	0.10	0.11	0.37	0.14	0.01
2000	0.36	0.32	0.39	0.18	0.14	0.16	0.36	0.18	0.01
2005	0.43	0.54	0.41	0.19	0.17	0.18	0.31	0.18	0.01
2010	0.48	0.86	0.43	0.19	0.21	0.22	0.31	0.18	0.02
2011	0.51	0.74	0.43	0.25	0.22	0.23	0.32	0.17	0.02
2012	0.53	0.78	0.45	0.24	0.23	0.24	0.32	0.17	0.02
2013	0.54	0.78	0.46	0.24	0.23	0.25	0.33	0.17	0.02
2020	0.61	0.84	0.57	0.27	0.17	0.20	0.33	0.17	0.025
2035	0.75	1.5	0.65	0.28	0.18	0.21	0.3	0.17	0.04

Table 7.10 Negative structural indicators (relative value, 2020 and 2035 for the predicted value)

Year	The primary industry employment rate	The ratio of ex-factory price index to purchase price index	Urban-rural income ratio	The asset-liabilities ratio	Per capita incomes of the 5 most backward provinces/per capita income of the most advanced 5 provinces
1990	0.60	1.59	0.36	0.70	0.08
1995	0.52	1.38	0.39	0.65	0.06
2000	0.50	1.33	0.41	0.61	0.06
2005	0.45	1.18	0.49	0.58	0.05
2010	0.37	1.09	0.48	0.57	0.05
2011	0.35	1.06	0.48	0.58	0.06
2012	0.34	1.06	0.47	0.58	0.06
2013	0.31	1.06	0.47	0.58	0.06
2020	0.27	1.2	0.46	0.58	0.06
2035	0.1	2.5	0.6	0.55	0.2

Table 7.11 Variables of enterprise structure reform (relative value, predicted in 2020 and 2035)

Year	The export value/GDP	Industry concentration	The size of each non-state-owned enterprise/the size of each state-owned enterprise
1990	0.15	0.33	0.02
1995	0.20	0.40	0.08
2000	0.21	0.45	0.06
2005	0.33	0.38	0.06
2010	0.26	0.34	0.05
2011	0.26	0.43	0.05
2012	0.24	0.4	0.05
2013	0.23	0.39	0.06
2020	0.25	0.55	0.16
2035	0.25	0.65	0.3

In the model of allocation efficiency of production factors in Table 7.13, $FS(t)$ represents the sum of the forward structure indicators multiplied by the weighted scores, $NS(t)$ represents the sum of the negative structure indicators multiplied by the weighted scores, $QS(t)$ represents the sum of score of the enterprise structure index multiplied by the weight.

Table 7.12 The weight of each indicator

Index	The first principal component	The second principal component	The third principal component	Weights
The permanent residents urbanization rate	0.289	0.103	−0.009	0.188
Information index	0.287	0.057	−0.031	0.181
Industrialization index (the proportion of tertiary industry)	0.282	0.018	0.119	0.179
The export value/GDP	0.234	−0.244	0.045	0.120
The primary industry employment ratio	−0.275	−0.13	0.306	−0.171
The ratio of ex-factory price index to purchase price index	−0.281	0.003	0.335	−0.160
Income gap between urban and rural areas	−0.257	0.268	−0.192	−0.137
The proportion of equipment	0.162	0.512	−0.458	0.136
Fiscal budget revenue/GDP	0.26	0.286	0.272	0.199
Fiscal expenditure/GDP	0.259	0.268	0.304	0.197
The asset-liability ratio	−0.273	0.175	0.163	−0.144
Resident income Gini coefficient	0.281	−0.129	0.116	0.163
The ratio of enterprise disposable income	0.231	−0.34	0.269	0.116
Per capita income of the 5 most backward provinces/per capita income of the most advanced 5 provinces	−0.204	0.443	0.444	−0.064
R&D expenditure/GDP	0.265	0.25	0.232	0.197

7.4.3 China's Economic Restructuring Prospects by 2035 and the Innovation-Driven Strategy

7.4.3.1 China's Economic Restructuring Prospects by 2035

After the World War II, the United States underwent tremendous changes in its economic and social structure. In social structure, as a result of science and technological progress and the continuous improvement of agricultural productivity and industrial productivity, the proportion of the tertiary industry continued to rise from 59% in 1947 to 80% in 2016 (see Fig. 7.15). In particular, the share of knowledge-intensive services (including information services, finance and real estate, leasing, professional and technical services, technology services, education and literary arts services) increased rapidly from 27% in 1947 to 50% in 2016, and become the leading industry.

In the urban-rural structure, the urbanization rate has risen rapidly, from about 60% in 1947 to 75% in 1990; the proportion of cities with 100 million population increased from 27% in 1947 to 50% in 1990; in 1950, the population in

Table 7.13 The model of allocation efficiency of production factors

Dependent variable: θ_t				
Method: least squares				
Sample(adjusted): 1992–2013				
Included observations: 22 after adjusting endpoints				
Convergence achieved after 9 iterations				
Variable	Coefficient	Std. error	t-Statistic	Prob.
$\theta(t-1)$	0.63	0.13	4.7	0.0002
$FS(\mathrm{t}) * \mathrm{QS(t)/NS(t)}$	0.015	0.0069	2.2	0.0398
C	0.57	0.194	2.9	0.0089
$AR(1)$	0.29	0.234	1.24	0.2301
R-squared	0.868403	Mean dependent var	0.984	
Adjusted R-squared	0.84647	S.D. dependent var	0.03	
S.E. of regression	0.011583	Akaike info criterion	−5.9	
Sum squared resid	0.002415	Schwarz criterion	−5.7	
Log likelihood	69.07124	Durbin-Watson stat	1.25	
Inverted AR Roots	0.29			

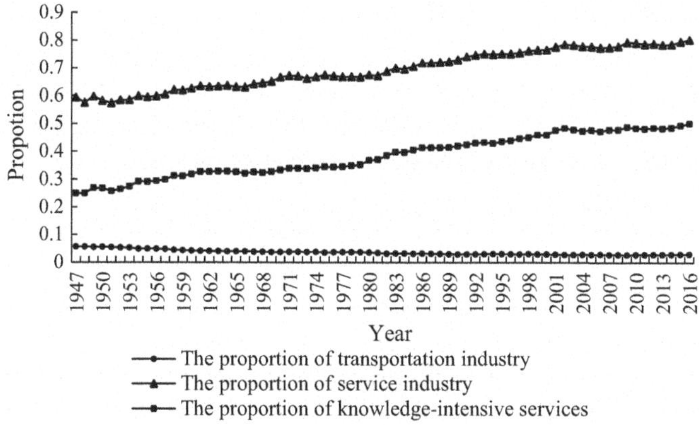

Fig. 7.15 Great changes in the industrial structure of the United States

northeastern United States accounted for 26% of the total population, and then down to 20% in 1990; in 1950, the proportion of the population in the central and western United States account for 29% of the total population, and then down to 24% in 1990; in 1950, the population of the southern United States accounted for 13% of the total population and rose to 21% in 1990; by 2020 and 2035, the main targets of China's economic restructuring are listed in Tables 7.9, 7.10, and 7.11. In the next 20 years, China's economic structure will undergo major changes, although China's economic structure will not reach the level of knowledgeable, post-industrialization and highly urbanization of the United States in 2010 through its economic structure by 2035.

7.4.3.2 The Innovation-Drive and Investment Interaction Strategy

(1) The trend of the factors' marginal rate of return: the necessity of the dual-drive strategy of innovation and investment

1. Formula for calculating the factors' marginal rate of return

China's economic growth model is as follows:

$$Y = aL^{\alpha}H^{\beta}S^{\gamma}D^{\delta} + bK + cSHD/K^2 + eD^2/L + u \tag{7.52}$$

Using model (7.52), the marginal return rate of labor, physical capital stock, investment in physical capital, research and development investment, and human capital can be measured by calculating the partial derivative of the gross domestic product (Y) to these elements.

Marginal rate of return of labor. Using model (7.52), taking partial derivative of Y with respect to L, and obtain the formula for calculating the marginal return rate of labor as

$$w = a_1(b_1 - b_2)(H)^{b_1}(SD)^{b_2}(L)^{b_1-b_2-1} - a_4\left(\frac{D}{L}\right)^2 \tag{7.53}$$

Marginal rate of the return of physical capital stock. Using model (7.52), taking partial derivative of Y with respect to K, and obtaining the formula for calculating the marginal rate of return r of physical capital stock is

$$R = \left[a_2 - 2a_3\frac{SDH}{(K)^3}\right] \tag{7.54}$$

Marginal rate of return of investment in physical capital. Using model (7.52), taking partial derivative of Y with respect to D_t, and obtaining the formula of marginal rate of return i_t on investment in physical capital as

$$i = a_1b_2(HL)^{b_1}\left(\frac{S}{L}\right)^{b2}(D)^{b_2-1} + a_3\frac{SH}{(K)^2} + 2a_4\frac{D}{L} \tag{7.55}$$

Marginal rate of return of research and development investment (science and technological progress). Using model (7.52), taking partial derivative of Y with respect to S, and obtaining the formula for calculating the marginal rate of return U_t on R&D investment as

$$u = a_1b_2(HL)^{b_1}\left(\frac{D}{L}\right)^{b2}(S)^{b_2-1} + a_3\frac{DH}{(K)^2} \tag{7.56}$$

Marginal rate of return of human capital. Using model (7.52), taking partial derivative of Y with respect to S, and obtaining the formula of marginal rate of return V on human capital as

$$v = a_1 b_1 (L)^{b_1} \left(\frac{SD}{L}\right)^{b2} (H)^{b_1 - 1} + a_3 \frac{SD}{(K)^2} \tag{7.57}$$

2. The evolution of marginal rate of return of various factors in China

Using the calculation Formulas (7.53)–(7.57) and the actual data of China in each year and the model (7.52), we can estimate the marginal rate of return of China's labor force, physical capital stock, investment in physical capital, research and development investment and human capital from 1978 to 2012, see Table 7.14 for details.

As can be seen from Table 7.14 and Fig. 7.16, the marginal rate of return of China's physical capital stock increased in scale from 1978 to 1990, fluctuating around 13% since 1990, and there was no decrease in returns to scale, which has become a favorable condition for attracting foreign investment in more than two decades. The marginal rate of return on investment in physical capital has been keeping at a one-sided declining trend since 1981, which shows that: first, the efficiency of investment in physical capital is declining; second, the influence of one-unit investment in physical capital for stimulating economic growth is declining, and the marginal rate of return on investment in physical capital has dropped to a very low level (down to 0.23 in 2012); third, the way of using the rapid growth of investment in physical capital alone to drive the economy growth is dangerous.

Table 7.14 The evolutionary trend of marginal rate of return of various factors in China (at 1990 prices)

Year	Marginal rate of return of labor	Marginal rate of return on physical capital stock	Marginal rate of return of investment in physical capital	Marginal rate of return of research and development	Marginal rate of return of human capital
1978	2.2	0.064	0.86	21	1.3
1980	2.7	0.053	0.91	24	1.4
1985	4.0	0.036	0.87	30	1.7
1990	5.0	0.140	0.65	30	1.4
1995	7.1	0.106	0.49	44	2.0
2000	9.5	0.146	0.38	47	2.4
2005	15.1	0.134	0.33	66	3.8
2010	24.7	0.122	0.27	103	6.1
2011	26.1	0.136	0.24	107	6.1

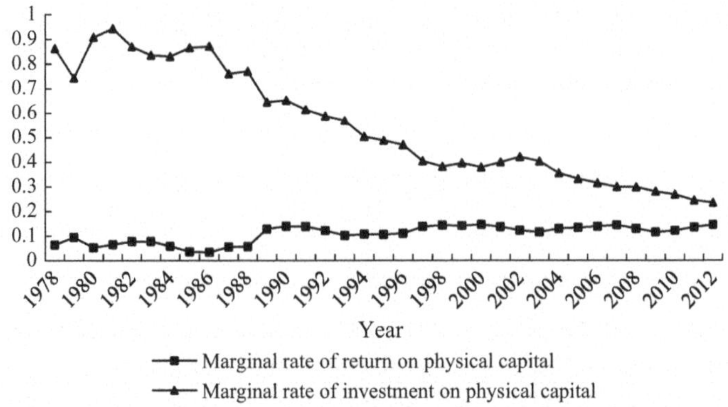

Fig. 7.16 Evolution of marginal rate of return on physical capital stock and investment in physical capital in China

The marginal rate of return of labor, research and development, and human capital are all increasing year by year. The marginal rate of return of labor in 2012 was 12.5 times as 1978; the marginal rate of return of human capital was 4.77 times as 1978; the marginal rate of return of research and development was 4.9 times as 1978; the rapid increase in marginal rate of return of labor indicate that China's labor market has gradually shifted from excess labor to labor shortages, and the wages of labor is increasing; the gradual increase in marginal rate of return of human capital and research and development input indicating that accelerating innovation (technology innovation, human capital innovation and institutional innovation) is not only necessary condition to change the unilateral stimulus of investment in physical capital, but increase research and development investment, human capital investment can also promote the marginal rate of return of investment in physical capital. This shows that, from the view of evolution of the marginal rate of return of various factors, adopting such an "innovation driven-interactive investment" strategy, which under the condition of innovation driven, the investment structure was adjusted and the investment efficiency was raised, and the investment growth rate remained basically stable, is not only necessary but also an inevitable trend.

According to the theory of the main driving force, Porter divided economic growth into four stages: the first stage is the factor-driven stage, the second stage is the investment-driven stage, the third stage is the innovation-driven stage and the fourth stage is the wealth-driven stage. *Chinese Regional Innovation Capability Report 2012*, funded by the Science and Technology Ministry and the National Soft Science Program, classifies the stage of economic growth as factor-driven, the transition from factor-driven to investment-driven, investment-driven, the transition from investment-driven to innovation-driven, and innovation-drive. According to the report's view, at present, the stage of economic development in China is in the transitional stage from investment-driven to innovation-driven. This study argues that at this stage, we should adopt the economic growth mode transformation strategy of innovation-driven—investment interaction, taking innovation as the primary driving force of economic growth. Although, the contribution of both investment in physical capital and physical capital stock is less than innovation, these factors also play an important role in stabilizing economic growth. We should maintain an appropriate growth rate of investment in physical capital, which lies in building a new system of investment, science and technology, and adjusting investment structure around innovation-driven investment so as to increase investment returns.

(2) The necessity, reality and importance of innovation-driven—investment interaction

1. Necessity

Under the environmental conditions that China have entered the upper middle-income level, if China continues to adopt the growth mode dominated by high investment growth, it will lead to the collapse of China's economy. The growth of investment is based on the growth of fiscal expenditure and money supply. From the view of money supply, M2 has risen sharply since 2009, bringing the money supply above its normal trend value, which resulted in that the government's fiscal expenditure also has to increase substantially. Along with this trend, once the international economic crisis happened, or the overcapacity happened, or the real estate prices fluctuates sharply, the economy would have a very serious crisis.

The share of investment in physical capital to GDP was 72% in 2012 and 78.6% in 2013. If the investment in physical capital increases at a rate of 12% per year and GDP grows at a rate of 7.5% per year, the share of investment in physical capital in GDP will reach at 105% by 2020, which means that serious inefficiencies and the investment risk arise. Studies of Li et al. (2012) showed that the investment rate in China's economy after 2002 is much higher than the investment rate at the time of maximizing social welfare. If the rate of investment is reduced and the efficiency of investment is improved at the same time, the rate of economic growth in China will not be a sharp decline.

Cai (2013) also showed that, with the rise of the "Lewis turning point" characterized by a shortage of labor and the rising wages, the diminishing phenomenon of returns to capital began to largely emerge, thus, relying on large-scale government-led investment to sustain economic growth will no longer be sustainable. Only by forming a policy environment of innovation-driven and obtaining higher efficiency from technology innovation and institutional improvement and the investment efficiency and investment returns be enhanced. However, Feldstein (2014) also pointed out that better policies and more new technologies can increase allocation efficiency of physical capital so as to increase production efficiency and achieve economic growth.

Keeping the economic growth rate at a reasonable range requires innovation-driven, and the proper rate of investment growth. For developed countries, the innovation-driven economy is a lower-growth economy. Taking the

United States as an example, an analysis of the factors of economic growth in the United States shows that the contribution of physical capital was only 35% during the 26 years from 1982 to 2008 (of which the contribution of physical capital stock growth was 24%, and the contribution of investment in physical capital growth was 11%), while the contribution of innovation was more than 50% (of which the contribution of human capital innovation was 19%, the contribution of science and technology progress was 23% and the contribution of system innovation was 10%). The contribution of labor force to economic growth was 8%, and the impact rate of economic externalities was 5%. This is a typical innovation-driven growth model. However, during the 26 years, the average economic growth rate was only 3.15%. The contribution of physical capital was −26% in Japan during the 16 years from 1993–2009 (of which the contribution of physical capital stock growth was 10% and the contribution of investment in physical capital was −36%), while the contribution of innovation was close to 100% (of which human capital contribution was 17%, the contribution of science and technological progress was 86% and the contribution of institutional innovation was −5%). The contribution of labor force to economic growth was −1%, and the impact rate of economic externalities was 28%. This is also a typical innovation-driven growth model, but the average rate of economic growth was only 0.75% during the 16 years.

In the case of developed economy, the rate of investment growth determines the rate of economic growth, and innovation determines the quality of economic growth. The steady and reasonable range of economic growth rates (e.g. 6.5–7.5%) requires the support of the corresponding investment growth rate. If we only rely on innovation, our economic growth rate will not exceed 5%. On the contrary, if we continue the previous investment-driven mode, the average rate of economic growth in the next 10 years will not exceed 5%, which maybe grow at a relatively high rate a few years and then fall below 5% in a few years.

The analysis of the economic growth factors of 15 countries, such as the United States and Japan, shows that the contribution of innovation is not linear with the rate of economic growth, but appears opposite trend with economic growth. The contribution of physical capital investment is basically linear with the economic growth rate, which shows that the growth rate of investment in physical capital is the first factor that determines the level of economic growth. This is a common rule of economic growth theory. The direct reason that Japan's economy stagnated after 1991 is the decline of investment in physical capital. The underlying reason is that Japan's economic system and mechanism is not suitable. Therefore, the innovative-drive must be combined with the adjustment of investment structure and the steady growth rate of investment so as to increase investment returns and avoid the fluctuation of investment.

2. Reality

If only driven by innovation, and there is no interaction between investment and innovation, and if investment growth rates is not stable, then, China's economic growth rate will decline significantly. It will take time for China to build itself into an innovation-oriented country, and its creativity is not strong enough. *The National Innovation Index Report 2013,* completed by China Science and Technology Development Strategy Institute, shows that China's innovation capability is steadily rising. China's National Innovation Index (NIS) ranks 19th among the 40 major countries in the world and increased by 1 than 2012. Research and experimental development (R&D) expenditures in 2013 amounted to 1.1986 trillion yuan, accounting for 2.09% of the GDP. The construction standard of innovative countries is that R&D accounts for more than 2.5% of GDP, the contribution of innovation exceeds 50%, the average years of schooling of laborers is more than 12 years and the rate of technology autonomy is over 60%. Judging from the construction standards of these innovative countries, China can enter the ranks of an innovative country by about 2025.

China's per capita GDP, per capita physical capital formation and technological level are still far behind those developed countries, and there is still some space for growth in the formation of per capita physical capital, as shown in Fig. 7.17.

Japan surpassed the United States in terms of physical capital per capita in 1970, and since then, Japan has ended its high growth. After reaching to 160% of US physical capital per capita in 1991, Japan's physical capital per capita began to decline and fell to only 90% of the United States in 2011. While during the 20 years from 1991 to 2011, the average rate of economic growth in Japan was only 0.7%. The ratio of China's per capita physical capital formation to the per capita physical capital formation in the United States is equivalent to Japan's 1967 level in 2011. There is still some space for growth in the process of formation of per capita physical capital in China. However, it is not eager to raise the level of per capita physical capital formation in China (rising rapidly in recent years), or repeat Japanese mistakes.

Figure 7.17 shows the evolution of the ratio of physical capital stock per capita in Japan to physical capital stock in the United States measured at the exchange rate

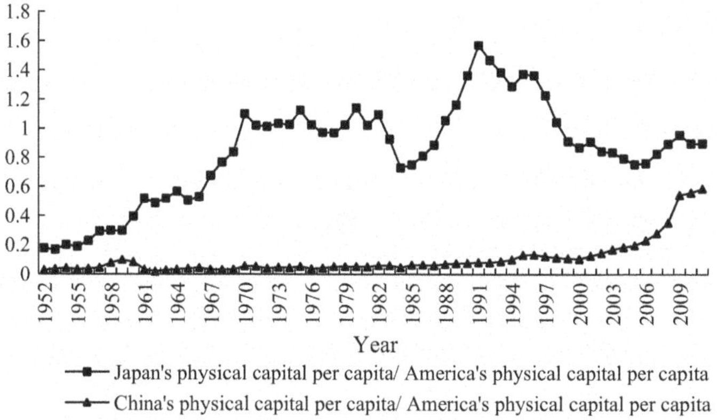

Fig. 7.17 China and Japan per capita physical capital formation compared to the United States (according to purchasing power parity)

(2005 constant-price U.S. dollar), and the evolution of the ratio of China's per capita physical capital to the per capita physical capital stock in the United States.

If the calculation of purchasing power parity exaggerates China's per capita physical capital formation, the calculation based on the exchange rate, to some extent, has underestimated the formation of physical capital per capita in China. By compromising two approaches, China's per capita physical capital formation in 2013 was equivalent to about 40% of the United States, and equivalent to Japan's level in 1961, so there is still room for improvement. In this way, the growth rate of investment in physical capital in China can still be maintained at a relatively high level by 2025. The simulation analysis, based on the economic growth model (7.52), established in this paper shows that while the economy is driven by innovation (the contribution of innovation to economic growth is greater than 55%), and at the same time, if the growth rate of investment in physical capital remains at 8–12%, the China's economy will be able to maintain an average annual growth rate of 6.5–7.5% from 2015 to 2025.

3. Importance

Whether the sustainable growth of investment demand can be sustained depends critically on creativity (Liu 2014b), or it will be hard for large amounts of physical capital to find effective investment opportunities without new products and new technologies. Investment is also important for speeding up the process of new urbanization, new-type industrialization and agricultural modernization in advanced industries, strategic emerging industries, energy-saving and emission-reduction, modern agriculture, energy and infrastructure, upgrading and transformation of traditional industries.

Innovation-driven and investment interaction will speed up China's economy shifting from an economic growth pattern of high energy consumption and polluting to a new investment-consumption growth mode with the equilibrium condition between investment and consumption low intensity of consumption, low pollution and low carbon emission (Jiang 2012). Studies of Chinese and foreign scholars show that innovation has an "anti-cyclical nature", and that the effective combination of investment and innovation can withstand the impact of economic fluctuations at home and abroad and effectively prevent the economic crisis well.

4. Strategic objectives

The improvement of human capital combined with the investment in physical capital and independent innovation is one of the major themes for China in transforming its economic development mode (Cui and Jiang 2011), while building an innovative country is an important way to promote this combination. In the process of building an innovation-oriented country, the share of China's R&D expenditure in GDP will steadily increase year by year, and by calculation it will reach at about 2.5% by 2020. By 2020, the average years of schooling of laborers in China will reach at about 12 years. China has a higher number of educated people, which has ranked top of the world, and China will speed up its transformation from a populous nation to a talent power (Li and Xia 2013).

Under the above conditions, according to the model (7.52), the simulation results of this paper, while using data from 2015 to 2030, shows that the reasonable range of China's economic growth rate is 6.5–7.5%. In terms of the economic growth rate of 7%, the contribution of physical capital stock and investment in physical capital is 27 and 19%, and the contribution of science and technological progress and human capital is 34 and 19%, and the contribution of labor force is 2%, and the contribution of institutional innovation is 5%, and the impact rate of economic externalities is −6%. Economic growth has shifted to the track of interaction of innovation and investment. This requires that further deepening the reform in an all-round way, carrying out institutional innovations, further increasing the resource allocation efficiency of production factors (Lin and Su 2012) and adapting itself to the increasingly diversified economic transformation environment under the conditions of globalization, which is a new historic proposition faced by China.

(3) The implementation of innovation-investment dual-drive strategy

About the implementation of innovation-driven interactive investment strategy, the paper made the following suggestions:

1. Accelerating the reform of investment, technology innovation, and building a new mechanism of innovation-driven interaction

Accelerating the reform of the investment system. The investment behavior in some places has caused the irrational investment structure of the entire country, which has a close relationship with the fiscal and taxation system and the promotion assessment mechanism (Zhang 2013). Therefore, we need to reform and improve the fiscal and taxation system and the promotion assessment mechanisms. By breaking the administrative monopoly and market monopoly, we can lower the threshold of private capital, reform the main body of state-owned investment, vigorously foster investors in non-public sectors of economy, develop a mixed ownership economy, enhance the functions of intermediary organizations and promote the equal competition of all types of investors according to the law. And through the innovative of investment and financing, regulating the issuance of local government debt, project bidding, tax relief and financial support, can we stimulate the vitality of private investment. Hsu (2014) used large data sets of 32 developed and emerging countries to analyze the impact of financial market developments (such as capital markets and credit markets) on technology innovation. High-tech industries in capitalist countries have shown a high level of innovation. However, the development of credit markets in emerging countries appears to hinder innovation. Our country accelerates financial system reform and financial innovation by the adjustment of financial policies, the innovation of financial intermediation services and the innovation of financial products. We should adjust the distribution of bank credit resources and support the combination and interaction of innovation and investment, encourage commercial banks to investment in private equity or investment companies, venture capital funds, technology incubators and other technology innovation platform. We deploy the innovation chain around the industry chain, improve the capital chain around the innovation chain, and create an open and collaborative and efficient innovation ecosystem.

Speeding up the reform of science and education system. The reform of science and technology system was carried out in response to the problems of the combination of innovation and investment structure being not close enough, the backwardness of science and technology management system, the diversification of investment in science and technology, the low degree of openness and sharing, and the inefficient use of resources (Wan 2014). China will gradually establish an organizational implementation mechanism, such as "enterprise decision-making, prior investment, collaborative research, market acceptance and government subsidies".

By facing the whole industry chain, constructing an organizational mechanism and operational system for synergistic innovation of CEEUSRO: adopting the synergistic and progressive organizational structure involved with governments, financial institutions, universities, research institutes and industries, we form a "three powers separation" governance mechanism for investors, scholars and managers, and form a transnational innovation network dynamic adjustment and optimization mechanism, form an operating mechanism of intellectual property rights based on patent pool, form an international resource allocation and linkage mechanism, form an international standards of distribution mechanism, and so on.

The vitality of an enterprise comes from the interaction between technology innovation and institutional innovation. Technology innovation and institutional innovation can be conducted simultaneously, in succession, or in different combinations. Large and medium-sized enterprises should establish and improve the intellectual property system, organizational system, decision-making system, supervision system, investment system, cooperation system, information system as well as training system, appointing system, appraisal system and distribution system for technological innovation.

Innovation is the process of multi-agent participation and multi-factor interaction. The creativity of an enterprise is inseparable with the social environment. Whether the acquisition of innovative resources or the carrying out of innovative activities, both need to rely on this social environment. In the whole process of innovation, innovation involved with enterprises, universities (research institutes), governments, intermediaries, business associates (upstream enterprises and service providers, downstream users, competitors, factors provider), external innovator (such as innovators outside the enterprise) and other entities, and also involved with the various elements of talent, capital, technology, raw materials, resources, and outsourcing. All kinds of subjects are in contact with each other inseparably. With the improvement of enterprise creativity, the technological content, the risks and benefits of physical capital investment will increase, and the corresponding demand for funds, policies, talents will also be higher and the dependence on the environment will be higher. Therefore, it is important to create a good multi-agent synergistic system for enterprises. The multi-agent synergistic system in the regional innovation and entrepreneurship center is composed of regional innovation system (enterprise + university + institute + government + agency + finance) and external innovators (international agencies or enterprises), business associates (upstream and downstream, factor providers, customers) built in the interaction.

2. Strengthen the government's macro-control, and effectively manage the duplication of investments and overcapacity at a low level of technology

The reason for overcapacity in some industries is the lack of new products and technologies that have good economic returns and the lack of new investment opportunities. The falling technical level has lowered the entry barrier to the industry (Wang and Gao 2012), many investors (probably with the support of local governments) invest almost simultaneously in hot spots in the absence of the necessary information, and then lead to a "surge" (Lin et al. 2010): there is consensus among many investors about the "good prospects" in some industries, triggering a flood of businesses and funding into one or more industries almost at the same time. However, during the process of investment and establishment of factories, it is difficult for all enterprises in the industry to coordinate with each other, and it is difficult to count the total amount of investment information, resulting in the occurrence of overcapacity afterwards. In addition, resulting in that enterprises in the industry generally start to work insufficiently, the prices of products fall, business bankruptcy and other serious consequences.

In accordance with the principle of combining government macro-control with the efficient allocation of investment resources in the market, China adopted a wide range of macro-control measures based on the actual situation of China as a rapidly developing major power, and adopted different policies in different industries and in different regions. In the industries that may have the issue of overcapacity, real estate and other industries, government need to strengthen the macro-control of the central government. While in the strategic emerging industries, high-tech industries, government should give full play to the initiative of localities and markets, and in particular, give full play to the initiative of the private economy.

3. Combining independent innovation with technological transformation and structure adjustment of investment in physical capital

Levena et al. (2014) compared the innovation efficiency among 35 countries from 2007 to 2011. Research shows that the efficiency of innovation depends on the combination level of technological innovation and investment in physical capital. However, Caiani (2014) used the post-Keynesian approach to analyze the effect of promotion, feedback and interaction between the real economy and the financial sector in the process of bringing innovation into the economy, and then analyze the relationship among technological innovation, market demand and investment behavior.

Constructing the close relationship between technology innovation, market demand and investment behavior starting from the source of the industrial chain, based on independent innovation, enterprise combines independent innovation and corresponding investment in physical capital in the process of product architecture design, key modules (including the production of raw materials), deep processing to assembly, synthesis and marketing services to improve the share of proprietary technology, materialized technical progress and embodied technological advancement in investment in physical capital. At the same time, we should deal with the issue of cross-industry cooperation and their multiple governance issues.

Promoting the integration of independent innovation with international technology trade, advanced equipment trade and undertaking international projects. Through those approaches (such as the internationalization of technology markets, establishing various types of public science and technology service platforms, speeding up the connection between foreign trade enterprises and domestic and overseas capital markets, to adjust the relationship between the introduction of foreign investment, foreign advanced equipment trade and independent innovation. We should give full play to the advantages of Chinese science and technology and talents, organize enterprises and research institutes to export their products, equipment and related production technologies and technologies with independent intellectual property rights to other countries, and also introduce advanced technologies and products from other countries to create a broader national innovation system with international space for development.

We should give full play to the role of economic tools in enhancing the capability of independent innovation, adjusting the structure of investment, and improving investment efficiency. We should also give full play to the advantages of the distribution of state-owned banks across the country, banks should do not provide loans for the enterprises that easy to cause overcapacity, not meet the standards of energy-saving emission reduction and not conducive to technological innovation. We should provide more funds to the traditional industries of transformation and upgrading, speed up the development of new industries, speed up the development of modern service industries, the reconstruction of shantytowns, the construction of central and western railways and urban infrastructure, wind power, hydropower, photovoltaic power generation and coastal nuclear power construction, especially the strategy emerging industries, science and technology, education, medical care, culture, energy conservation and environmental protection, ecological environment, health and pension services, tourism and other projects.

4. Innovation-drive in the eastern advanced regions, and the investment-drive in the central and western regions

Chinese Regional Innovation Capacity Report in 2012, funded by the Ministry of Science and Technology and National Soft Science Program, classify various provinces and cities into four categories: Shanghai, Beijing and other areas has entered the stage of innovation-driven; Shandong, Hubei and Liaoning are transitioning from investment-driven to innovation-driven. Most of the central and western regions are in investment-driven or factor-driven phase. Therefore, it is necessary to combine innovation-driven in the eastern advanced regions with investment-driven in the central and western regions according to local conditions, which needs to achieve the integration and linkage of technology, investment and human resources in the eastern, central and western regions.

5. Speeding up the internationalization of the national innovation system and building up a strong power for science and technology

To achieve the change of the mode of technology innovation from the introduction-digestion and absorption-innovation to integrated innovation and independent innovation, we need to accelerate the internationalization of the national innovation system, and establish some new science and technology policy, and with the existing science and technology laws, regulations, and policy measures, constitute the multi-dimensional system of science and technology policies and regulations that are in line with the international standards. Among the reform of science and technology system, science and technology investment policy, tax policy, financial policy, government procurement, international cooperation policy in science and technology, innovation service internationalization policy, international technology market and international technology trade policy, international personnel policy, international intellectual property protection and management policy, science and technology reward system and so on, need to set up science and technology policy system in corresponding to the internationalization of national innovation system.

The six main actors of the national innovation system are the enterprise sector, the university sector (including independent research institutes), the government sector, the financial sector, the intermediary sector and the external sector related to international technology transfer, technology trade, etc. Based on related theory, we build the innovation behavior model of these six departments. Combining the expected utility function with the innovation behavior models of six departments and the volatility models of random variables, finally form the basis of the DSGE model system. On this basis, the model is solved and the model parameters are determined by the Bayesian method and econometric method. The combined analysis of stochastic shocks shows that compared with GDP and government investment in R&D, there will be a rapid increase in research and development funds of the whole society, the use of R&D funds in the enterprises and new product sales revenue, and the marginal cost of patents will grow faster. As a result, the growth rate of Chinese patent grants will be moderately reduced, while the number of international patents granted by China will accelerate its growth. By 2025, the number of papers published in China counted by international authorization (such as SCI) will account for more than 20% of the world's totals, China will receive more than 150,000 international patents, and the ratio of research and development funds to GDP will exceed 3%, while the number of personnel engaged in research and development will reach over 7 million, thus, China will develop from a science and technology country to a technological power (Table 7.15).

The first transition of China's economy: from factor-driven to investment-driven. From 1953 to 1976, China's economy belonged to a factor-driven growth mode that relied on the accumulation of laborers and physical capital. The contributions of human capital and labor force to economic growth reached at 42 and 23%

Table 7.15 Prediction of development of variables of national innovation system based on DSGE model

State variables and control variables of national innovation system	In 2010	In 2020	In 2025	Stochastic variables of national innovation system	In 2010	In 2020	In 2025
Invention patents acquired in China (Item)	79,767	199,418	250,000	GDP (trillion yuan)	36	75	100
Research and development funding (100 million yuan)	7062	18,755	32,372	Government investment in science and technology (100 million yuan)	3818	11,454	22,908
Enterprise R&D investment (100 million yuan)	5084	13,691	23,955	Technology introduction (100 million yuan)	386	800	1500
R&D personnel (10 thousand people)	255	537	876	Continuous innovation rate	0.88	0.95	0.95
New product sales revenue (100 million yuan)	72,864	200,134	336,000	Technology market turnover (100 million yuan)	3907	10,158	15,000
International paper ratio	0.117	0.16	0.27	Innovation system	0.72	0.73	0.74
International patent (item)	15,505	105,000	239,000	International R&D personnel per 10,000 staff (per person/million)	95	120	150
The ratio of technology output to technology introduction	0.61	1.5	1.5	The ratio of high-tech import to export ratio	1.2	2	3
The cost of each patent (10 thousand yuan)	319	560	777	The ratio of CEEUSRO cooperation papers	6.6%	8%	10%
R&D personnel costs (10 thousand yuan)	26	33	36	The ratio of CEEUSRO cooperation patents	4.9%	7%	8%

(continued)

Table 7.15 (continued)

State variables and control variables of national innovation system	In 2010	In 2020	In 2025	Stochastic variables of national innovation system	In 2010	In 2020	In 2025
R&D funds used by enterprises (100 million yuan)	5105	18,006	23,000	The ratio of international paper of cross-agency cooperation	68%	70%	75%
High-tech industry output (100 million yuan)	74,709	123,719	184,494	The proportion of patents granted by foreign applicants in China to the total amount authorized by China	41%	35%	30%
				Venture capital investment (100 million yuan)	2407	8500	12,750
				FDI (billion yuan)	7367	10,000	12,000

respectively, which together accounted for 65% of the total. The growth of human factors became the primary drive force. The contribution of physical capital stock growth was 28%, that of investment in physical capital growth was 20%, while the contribution of science and technological progress and institutional innovation was negative.

China's economy turned to investment-driven from 1978 to 2012. The contribution of the growth of physical capital stock reached at 39.5%, the contribution of investment in physical capital growth was 27.7%, and the sum of these two was 67.2%. The contribution of human capital was 20.3%; the contribution of science and technology progress was 22%; the contribution of the institutional innovation was 8%, and the contribution of these three factors together was 50.3%.

The second transition of China's economy: turning to the mode of innovation-driven and interacting with Investment. In this paper, we use the established model of economic growth and draw lessons from relevant studies of domestic and foreign scholars, to predict that from 2015 to 2030, the reasonable range of China's economic growth rate will be 5.5–7.5%. In terms of economic growth rate of 7%, the contribution of innovation (the contribution of science and technological progress and human capital will reach at 34 and 19%, and the contribution of institutional innovation will be 5%) adds up to 58%. The combined contribution of physical capital stock and investment in physical capital was accounted to be 46% of the total. The China's economy will turn to the mode of innovation-driven and interactive growth path.

Under the conditions of entering the upper middle-income level, the growth mode dominated by high investment growth has been unsustainable. In the absence of new products and processes, there is a lack of investment demand and opportunities, and can only invest in low-tech which would trigger the overcapacity, so as to the fluctuation of economic cycles, therefore, there is a need of innovation-drive. However, if the economy is driven by innovation alone, and there is no interaction between investment and innovation, and the investment growth rate does not remain basically stable, thus China's economic growth rate will reduce sharply. Therefore, it is necessary to implement the strategy of China's economic transformation of innovation-driven and investment interaction and combine innovation-driven with adjustment of investment structure, stabilization of investment growth and enhancement of investment returns.

7.5 Summary

Structural reform and institutional innovation have played a powerful role in promoting economic growth. Since the reform and opening up, the China's economy has created a miracle of sustained high-speed, medium to high-speed growth for more than 40 years. The gradual structural reform of China's economic dual-track system is the result of five levels of synergy (the overall design of the reform, the four dimensions of the dual-track reform, the pulling and driving layers of multiple dynamics, the reform behaviors of various entities, and the political and social basis of reform).

For the structural reform that promote the improvement of allocation efficiency of production factors, the positive indicators include the urbanization rate of permanent residents, information index, and industrialization index (the proportion of tertiary industry), total exports/GDP, the proportion of equipment, fiscal budget revenue/GDP, fiscal expenditure/GDP, residents' income Gini coefficient, the proportion of disposable income of enterprises, R&D expenditure/GDP; The negative structural indicators include the employment ratio of the primary industry, the ratio of the ex-factory index to the purchase index, the urban-rural income gap, the asset-liability ratio, the ratio of per capita income of the most backward five provinces to the per capita income of the five most advanced provinces; The corporate structure indicators include total exports/GDP, industry concentration, the size of each non-state-owned enterprise/the size of each state-owned enterprise. Quantitatively, structural reform is to adjust these indicators.

When we implement the innovation-driven and investment interaction strategy, the key is to promote the institutional innovation by comprehensively deepening reform, construct the new investment system and the new science and technology system, and promote the combination of technology innovation and human capital innovation and investment, combine the government's macroeconomic control with market regulation, combine innovation-drive in the eastern advanced regions with the investment-drive in mid-west regions together, and fully use the economic means (such as financial, fiscal, monetary), strive to solve the issue of low technical level in traditional industry, the issue of the excess investment and the issue of lacking inadequate investment in strategic emerging industries and knowledge intensive services, etc.; we should further emancipate the mind, seeking truth from facts, according to China's current national conditions and environmental conditions, we should not imitate the American market economy mode, but carry out the Chinese characteristic socialist market economy mode, and combine the macro regulation with market mechanism better, and we should appropriately enhance the function of central government on the issue of excess capacity in traditional industries (such as real estate, steel and other industries), and promote the transformation of the traditional industries; accelerating the internationalization of the national innovation system, and achieving the transformation of technological innovation from the introduction-digestion and absorption-innovation to integrated innovation and independent innovation.

References

Bertinelli, L., & Black, D. (2004). Urbanization and growth. Journal of Urban Economics, 56(1), 80–96.

Berry B.J.L. (1981). Comparative urbanisation: divergent paths in the twentieth century[M]. London: Macmillan.

Cai, F. (2013). How China's economic growth turns to total factor productivity driven. Chinese Social Sciences, (1), 56–71.

Caiani, A., Godin, A., & Lucarelli, S. (2014). Innovation and finance: a stock flow consistent analysis of great surges of development. Journal of Evolutionary Economics, 24(2), 421–448.

Chen, Y.L., & Ruan, S.F. (2009). China's consumer intertemporal elasticity of substitution and savings analysis. Science and Technology of West China, (2), 68–68.

Cheng Dening (2007). Urbanization, Increasing Returns and Economic Growth. Nandu Tribune: Journal of Nanyang Normal University, (1): 131–136.

Cheng Kaiming (2009). Urbanization, Technological Innovation and Economic Growth: An Empirical Study Based on the Effect of Innovation Intermediary. Statistical Analysis, (5): 40–46.

Cui, X., & Jiang, Z.H. (2011). Contribution of human capital in China's economic growth. Science and Technology Management, 32 (12), 168–172.

Cui, Y., & Shi, L. (2011). Study on cost control hyper cycle model of third party logistics. China Logistics and Purchasing, (5), 66–67.

Eaton, J., & Eckstein, Z. (1997). Cities and growth: theory and evidence from France and Japan. Regional Science & Urban Economics, 27(4), 443–474.

Feldstein, M. (2014). How to achieve stronger US growth. Journal of Policy Modeling, 36(4), 649–53.

Forni, L., Monteforte, L., & Sessa, L. (2009). The general equilibrium effects of fiscal policy: Estimates for the Euro area. Public Economics, 93(3), 559–585.

Fu, M.J. (2016). Twenty years of tax sharing system: evolutionary vein and reform direction. Sociological Research, 31(05), 215–240 + 245–246.

Henderson, V. (2003). The urbanization process and economic growth: the so-what question. Journal of Economic Growth, 8(1), 47–71.

Hsu, P.H, Xuan, T., & Yan, X. (2014), Financial development and innovation: Cross-country evidence. Journal of Financial Economics, 112(1), 116–135.

Hu, D.L. (2006). Relationship between the gap between regional economic development and private economy in China. Shanghai Economic Research, (2), 17–25.

Hu, A.G., Liu, S.L., & Ma, Z.G. (2012). Population aging, population growth and economic growth - empirical evidence from provincial panel data in China. Population Research, (3), 14–26.

Hu, A.G., Zhou, S.J., & Ren, H. (2016). Supply-side structural reform—Adapting and leading the new normal of China's economy, Journal of Tsinghua University (Philosophy and Social Sciences), 31(02):17–22+195.

Ireland, P.N. (2004). A method for taking models to the data. Economic Dynamics and Control, 28 (6), 1205–1226.

Jiang, Z.H. (2012). Regional innovation and eco-efficiency revolution. Beijing: Science Press.

Jing, Y.J., & Wang, X.F. (2006). Analysis on present situation and future tendency of US industrial structures. Northeast Asia Forum, 15(1), 111–115.

Krugman, P. (1991). Increasing Returns and Economic Geography. Journal of Political Economy, 99(3), 483–499.

Kydland, F.E., & Prescott, E.C. (1982). Time to build and aggregate fluctuations. Econometrica, 50(6), 1345–1370.

Levén, P., Holmström, J., & Mathiassen, L. (2014). Managing research and innovation networks: Evidence from a government sponsored cross-industry program. Research Policy, 43(1), 156–168.

Li, D.H., & Xia, E.J. (2013). The impact of human capital on China's economic growth - a study based on expanded Solow expansion model. Journal of China Population, Resources and Environment, 23(8), 100–106.

Li, D.K., Kui, X.X., & Jiang, H.P. (2012). Welfare economics analysis of national investment rate in China. Journal of Economic Research, (9), 46–56.

Lin, Y.F., & Su, J. (2012). New structural economics: the theoretical framework of reflection on economic development and policy. Beijing: Peking University Press.

Lin, Y.F., Wu, H.M., & Xing, Y.Q. (2010). Mechanism of the "surge phenomenon" and overcapacity. Journal of Economic Research, (10), 118–118.

Liu, W. (2010). From demand management to supply management (China economic growth report 2010). Beijing: China Development Press.

Liu, W. (2013). Promoting economic growth and balanced development pattern. Academic Monthly, (2), 70–81.

Liu, S.J., et al. (2014). Form a new normal of growth in the reform. Beijing: Citic Press Group.

Liu, X.H. (2014a). The supply-side structural reforms will promote China's economic growth–macroeconomic analysis and reflections of 2015. Academic Monthly, (4), 54–62.

Liu, W. (2014b). The fundamental way to change the mode of development lies in innovation. Journal of Peking University (Philosophy and Social Science), 51 (1), 14–20.

Liu, W. (2016). Explain the new economic normal. People's Daily, 2016-8-18, Beijing, 07.

Liu, J.H, & Jiang, Z.H. (2015). Innovation-driven and investment supportive strategies for China's economic transformation based on collaborative theory. Science of Science and Management of S.&.T., (2), 25–33.

Liu, J.H, & Jiang, Z.H. (2016). Innovation drive, transformation and upgrade under the new normal: Henan province as an example. Beijing: Science Press.

Liu, W., Cai, Z.Z., et al. (2005). China economic growth report 2005: economic growth under macro-control. Beijing: Economic Publishing House.

Liu, W., & Li, S.R. (2001). The ownership change and the economic growth and upgrading of factors efficiency. Economic Research Journal, (1), 3–9+93.

Ma, X.J., & Chen, T. (2009). Research on the mechanism of urbanization affecting economic growth. Modern Management Science, (2), 56–58.

Mao, X.Y., & Peng, X.Z. (2012). Urbanization, opening to the outside world and demographic bonus - an empirical study of economic growth in China from 1979 to 2010. Nanjing Social Sciences, (4), 31–38.

Omri, A. (2013). CO_2 emissions, energy consumption and economic growth nexus in MENA countries: evidence from simultaneous equations models. Energy Economics, 40(2), 657–664.

Rabanal, P., & Tuesta, V. (2006). Euro-dollar real exchange rate dynamics in an estimated two-country model: what is important and what is not. C.E.P.R. Discussion Papers.

Ren, Y.W., Jiang, G.Z., & Xu, X.B. (2014). The impact of urbanization level on economic growth in China based on the structural equation model. Business Times, (10), 46–47.

Shen, K.R., & Jiang, R. (2007). An empirical study of the impact of urbanization on economic growth in China. Statistical Analysis, (6), 9–15.

Shen, K.R., & Zhou, M. (2013). Economic growth theory and China's economic growth - an interview with Prof. Shen Kunrong. Academic Monthly, (6), 173–176.

Smets, F., & Wouters, R. (2005). Comparing shocks and frictions in US and Euro area Business cycles: a Bayesian DSGE approach. Applied Econometrics, 20(2), 161–183.

Smets, F., & Wouters, R. (2007). Shocks and frictions in US business cycles: a Bayesian DSGE approach. American Economic Review, 97, 586–606.

Sun, X.M., & Zhou F.Z. (2013). Land finance and tax sharing system: an empirical explanation. Chinese Social Sciences, (04), 40–59 + 205.

Walque, G., Wouters, R., & Smets, F. (2005). An open economy DSGE model linking the euro area and the US economy. National Bank of Belgium.

Wan, G. (2014). Optimize the allocation of science and technology resources and implement the strategy of innovation-driven development. China Science and Technology Industry, (8), 11–13.

Wang, L.G., & Gao, Y.Q. (2012). Study on the problem of overcapacity based on the perspective of technological progress. Proceedings of Finance and Economics, (2), 26–32.

Wu, F.X., & Liu, Z.B. (2008). Research on the mechanism of urbanization community driving economic growth - empirical evidence from 16 cities in the Yangtze river delta. Economic Research, (11), 126–136.

Xiang, B.W., & Zhang, H.W. (2013). The relationship between the long-run equilibrium and short-run dynamic effects of urbanization and economic growth—an empirical analysis based on penal data of provincial level in China. Journal of Huazhong Normal University (Humanities and Social Sciences), (2), 47–54.

Xu, X.Q., & Yuan, K.H. (2013). Research on mechanism and characteristics of urbanization driving economic growth - empirical evidence from provincial panel data. Institute of Economic Exploration, (5), 134–140.

Yu, L., & Wang, J.L. (2008). Vertical price dual-track system: "electricity shortage" economic analysis and outlet. China Industrial Economics, (10), 43–52.

Zhang, C.C. (2013). Investment structure should be reasonable and can be dynamically optimized. China Economic Herald, 2013-8-23, Beijing, Version A02, http://www.ceh.com.cn/xwpd/2013/08/236693.shtml.

Zhang, S.Y. (2014). Reflections on China's dual-track economic reform. Economist, (01), 67 + 70.

Zhang, P., Liu, X.H., & Wang, H.M. (2011). The frontier of China's economic growth - a theoretical and policy study on the balanced growth of the structure. Beijing: China social sciences press.

Chapter 8
Conclusion

This book discusses the synergy theory and the model of economic growth. It also discussed different empirical research conducted on the economic growth of China, the United States and other countries, and builds up their economic growth models with the support of relevant data, and finally analyzes its economic growth factors.

8.1 Theoretical Achievements

This book studies the theoretical basis of many countries' economic growth, the modeling method based on the synergy theory, the method of calculating the contribution of various determining factors to economic growth, and obtains the results that fit the actual situation. From the viewpoint of the accounting results and the logical structure of the synergy theory, the synergy theory and the value decomposition method of economic growth organically combine the new growth theory with new institutional economics, which has a solid theoretical basis. These methods are empirically tested and can be applied to account for economic growth of other countries or regions and industries.

(1) Through the meaning of synergy, this book summarizes the interaction among the technology spillovers, innovation and investment and economic environment.

The meaning of synergy used in this book are as follows: innovation (science and technology progress, human capital innovation — the innovation of knowledge and intelligence in the mind, institutional innovation) and investment in physical capital interact with each other through bidirectional knowledge spillovers and knowledge sharing. This "synergy" includes both the endogenous (technology is endogenous to investment) and exogenous (R&D, education) contribution to investment and economic growth. The basis of "synergy" is knowledge sharing, and the synergistic benefit is the basis for the existence and development of economic organizations.

J. H. Liu and Z. H. Jiang, *The Synergy Theory on Economic Growth: Comparative Study Between China and Developed Countries*,
https://doi.org/10.1007/978-981-13-1885-6_8

To some extent, there is a synergy relationship between economic system and its environment. A good external environment will promote economic growth, while poor external environment will inhibit economic growth. And the rapid economic growth will helps to form a good external environment, low-speed economic growth may bring a poor external environment.

(2) Theoretical innovation.

If the theoretical basis of Harold model and Solow model were the Keynes's equilibrium theory, then the new growth theory would be lack of necessary theoretical basis, which is to say that the new growth theory lacks the theoretical basis for building production functions. Therefore, according to the synergy theory, this book decomposes the GDP into compensation of employees, investment income and synergistic benefit, and then establishes the compensation function of employees, the investment income function and the synergistic benefit function so as to deduce the formula for calculating the contribution of impact factors like the progress of science and technology, human capital, etc. to economic growth.

(3) A more comprehensive analysis of the determining factors of economic growth.

The determining factors analyzed in this book not only include labor, physical capital stock, investment in the physical capital, human capital, science and technology, but also include the institutional innovation and economic externalities. These two variables of "investment in the physical capital (current-period)" and "physical capital stock (last period)" are equivalent to the previous "physical capital stock (current-period)". And by absorbing scientific thinking of the new institutional economics, this book introduces the factor of the economic externalities, which makes the new theory has more capable of explaining the practical problems.

(4) The economic growth models established in this book have accepted the econometric test and are consistent with the facts of economic growth in various countries.

In the economic growth models of all countries, the types of the models of compensation of employees and the capital income models are basically the same except that the parameters are different. However, the synergistic benefit models are different from country to country. And one country may have different models of synergistic benefit in different periods. It depends on the richness of production factors, economic structure and economic system of different countries.

8.2 New Findings of Several Typical Facts in Contemporary Economic Growth

According to the summary of convergence hypothesis and economic growth by Barro, Temple, Zhu Yong, Zhu Baohua, Shen Kunrong and other scholars, the main conclusions of convergence hypothesis and economic growth can be summarized as follows: the economic growth rate is negatively correlated with the initial value of per capita income, and the average annual economic growth rate of the world is about 2%. There is a tendency of diminishing marginal returns in physical capital investment, the relationship between human capital and economic growth is weak, and has a certain feature of endogenous and time lag. The relationship between the scale of development and economic growth is weak and the relationship between government scale and economic growth is not certain because of the facts that balance indicators are different and inequality in income distribution will hinder economic growth, but the mechanism is not clear. While the relationship between foreign trade and economic growth depends on indicators that measure the extent of foreign trade and political stability is closely related to economic growth (Zhu 1999).

Kaldor puts forward 6 features of modern economic growth, which are, the per capita output continues to increase, and its growth rate does not tend to decline, per capita physical capital continues to increase, the rate of return on capital is almost stable, the ratio of physical capital—output is almost stable, the share of labor and physical capital in GDP is almost stable and the growth rate of per capita output varies greatly among countries.

The conclusions of this book are as follows:

(1) Comparison of determining factors of economic growth among fifteen countries:

Table 8.1 shows the contribution of various factors to economic growth among fifteen countries. In different countries, the contribution of various factors to economic growth is quite different. In many countries, the contribution of institutional innovation is zero, or very small. This does not mean that institutional innovation is ineffective in the economy, but shows that the institutional innovation ensures that the economic efficiency does not decline.

For the calculation of the above countries, the average economic growth rate is 4%, the contribution of institutional innovation to economic growth is 3.3% on average, the contribution of physical capital stock to economic growth is 26.7% on average, the contribution of physical capital investment to economic growth is 15.9% on average, the contribution of science and technological progress to economic growth is 30.5% on average, the contribution of human capital growth to economic growth is 21.3% on average and the contribution of labor to economic growth is 6.2% on average. While the impact rate of economic externalities to the economic growth is -3.9% on average, which shows that the economic environment is conducive to economic growth on average.

(2) An important way to achieve higher economic growth is to strengthen institutional innovation.

The breakthrough point for backward countries to catch up with advanced countries lies in institutional innovation. The most basic and essential function of institutional innovation to economic growth is to improve the allocation efficiency of production resources. From the point of view above, this book uses the efficiency analysis

Table 8.1 Analysis on economic growth factors among 15 countries (average annual, %)

Country	Period	Economic growth rate	The contribution of physical capital stock	The contribution of investment in physical capital	The contribution of science and technology progress	The contribution of human capital	The contribution of labor	The contribution of institutional innovation	The impact rate of economic externalities
China	1953–1975	5.5	28	20	−8	42	23	−17	12
China	1977–2000	9.7	39	14	9	17	5	31	−15
China	2001–2012	9.8	57	21	29	7	1	5	−20
UK	1961–1980	2.2	24	14	39	32	0	−23	14
UK	1981–2010	2.4	13	30	18	27	10	17	−15
Italy	1981–2010	1.5	9	23	11	41	2	0	14
New Zealand	1981–2010	2.5	25	17	15	15	24	10	−6
Singapore	1981–2010	6.5	37	19	35	18	1	0	−10
Sweden	1993–2010	2.2	26	26	56	9	0	0	−17
Japan	1960–1973	9.7	12	40	39	4	1	-2	6
Japan	1973–1993	3.4	4	27	63	12	2	6	−14
Japan	1993–2009	0.75	10	−36	86	17	−1	−5	29
USA	1900–1929	3.1	58	11	8	24	6	−1	-6
USA	1930–1953	3.7	32	13	17	21	5	22	−10
USA	1954–1981	3.4	26	17	30	22	4	3	−2
USA	1982-2000	3.3	17	25	21	24	6	17	−10
USA	2001–2008	2.2	21	3	35	19	5	5	12
Canada	1980–2010	2.5	22	18	26	4	31	1	−2
South Korea	1960–1972	8	21	14	7	17	6	4	31
South Korea	1973–1997	7.9	24	35	20	18	7	-10	6

(continued)

Table 8.1 (continued)

Country	Period	Economic growth rate	The contribution of physical capital stock	The contribution of investment in physical capital	The contribution of science and technology progress	The contribution of human capital	The contribution of labor	The contribution of institutional innovation	The impact rate of economic externalities
South Korea	1998–2010	4	48	7	25	22	6	10	−18
Finland	1981–2010	2.3	8	14	62	16	1	10	−11
France	1981–2010	1.9	18	19	28	24	8	0	3
Germany	1990–2000	1.9	49	23	24	7	2	0	−5
Germany	2001–2010	1	41	−6	49	19	2	0	−5
Australia	1981–2010	4.5	31	23	34	17	10	0	−15
Ireland	1981–2010	4.8	28	14	19	16	2	9	12
Average		4.0	26.7	15.9	30.5	21.3	6.2	3.3	−3.9

method (Data Envelopment Analysis) to measure the contribution of institutional innovation to economic growth, obtains the results which accord with the reality (1978–2002 China, 1992–2002 United States, 1980–2000 UK, 1987–2000 New Zealand, 1980–2000 Ireland, etc.), and finds out the reason that why the allocation efficiency of production resources increases or decreases at the same time.

(3) To some extent, the economic externalities reflect the investment environment.

In the calculation, the countries, in which the investment environment is good (or the investment environment is improved) and economic externalities are negative for economic growth, always have higher economic growth rate, such as China (1978–2000), the United States (1992–2000), Ireland (1974–2000), South Korea (1974–2000) and other countries.

(4) Economic growth rate is closely related to savings rate and investment rate. The growth rate of investment in fixed assets is the decisive factor in the economic growth rate. The high growth rate of fixed capital is the determining factor of economic growth, and the high growth rate of investment in science and technology does not necessarily bring about the high economic growth. Those countries with higher economic growth rates (such as China and South Korea) have high savings rates and investment rates, while those with high growth rates in science and technology and those with R & D expenditures as a high proportion of GDP do not necessarily accompanied by high economic growth, such as Japan, Finland, Sweden after 1990. Only if investment in science and technology and investment in fixed assets continue to grow rapidly at the time can we ensure the economy grows faster and better, which is of crucial importance to China.
(5) The average income of each worker is increasing. The wage rate increases constantly with the growth of the fixed assets investment, investment in science and technology, and human capital. And the ratio of workers' remuneration to gross domestic product tends to be stable, and it maintains between 45% and 60% in many countries at present.
(6) In the calculation process, the ratio of investment in science and technology to gross domestic product among the 15 countries are less than 4.5%; the ratio of "science and technology income" to gross domestic product among 15 countries are more than 20%. For example, the average ratio of investment in science and technology to GDP in the United Kingdom from 1980 to 2000 was 2.1%, while at the same period, the average ratio of the "science and technology income" to GDP was as high as 20%, which resulted from the interaction between R&D investment and fixed-asset investment. By investing in fixed assets, enterprises spill external knowledge into the enterprise and combine them with their own innovations, which greatly increase the output efficiency of science and technology and the "science and technology income". This is consistent with the view of endogenous growth theory that "knowledge is inherent in fixed assets investment".

(7) The level of human capital prices depends on the investment in fixed assets and investment in science and technology firstly. If there is more investment in fixed assets (more developed economy) and more investment in science and technology (more advanced science and technology), the price of human capital will be higher. Therefore, talent tends to flow into the developed areas forming a "pool", so that the economy grows faster. And because of the faster and better economy growth, more capital will be invested in fixed assets and in science and technology so as to attract more talents, which form a recycling mechanism (Jiang 2006).

(8) Similar to the conclusion of Kaldor, this book's calculations show that the capital return is almost stable, and the labor and physical capital take stable share of GDP.

(9) In recent years, the proportion of innovation investment (investment in science and technology, physical capital, and human capital) in the gross domestic product (GDP) trends to increase in many countries. For example, the ratio of the $(\mathrm{SHD}/K^2)/Y$ (s represents investment in science & technology, H represents investment in human capital, D represents investment in physical capital, K represents physical capital stock in last period, Y represents GDP) in the United States increased from 0.023 in 1947 to 0.088 in 2008. This shows that science and technology and human capital play a more important role in economic growth.

8.3 Analysis of Several Controversial Issues in the Study of Economic Growth

This book analyzes a number of important controversial issues of economic growth, such as supply-side structural reform and new structural economics, IT investment and productivity paradox, motive of economic growth miracle in East Asia.

(1) supply-side structural reform and new structural economics

This book contains the theory of supply-side structural reform and new structural economics, and also contains a model of standard supply-side structural reform and new structural economics. Taking the model (4-3) as an example, we now write as (8.1)

$$Y = 1.16(HL)^{0.53}(SD/L)^{0.18} + 0.189K + 19SD/K + 11.5LD/K + 1810 \quad (8.1)$$

In (8.1), SD/L, SD/K, LD/K respectively represent the endowment degree of technology compared to labor, the endowment degree of new investment compared to capital, the endowment degree of labor compared to capital. While the average years of schooling of laborers is the main structural factor of labor force, investment in physical capital is the main structural factor for the growth of physical capital stock. The process of economic growth is also a relatively richer process of technology and new investment, thus the characteristic of the economy would evolve from labor-intensive to investment-intensive and technology-intensive. Institutional innovation and the economic externalities are the key factors of accelerating or delaying this evolutionary process.

(2) IT investment and productivity paradox

Since the 1960s and 1970s, information technology (IT), such as computers etc., has been rapidly developed and has been widely used in various fields of national economy (Li 2004). However, some scholars pointed out, although the proportion of investment in information technology in total investment has risen sharply, there is no obvious connection between information system investment and corporate performance. In 1987, Robert Solow, a famous American economist and Nobel laureate in economics, concluded: "We can see the advent of the computer age everywhere, but it is hard to see its effect in productivity statistics alone." As a result, academics call the phenomenon of lack of a significant link between increased IT investment and improved productivity or improved corporate performance as a "productivity paradox".

However, Jorgenson and Stiroh has pointed out, that from 1948 to 1999, the average annual growth rate of U.S. GDP was 3.46%, of which the contribution of information technology was 0.4%; From 1990 to 1995, the average annual growth rate of GDP was 2.36%, of which the contribution of information technology was 0.57%. From 1995 to 1999, the average annual growth rate of GDP was 4.08%, of which the contribution of information technology was 1.18% (Li 2004).

From the study of this book, taking Fig. 8.1 as an example, we can say the growth rate of productivity is mainly determined by the change of investment rate. When the investment rate is increased, the growth rate of productivity is high; in the period of 1992–2000, the investment rate was driven by IT investment, so the productivity also tended to increase (also called "new economy" period); however, from 2000 to 2003, the Internet bubble burst, then, the investment rates declined, finally productivity also tended to decline. Therefore, high and new technology do not necessarily bring about high economic growth. Only when new investment and new technology are cooperated, the investment rate tends to rise, then, the growth rate of productivity tends to increase. Therefore, the rapid development of technology (necessary conditions) is not a sufficient condition for economic growth, rapid and synergy development of investment and technology is the sufficient condition for higher productivity growth. As in China, the information technology has been rapidly developed (although most of them are introduced, there is no shortage of independent innovation), at the same time, investments have also increased substantially, resulting in substantial growth in production (Fig. 8.1).

(3) The motive of economic growth miracle in East Asia

From the analysis of this book, it is not merely the contribution of "sweat" and capital to the rapid growth momentum that China, Japan, South Korea and

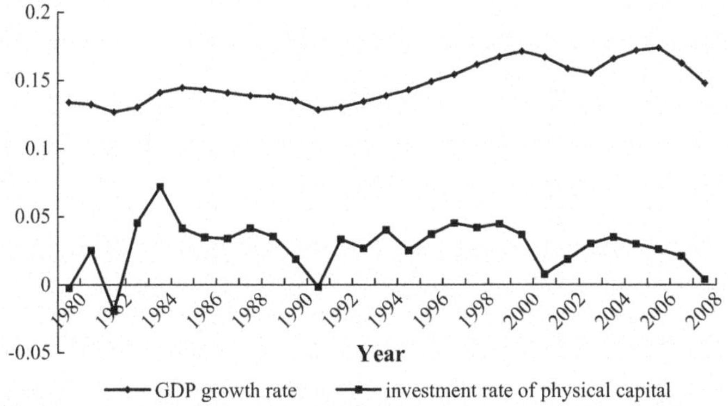

Fig. 8.1 Relationship between GDP growth rate and investment rate of physical capital

Singapore have experienced or are experiencing. Although the contribution of the sum of investment in physical capital and capital stock is the first drive force, the sum of the contribution of science and technology progress, human capital and institutional innovation also plays a significant role. The dual power model of economic growth shows that investment as the first driving force and innovation as the second driving force.

In 1960–1972, the economic growth rate in South Korea was 8%, of which 6% was contributed by the growth of labor force and 35% by the growth of physical capital. Meanwhile, the contribution of science and technology progress to economic growth was 7%, the contribution of human capital growth to economic growth was 17%, and the contribution of institutional innovation was 4%. Therefore, from 1960 to 1972, South Korea's economic growth belonged to the dual power model that material capital as the first driving force and innovation (science and technology progress, human capital and institutional innovation) as the second driving force.

In 1955–1973, Japan's economic growth rate was averaged at 9.65%. The factors behind its economic growth were analyzed, which showed that the contribution of physical capital stock growth was 12%, the contribution of investment in physical capital was 40%, and the sum of this two was the contribution of physical capital (52%). The contribution of human capital growth was 4%, the contribution of science and technology progress was 39%, and the contribution of institutional innovation was −2%, and the sum of these three was the contribution of innovation (41%), while the impact rate of economic externalities was 6%, which showed that Japan's economic externalities have little effect on the economic growth. During this period, Japan's economy belonged to the type of capital - innovative dual-driven.

In 1980–2009, the average rate of economic growth in Singapore reached at 6.5%. The contribution of physical capital stock growth was 37%, the contribution of investment in physical capital was 19%, the contribution of human capital growth was 18%, the contribution of science and technology progress was 35%, and the contribution of institutional innovation was 0. During this period, the higher growth of Singapore's economy belonged to the type of capital - innovative dual-driven.

In 1978–2012, the average rate of economic growth in China was nearly at 10%. The contribution of physical capital stock growth was 39%, the contribution of investment in physical capital was 14%, the contribution of human capital growth was 17%, the contribution of science and technological progress was 9%, the contribution of institutional innovation was 31%, the contribution of labor growth reached at 5%, and the impact rate of economic externalities was −15%. In 2001–2012, the contribution of physical capital stock growth was 57%, the contribution of investment in physical capital was 21%, the contribution of human capital growth was 7%, the contribution of science and technology progress was 29%, the contribution of institutional innovation was 5%, the contribution of labor growth reached at 1%, and the impact rate of economic externalities was −20%. During this period, China's economy belonged to the type of capital—innovative dual-driven.

References

Jiang, Z.H. (2006). The distributive analysis theory of S&T progress and economic growth - a test of fifteen countries. Science of Science and Management of S. &. T., (9), 113–118.

Li Zhitang. 2004. Research on "Productivity Paradox" of Information Technology Investment and Its Latest Development. Foreign Economies and Management. 27(9), pp:2–7,20.

Zhu, B.H. (1999). New economic growth theory. Shanghai: Shanghai University of Finance and Economics Press.

Appendix A
The Data and Model of China's Economic Growth

1. **1952–1976**

(1) Data

Data Sources: The data of physical capital stock before 1978 adopt the data of Zou (1995). The data of investment in physical capital, labor, R&D expenditure before 1978 come from the *China Statistical Yearbook*. The data of R&D expenditure from 1952 to 1976 adopt the data of government financial input in science and technology. The data of physical capital stock and average years of schooling of laborers after 1977 comes from the book named *Capital Deepening, Human Capital Accumulation and China's Economic Sustained Growth* written by Tang (see Attached list A.1).

(2) China's economic growth model (Add A.1)

$$Y = 537(HL)^{0.76}(SD/L)^{-0.23} + 0.33K + 0.867SD/K - 13.5S + 152 \quad \text{(Add A.1)}$$

Attached list A.2.
Attached list A.3.

2. **1977–2012**

(1) Data (Attached list A.4).

(2) China's economic growth model (Add A.2).

J. H. Liu and Z. H. Jiang, *The Synergy Theory on Economic Growth: Comparative Study Between China and Developed Countries*,
https://doi.org/10.1007/978-981-13-1885-6

Attached list A.1 The data of China's economic growth (the prices at 1990, per hundred million yuan; per million people; years)

Year	GDP (100 million yuan)	Physical capital stock (100 million yuan)	Labor (million people)	Compensation of employees/GDP	Average years of schooling of laborers (years)	Investment in physical capital/GDP	R&D expenditure/GDP (%)
1953	1615.61	420.8	213	0.58	2.7	0.12	0.08
1954	1683.46	455.3	218	0.58	2.78	0.14	0.18
1955	1798.01	488	223	0.6	2.86	0.16	0.28
1956	2067.65	526.4	230	0.57	2.95	0.16	0.38
1957	2173.15	567.6	237	0.59	3.04	0.21	0.51
1958	2635.86	634.5	266	0.5	3.13	0.18	0.63
1959	2867.86	733.2	261	0.43	3.22	0.25	0.75
1960	2859.3	821.7	259	0.46	3.32	0.3	0.87
1961	2078.64	856.2	256	0.62	3.42	0.32	0.99
1962	1962.31	873.7	259	0.69	3.52	0.19	1.13
1963	2162.49	906	266	0.64	3.63	0.15	1.36
1964	2558.15	952.5	277	0.57	3.74	0.17	1.59
1965	2993.07	1017	287	0.52	3.89	0.2	1.87
1966	3313.28	1100.1	298	0.51	4.04	0.2	1.8
1967	3124.42	1153.8	308	0.58	4.2	0.22	1.73
1968	2996.3	1206.5	319	0.59	4.37	0.18	1.66
1969	3502.79	1269.6	332	0.55	4.55	0.17	1.59
1970	4182.32	1378.8	344	0.51	4.73	0.21	1.55
1971	4475.07	1499.7	356	0.5	4.92	0.24	1.53
1972	4645.19	1614.3	359	0.51	5.12	0.25	1.51
1973	5012.09	1745.3	367	0.51	5.32	0.25	1.49
1974	5127.29	1876.2	374	0.51	5.53	0.24	1.47
1975	5573.36	2022.9	382	0.49	5.75	0.27	1.44
1976	5484.34	2055.1	389	0.53	5.89	0.29	1.49

Attached list A.2 China's model of compensation of employees (1953–1976)

Dependent Variable: log *V*				
Variable	Coefficient	Std. Error	T-Statistic	Prob.
C	2.730231	0.169864	16.07307	0.0000
log *HL*	0.757707	0.133338	5.682596	0.0000
log *SD*/*L*	−0.233484	0.120964	−1.930186	0.0704
AR(1)	0.767804	0.225318	3.407653	0.0034
AR(2)	−0.431496	0.209817	−2.056530	0.0554
R-squared	0.915817	Mean dependent var	2.893723	
Adjusted R-squared	0.896009	S.D. dependent var	0.139747	
S.E. of regression	0.045065	Akaike info criterion	−3.164699	
Sum squared resid	0.034525	Schwarz criterion	−2.916735	
Log likelihood	39.81169	F-statistic	46.23497	
Durbin-Watson stat	1.844689	Prob(F-statistic)	0.000000	

Attached list A.3 $Y - B$ model and its test (1953–1976)

Dependent variable: $Y - B$				
Variable	Coefficient	Std. Error	T-Statistic	Prob.
C	152.1957	42.64249	3.569109	0.0028
K	0.3261324	10.35525	3.149440	0.0066
SD/*K*	0.866791	0.162929	5.320061	0.0001
S	−13.50080	3.511089	−3.845188	0.0016
R-squared	0.983734	Mean dependent var	723.8269	
Adjusted R-squared	0.980480	S.D. dependent var	338.5944	
S.E. of regression	47.30601	Akaike info criterion	10.73582	
Sum squared resid	33567.87	Schwarz criterion	10.93464	
Log likelihood	−97.99025	F-statistic	302.3818	
Durbin-Watson stat	1.378476	Prob(F-statistic)	0.000000	

$$Y = 0.001243(HL)^{0.803}(SD/L)^{0.228} + 0.19K + 1334HSD/K^2 - 16.95 \quad \text{(Add A.2)}$$

Attached list A.5.
Attached list A.6.
Attached list A.7.

Attached list A.4 The data of China' economic growth (the prices at 1990, per ten billion yuan; per million people; years)

Year	GDP (10 billion yuan)	Labor (million people)	Physical capital stock (lag one year; 10 billion yuan)	Science and technology (lag two years; 10 billion yuan)	Investment in physical capital (10 billion yuan)	Average years of schooling of laborers (years)	The share of compensation of employees
1977	59.01	394	208	0.795	16.81	5.90	0.50
1978	65.92	401	216	0.894	25.06	5.87	0.50
1979	70.93	410	218	0.767	25.90	5.78	0.51
1980	76.32	424	227	0.989	26.86	5.76	0.51
1981	80.29	437	237	1.064	26.10	5.79	0.53
1982	87.59	453	250	0.992	29.11	5.84	0.54
1983	97.14	464	265	1.044	32.82	5.90	0.54
1984	111.91	482	285	1.139	38.52	5.97	0.54
1985	127.02	499	317	1.360	47.98	6.06	0.53
1986	138.19	513	353	1.567	52.10	6.16	0.53
1987	154.22	528	391	1.524	55.72	6.27	0.52
1988	171.65	543	435	1.796	63.18	6.47	0.52
1989	178.69	553	478	1.542	64.42	6.67	0.52
1990	185.48	639	515	1.373	64.44	6.86	0.53
1991	202.54	648	555	1.430	70.42	6.95	0.52
1992	231.30	656	602	1.484	83.66	7.04	0.51
1993	263.68	664	672	1.620	114.17	7.12	0.52
1994	298.22	672	756	1.619	122.84	7.21	0.52
1995	330.73	680	852	1.846	135.04	7.29	0.53
1996	363.80	689	954	2.088	143.99	7.45	0.53
1997	397.64	696	1061	1.984	151.98	7.60	0.53
1998	428.65	700	1149	2.183	161.65	7.74	0.53
1999	461.23	706	1234	2.704	172.55	7.87	0.52
2000	499.97	712	1294	3.001	181.64	8.01	0.51
2001	541.47	721	1354	3.828	208.41	8.13	0.51
2002	590.75	728	1359	5.000	238.78	8.26	0.51
2003	653.58	733	1365	5.902	267.39	8.43	0.50
2004	719.60	738	1396	6.321	317.21	8.61	0.49
2005	794.44	743	1460	7.386	383.56	8.79	0.49
2006	886.59	749	1559	8.851	462.48	8.97	0.48
2007	1001.85	754	1699	11.000	557.51	9.16	0.48
2008	1098.02	756	1873	12.320	650.06	9.41	0.48
2009	1199.04	758	2142	13.798	861.32	9.66	0.48
2010	1323.74	761	2474	16.690	1029.28	9.92	0.48
2011	1446.85	764	2859	19.424	1192.94	10.17	0.48
2012	1559.70	767	3325	23.165	1419.60	10.44	0.48

Attached list A.5 The logarithm model of compensation of employees (log *V*) and its test in China (1977–2012)

Dependent variable: log *V*				
Method: Least Squares				
Sample(adjusted): 1981 2012				
Included observations: 32 after adjusting endpoints				
Convergence achieved after 9 iterations				
Variable	Coefficient	Std. Error	T-Statistic	Prob.
C	−2.90546	0.447708	−6.48963	0
log *HL*	0.803157	0.068434	11.73617	0
log *SD*/*L*	0.22755	0.017545	12.96943	0
AR(3)	−0.36579	0.231261	−1.58173	0.1254
AR(4)	0.890066	0.235719	3.775962	0.0008
R-squared	0.996792	Mean dependent var	2.228862	
Adjusted R-squared	0.996317	S.D. dependent var	0.373678	
S.E. of regression	0.022678	Akaike info criterion	−4.59227	
Sum squared resid	0.013885	Schwarz criterion	−4.36325	
Log likelihood	78.47635	F-statistic	2097.511	
Durbin-Watson stat	1.106366	Prob(F-statistic)	0	
Inverted AR Roots	.55 −.16i	.55+.16i	−1.11	

Attached list A.6 Investment value model and its test (1978–2012)

Dependent Variable: *M*				
Method: Least Squares				
Sample(adjusted): 1980 2012				
Included observations: 31 after adjusting endpoints				
Convergence achieved after 9 iterations				
Variable	Coefficient	Std. Error	T-Statistic	Prob.
C	−16.9506	10.47311	−1.61849	0.116
K	0.189535	0.018582	10.20018	0
HSD/K^2	1334.287	225.6204	5.913861	0
AR(2)	0.457366	0.323686	1.412994	0.1679
R-squared	0.996045	Mean dependent var	248.367	
Adjusted R-squared	0.995649	S.D. dependent var	227.3159	

(continued)

Attached list A.6 (continued)

Dependent Variable: *M*				
S.E. of regression	14.994	Akaike info criterion	8.363308	
Sum squared resid	6744.602	Schwarz criterion	8.54288	
Log likelihood	−138.176	F-statistic	2518.234	
Durbin-Watson stat	1.126434	Prob (F-statistic)	0	
Inverted AR Roots	0.68	−0.68		

Attached list A.7 The analysis of the resource allocation efficiency of production factors

Year	Efficiency	Waste rate of physical capital	Waste rate of Labor	Waste rate of human capital
1977	0.5411	0	0.44	0.38
1978	0.5517	0	0.44	0.37
1979	0.5628	0	0.44	0.37
1980	0.581	0	0.46	0.38
1981	0.5847	0	0.46	0.38
1982	0.6055	0	0.47	0.39
1983	0.6331	0	0.49	0.40
1984	0.6777	0	0.52	0.43
1985	0.6924	0	0.52	0.42
1986	0.6759	0	0.49	0.39
1987	0.6804	0	0.48	0.38
1988	0.6809	0	0.46	0.36
1989	0.6459	0	0.42	0.33
1990	0.6216	0	0.42	0.35
1991	0.6305	0	0.42	0.34
1992	0.6628	0	0.42	0.34
1993	0.6772	0	0.40	0.32
1994	0.6812	0	0.38	0.28
1995	0.6702	0	0.34	0.24
1996	0.658	0	0.29	0.20
1997	0.6471	0	0.25	0.16
1998	0.6442	0	0.22	0.13
1999	0.6452	0	0.20	0.11
2000	0.6669	0	0.18	0.10
2001	0.6905	0	0.17	0.09
2002	0.7505	0	0.19	0.11
2003	0.8186	0	0.21	0.13

(continued)

Attached list A.7 (continued)

Year	Efficiency	Waste rate of physical capital	Waste rate of Labor	Waste rate of human capital
2004	0.8734	0	0.20	0.14
2005	0.9164	0	0.18	0.13
2006	0.9561	0	0.14	0.10
2007	0.9991	0	0.08	0.06
2008	1	0	0	0
2009	0.9941	0	0	0
2010	1	0	0	0
2011	1	0	0	0
2012	1	0	0	0

Appendix B
The Data and Model of America's Economic Growth

(1) Data

Data Sources: The data of GDP, labor, compensation of employees, physical capital stock, investment in physical capital come from the book of *United States Statistical Abstract*. The data of average years of schooling of laborers comes from the book of *Human Capital Accumulation, Technological Change and International Spillovers: Comparative Growth Experience from Japan, Korea and the United States* written by Yamauchi F and Godo Y. The data of R&D expenditure comes from the book of *Statistical Abstract of the United States*, and the research report *International Technological Progress* written by Hamilton R.T and Strausz-Hupe R, and the book of *Science & Engineering Indicators–2000*. The data of R&D expenditure data before 1953 was estimated by the author of this book (Attached list B.1).

(2) America's economic growth model (Add B.1)

$$Y = 0.00316(HL)^{0.482} * (SD/L)^{0.001461t - 0.0000000488t^3} + 0.12K + 0.0007SH/K + 0.007HD/K + 11.7 \quad \text{(Add B.1)}$$

In the model, t represents year, and 1900 = 1, 1978 = 79, … 2008 = 109.

In the equation, Y is GDP. K is physical capital stock. D represents investment in physical capital. S stands for science and technology progress. H is human capital and L is labor.

Attached list B.2.
Attached list B.3.
Attached list B.4.

J. H. Liu and Z. H. Jiang, *The Synergy Theory on Economic Growth: Comparative Study Between China and Developed Countries*,
https://doi.org/10.1007/978-981-13-1885-6

Attached list B.1 The data of America's economic growth (the prices at 2000, per billion dollars; per thousand people; years)

Year	GDP (billion dollars)	Investment in physical capital (billion dollars)	Physical capital stock (lag one year) (billion dollars)	Compensation of employees (billion dollars)	Labor (thousand people)	Average years of schooling of laborers (years)	R&D expenditure (lag two years; billion dollars)	t
1900	326.49	35.91		156.06	29269	6.85		1
1901	365.67	40.22	808.1873	174.79	30201	6.91	27.75	2
1902	368.93	40.58	840.5148	178.19	31008	6.97	32.18	3
1903	385.26	42.38	889.006	186.08	31654	7.03	33.57	4
1904	381.99	42.02	937.4972	184.5	31894	7.09	36.21	5
1905	408.11	44.89	977.9066	197.12	32992	7.15	37.05	6
1906	457.09	54.85	1018.316	220.77	34608	7.21	40.81	7
1907	463.62	55.63	1058.725	229.03	35172	7.27	47.08	8
1908	424.44	50.93	1107.217	209.67	34137	7.33	49.14	9
1909	496.27	59.55	1155.708	245.16	35791	7.39	46.26	10
1910	509.33	61.12	1204.199	251.61	36413	7.5	55.58	11
1911	522.38	62.69	1260.772	258.06	36790	7.57	56.03	12
1912	551.77	66.21	1317.345	268.71	37930	7.64	59.55	13
1913	558.3	67	1373.918	271.89	38711	7.71	65.11	14
1914	532.18	58.54	1422.41	259.17	38003	7.78	68.11	15
1915	528.91	58.18	1462.819	257.58	37947	7.85	67.05	16
1916	568.09	62.49	1495.146	276.66	39699	7.92	68.76	17
1917	574.62	63.21	1535.556	297.08	39857	7.99	76.12	18
1918	643.19	70.75	1559.801	332.53	40214	8.06	79.3	19
1919	620.33	68.24	1584.047	320.71	40811	8.13	91.33	20
1920	594.21	65.36	1608.293	307.21	40868	8.2	90.57	21
1921	541.97	48.78	1656.784	280.2	38767	8.27	86.16	22

(continued)

Attached list B.1 (continued)

Year	GDP (billion dollars)	Investment in physical capital (billion dollars)	Physical capital stock (lag one year) (billion dollars)	Compensation of employees (billion dollars)	Labor (thousand people)	Average years of schooling of laborers (years)	R&D expenditure (lag two years; billion dollars)	t
1922	626.86	56.42	1697.193	324.09	41288	8.34	81.84	23
1923	705.22	77.57	1745.684	364.6	43987	8.41	98.42	24
1924	701.95	77.21	1794.176	362.91	43645	8.48	114.95	25
1925	760.72	83.68	1850.749	393.29	45280	8.55	118.63	26
1926	806.43	88.71	1907.322	416.92	46368	8.62	133.13	27
1927	806.43	88.71	1963.895	427.41	46396	8.69	145.96	28
1928	809.7	89.07	2028.55	429.14	46657	8.76	150.8	29
1929	865.2	103.82	2093.205	432.6	47718	8.83	156.27	30
1930	790.7	86.98	2157.86	406.66	44726	9	172.17	31
1931	739.9	66.59	2223.12	384.97	40630	9.08	158.14	32
1932	643.7	45.06	2249.03	341.03	35906	9.16	159.08	33
1933	635.5	38.13	2239.91	333.51	35926	9.24	148.05	34
1934	704.2	49.29	2221.52	365.97	39191	9.32	155.7	35
1935	766.9	53.68	2222.48	391.27	41162	9.4	183.09	36
1936	866.6	77.99	2238.31	443.61	44511	9.48	210.9	37
1937	911.1	82	2288.06	475.87	47517	9.56	251.31	38
1938	879.7	70.38	2344.36	459.73	44732	9.64	277.89	39
1939	950.7	85.56	2380.19	495.98	46534	9.72	281.5	40
1940	1034.1	93.07	2427.05	532.35	48545	9.8	318.48	41
1941	1211.1	133.22	2484.79	619.36	51739	9.91	361.94	42
1942	1435.4	200.96	2616.75	756.31	55577	10.02	520.77	43
1943	1670.9	233.93	2878.42	920.5	56390	10.13	732.05	44

(continued)

Attached list B.1 (continued)

Year	GDP (billion dollars)	Investment in physical capital (billion dollars)	Physical capital stock (lag one year) (billion dollars)	Compensation of employees (billion dollars)	Labor (thousand people)	Average years of schooling of laborers (years)	R&D expenditure (lag two years; billion dollars)	*t*
1944	1806.5	252.91	3184.4	997.73	55814	10.24	985.83	45
1945	1786.3	214.36	3451.36	986.39	54527	10.35	1210.36	46
1946	1589.4	143.05	3573.72	855.1	57270	10.46	1250.41	47
1947	1574.5	173.2	3492.78	838.89	60162	10.57	1220.66	48
1948	1643.2	197.18	3452	866.13	60763	10.68	1316.28	49
1949	1634.6	196.15	3446.24	867.81	59978	10.79	1485.45	50
1950	1777.3	231.05	3474.87	939.48	61413	10.9	1588.83	51
1951	1915	248.95	3520.46	1023.76	65017	11.04	1848.39	52
1952	1988.3	258.48	3649.21	1088.79	66158	11.13	2121.82	53
1953	2079.5	270.34	3792.21	1152.11	67126	11.3	2338.24	54
1954	2065.4	278.03	3950.56	1135.86	65459	11.33	2680.5	55
1955	2212.8	297.1	4086.83	1204.02	66877	11.37	2891.2	56
1956	2255.8	298.11	4228.07	1260.67	68365	11.372	3175.6	57
1957	2301.1	297	4378.9	1285.04	68577	11.408	4156.5	58
1958	2279.2	288.1	4526.37	1265.95	66863	11.448	4689.2	59
1959	2441.3	324.82	4649.37	1354.14	68317	11.49	5043.9	60
1960	2501.8	324.11	4796.2	1408.69	69195	11.528	5708.2	61
1961	2560	332.31	4945.43	1434.86	69090	11.64	6179	62
1962	2715.2	357.9	5101.06	1516.64	70374	11.712	6490.3	63
1963	2834	377.36	5278.12	1583.77	70930	11.722	6876.1	64
1964	2998.6	405.65	5458.87	1675.08	72290	11.774	7616.9	65
1965	3191.1	437.72	5666.32	1772.83	74289	11.808	8184.6	66

(continued)

Attached list B.1 (continued)

Year	GDP (billion dollars)	Investment in physical capital (billion dollars)	Physical capital stock (lag one year) (billion dollars)	Compensation of employees (billion dollars)	Labor (thousand people)	Average years of schooling of laborers (years)	R&D expenditure (lag two years; billion dollars)	*t*
1966	3399.1	465.94	5915.2	1910.11	77540	11.846	8516.5	67
1967	3484.6	465.45	6201.18	1988.39	79129	11.904	9023.6	68
1968	3652.7	486.36	6468.46	2104.52	80943	11.944	9260.8	69
1969	3765.4	501.05	6727.89	2208.91	82985	11.996	9378.8	70
1970	3771.9	485	6988.13	2241.71	82607	12.04	9422.2	71
1971	3898.6	501.72	7213.81	2279.11	82278	12.13	9040.4	72
1972	4105	543.29	7405.27	2403.73	84095	12.17	8830.8	73
1973	4341.5	586.93	7616.08	2547.06	87391	12.232	9032.1	74
1974	4319.6	561.58	7873.76	2563.54	88794	12.308	9211.8	75
1975	4311.2	514.83	8119.12	2497.56	87257	12.416	9109.5	76
1976	4540.9	556.55	8300.98	2635.28	89371	12.446	8911.2	77
1977	4750.5	618.02	8489.72	2761.32	92358	12.468	9322.7	78
1978	5015	688.39	8706.29	2920.01	96772	12.496	9644.9	79
1979	5173.4	727.81	8987.48	3029	100332	12.558	10112.7	80
1980	5161.7	691.21	9306.57	3056.5	100850	12.616	10613.7	81
1981	5291.7	700.34	9595.92	3088.35	101731	12.694	11092.7	82
1982	5189.3	657.87	9891.02	3070.22	100516	12.778	11586.8	83
1983	5423.8	706.34	10123.91	3132.48	101595	12.824	12203.4	84
1984	5813.6	819.96	10334.88	3333.97	106054	12.876	13077	85
1985	6053.7	874.99	10648.7	3478.05	108330	12.898	14325.9	86
1986	6263.6	897.81	10998.82	3607.17	110093	12.926	15575.7	87
1987	6475.1	911.5	11303.53	3757.32	113061	12.962	15978.9	88

(continued)

Attached list B.1 (continued)

Year	GDP (billion dollars)	Investment in physical capital (billion dollars)	Physical capital stock (lag one year) (billion dollars)	Compensation of employees (billion dollars)	Labor (thousand people)	Average years of schooling of laborers (years)	R&D expenditure (lag two years; billion dollars)	t
1988	6742.7	934.68	11592.07	3920.01	116092	12.984	16279.8	89
1989	6981.4	964.5	11881.58	4003.7	118634	13.03	16697.4	90
1990	7112.5	960.05	12176.52	4091.42	120071	13.066	17042.7	91
1991	7100.5	911.34	12472.75	4079.9	119124	13.162	17576.1	92
1992	7336.6	955.55	12697.31	4208.38	120039	13.28	17947.1	93
1993	7532.7	1012.55	12906.04	4301.2	121955.5	13.312	18005	94
1994	7835.5	1086.33	13151.4	4428.62	124923	13.358	17619.8	95
1995	8031.7	1148.39	13413.4	4552.68	126916	13.362	17624.6	96
1996	8328.9	1241.37	13738.41	4678.07	128887	13.39	18716.7	97
1997	8703.5	1341.27	14113.81	4885.79	131912	13.382	19733	98
1998	9066.9	1463.11	14529.52	5202.97	133986	13.418	20831.6	99
1999	9470.3	1583.13	14987.13	5473.8	136186	13.388	21979.4	100
2000	9817	1679	15477.21	5782.7	138151	13.53	23302.7	101
2001	9890.7	1649.63	15994.8	5802.88	138283	13.58	24751.9	102
2002	10074.8	1595.81	16387.47	5830.93	137916	13.6	26715.3	103
2003	10377.04	1610.93	16876.13	5930.48	138987	13.63	27602.93	104
2004	10740.24	1781.56	17276.93	6071.46	140493.1	13.66	27280.21	105
2005	11062.45	1901.34	17676.16	6179.48	142991	13.69	28430.5	106
2006	11350.07	1971.35	18119.4	6332.2	145682	13.72	29623.68	107
2007	11588.42	1883.85	18504.48	6472.13	147304	13.75	30825.2	108
2008	11634.77	1720.96	18974.44	6479.4	146639	13.78	32228.31	109

Attached list B.2 America's model of compensation of employees

Dependent Variable: log *V*				
Method: Least Squares				
Sample(adjusted): 1902 2002				
Included observations: 101 after adjusting endpoints				
Convergence achieved after 5 iterations				
Variable	Coefficient	Std. Error	T-Statistic	Prob.
C	−2.490222	0.643256	−3.87127	0.0002
log *HL*	0.481456	0.06472	7.439013	0
t^3 log *SD*/*L*	−4.88E-08	8.93E-09	−5.46037	0
t log *SD*/*L*	0.001461	0.00018	8.110894	0
AR(1)	0.789106	0.064115	12.30758	0
R-squared	0.998978	Mean dependent var	3.012006	
Adjusted R-squared	0.998935	S.D. dependent var	0.46807	
S.E. of regression	0.015275	Akaike info criterion	−5.47691	
Sum squared resid	0.0224	Schwarz criterion	−5.34745	
Log likelihood	281.5839	F-statistic	23449.42	
Durbin-Watson stat	1.283108	Prob(F-statistic)	0	
Inverted AR Roots	0.79			

Attached list B.3 Investment value model

Dependent Variable: *M*				
Method: Least Squares				
Date: 03/22/10 Time: 08:24				
Sample: 1900 1945				
Included observations: 46				
Variable	Coefficient	Std. Error	T-Statistic	Prob.
C	11.72797	11.03289	1.063001	0.2939
K	0.115745	0.00644	17.97427	0
M	0.000696	0.000117	5.963635	0
HD/*K*	0.006999	0.000431	16.24785	0
R-squared	0.991766	Mean dependent var	366.9098	
Adjusted R-squared	0.991178	S.D. dependent var	161.7081	
S.E. of regression	15.18876	Akaike info criterion	8.36193	
Sum squared resid	9689.334	Schwarz criterion	8.520942	
Log likelihood	−188.324	F-statistic	1686.24	
Durbin-Watson stat	1.043807	Prob(F-statistic)	0	

Attached list B.4 The analysis of the resource allocation efficiency of production factors

Year	Efficiency	Waste rate of physical capital	Waste rate of labor	Waste rate of human capital
1901	0.73	0.00	0.58	0.42
1902	0.73	0.00	0.58	0.45
1903	0.58	0.00	0.44	0.31
1904	0.58	0.00	0.44	0.31
1905	0.78	0.00	0.59	0.44
1906	0.78	0.00	0.61	0.44
1907	0.65	0.00	0.48	0.34
1908	0.65	0.00	0.47	0.31
1909	0.65	0.00	0.48	0.34
1910	0.65	0.00	0.48	0.36
1911	0.55	0.00	0.39	0.27
1912	0.69	0.00	0.50	0.33
1913	0.69	0.00	0.50	0.36
1914	0.69	0.00	0.50	0.36
1915	0.61	0.00	0.41	0.27
1916	0.61	0.00	0.42	0.29
1917	0.61	0.00	0.42	0.29
1918	0.73	0.00	0.50	0.35
1919	0.61	0.00	0.43	0.29
1920	0.61	0.00	0.43	0.31
1921	0.54	0.00	0.34	0.22
1922	0.54	0.00	0.36	0.24
1923	0.65	0.00	0.44	0.31
1924	0.65	0.00	0.44	0.31
1925	0.68	0.00	0.45	0.31
1926	0.68	0.00	0.46	0.33
1927	0.68	0.00	0.46	0.33
1928	0.62	0.00	0.40	0.26
1929	0.62	0.00	0.40	0.28
1930	0.62	0.00	0.39	0.26
1931	0.48	0.00	0.27	0.15
1932	0.48	0.00	0.23	0.11
1933	0.40	0.00	0.19	0.09
1934	0.48	0.00	0.26	0.15
1935	0.57	0.00	0.31	0.19
1936	0.57	0.00	0.33	0.23
1937	0.65	0.00	0.39	0.28
1938	0.65	0.00	0.39	0.26
1939	0.60	0.00	0.34	0.23

(continued)

Attached list B.4 (continued)

Year	Efficiency	Waste rate of physical capital	Waste rate of labor	Waste rate of human capital
1940	0.67	0.00	0.40	0.29
1941	0.75	0.00	0.46	0.34
1942	0.83	0.00	0.51	0.40
1943	0.90	0.00	0.53	0.40
1944	0.91	0.00	0.49	0.34
1945	0.81	0.00	0.40	0.27
1946	0.71	0.00	0.35	0.24
1947	0.75	0.00	0.41	0.30
1948	0.75	0.00	0.41	0.31
1949	0.75	0.00	0.41	0.31
1950	0.81	0.00	0.45	0.35
1951	0.82	0.00	0.45	0.37
1952	0.87	0.00	0.49	0.39
1953	0.87	0.00	0.48	0.39
1954	0.83	0.00	0.43	0.34
1955	0.84	0.00	0.42	0.33
1956	0.84	0.00	0.43	0.33
1957	0.84	0.00	0.41	0.32
1958	0.81	0.00	0.37	0.28
1959	0.81	0.00	0.36	0.27
1960	0.85	0.00	0.38	0.28
1961	0.82	0.00	0.35	0.26
1962	0.83	0.00	0.34	0.26
1963	0.83	0.00	0.33	0.24
1964	0.87	0.00	0.33	0.24
1965	0.87	0.00	0.34	0.24
1966	0.91	0.00	0.35	0.26
1967	0.88	0.00	0.32	0.24
1968	0.88	0.00	0.31	0.23
1969	0.89	0.00	0.32	0.23
1970	0.84	0.00	0.26	0.18
1971	0.87	0.00	0.25	0.17
1972	0.87	0.00	0.25	0.18
1973	0.90	0.00	0.27	0.19
1974	0.87	0.00	0.26	0.18
1975	0.83	0.00	0.21	0.14
1976	0.86	0.00	0.21	0.14
1977	0.88	0.00	0.23	0.16
1978	0.91	0.00	0.25	0.18

(continued)

Attached list B.4 (continued)

Year	Efficiency	Waste rate of physical capital	Waste rate of labor	Waste rate of human capital
1979	0.91	0.00	0.25	0.19
1980	0.87	0.00	0.23	0.16
1981	0.86	0.00	0.20	0.15
1982	0.84	0.00	0.18	0.13
1983	0.86	0.00	0.17	0.12
1984	0.90	0.00	0.20	0.15
1985	0.90	0.00	0.19	0.14
1986	0.90	0.00	0.18	0.12
1987	0.90	0.00	0.17	0.13
1988	0.92	0.00	0.18	0.14
1989	0.92	0.00	0.17	0.13
1990	0.92	0.00	0.17	0.13
1991	0.90	0.00	0.14	0.11
1992	0.91	0.00	0.14	0.11
1993	0.93	0.00	0.14	0.11
1994	0.94	0.00	0.15	0.13
1995	0.94	0.00	0.14	0.11
1996	0.97	0.00	0.14	0.11
1997	0.98	0.00	0.14	0.11
1998	0.98	0.00	0.12	0.10
1999	0.99	0.00	0.11	0.08
2000	0.99	0.00	0.09	0.08
2001	0.98	0.00	0.07	0.06
2002	0.98	0.00	0.05	0.04
2003	0.97	0.00	0.02	0.01
2004	0.98	0.00	0.01	0.00
2005	0.99	0.00	0.01	0.00
2006	1.00	0.00	0.00	0.00
2007	1.00	0.00	0.00	0.00
2008	1.00	0.00	0.00	0.00

Appendix C
The Data and Model of Britain's Economic Growth

(1) Data

Data Sources: The data of R&D expenditure comes from the book of *Main Science and Technology Indicators Database* and *National Science Foundation* published by Organization for Economic Co-operation and Development (OEDC). The data of average years of schooling of laborers comes from the book of *Does Human Capital Matter for Growth in OECD Countries? Evidence from Poole Mean-group Estimates* written by Bassanini A and Scarpetta S. The data of compensation of employees comes from World Bank. The data of GDP and other data come from these databases of British Bureau of Statistics, Groningen Growth and Development Centre, and The Conference Board (Attached list C.1).

(2) British economic growth model (Add C.1)

$$Y = 0.000002(HL)^{0.83}(SD/L)^{0.115} + 0.12K + 139SD/K - 9.6 \quad \text{(Add C.1)}$$

Attached list C.2.
Attached list C.3
Attached list C.4.

J. H. Liu and Z. H. Jiang, *The Synergy Theory on Economic Growth: Comparative Study Between China and Developed Countries*,
https://doi.org/10.1007/978-981-13-1885-6

Attached list C.1 The data of Britain's economic growth (the prices at 2000, per billion pounds; per thousand people; years)

Year	GDP (billion pounds)	R&D expenditure / GDP (%)	Average years of schooling of laborers (Years)	Labor (thousand people)	The share of compensation of employees	Investment in physical capital / GDP	Net capital (lag one year; billion pounds)
1960	313.21	1.47	7.59	24178	0.588019	0.138554	
1961	321	1.48	7.67	24452	0.599694	0.145846	650
1962	324.99	1.48	7.66	24627	0.601992	0.144226	676
1963	340.3	1.48	7.7	24657	0.597113	0.140985	706
1964	358.9	1.46	7.75	24946	0.592386	0.153138	734
1965	368	1.52	7.82	25199	0.593844	0.153949	762
1966	375.18	1.58	7.88	25351	0.597999	0.154759	797
1967	383.79	1.68	7.94	24987	0.591807	0.160431	834
1968	399.49	1.7	8.01	24836	0.584324	0.162862	871
1969	407.66	1.7	8.07	24858	0.580782	0.15719	912
1970	417.4	1.6	9.2	24753	0.595089	0.158	955
1971	425.77	1.6	9.3	24533	0.585057	0.158431	997
1972	441.21	1.5	9.4	24510	0.589813	0.152826	1038
1973	473.48	1.5	9.5	25076	0.594675	0.151728	1080
1974	465.53	1.5	9.6	25148	0.627848	0.15131	1119
1975	462.37	1.5	9.7	25055	0.62	0.149459	1162
1976	475.34	1.5	9.8	24845	0.625323	0.147892	1202
1977	486.58	1.6	9.9	24865	0.595804	0.142265	1238
1978	503.14	1.8	10	25014	0.589558	0.14104	1273
1979	516.96	2	10.1	25394	0.588216	0.140865	1306
1980	505.69	2.2	10.2	25327	0.598292	0.137164	1339
1981	499.26	2.39	10.3	24345	0.592368	0.126866	1372
1982	508.24	2.3	10.4	23908	0.573607	0.131735	1399
1983	527.29	2.21	10.4	23626	0.562665	0.133543	1418
1984	540.2	2.2	10.5	24019	0.561039	0.141898	1440
1985	560.64	2.25	10.6	24390	0.556022	0.142678	1464
1986	584.24	2.27	10.7	24545	0.558284	0.140185	1494
1987	608.6	2.2	10.7	24931	0.548993	0.146776	1525
1988	640.22	2.15	10.8	25859	0.549244	0.160489	1556
1989	654.02	2.16	10.9	26689	0.556765	0.166477	1594
1990	659.17	2.16	11	26935	0.567203	0.161538	1643
1991	650.09	2.08	11.2	26153	0.572728	0.150517	1696
1992	651.57	2.09	11.3	25573	0.569224	0.148938	1743
1993	667.8	2.12	11.6	25342	0.556822	0.145344	1777
1994	698.92	2.08	11.6	25543	0.542537	0.14578	1807
1995	719.18	1.99	11.7	25856	0.537724	0.145629	1834
1996	738.05	1.92	11.8	26099	0.531962	0.149244	1865
1997	763.47	1.84	11.9	26567	0.533815	0.154294	1896

(continued)

Attached list C.1 (continued)

Year	GDP (billion pounds)	R&D expenditure / GDP (%)	Average years of schooling of laborers (Years)	Labor (thousand people)	The share of compensation of employees	Investment in physical capital / GDP	Net capital (lag one year; billion pounds)
1998	786.3	1.83	11.9595	26838	0.541153	0.169414	1930
1999	803.02	1.88	12.0193	27212	0.545979	0.168709	1969
2000	827.43	1.86	12.07939	27528	0.552275	0.166014	2022
2001	845.69	1.74	12.13979	27756	0.563166	0.165596	2070
2002	866.58	1.72	12.20049	27966	0.56	0.167651	2120
2003	899.64	1.7	12.26149	28230	0.56	0.163355	2181.769
2004	925.8	1.68	12.3228	28530	0.55	0.166669	2233.671
2005	951.49	1.73	12.38441	28819	0.54	0.166063	2289.286
2006	976.23	1.75	12.44634	29076	0.54	0.172116	2332.319
2007	1011.69	1.78	12.50857	29277	0.54	0.179621	2385.579
2008	1001.9	1.77	12.7	29488	0.53	0.172976	2461.067
2009	962.08	1.85	12.7635	29003	0.55	0.155464	2536.295
2010	979.39	1.77	12.82732	29067	0.55	0.158066	2588.883

Attached list C.2 UK's model of compensation of employees

Dependent Variable: log *V*				
Method: Least Squares				
Sample(adjusted): 1963 2005				
Included observations: 43 after adjusting endpoints				
Convergence achieved after 7 iterations				
Variable	Coefficient	Std. Error	T-Statistic	Prob.
C	−5.72083	0.617573	−9.26341	0
log *HL*	0.831099	0.063987	12.98847	0
log *SD/L*	0.115351	0.022089	5.222099	0
AR(3)	−0.36288	0.194397	−1.86669	0.0697
AR(2)	0.487679	0.198219	2.460302	0.0185
R-squared	0.991273	Mean dependent var	2.510972	
Adjusted R-squared	0.990355	S.D. dependent var	0.111559	
S.E. of regression	0.010956	Akaike info criterion	−6.08086	
Sum squared resid	0.004562	Schwarz criterion	−5.87607	
Log likelihood	135.7384	F-statistic	1079.108	
Durbin-Watson stat	1.050439	Prob(F-statistic)	0	
Inverted AR Roots	.47+.41i	.47−.41i	−0.94	

Attached list C.3 UK's investment value model

Dependent Variable: *M*				
Method: Least Squares				
Sample(adjusted): 1962 2010				
Included observations: 49 after adjusting endpoints				
Convergence achieved after 5 iterations				
Variable	Coefficient	Std. Error	T-Statistic	Prob.
C	−9.57817	18.36039	−0.52168	0.6045
K	0.118932	0.015408	7.718833	0
SD/*K*	139.2583	25.78875	5.399963	0
AR(1)	0.787707	0.093282	8.444388	0
R-squared	0.993432	Mean dependent var	272.822	
Adjusted R-squared	0.992994	S.D. dependent var	102.5097	
S.E. of regression	8.580171	Akaike info criterion	7.214892	
Sum squared resid	3312.87	Schwarz criterion	7.369327	
Log likelihood	−172.765	F-statistic	2268.801	
Durbin-Watson stat	1.424981	Prob(F-statistic)	0	
Inverted AR Roots	0.79			

Attached list C.4 The analysis of the resource allocation efficiency of production factors

Year	Efficiency	Waste rate of physical capital	Waste rate of labor	Waste rate of human capital
1960	1.00	0.00	0.00	0.00
1961	0.99	0.00	0.00	0.01
1962	0.97	0.00	0.00	0.00
1963	0.98	0.00	0.00	0.00
1964	1.00	0.00	0.00	0.00
1965	0.99	0.00	0.01	0.00
1966	0.97	0.00	0.02	0.00
1967	0.97	0.00	0.04	0.00
1968	0.97	0.00	0.06	0.00
1969	0.96	0.00	0.07	0.00
1970	0.93	0.00	0.00	0.06
1971	0.92	0.00	0.00	0.05
1972	0.92	0.00	0.00	0.04
1973	0.96	0.00	0.00	0.05
1974	0.91	0.00	0.00	0.04

(continued)

Attached list C.4 (continued)

Year	Efficiency	Waste rate of physical capital	Waste rate of labor	Waste rate of human capital
1975	0.88	0.00	0.00	0.04
1976	0.88	0.00	0.00	0.03
1977	0.88	0.00	0.00	0.03
1978	0.89	0.00	0.00	0.03
1979	0.89	0.00	0.00	0.03
1980	0.86	0.00	0.00	0.03
1981	0.84	0.00	0.00	0.01
1982	0.84	0.00	0.00	0.01
1983	0.86	0.00	0.01	0.00
1984	0.87	0.00	0.00	0.00
1985	0.89	0.00	0.00	0.01
1986	0.91	0.00	0.00	0.01
1987	0.92	0.00	0.00	0.01
1988	0.95	0.00	0.00	0.03
1989	0.94	0.00	0.00	0.03
1990	0.92	0.00	0.00	0.03
1991	0.89	0.00	0.00	0.02
1992	0.88	0.00	0.00	0.01
1993	0.89	0.00	0.00	0.02
1994	0.91	0.00	0.00	0.01
1995	0.93	0.00	0.00	0.02
1996	0.93	0.00	0.00	0.02
1997	0.95	0.00	0.00	0.03
1998	0.96	0.00	0.00	0.03
1999	0.96	0.00	0.00	0.03
2000	0.96	0.00	0.00	0.03
2001	0.96	0.00	0.00	0.02
2002	0.96	0.00	0.00	0.02
2003	0.97	0.00	0.00	0.02
2004	0.98	0.00	0.00	0.01
2005	0.99	0.00	0.00	0.01
2006	0.99	0.00	0.00	0.01
2007	1.00	0.00	0.00	0.00
2008	0.98	0.02	0.00	0.01
2009	0.96	0.06	0.00	0.02
2010	0.98	0.06	0.00	0.02

Appendix D
The Data and Model of South Korea's Economic Growth

(1) Data

Data Sources: The data of GDP, labor, compensation of employees, physical capital stock, investment in physical capital come from the South Korea Statistical Information Network. The data of average years of schooling of laborers comes from Yamauchi F and Godo Y's *Human Capital Accumulation, Technological Change and International Spillovers: Comparative Growth Experience from Japan, North Korea and the United States*. The data of R&D expenditure comes from Pyo H K and Ha B's *Technology and Long-run Economic Growth in Korea*. The data of compensation of employees comes from Yoo J's *Neoclassical versus Revisionist View of Korean Economic Growth*, and Pyo H K's A*n Episode of Rapid Productivity Convergence and Stagnation: Korea (1954–2002)*. The data of physical capital stock refer to Pyo H K's *Estimates of Reproducible Tangible Physical Capital in the Republic of Korea, 1953–1996* (Attached list D.1).

(2) South Korea's economic growth model (Add D.1)

$$Y = 1.16(HL)^{0.53}(SD/L)^{0.18} + 0.189K + 19SD/K + 11.5LD/K + 1810 \tag{Add D.1}$$

Attached list D.2.
Attached list D.3.
Attached list D.4.

J. H. Liu and Z. H. Jiang, *The Synergy Theory on Economic Growth: Comparative Study Between China and Developed Countries*,
https://doi.org/10.1007/978-981-13-1885-6

Attached list D.1 The data of South Korea's economic growth (the prices at 2005, per hundred million won; per thousand people; years)

Year	GDP (100 million won)	Gross physical capital formation (100 million won)	Average years of schooling of laborers (years)	Physical capital stock (100 million won)	Labor (thousand people)	Compensation of employees (100 million won)	R&D expenditure (lag three years; 100 million won)
1960	30908.55	1327.55	3.23	28436	6829	9272.565	6.594621
1961	32206.71	1579.61	3.33	30729	7074	9984.08	6.858406
1962	33333.94	2119.45	3.43	32317	7318	10666.86	7.132742
1963	36367.33	2701.31	3.53	34295	7563	12001.22	7.418052
1964	39858.59	2871.45	3.64	37045	7698	13551.92	7.72961
1965	42170.39	3180.23	3.75	40001	8112	14337.93	8.333485
1966	47526.03	4627.51	3.86	43328	8325	16158.85	9.091833
1967	50662.75	5669.38	3.98	48180	8624	17225.34	10.36323
1968	56387.64	7744.73	4.1	54559	9061	19171.8	11.38601
1969	64169.14	10397.72	4.22	62831	9285	21817.51	13.30729
1970	69046	10320.3	4.5	74167	9617	23931.34	14.6922
1971	74737.5	10798.2	4.715	82689	9946	25724.65	16.91629
1972	78076.7	10983.3	4.93	88975	10379	26514.85	20.53412
1973	87472.7	13866.3	5.145	102673	10942	29600.76	26.35035
1974	93755.1	15824.6	5.36	113349	11421	29926.63	23.31135
1975	99331.3	17240.5	5.575	123693	11691	32044.28	22.26479
1976	109832.9	20816.2	5.79	140873	12412	36233.87	25.06644
1977	120810.5	27095.7	6.005	159602	12812	41812.51	46.02591
1978	132040	36423.1	6.22	179670	13412	48260.62	40.80329
1979	140996.2	40077.6	6.435	197613	13602	53691.35	46.76028
1980	138897.9	35783	6.65	200512	13683	54309.08	71.26716
1981	147458.2	34676.6	6.865	219256	14023	56653.44	81.33165
1982	158259.7	38531.6	7.08	242376	14379	61942.85	77.33176
1983	175312	45254.6	7.295	276546	14505	70668.27	75.844
1984	189516.2	50168.1	7.51	307921	14429	76526.64	111.726
1985	202408	52813.4	7.725	338734	14970	81570.42	151.4027
1986	223901.5	58901.3	7.94	385944	15505	89829.28	166.2625
1987	248763.9	69556.9	8.155	441664	16354	101296.7	210.361
1988	275235.3	79032.1	8.37	503323	16869	115791.5	278.1466
1989	293798.5	91669.7	8.585	553387	17560	130270.3	366.7198
1990	320696.4	114989	8.8	622172	18085	144473.7	428.8239
1991	350819.9	131589.2	9.07	701032	18623	162043.7	492.6423
1992	371433	132313	9.34	764490	18985	171416.3	534.8545
1993	394215.8	142536.9	9.61	835723	19211	182403.7	575.4374
1994	427868.2	160340.6	9.88	934277	19829	197846.3	645.4933
1995	467099.2	181345.2	10.15	1050538	20397	219116.2	719.5759

(continued)

Attached list D.1 (continued)

Year	GDP (100 million won)	Gross physical capital formation (100 million won)	Average years of schooling of laborers (years)	Physical capital stock (100 million won)	Labor (thousand people)	Compensation of employees (100 million won)	R&D expenditure (lag three years; 100 million won)
1996	499789.8	196550.1	10.42	1157784	20838	238949.5	834.4708
1997	523034.7	192033.8	10.69	1247980	21201	241380.5	992.8949
1998	487183.5	147991.7	10.96	1197311	19920	218355.6	1105.638
1999	533399.3	160336.3	11.23	1350219	20275	229575.1	1211.944
2000	578664.5	179907.7	11.5	1508745	21137	248247.1	1297.729
2001	600865.9	179576.3	11.77	1567622	21557	261316.6	1140.876
2002	642748.1	191464.6	12.04	1633677	22151	276574.5	1200.955
2003	662654.8	199047.9	12.31	1702031	22116.3	292562.1	1384.85
2004	693995.5	203187.9	12.42	1769056	22557.1	306884.8	1556.006
2005	723126.8	208054.8	12.51	1835586	22856.1	325696.3	1627.394
2006	759234.4	214624.7	12.61	1903364	23150.8	344464.6	1743.672
2007	776696.8	210546.8	12.9	1961642	23432.8	354173.7	1859.908
2008	779026.9	208441.4	13.2	2013152	23577.3	358352.4	2155.1
2009	828105.6	220531	13.4	2072631	23505.6	380928.6	2277.703
2010	857917.4	218105.1	13.6	2124926	23828.8	394642	2493.197

Attached list D.2 South Korea's model of compensation of employees

Dependent Variable: log *V*				
Method: Least Squares				
Sample(adjusted): 1963–2010				
Included observations: 48 after adjusting endpoints				
Convergence achieved after 52 iterations				
Variable	Coefficient	Std. Error	T-Statistic	Prob.
C	0.062808	0.680	0.09	0.9267
log *HL*	0.532579	0.090	5.99	0
log *SD*/*L*	0.180383	0.030	6.22	0
AR(3)	0.733073	0.120	6.19	0
R-squared	0.997938	Mean dependent var	6.082917	
Adjusted R-squared	0.997797	S.D. dependent var	0.485114	
S.E. of regression	0.022768	Akaike info criterion	−4.647251	
Sum squared resid	0.022809	Schwarz criterion	−4.491317	
Durbin-Watson stat	0.8	F-statistic	7098	

Attached list D.3 Investment value model

Dependent Variable: Y - V				
Method: Least Squares				
Sample (adjusted): 1963–2006				
Included observations: 44 after adjustments				
Convergence achieved after 8 iterations				
	Coefficient	Std. Error	T-Statistic	0.03
C	1810	8034.452	2.25486	0
K	0.189112	0.013328	14.18877	0.0331
SD/K	19	86.84337	2.211049	0.0007
LD/K	11.4759	3.120802	3.677228	0
AR(1)	1.089222	0.099214	10.97853	0.0026
AR(3)	−0.324086	0.100674	−3.219166	
R-squared	0.9.98	Mean dependent var	160714	
Adjusted R-squared	0.998	S.D. dependent var	120498	
S.E. of regression	5224	Akaike info criterion	20.1	
Sum squared resid	1.04E+09	Schwarz criterion	20.3	
Durbin-Watson stat	2.18	F-statistic	4567	

Attached list D.4 The analysis of the resource allocation efficiency of production factors

Year	Efficiency	Waste rate of physical capital	Waste rate of labor	Waste rate of human capital
1960	0.99	0.00	0.04	0.20
1961	0.96	0.00	0.03	0.16
1962	0.94	0.00	0.04	0.14
1963	0.97	0.00	0.05	0.12
1964	0.98	0.00	0.02	0.07
1965	0.96	0.00	0.02	0.05
1966	1.00	0.00	0.00	0.00
1967	0.98	0.00	0.01	0.00
1968	0.98	0.00	0.01	0.00
1969	1.00	0.00	0.00	0.00
1970	0.98	0.00	0.00	0.00
1971	0.99	0.00	0.01	0.00
1972	0.98	0.00	0.04	0.00

(continued)

Attached list D.4 (continued)

Year	Efficiency	Waste rate of physical capital	Waste rate of labor	Waste rate of human capital
1973	0.99	0.00	0.03	0.00
1974	0.99	0.00	0.04	0.00
1975	0.99	0.00	0.05	0.00
1976	0.99	0.00	0.04	0.00
1977	1.00	0.00	0.03	0.00
1978	1.00	0.00	0.02	0.00
1979	1.00	0.00	0.00	0.00
1980	0.97	0.00	0.03	0.00
1981	0.97	0.00	0.04	0.00
1982	0.97	0.00	0.04	0.00
1983	0.99	0.00	0.02	0.00
1984	1.00	0.00	0.00	0.00
1985	0.99	0.00	0.01	0.00
1986	1.00	0.00	0.01	0.00
1987	1.00	0.00	0.01	0.00
1988	1.00	0.00	0.00	0.00
1989	0.99	0.00	0.01	0.00
1990	0.99	0.00	0.00	0.00
1991	1.00	0.00	0.00	0.00
1992	0.99	0.00	0.01	0.00
1993	0.98	0.00	0.00	0.00
1994	0.98	0.00	0.00	0.00
1995	0.98	0.00	0.00	0.00
1996	0.97	0.00	0.00	0.00
1997	0.96	0.00	0.00	0.00
1998	0.93	0.00	0.00	0.00
1999	0.93	0.00	0.00	0.00
2000	0.92	0.00	0.00	0.02
2001	0.92	0.00	0.00	0.00
2002	0.94	0.00	0.00	0.00
2003	0.94	0.00	0.00	0.00
2004	0.95	0.00	0.00	0.00
2005	0.97	0.00	0.00	0.02
2006	0.99	0.00	0.00	0.06
2007	0.98	0.00	0.00	0.02
2008	0.95	0.00	0.00	0.00
2009	0.99	0.00	0.00	0.01
2010	1.00	0.00	0.00	0.00

Appendix E
The Data and Model of France's Economic Growth

(1) Data

Data Sources: The data of GDP, labor, compensation of employees, physical capital stock, investment in physical capital come from the book of *France Statistical Yearbook*, and databases of Groningen Growth and Development Centre, The World Bank, The Conference Board and United Nations Statistics Division. The data of average years of schooling of laborers comes from *Does Human Capital Matter for Growth in OECD Countries? Evidence from Poole Mean-group Estimates Written by* Bassanini A and Scarpetta S, *The Comparative Postwar Economic Performance of The G-7 Countries* written by Boskin M J and Lau L J, and Organization for Economic Co-operation and Development (OECD). The index of R&D expenditure comes from Organization for Economic Co-operation and Development (OECD) (Attached list E.1).

(2) France's economic growth model (Add E.1)

$$Y = 0.013(HL)^{0.57}(SD/L)^{0.08} + 0.142K + 74SD/K + 603 \qquad \text{(Add E.1)}$$

Attached list E.2.
Attached list E.3.
Attached list E.4.

J. H. Liu and Z. H. Jiang, *The Synergy Theory on Economic Growth: Comparative Study Between China and Developed Countries*,
https://doi.org/10.1007/978-981-13-1885-6

Attached list E.1 The data of France's economic growth (the prices at 2005, per hundred million euros; per thousand people; years)

Year	GDP (100 million euros)	Compensation of employees (100 million euros)	Average years of schooling of laborers (years)	R&D expenditure (100 million euros)	Physical capital stock (100 million euros)	Investment in physical capital (100 million euros)	Labor (thousand people)
1980	10322	5809	9.5	175		2000	22845
1981	10423	5837	9.6	182	16482	1962	22806
1982	10675	6089	9.6	195	17220	1933	22849
1983	10807	6121	9.7	209	17883	1863	22825
1984	10968	6135	9.7	222	18541	1836	22691
1985	11145	6175	9.8	230	19162	1880	22633
1986	11396	6158	9.8	246	19809	1966	22750
1987	11668	6235	9.8	259	20426	2062	22941
1988	12213	6404	9.9	270	21125	2256	23160
1989	12724	6607	9.9	285	21937	2426	23557
1990	13058	6853	10	292	22913	2523	23766
1991	13193	6957	10	302	23977	2516	23798
1992	13388	7081	10.2	317	25070	2466	23634
1993	13299	7043	10.3	315	26076	2319	23360
1994	13598	7081	10.4	324	26981	2357	23459
1995	13876	7228	10.5	333	27686	2400	23679
1996	14024	7313	10.6	328	28417	2416	23812
1997	14331	7440	10.6	331	29067	2430	23973
1998	14815	7631	10.6	341	29735	2611	24383
1999	15302	7937	10.7	338	30315	2833	24943
2000	15866	8246	10.9	346	31069	3024	25588
2001	16157	8481	11.0	354	31909	3086	25970
2002	16307	8568	11.2	351	32818	3023	26105
2003	16454	8677	11.3	347	33687	3087	26137
2004	16872	8774	11.5	356	34700	3192	26176
2005	17180	8934	11.6	363	35660	3333	26349
2006	17604	9154	11.8	371	36140	3464	26634
2007	18007	9363	11.9	380	36713	3682	27006
2008	17992	9536	12.2	380	37458	3693	27137
2009	17426	9236	12.4	368	38154	3300	26783
2010	17716	9389	12.5	374	37639	3341	26766

Attached list E.2 France's model of compensation of employees

Dependent Variable: log *V*				
Method: Least Squares				
Sample(adjusted): 1982 2010				
Included observations: 29 after adjusting endpoints				
Convergence achieved after 11 iterations	Coefficient	Std. Error	T-Statistic	Prob.
C	−1.86611	0.679232	−2.74738	0.011
log *HL*	0.573278	0.072968	7.856555	0
log *SD*/*L*	0.080741	0.041026	1.968044	0.0602
AR(1)	0.818749	0.114573	7.146123	0
R-squared	0.996822	Mean dependent var	3.869587	
Adjusted R-squared	0.996441	S.D. dependent var	0.067342	
S.E. of regression	0.004018	Akaike info criterion	−8.06881	
Sum squared resid	0.000404	Schwarz criterion	−7.88022	
Log likelihood	120.9977	F-statistic	2613.894	
Durbin-Watson stat	1.73171	Prob(F-statistic)	0	
Inverted AR Roots	0.82			

Attached list E.3 France's investment value model

Dependent variable: *M*				
Method: Least Squares				
Sample(adjusted): 1982 2010				
Included observations: 29 after adjusting endpoints				
Convergence achieved after 14 iterations				
Variable	Coefficient	Std. Error	T-Statistic	Prob.
C	603.0788	300.3448	2.007955	0.0556
K	0.141904	0.008137	17.43989	0
SD/*K*	73.74014	11.41406	6.460467	0
AR(1)	0.668473	0.199549	3.34992	0.0026
R-squared	0.996478	Mean dependent var	6800.487	
Adjusted R-squared	0.996055	S.D. dependent var	1258.243	
S.E. of regression	79.03043	Akaike info criterion	11.70499	
Sum squared resid	156145.2	Schwarz criterion	11.89358	
Log likelihood	−165.722	F-statistic	2357.462	
Durbin-Watson stat	1.594888	Prob(F-statistic)	0	
Inverted AR Roots	0.67			

Attached list E.4 The analysis of the resource allocation efficiency of production factors

Year	Efficiency	Waste rate of physical capital	Waste rate of labor	Waste rate of human capital
1980	1.00	0.00	0.00	0.00
1981	0.99	0.00	0.00	0.00
1982	0.99	0.00	0.00	0.00
1983	0.98	0.00	0.00	0.01
1984	0.98	0.00	0.00	0.00
1985	0.97	0.00	0.00	0.01
1986	0.97	0.00	0.00	0.00
1987	0.98	0.00	0.00	0.00
1988	0.99	0.00	0.00	0.00
1989	1.00	0.00	0.00	0.00
1990	1.00	0.00	0.00	0.00
1991	1.00	0.00	0.03	0.00
1992	0.99	0.00	0.03	0.00
1993	0.98	0.00	0.04	0.00
1994	0.98	0.00	0.04	0.00
1995	0.98	0.00	0.03	0.00
1996	0.97	0.00	0.02	0.00
1997	0.98	0.00	0.00	0.00
1998	1.00	0.00	0.00	0.00
1999	1.00	0.00	0.00	0.00
2000	1.00	0.00	0.00	0.00
2001	0.99	0.00	0.00	0.00
2002	0.99	0.00	0.00	0.00
2003	0.98	0.00	0.00	0.00
2004	1.00	0.01	0.00	0.00
2005	1.00	0.01	0.00	0.00
2006	1.00	0.00	0.00	0.00
2007	1.00	0.00	0.00	0.00
2008	0.99	0.01	0.00	0.02
2009	0.98	0.01	0.00	0.04
2010	0.99	0.02	0.00	0.05

Appendix F
The Data and Model of Germany's Economic Growth

(1) Data

Data Sources: The data of GDP, labor, compensation of employees, physical capital stock, investment in physical capital come from the book of *German Statistical Yearbook*, and databases of Groningen Growth and Development Centre, The World Bank, The Conference Board and United Nations Statistics Division. The data of average years of schooling of laborers comes from *Does Human Capital Matter for Growth in OECD Countries? Evidence from Poole Mean-group Estimates* written by Bassanini A and Scarpetta S, *The Comparative Postwar Economic Performance of The G-7 Countries* written by Boskin M. J. and Lau L. J., and Organization for Economic Co-operation and Development (OECD). The index of research and development expenditure comes from Organization for Economic Co-operation and Development (OECD) (Attached list F.1).

(2) Germany's economic growth model (Add F.1)

$$Y = 0.038(HL)^{0.292}(SD)^{0.15} + 0.235K + 0.48SD/K - 2326 \qquad \text{(Add F.1)}$$

Attached list F.2.
Attached list F.3.
Attached list F.4.

J. H. Liu and Z. H. Jiang, *The Synergy Theory on Economic Growth: Comparative Study Between China and Developed Countries*,
https://doi.org/10.1007/978-981-13-1885-6

Attached list F.1 The data of Germany's economic growth (the prices at 1990, per hundred million euros; per thousand people; y ears)

Year	GDP (100 million euros)	Compensation of employees (100 million euros)	Physical capital stock (100 million euros)	Physical capital investment (100 million euros)	R&D expenditure (lag two years; 100 million euros)	Average years of schooling of laborers (years)	Labor (thousand people)
1990	17821	9980	33038	3487	407	11.5	37404
1991	18732	10302	34095	3661	423	11.5	38712
1992	19090	10611	35194	3836	453	11.6	38183
1993	18899	10455	36286	3678	472	11.6	37695
1994	19366	10450	37440	3831	448	11.6	37667
1995	19690	10619	38322	3819	434	11.7	37802
1996	19846	10643	39139	3800	440	11.7	37772
1997	20191	10649	39949	3837	439	11.7	37716
1998	20567	10793	40805	3986	453	11.8	38148
1999	20952	11025	41559	4163	471	11.8	38721
2000	21592	11515	42456	4272	504	11.8	39382
2001	21919	11632	43630	4132	527	11.9	39485
2002	21921	11618	44295	3878	544	11.9	39257
2003	21839	11356	44702	3830	554	12.0	38918
2004	22093	11488	44917	3821	554	12.1	39034
2005	22244	11344	45091	3852	552	12.2	38976
2006	23067	11764	45335	4171	553	12.4	39192
2007	23821	12149	45879	4367	557	12.5	39857
2008	24079	12040	46576	4423	586	12.7	40348
2009	22845	11879	47273	3919	603	12.8	40370
2010	23794	12135	47411	4147	648	13.0	40603

Attached list F.2 Germany's model of compensation of employees

Dependent Variable: log V				
Method: Least Squares				
Sample(adjusted): 1991 2010				
Included observations: 20 after adjusting endpoints				
Convergence achieved after 9 iterations				
Variable	Coefficient	Std. Error	T-Statistic	Prob.
C	0.808033	1.29516	0.623887	0.5415

(continued)

Attached list F.2 (continued)

Dependent Variable: log *V*				
log *HL*	0.291655	0.135362	2.154622	0.0468
log *SD*	0.144784	0.06956	2.081424	0.0538
AR(1)	0.581123	0.17059	3.406545	0.0036
R-squared	0.945822	Mean dependent var	4.049502	
Adjusted R-squared	0.935664	S.D. dependent var	0.023937	
S.E. of regression	0.006072	Akaike info criterion	−7.19355	
Sum squared resid	0.00059	Schwarz criterion	−6.9944	
Log likelihood	75.93548	F-statistic	93.10759	
Durbin-Watson stat	2.13404	Prob (F-statistic)	0	
Inverted AR Roots	0.58			

Attached list F.3 Germany's investment value model

Dependent Variable: *M*				
Method: Least Squares				
Sample: 1990 2010				
Included observations: 21				
Variable	Coefficient	Std. Error	T-Statistic	Prob.
C	−2325.69	563.2719	−4.12889	0.0006
K	0.23538	0.016766	14.03913	0
SD/*K*	0.479968	0.138263	3.471427	0.0027
R-squared	0.965623	Mean dependent var	9996.099	
Adjusted R-squared	0.961803	S.D. dependent var	1198.594	
S.E. of regression	234.2544	Akaike info criterion	13.88226	
Sum squared resid	987752.1	Schwarz criterion	14.03147	
Log likelihood	−142.764	F-statistic	252.7993	
Durbin-Watson stat	1.059194	Prob(F-statistic)	0	

Attached list F.4 The analysis of the resource allocation efficiency of production factors

Year	Efficiency	Waste rate of physical capital	Waste rate of labor	Waste rate of human capital
1990	0.98	0.00	0.01	0.00
1991	1.00	0.00	0.00	0.00
1992	0.99	0.00	0.03	0.00
1993	0.96	0.00	0.04	0.00
1994	0.97	0.00	0.06	0.00
1995	0.97	0.00	0.06	0.00
1996	0.96	0.00	0.07	0.00
1997	0.96	0.00	0.06	0.00
1998	0.96	0.00	0.06	0.00
1999	0.96	0.00	0.05	0.00
2000	0.97	0.00	0.05	0.00
2001	0.98	0.00	0.05	0.00
2002	0.98	0.01	0.04	0.00
2003	0.98	0.02	0.04	0.00
2004	0.98	0.01	0.03	0.00
2005	0.97	0.01	0.02	0.00
2006	0.99	0.01	0.01	0.00
2007	1.00	0.00	0.00	0.00
2008	1.00	0.00	0.00	0.00
2009	0.95	0.00	0.00	0.02
2010	0.98	0.00	0.00	0.04

Appendix G
The Data and Model of Canada's Economic Growth

(1) Data

Data Sources: The data of GDP, labor, compensation of employees, physical capital stock, investment in physical capital come from the book of *Canadian Statistical Yearbook*, and databases of Groningen Growth and Development Centre, The World Bank, The Conference Board and United Nations Statistics Division. The data of average years of schooling of laborers comes from *Does Human Capital Matter for Growth in OECD Countries? Evidence from Poole Mean-group Estimates* written by Bassanini A and Scarpetta S, and *The Comparative Postwar Economic Performance of The G-7 Countries* written by Boskin M. J. and Lau L. J. The index of research and development expenditure comes from Statistics Canada and Organization for Economic Co-operation and Development (OECD) (Attached list G.1).

(2) Canada's economic growth model (Add G.1)

$$Y = 0.0436H^{1.04}(SDH)^{0.091} + 0.115K + 83.7SD/K + 818 \qquad \text{(Add G.1)}$$

Attached list G.2.
Attached list G.3.
Attached list G.4.

J. H. Liu and Z. H. Jiang, *The Synergy Theory on Economic Growth: Comparative Study Between China and Developed Countries*,
https://doi.org/10.1007/978-981-13-1885-6

Attached list G.1 The data of Canada's economic growth (the prices at 2005, per hundred million Canadian dollar; per thousand people; years)

Year	GDP (100 million Canadian dollar)	Physical capital stock (lag one year) (100 million Canadian dollar)	Investment in physical capital (100 million Canadian dollar)	R&D expenditure / GDP (lag two years; %)	Average years of schooling o laborers (years)	Labor (thousand people)
1980	6886		1256			11057
1981	7127	15425	1349	1.2	10.6	11379
1982	6923	16254	1194	1.2	10.7	11019
1983	7111	17133	1183	1.2	10.7	11098
1984	7525	17806	1211	1.4	10.8	11377
1985	7885	18429	1317	1.4	10.8	11704
1986	8076	19062	1378	1.4	10.9	12064
1987	8419	19763	1522	1.4	11.0	12412
1988	8838	20496	1664	1.5	11.1	12788
1989	9069	21350	1758	1.4	11.1	13075
1990	9087	22314	1689	1.4	11.1	13165
1991	8897	23318	1597	1.5	11.3	12935
1992	8975	24207	1553	1.5	11.4	12807
1993	9184	24942	1522	1.6	11.6	12868
1994	9626	25570	1636	1.6	11.9	13132
1995	9896	26161	1601	1.7	12.1	13365
1996	10056	26816	1671	1.8	12.2	13484
1997	10481	27407	1926	1.7	12.4	13769
1998	10911	28002	1973	1.7	12.5	14107
1999	11514	28883	2116	1.7	12.6	14462
2000	12117	29836	2215	1.8	12.7	14817
2001	12333	30987	2303	1.8	12.8	14994
2002	12694	31000	2339	1.9	12.8	15352
2003	12932	31169	2484	2.1	12.9	15718
2004	13336	31783	2677	2.0	13.0	15977
2005	13738	32553	2926	1.9	13.0	16184
2006	14126	33526	3133	1.9	13.1	16471
2007	14437	34648	3244	1.9	13.2	16867
2008	14537	35813	3310	2.1	13.3	17150
2009	14134	36974	2881	2	13.3	16877
2010	14588	37637	3170	2	13.3	17105

Attached list G.2 Canada's logarithm model log *V* of compensation of employees

Sample: 1981 2010				
Included observations: 30				
Variable	Coefficient	Std. Error	T-Statistic	Prob.
C	−1.36276	0.732348	−1.86081	0.0737
log *L*	1.04258	0.274781	3.79422	0.0008
log *SDH*	0.091424	0.047492	1.92504	0.0648
R-squared	0.993611	Mean dependent var	3.739303	
Adjusted R-squared	0.993138	S.D. dependent var	0.094553	
S.E. of regression	0.007833	Akaike info criterion	−6.76638	
Sum squared resid	0.001656	Schwarz criterion	−6.62626	
Log likelihood	104.4958	F-statistic	2099.483	
Durbin-Watson stat	0.854362	Prob(F-statistic)	0	

Attached list G.3 Canada's investment value model

Dependent Variable: *M*				
Method: Least Squares				
Sample(adjusted): 1983 2010				
Included observations: 28 after adjusting endpoints				
Convergence achieved after 7 iterations				
Variable	Coefficient	Std. Error	T-Statistic	Prob.
C	818.1056	303.6265	2.694448	0.0129
K	0.114661	0.014511	7.901497	0
SD/*K*	83.67011	10.60507	7.889634	0
AR(2)	−0.49159	0.197145	−2.49353	0.0203
AR(1)	1.144191	0.186098	6.148319	0
R-squared	0.994637	Mean dependent var	5141.276	
Adjusted R-squared	0.993704	S.D. dependent var	1277.473	
S.E. of regression	101.366	Akaike info criterion	12.23578	
Sum squared resid	236326.4	Schwarz criterion	12.47368	
Log likelihood	−166.301	F-statistic	1066.319	
Durbin-Watson stat	1.790061	Prob (F-statistic)	0	
Inverted AR Roots	.57 −.41i	.57+.41i		

Attached list G.4 The analysis of the resource allocation efficiency of production factors

Year	Efficiency	Waste rate of physical capital	Waste rate of labor	Waste rate of human capital
1981	1.00	0.00	0.00	0.00
1982	0.95	0.00	0.00	0.10
1983	0.95	0.00	0.00	0.12
1984	0.98	0.00	0.00	0.13
1985	0.99	0.00	0.00	0.12
1986	0.98	0.00	0.00	0.12
1987	0.98	0.00	0.00	0.11
1988	0.99	0.00	0.00	0.11
1989	0.98	0.00	0.00	0.13
1990	0.95	0.00	0.00	0.17
1991	0.93	0.03	0.00	0.16
1992	0.94	0.05	0.00	0.14
1993	0.94	0.06	0.00	0.12
1994	0.94	0.04	0.00	0.10
1995	0.94	0.03	0.00	0.08
1996	0.93	0.03	0.00	0.07
1997	0.94	0.02	0.00	0.06
1998	0.95	0.02	0.00	0.05
1999	0.97	0.02	0.00	0.04
2000	0.99	0.03	0.00	0.03
2001	0.99	0.01	0.00	0.03
2002	0.99	0.00	0.00	0.01
2003	0.99	0.00	0.00	0.00
2004	1.00	0.00	0.00	0.00
2005	1.00	0.00	0.00	0.00
2006	1.00	0.00	0.00	0.00
2007	1.00	0.01	0.01	0.00
2008	0.99	0.02	0.01	0.00
2009	0.98	0.06	0.01	0.00
2010	0.99	0.07	0.02	0.00

Appendix H
The Data and Model of Japan's Economic Growth

(1) Data

Data Sources: The data of GDP, labor, compensation of employees, physical capital stock, investment in physical capital comes from *Japan Statistical Yearbook*, and databases of Groningen Growth and Development Centre, The World Bank, The Conference Board and United Nations Statistics Division. The data of average years of schooling of laborers come from Yamauchi F and Godo Y's *Human Capital Accumulation, Technological Changed International Spillovers: Comparative Growth Experience from Japan, Korea and the United States1*, Boskin M. J. and Lau L. J.'s *The Comparative Postwar Economic Performance of the G-7 Countries* and Organization for Economic Co-operation and Development (OECD), *Education at a Glance 2010*. The index of research and development expenditure comes from Statistics Canada and Organization for Economic Co-operation and Development (OECD) (Attached list H.1).

Note The physical capital stock from 2001 to 2009 is measured at the depreciation rate of 8%.

(2) Japan's economic growth model (Add H.1)

$$Y = 0.11788(HL)^{0.4}(SD/L)^{0.36} + 0.117K + 99.5SD/K - 332SD/L + 19.95 \quad \text{(Add H.1)}$$

Attached list H.2.
Attached list H.3.
Attached list H.4.

J. H. Liu and Z. H. Jiang, *The Synergy Theory on Economic Growth: Comparative Study Between China and Developed Countries*,
https://doi.org/10.1007/978-981-13-1885-6

Attached list H.1 The data of Japan's economic growth (the prices at 2005, per trillion yen; per ten thousand people; years)

Year	Investment in physical capital (trillion yen)	Compensation of employees (trillion yen)	GDP (trillion yen)	Labor (10 thousand people)	R&D expenditure (trillion yen)	Physical capital stock (trillion yen)	Average years of schooling of laborers (years)
1955	12	20	45.64	3926	0.25	50.88	8.2
1956	11	21	49.06	4032	0.27	64.50	8.4
1957	13	24	52.89	4138	0.29	78.24	8.5
1958	14	27	56.16	4244	0.36	94.20	8.6
1959	15	31	61.44	4350	0.44	112.03	8.7
1960	15	28	69.49	4436	0.74	131.41	8.8
1961	16	31	77.86	4498	0.85	151.97	9.0
1962	21	36	84.80	4556	1.06	177.51	9.1
1963	24	39	91.99	4595	1.17	200.28	9.2
1964	28	44	102.73	4655	1.28	223.54	9.3
1965	29	48	108.70	4730	1.45	266.21	9.4
1966	33	52	120.27	4827	1.60	288.48	9.4
1967	40	57	133.60	4920	1.72	316.45	9.6
1968	48	63	150.81	5002	2.00	351.52	9.7
1969	56	72	169.63	5040	2.39	395.37	9.8
1970	68	83	187.79	5094	2.73	451.10	9.9
1971	68	92	196.61	5121	3.30	498.24	10.0
1972	75	101	213.16	5126	3.54	531.66	10.1
1973	83	113	230.28	5259	3.67	591.75	10.1
1974	78	121	227.46	5237	3.75	626.22	10.2
1975	74	129	234.49	5223	4.29	602.05	10.3
1976	77	134	243.81	5271	4.35	601.54	10.4
1977	80	140	254.51	5342	4.55	606.09	10.4
1978	86	145	267.93	5408	4.79	631.06	10.5
1979	91	153	282.62	5479	5.16	655.37	10.6
1980	91	157	290.59	5536	5.55	705.31	10.7
1981	93	165	299.80	5581	6.10	742.90	10.8
1982	93	172	308.97	5638	6.83	791.65	10.9
1983	91	176	316.14	5733	7.33	827.01	10.9
1984	96	181	328.53	5766	7.85	862.27	11.0
1985	102	186	342.99	5807	8.45	891.48	11.1
1986	106	190	352.92	5853	9.35	933.77	11.1
1987	115	196	367.60	5911	9.66	972.22	11.1
1988	130	206	390.37	6011	10.27	1028.53	11.3
1989	140	217	409.24	6128	10.87	1093.91	11.4
1990	151	229	430.04	6249	11.82	1188.43	11.5

(continued)

Attached list H.1 (continued)

Year	Investment in physical capital (trillion yen)	Compensation of employees (trillion yen)	GDP (trillion yen)	Labor (10 thousand people)	R&D expenditure (trillion yen)	Physical capital stock (trillion yen)	Average years of schooling of laborers (years)
1991	156	242	446.37	6369	12.74	1259.74	11.6
1992	151	247	450.98	6436	13.19	1335.14	11.7
1993	145	251	452.34	6450	13.23	1394.49	11.8
1994	142	258	455.26	6453	13.02	1415.55	11.9
1995	145	260	462.04	6457	13.00	1436.37	11.9
1996	157	267	480.07	6486	13.83	1475.44	12.0
1997	158	275	487.75	6557	14.43	1535.14	12.1
1998	149	274	482.87	6514	15.25	1566.39	12.2
1999	146	263	486.25	6462	15.46	1611.71	12.3
2000	150	268	496.95	6446	15.50	1643.53	12.4
2001	124	259	497.15	6412	15.79	1636.33	12.5
2002	129	249	497.20	6330	16.41	1634.70	12.6
2003	114	244	497.60	6316	16.79	1618.37	12.7
2004	117	244	509.04	6329	17.19	1605.98	12.8
2005	125	245	522.28	6356	17.61	1602.85	12.9
2006	125	276	534.34	6382	17.96	1599.13	13.0
2007	124	277	544.07	6412	19.47	1594.99	13.1
2008	123	276	521.78	6385	20.09	1590.36	13.2
2009	122	270	509.45	6282	20.20	1585.01	13.3

Attached list H.2 Japan's compensation of employees model

Dependent Variable: log V				
Method: Least Squares				
Sample(adjusted): 1958 2009				
Included observations: 52 after adjusting endpoints				
Convergence achieved after 24 iterations				
Variable	Coefficient	Std. Error	T-Statistic	Prob.
C	−0.9289	1.991792	−0.46636	0.6431
log HL	0.404921	0.226382	1.788662	0.0801
log SD/L	0.3627	0.058007	6.252709	0
AR(2)	0.824307	0.177945	4.632365	0
AR(3)	−0.22271	0.176883	−1.25908	0.2142
R-squared	0.992958		2.136302	

(continued)

Attached list H.2 (continued)

Dependent Variable: log *V*				
		Mean dependent var		
Adjusted R-squared	0.992358	S.D. dependent var	0.320654	
S.E. of regression	0.028031	Akaike info criterion	−4.21983	
Sum squared resid	0.036928	Schwarz criterion	−4.03221	
Log likelihood	114.7156	F-statistic	1656.724	
Durbin-Watson stat	1.159227	Prob (F-statistic)	0	
Inverted AR Roots	0.72	0.3	−1.02	
	Estimated AR process is nonstationary			

Attached list H.3 Japan's investment value model

Dependent Variable: *M*				
Method: Least Squares				
Sample(adjusted): 1957 2009				
Included observations: 53 after adjusting endpoints				
Convergence achieved after 25 iterations				
Variable	Coefficient	Std. Error	T-Statistic	Prob.
C	19.95185	38.06488	0.524154	0.6025
K	0.116835	0.033885	3.447958	0.0012
SD/*K*	99.4963	40.69508	2.444922	0.0181
SD/*L*	−332.158	193.7689	−1.7142	0.0928
AR(1)	0.925468	0.058853	15.72516	0
R-squared	0.992961	Mean dependent var	148.7911	
Adjusted R-squared	0.992387	S.D. dependent var	74.35621	
S.E. of regression	6.487816	Akaike info criterion	6.665751	
Sum squared resid	2062.496	Schwarz criterion	6.849916	
Log likelihood	−174.975	F-statistic	1728.167	
Durbin-Watson stat	1.756441	Prob (F-statistic)	0	
Inverted AR Roots	0.93			

Attached list H.4 The analysis of the resource allocation efficiency of production factors

Year	Efficiency	Waste rate of physical capital	Waste rate of labor	Waste rate of human capital
1955	1.00	0.00	0.00	0.00
1956	0.95	0.00	0.00	0.01
1957	0.92	0.00	0.00	0.01
1958	0.88	0.00	0.00	0.02
1959	0.86	0.00	0.00	0.02
1960	0.88	0.00	0.00	0.02
1961	0.89	0.00	0.00	0.03
1962	0.87	0.00	0.00	0.03
1963	0.87	0.00	0.00	0.02
1964	0.89	0.00	0.00	0.02
1965	0.83	0.00	0.00	0.01
1966	0.85	0.00	0.00	0.01
1967	0.88	0.00	0.00	0.02
1968	0.91	0.00	0.00	0.01
1969	0.93	0.00	0.00	0.01
1970	0.92	0.00	0.01	0.00
1971	0.89	0.00	0.02	0.00
1972	0.91	0.00	0.02	0.00
1973	0.90	0.00	0.04	0.00
1974	0.86	0.00	0.04	0.00
1975	0.90	0.00	0.03	0.00
1976	0.94	0.00	0.02	0.00
1977	0.97	0.00	0.00	0.00
1978	0.98	0.00	0.00	0.00
1979	1.00	0.00	0.00	0.00
1980	0.98	0.00	0.00	0.00
1981	0.98	0.00	0.00	0.00
1982	0.96	0.00	0.00	0.00
1983	0.95	0.00	0.00	0.00
1984	0.96	0.00	0.00	0.00
1985	0.98	0.00	0.00	0.00
1986	0.98	0.00	0.01	0.00
1987	0.99	0.00	0.01	0.00
1988	1.00	0.00	0.00	0.00
1989	1.00	0.00	0.00	0.00
1990	1.00	0.00	0.00	0.00
1991	1.00	0.00	0.00	0.00
1992	0.98	0.00	0.01	0.00
1993	0.96	0.00	0.02	0.00

(continued)

Attached list H.4 (continued)

Year	Efficiency	Waste rate of physical capital	Waste rate of labor	Waste rate of human capital
1994	0.96	0.00	0.02	0.00
1995	0.96	0.00	0.02	0.00
1996	0.98	0.00	0.02	0.00
1997	0.97	0.00	0.02	0.00
1998	0.96	0.00	0.03	0.00
1999	0.96	0.00	0.04	0.00
2000	0.97	0.00	0.04	0.00
2001	0.96	0.00	0.04	0.00
2002	0.96	0.00	0.04	0.00
2003	0.96	0.00	0.02	0.00
2004	0.98	0.00	0.01	0.00
2005	0.99	0.00	0.00	0.00
2006	1.00	0.00	0.00	0.00
2007	1.00	0.00	0.00	0.00
2008	0.96	0.01	0.00	0.01
2009	0.955	0.03	0.00	0.01

Appendix I
The Data and Model of Australia's Economic Growth

(1) Data

Data Sources: The data of GDP, labor, compensation of employees, physical capital stock, investment in physical capital come from *Australia Statistical Yearbook*, databases of Groningen Growth and Development Centre, The World Bank, The Conference Board and United Nations Statistics Division., *New Estimates of Net Capital Stocks for 22 OECD Countries 1960–2001* written by Kamps C, and *Australia's Productivity Growth and the Role of Information and Communications Technology: 1960–2004* written by Diewert E and Lawrence D. The data of average years of schooling of laborers come from *Does Human Capital Matter for Growth in OECD Countries? Evidence from Poole Mean-group Estimates* written *by* Bassanini A and Scarpetta S, and Organization for Economic Co-operation and Development (OECD). The index of research and development expenditure comes from Organization for Economic Co-operation and Development (OECD) (Attached list I.1).

(2) Australia's economic growth model (Add I.1)

$$Y = 0.102(HL)^{0.487}(SD/L)^{0.13} + 0.14K + 83SD/K + 208 \qquad \text{(Add I.1)}$$

Attached list I.2.
Attached list I.3.
Attached list I.4.

J. H. Liu and Z. H. Jiang, *The Synergy Theory on Economic Growth: Comparative Study Between China and Developed Countries*,
https://doi.org/10.1007/978-981-13-1885-6

Attached list I.1 The data of Australia's economic growth (the prices at 2005, per hundred million Australian dollar; per thousand people; years)

Year	GDP (100 million Australian dollar)	Physical capital stock (lag one year; 100 million Australian dollar)	Labor (thousand people)	Investment in physical capital (100 million Australian dollar)	R&D expenditure (lag two years; 100 million Australian dollar)	Compensation of employees (100 million Australian dollar)	Average years of schooling of laborers (years)
1980	4375		6287	905		2251	11.6
1981	4516	12130	6416	971	38	2338	11.6
1982	4412	12444	6418	878	41	2351	11.7
1983	4621	12794	6301	923	42	2307	11.8
1984	4855	13476	6494	1012	43	2415	11.8
1985	5078	14142	6701	1071	48	2521	11.9
1986	5211	14843	6974	1075	52	2567	11.9
1987	5505	15115	7128	1155	58	2614	12
1988	5721	15666	7398	1280	65	2681	12
1989	5926	16047	7720	1291	68	2851	12.1
1990	5905	16769	7859	1169	70	2861	12.1
1991	5930	17406	7674	1122	75	2852	12.2
1992	6173	18133	7636	1198	77	2946	12.2
1993	6424	18787	7684	1267	84	3048	12.2
1994	6682	19206	7921	1415	94	3190	12.3
1995	6949	19643	8236	1457	100	3342	12.3
1996	7220	20075	8346	1555	106	3528	12.3
1997	7547	20505	8427	1700	113	3630	12.3
1998	7921	21455	8617	1779	120	3850	12.3
1999	8225	21833	8762	1925	120	3986	12.4
2000	8381	22750	8990	1772	120	4025	12.4

(continued)

Attached list I.1 (continued)

Year	GDP (100 million Australian dollar)	Physical capital stock (lag one year; 100 million Australian dollar)	Labor (thousand people)	Investment in physical capital (100 million Australian dollar)	R&D expenditure (lag two years; 100 million Australian dollar)	Compensation of employees (100 million Australian dollar)	Average years of schooling of laborers (years)
2001	8709	23466	9091	1933	126	4120	12.5
2002	8984	24474	9270	2179	130	4256	12.5
2003	9357	25155	9485	2375	138	4365	12.6
2004	9655	26105	9661	2538	145	4634	12.6
2005	9948	27226	9998	2775	154	4775	12.7
2006	10324	27823	10258	2916	166	4956	12.8
2007	10714	28513	10578	3196	184	5143	12.8
2008	10860	29428	10875	3240	205	5213	12.9
2009	11113	30314	10953	3314	236	5334	13.0
2010	11325	31203	11189	3444	261	5436	13.0

Attached list I.2 Australia's compensation of employees model

Dependent Variable: log *V*				
Method: Least Squares				
Sample(adjusted): 1983 2010				
Included observations: 28 after adjusting endpoints				
Convergence achieved after 6 iterations				
Variable	Coefficient	Std. Error	T-Statistic	Prob.
C	−0.98716	0.580964	−1.69917	0.1028
log *HL*	0.486598	0.069239	7.027858	0
log *SD*/*L*	0.134122	0.033439	4.010939	0.0005
AR(1)	1.086779	0.122675	8.859013	0
AR(3)	−0.31885	0.125441	−2.5418	0.0182
R-squared	0.997137	Mean dependent var	3.552254	
Adjusted R-squared	0.996639	S.D. dependent var	0.117621	
S.E. of regression	0.006819	Akaike info criterion	−6.97773	
Sum squared resid	0.00107	Schwarz criterion	−6.73983	
Log likelihood	102.6882	F-statistic	2002.451	
Durbin-Watson stat	2.283099	Prob(F-statistic)	0	
Inverted AR Roots	.77+.33i	.77 −.33i	−0.45	

Attached list I.3 Australia's investment value model

Dependent Variable: *M*				
Method: Least Squares				
Sample: 1981 2000				
Included observations: 20				
Variable	Coefficient	Std. Error	T-Statistic	Prob.
C	208.2224	177.6043	1.172395	0.2572
K	0.143876	0.017474	8.233876	0
SD/*K*	83.43167	23.183	3.59883	0.0022
R-squared	0.98764	Mean dependent var	3164.915	
Adjusted R-squared	0.986186	S.D. dependent var	680.2792	
S.E. of regression	79.95402	Akaike info criterion	11.73826	
Sum squared resid	108675	Schwarz criterion	11.88762	
Log likelihood	−114.383	F-statistic	679.229	
Durbin-Watson stat	1.057995	Prob(F-statistic)	0	

Attached list I.4 The analysis of the resource allocation efficiency of production factors

Year	efficiency	Waste rate of physical capital	Waste rate of labor	Waste rate of human capital
1980	0.99	0.00	0.20	0.34
1981	1.00	0.00	0.20	0.34
1982	0.95	0.00	0.18	0.30
1983	0.94	0.00	0.14	0.24
1984	0.94	0.00	0.13	0.23
1985	0.94	0.00	0.12	0.21
1986	0.95	0.00	0.14	0.23
1987	0.97	0.00	0.14	0.22
1988	0.98	0.00	0.15	0.24
1989	0.97	0.00	0.15	0.23
1990	0.93	0.00	0.13	0.21
1991	0.90	0.00	0.09	0.15
1992	0.90	0.00	0.06	0.11
1993	0.92	0.00	0.05	0.10
1994	0.93	0.00	0.06	0.11
1995	0.95	0.00	0.08	0.13
1996	0.97	0.00	0.07	0.12
1997	0.97	0.00	0.04	0.09
1998	1.00	0.00	0.05	0.09
1999	0.99	0.00	0.03	0.07
2000	0.98	0.00	0.03	0.06
2001	0.98	0.00	0.00	0.03
2002	0.98	0.00	0.00	0.03
2003	0.99	0.00	0.00	0.02
2004	1.00	0.00	0.00	0.00
2005	0.99	0.00	0.00	0.00
2006	1.00	0.00	0.00	0.00
2007	1.00	0.00	0.00	0.00
2008	0.99	0.00	0.00	0.00
2009	1.00	0.00	0.00	0.00
2010	1.00	0.00	0.00	0.00

Appendix J
The Data and Model of Singapore's Economic Growth

(1) Data

Data Sources: The data of GDP, labor, compensation of employees, physical capital stock, investment in physical capital, R&D expenditure come from *Singapore Statistical Yearbook*, United Nations Statistics Division and *Total Factor Productivity Growth: Survey Report* written by Thangavelu S M. The data of average years of schooling of laborers come from Lau L J's *The Sources of Long-Term Economic Growth* (Attached list J.1).

(2) Singapore's economic growth model (Add J.1)

$$Y = 0.038(HL)^{0.276}(SD/L)^{0.247} + 0.27K + 112.3HSD/K^2 - 8.69S - 0.84 \quad \text{(Add J.1)}$$

Attached list J.2.
Attached list J.3.
Attached list J.4.

J. H. Liu and Z. H. Jiang, *The Synergy Theory on Economic Growth: Comparative Study Between China and Developed Countries*,
https://doi.org/10.1007/978-981-13-1885-6

Attached list J.1 The data of Singapore's economic growth(the prices at 2000, per hundred million Singapore dollar; per thousand people; years)

Year	GDP (100 million Singapore dollar)	Physical capital stock (lag one year; 100 million Singapore dollar)	Investment in physical capital (100 million Singapore dollar)	R&D expenditure (lag two years; 100 million Singapore dollar)	Labor (thousand people)	Average years of schooling of laborers (years)	Compensation of employees (100 million Singapore dollar)
1980	371		113	0	102	8	
1981	401	679	127	1	107	8.2	168
1982	430	769	153	1	115	8.3	180
1983	478	874	173	1	122	8.4	201
1984	508	999	186	2	125	8.5	213
1985	491	1137	159	2	127	8.7	206
1986	495	1277	139	3	123	8.8	208
1987	543	1370	137	3	121	8.9	228
1988	619	1430	147	4	127	9.1	260
1989	679	1494	169	5	133	9.2	285
1990	805	1577	202	5	139	9.3	338
1991	863	1688	230	6	147	9.5	363
1992	908	1792	252	7	152	9.6	381
1993	1033	1918	284	9	158	9.8	434
1994	1151	2069	314	11	159	9.9	483
1995	1261	2244	358	11	165	10.1	530
1996	1322	2429	431	13	170	10.2	555
1997	1417	2627	470	14	175	10.4	595
1998	1395	2899	446	18	183	10.5	586
1999	1418	3187	406	21	187	10.7	596
2000	1599	3422	466	25	189	11.0	672

(continued)

Attached list J.1 (continued)

Year	GDP (100 million Singapore dollar)	Physical capital stock (lag one year; 100 million Singapore dollar)	Investment in physical capital (100 million Singapore dollar)	R&D expenditure (lag two years; 100 million Singapore dollar)	Labor (thousand people)	Average years of schooling of laborers (years)	Compensation of employees (100 million Singapore dollar)
2001	1519	3591	440	26	209	11.1	638
2002	1583	3694	390	30	222	11.2	665
2003	1655	3770	371	32	221	11.4	695
2004	1807	3877	409	34	224	11.5	759
2005	1940	3977	410	35	227	11.6	815
2006	2110	4124	466	39	251	11.7	886
2007	2297	4341	547	43	263	12.0	965
2008	2336	4612	618	46	286	12.1	981
2009	2313	4844	600	55	291	12.2	972

Attached list J.2 Singapore's compensation of employees model

Dependent Variable: log *V*				
Method: Least Squares				
Sample: 1981 2005				
Included observations: 25				
Variable	Coefficient	Std. Error	T-Statistic	Prob.
C	0.843274	0.46382	1.818105	0.0827
log *HL*	0.275616	0.093325	2.953283	0.0073
log *SD/L*	0.247201	0.037129	6.657927	0
R-squared	0.982575	Mean dependent var	2.593506	
Adjusted R-squared	0.980991	S.D. dependent var	0.224872	
S.E. of regression	0.031003	Akaike info criterion	-3.99727	
Sum squared resid	0.021147	Schwarz criterion	-3.85101	
Log likelihood	52.96592	F-statistic	620.2948	
Durbin-Watson stat	0.687342	Prob(F-statistic)	0	

Attached list J.3 Singapore's investment value model

Dependent Variable: *M*				
Method: Least Squares				
Sample(adjusted): 1985 2005				
Included observations: 21 after adjusting endpoints				
Convergence achieved after 17 iterations				
Variable	Coefficient	Std. Error	T-Statistic	Prob.
C	−0.83908	60.48565	−0.01387	0.9891
K	0.271161	0.049336	5.496187	0
SHD/K^2	112.3432	56.98123	1.971583	0.0627
S	−8.69051	4.602327	−1.88829	0.0736
AR(1)	0.874405	0.187679	4.659033	0.0002
AR(3)	−0.46458	0.16666	−2.78759	0.0114
R-squared	0.991823	Mean dependent var	676.7143	
Adjusted R-squared	0.989779	S.D. dependent var	0.9891	
S.E. of regression	34.84135	Akaike info criterion	0	
Sum squared resid	24278.4	Schwarz criterion	0.0627	
Log likelihood	−125.803	F-statistic	0.0736	
Durbin-Watson stat	2.369576	Prob (F-statistic)	0.0002	
Inverted AR Roots	.72 −.55i	.72+.55i	−0.57	

Attached list J.4 The analysis of the resource allocation efficiency of production factors

Year	efficiency	Waste rate of physical capital	Waste rate of labor	Waste rate of human capital
1981	1.00	0.00	0.00	0.00
1982	0.94	0.00	0.00	0.00
1983	0.92	0.00	0.00	0.00
1984	0.86	0.00	0.01	0.00
1985	0.74	0.00	0.03	0.00
1986	0.70	0.00	0.04	0.00
1987	0.73	0.00	0.04	0.00
1988	0.80	0.00	0.03	0.00
1989	0.83	0.00	0.02	0.00
1990	0.92	0.00	0.01	0.00
1991	0.93	0.00	0.00	0.01
1992	0.91	0.00	0.00	0.01
1993	0.96	0.00	0.00	0.01
1994	0.99	0.00	0.00	0.00
1995	1.00	0.00	0.00	0.00
1996	0.99	0.00	0.00	0.00
1997	1.00	0.00	0.00	0.00
1998	0.93	0.01	0.00	0.00
1999	0.91	0.02	0.00	0.00
2000	1.00	0.00	0.00	0.00
2001	0.86	0.00	0.00	0.00
2002	0.85	0.00	0.00	0.00
2003	0.88	0.00	0.00	0.00
2004	0.94	0.00	0.00	0.00
2005	0.99	0.01	0.00	0.00
2006	0.98	0.00	0.00	0.00
2007	1.00	0.00	0.00	0.00
2008	0.96	0.00	0.00	0.04
2009	0.91	0.00	0.00	0.02

Appendix K
The Data and Model of New Zealand's Economic Growth

(1) Data

Data Sources: The data of GDP, labor, compensation of employees, physical capital stock, investment in physical capital come from *New Zealand Statistical Yearbook*, and databases of Groningen Growth and Development Centre, The World Bank, The Conference Board and United Nations Statistics Division. The data about average years of schooling of laborers come from *Does Human Capital Matter for Growth in OECD Countries? Evidence from Poole Mean-Group Estimates* written by Bassanini A and Scarpetta S, and Organization for Economic Co-operation and Development (OECD). The index of R&D expenditure comes from Organization for Economic Co-operation and Development (OECD) (Attached list K.1).

(2) New Zealand's economic growth model (Add K.1)

$$Y = 6.6(HL)^{0.32}(SD/L)^{0.14} + 0.105K + 84.9SD/K + 1.64L + 48.7 \quad \text{(Add K.1)}$$

Attached list K.2.
Attached list K.3.
Attached list K.4.

J. H. Liu and Z. H. Jiang, *The Synergy Theory on Economic Growth: Comparative Study Between China and Developed Countries*,
https://doi.org/10.1007/978-981-13-1885-6

Attached list K.1 The data of New Zealand's economic growth (the prices at 2005, per hundred million dollar of New Zealand; per hundred thousand people; years)

Year	GDP (100 million dollar of New Zealand)	Average years of schooling of laborers (years)	Compensation of employees (100 million dollar of New Zealand)	Investment in physical capital (100 million dollar of New Zealand)	Physical capital stock (100 million dollar of New Zealand)	Labor (thousand people)	R&D expenditure (100 million dollar of New Zealand)
1980	809	10.9	405	92	1715	127	6.5
1981	836	11	418	111	1719	127	7.0
1982	872	11	436	119	1719	129	7.6
1983	896	11.1	443	125	1737	128	7.6
1984	940	11.1	451	141	1761	129	7.4
1985	947	11.2	465	136	1787	134	7.4
1986	967	11.2	469	133	1819	145	7.6
1987	971	11.2	468	127	1856	156	7.1
1988	989	11.3	463	139	1896	151	6.9
1989	994	11.3	453	137	2123	147	6.7
1990	997	11.4	449	149	2335	148	6.7
1991	987	11.4	441	144	2503	146	6.8
1992	997	11.5	441	120	2644	147	7.2
1993	1061	11.5	454	126	2633	150	7.4
1994	1114	11.6	474	150	2611	156	7.7
1995	1161	11.7	494	177	2693	163	8.1
1996	1198	11.7	518	199	2822	169	8.4
1997	1231	11.7	535	208	2978	169	8.8
1998	1247	11.8	545	205	3101	173	11.0
1999	1311	11.9	553	194	3305	175	11.0

(continued)

Attached list K.1 (continued)

Year	GDP (100 million dollar of New Zealand)	Average years of schooling of laborers (years)	Compensation of employees (100 million dollar of New Zealand)	Investment in physical capital (100 million dollar of New Zealand)	Physical capital stock (100 million dollar of New Zealand)	Labor (thousand people)	R&D expenditure (100 million dollar of New Zealand)
2000	1340	12.1	562	213	3259	178	10.6
2001	1388	12.2	580	219	3363	182	10.6
2002	1456	12.2	618	233	3572	188	12.3
2003	1513	12.3	647	264	3657	197	13.4
2004	1566	12.4	673	287	3761	203	13.9
2005	1616	12.5	695	309	3882	209	14.4
2006	1644	12.6	723	300	3988	214	14.8
2007	1702	12.7	766	323	4112	218	15.0
2008	1671	12.8	752	302	4208	220	16.2
2009	1687	12.9	759	261	4259	217	16.3
2010	1691	13.0	761	278	4323	219	17.6

Attached list K.2 New Zealand's compensation of employees model

Dependent Variable: log V				
Method: Least Squares				
Sample(adjusted): 1981 2010				
Included observations: 30 after adjusting endpoints				
Convergence achieved after 17 iterations				
Variable	Coefficient	Std. Error	T-Statistic	Prob.
C	0.822479	0.25072	3.280465	0.0029
log HL	0.319992	0.046884	6.825137	0
log SD/L	0.141349	0.030197	4.680869	0.0001
AR(1)	0.849799	0.106821	7.955343	0
R-squared	0.992904	Mean dependent var	2.731614	
Adjusted R-squared	0.992086	S.D. dependent var	0.088119	
S.E. of regression	0.007839	Akaike info criterion	−6.73576	
Sum squared resid	0.001598	Schwarz criterion	−6.54894	
Log likelihood	105.0364	F-statistic	1212.741	
Durbin-Watson stat	2.139213	Prob(F-statistic)	0	
Inverted AR Roots	0.85			

Attached list K.3 New Zealand's investment value model

Dependent Variable: M				
Method: Least Squares				
Sample(adjusted): 1982 2010				
Included observations: 29 after adjusting endpoints				
Convergence achieved after 32 iterations				
Variable	Coefficient	Std. Error	T-Statistic	Prob.
C	48.72434	91.49805	0.532518	0.5993
K	0.104768	0.022514	4.653467	0.0001
LD/K	84.93527	51.05445	1.663621	0.1092
L	1.643709	0.817041	2.011783	0.0556
AR(2)	0.519383	0.226774	2.290309	0.0311
R-squared	0.983711	Mean dependent var	691.9564	
Adjusted R-squared	0.980996	S.D. dependent var	174.0454	
S.E. of regression	23.99325	Akaike info criterion	9.349008	

(continued)

Attached list K.3 (continued)

Dependent Variable: M				
Sum squared resid	13816.23	Schwarz criterion	9.584749	
Log likelihood	−130.561	F-statistic	362.3364	
Durbin-Watson stat	0.905374	Prob(F-statistic)	0	
Inverted AR Roots	0.72	−0.72		

Attached list K.4 The analysis of the resource allocation efficiency of production factors

Year	Efficiency	Waste rate of physical capital	Waste rate of labor	Waste rate of human capital
1980	0.89	0.01	0.02	0.00
1981	0.91	0.00	0.01	0.00
1982	0.95	0.00	0.02	0.01
1983	0.97	0.00	0.00	0.00
1984	1.00	0.00	0.00	0.00
1985	0.99	0.00	0.02	0.03
1986	1.00	0.00	0.08	0.09
1987	0.98	0.00	0.12	0.13
1988	0.90	0.00	0.00	0.01
1989	0.92	0.07	0.00	0.00
1990	0.91	0.09	0.00	0.00
1991	0.91	0.15	0.00	0.00
1992	0.91	0.11	0.00	0.00
1993	0.95	0.09	0.00	0.00
1994	0.95	0.05	0.00	0.00
1995	0.94	0.03	0.00	0.00
1996	0.94	0.04	0.00	0.00
1997	0.97	0.08	0.00	0.00
1998	0.95	0.09	0.00	0.00
1999	0.98	0.04	0.00	0.00
2000	0.98	0.00	0.00	0.00
2001	0.98	0.01	0.00	0.00
2002	1.00	0.00	0.00	0.00
2003	0.99	0.00	0.00	0.00
2004	0.99	0.00	0.00	0.00
2005	0.99	0.00	0.00	0.00
2006	0.99	0.00	0.00	0.00
2007	1.00	0.00	0.00	0.00
2008	0.97	0.00	0.00	0.01
2009	0.99	0.03	0.00	0.02
2010	0.99	0.05	0.00	0.02

Appendi L
The Data and Model of Italy's Economic Growth

(1) Data

Data Sources: The data of GDP, labor, compensation of employees, physical capital stock, investment in physical capital come from *Italy Statistical Yearbook*, and databases of Groningen Growth and Development Centre, The World Bank, The Conference Board and United Nations Statistics Division. The data of average years of schooling of laborers comes from *Does Human Capital Matter for Growth in OECD Countries? Evidence from Poole Mean-Group Estimates* written by Bassanini A and Scarpetta S, and Organization for Economic Co-operation and Development (OECD). The index of R&D expenditure comes from Organization for Economic Co-operation and Development (OECD) (Attached list L.1).

(2) Italy's economic growth model (Add L.1)

$$Y = 95.5(HLSD)^{0.12} + 0.168K + 0.106SD/K + 569.7 \qquad \text{(Add L.1)}$$

Attached list L.2.
Attached list L.3.
Attached list L.4.

J. H. Liu and Z. H. Jiang, *The Synergy Theory on Economic Growth: Comparative Study Between China and Developed Countries*,
https://doi.org/10.1007/978-981-13-1885-6

Attached list L.1 Italy's economic growth model (the prices at 2005, per hundred million euros; per thousand people; years)

Year	GDP (100 million euros)	Investment in physical capital (100 million euros)	Compensation of employees (100 million euros)	R&D expenditure (lag two years; 100 million euros)	Physical capital (lag one year; 100 million euros)	Labor (thousand people)	Average years of schooling of laborers (years)
1980	9202	1998	4655			21373	3.3
1981	9279	1967	4739	78	13493	21356	7.4
1982	9318	1901	4743	79	14032	21399	7.5
1983	9427	1873	4755	82	14454	21468	7.6
1984	9731	1948	4780	85	14825	21467	7.7
1985	10003	1968	4884	90	15253	21670	7.8
1986	10289	2023	4909	98	15608	21819	7.9
1987	10618	2120	5066	113	16082	21869	8.0
1988	11063	2273	5245	116	16567	22104	8.1
1989	11438	2372	5419	126	17114	22255	8.2
1990	11673	2474	5628	135	17784	22609	8.4
1991	11852	2506	5768	142	18451	23032	8.5
1992	11943	2471	5795	151	19126	22865	8.6
1993	11841	2188	5700	146	19723	22251	8.8
1994	12096	2198	5658	141	20152	21885	9.0
1995	12445	2350	5628	134	20429	21841	9.2
1996	12587	2394	5679	127	20727	21965	9.4
1997	12821	2430	5843	124	21184	22035	9.6
1998	13007	2525	5677	127	21588	22252	9.8
1999	13196	2625	5814	127	22004	22494	10.2
2000	13678	2793	5992	133	22530	22930	10.4

(continued)

Attached list L.1 (continued)

Year	GDP (100 million euros)	Investment in physical capital (100 million euros)	Compensation of employees (100 million euros)	R&D expenditure (lag two years; 100 million euros)	Physical capital (lag one year; 100 million euros)	Labor (thousand people)	Average years of schooling of laborers (years)
2001	13933	2870	6109	137	23307	23394	10.6
2002	13996	2968	6088	146	24061	23794	10.7
2003	13989	2930	6015	155	24817	24150	10.9
2004	14231	2989	5977	155	25394	24256	11.0
2005	14364	3027	6033	155	26091	24396	11.2
2006	14680	3129	6165	155	26509	24875	11.3
2007	14927	3186	6269	156	26987	25188	11.5
2008	14754	3067	6197	165	27475	25256	11.6
2009	13943	2707	5996	175	27794	24840	11.8
2010	14196	2765	5962	178	27722	24661	11.9

Attached list L.2 Italy's compensation of employees model

Dependent Variable: log *V*				
Method: Least Squares				
Sample(adjusted): 1982 2010				
Included observations: 29 after adjusting endpoints				
Convergence achieved after 8 iterations				
Variable	Coefficient	Std. Error	T-Statistic	Prob.
C	1.979786	0.444194	4.457027	0.0001
log *SDHL*	0.116474	0.028857	4.036287	0.0004
AR(1)	0.862757	0.100285	8.603078	0
R-squared	0.971963	Mean dependent var	3.750363	
Adjusted R-squared	0.969806	S.D. dependent var	0.037709	
S.E. of regression	0.006553	Akaike info criterion	−7.12024	
Sum squared resid	0.001116	Schwarz criterion	−6.97879	
Log likelihood	106.2434	F-statistic	450.6675	
Durbin-Watson stat	1.684815	Prob (F-statistic)	0	
Inverted AR Roots	0.86			

Attached list L.3 Italy's investment value model

Dependent Variable: *M*				
Method: Least Squares				
Sample(adjusted): 1984 2010				
Included observations: 27 after adjusting endpoints				
Convergence achieved after 22 iterations				
Variable	Coefficient	Std. Error	T-Statistic	Prob.
C	569.7427	938.7825	0.606895	0.5501
K	0.168292	0.037887	4.441989	0.0002
SD/*K*	0.105655	0.019859	5.320171	0
AR(1)	0.928283	0.149774	6.197895	0
AR(3)	−0.169	0.157737	−1.0714	0.2956
R-squared	0.989267	Mean dependent var	6999.9	
Adjusted R-squared	0.987316	S.D. dependent var	1156.869	

(continued)

Attached list L.3 (continued)

Dependent Variable: *M*				
S.E. of regression	130.291	Akaike info criterion	12.74299	
Sum squared resid	373466.2	Schwarz criterion	12.98296	
Log likelihood	−167.03	F-statistic	506.9517	
Durbin-Watson stat	1.772851	Prob (F-statistic)	0	
Inverted AR Roots	.65+.23i	.65 −.23i	−0.36	

Attached list L.4 The analysis of the resource allocation efficiency of production factors

Year	Efficiency	Waste rate of physical capital	Waste rate of labor	Waste rate of human capital
1981	1.00	0.00	0.00	0.00
1982	0.97	0.00	0.01	0.00
1983	0.96	0.00	0.01	0.00
1984	0.97	0.00	0.01	0.00
1985	0.97	0.00	0.01	0.00
1986	0.98	0.00	0.00	0.00
1987	0.98	0.00	0.00	0.00
1988	1.00	0.00	0.00	0.00
1989	1.00	0.00	0.00	0.00
1990	0.99	0.00	0.00	0.00
1991	0.98	0.00	0.00	0.00
1992	0.97	0.00	0.00	0.00
1993	0.97	0.02	0.00	0.00
1994	0.99	0.02	0.00	0.00
1995	1.00	0.00	0.00	0.00
1996	1.00	0.00	0.00	0.00
1997	1.00	0.00	0.00	0.00
1998	1.00	0.00	0.00	0.00
1999	0.99	0.00	0.00	0.00
2000	1.00	0.00	0.00	0.00
2001	1.00	0.01	0.00	0.02
2002	0.99	0.03	0.00	0.03
2003	0.97	0.04	0.00	0.04
2004	0.98	0.06	0.00	0.06
2005	0.99	0.08	0.00	0.07
2006	0.99	0.08	0.00	0.08
2007	0.99	0.08	0.00	0.09
2008	0.98	0.09	0.00	0.10
2009	0.94	0.11	0.00	0.11
2010	0.97	0.12	0.00	0.12

Appendix M
The Data and Model of Ireland's Economic Growth

(1) Data

Data Sources: The data of GDP, labor, compensation of employees, physical capital stock, investment in physical capital come from *Ireland Statistical Yearbook*, and databases of Groningen Growth and Development Centre, The World Bank, The Conference Board and United Nations Statistics Division. The data of average years of schooling of laborers come from *Does Human Capital Matter for Growth in OECD Countries? Evidence from Poole Mean-Group Estimates* written by Bassanini A and Scarpetta S, and Organization for Economic Co-operation and Development (OECD). The index of R&D expenditure comes from Organization for Economic Co-operation and Development (OECD) (Attached list M.1).

(2) Ireland's Economic growth model (Add M.1)

$$Y = 7.56(HL)^{0.4}(SD/L)^{0.15} + 0.316K + 0.144SDH/K^2 + 4289.7 \quad \text{(Add M.1)}$$

Attached list M.2.
Attached list M.3.
Attached list M.4.

J. H. Liu and Z. H. Jiang, *The Synergy Theory on Economic Growth: Comparative Study Between China and Developed Countries*,
https://doi.org/10.1007/978-981-13-1885-6

Attached list M.1 The data of Ireland's economic growth (the prices at 1995, per million pound; per ten thousand people; years)

Year	GDP (million pound)	R&D expenditure (million pound)	Compensation of employees (GDP)	Physical capital stock (million pound)	Labor (ten thousand)	Investment in physical capital (million pound)	Average years of schooling of laborers (years)
1980	21587	108			1141	3928	8.5
1981	22294	111	0.55	29734	1138	3364	8.6
1982	22788	137	0.53	31827	1133	3220	8.7
1983	22535	139	0.52	33921	1124	3670	8.8
1984	23497	145	0.51	35533	1103	3487	8.9
1985	24222	146	0.51	36684	1094	3200	9
1986	24080	163	0.51	37531	1092	3215	9
1987	25283	180	0.50	38203	1099	3234	9.1
1988	26708	198	0.48	38870	1099	3508	9.2
1989	28356	213	0.46	39661	1099	3937	9.3
1990	30869	258	0.46	40763	1151	4686	9.4
1991	31430	287	0.47	42369	1147	4214	9.5
1992	32482	327	0.48	43988	1155	4132	9.6
1993	33348	337	0.48	45239	1174	4025	9.7
1994	35326	342	0.47	46349	1213	4302	9.8
1995	38960	393	0.46	47500	1272	5035	10
1996	42187	422	0.45	49084	1319	5986	10.1
1997	46927	436	0.43	51357	1372	7233	10.2
1998	51159	532	0.42	54485	1487	8835	10.3
1999	57020	667	0.41	58720	1583	10401	10.4
2000	62814	823	0.41	64098	1664	11715	10.5
2001	66386	850	0.41	70292	1710	11620	10.7

(continued)

Attached list M.1 (continued)

Year	GDP (million pound)	R&D expenditure (million pound)	Compensation of employees (GDP)	Physical capital stock (million pound)	Labor (ten thousand)	Investment in physical capital (million pound)	Average years of schooling of laborers (years)
2002	69902	923	0.39	75054	1749	16509	10.9
2003	73842	945	0.40	79385	1776	16917	11.2
2004	76711	959	0.41	83440	1809	17977	11.4
2005	80057	953	0.43	87467	1870	19694	11.7
2006	84762	975	0.44	92428	1962	22650	11.9
2007	89343	1027	0.46	98344	2048	23764	12.2
2008	94208	1112	0.47	104825	2123	24320	12.5
2009	92221	1107	0.49	111298	2100	21879	12.7
2010	87189	1066	0.50	116773	1929	15839	13.0

Attached list M.2 Ireland's compensation of employees model

Dependent Variable: log *V*				
Method: Least Squares				
Sample: 1981 2006				
Included observations: 26				
Variable	Coefficient	Std. Error	T-Statistic	Prob.
C	0.878642	0.479712	1.831603	0.08
log *HL*	0.399975	0.081766	4.891682	0.0001
log *SD/L*	0.148512	0.035479	4.18585	0.0004
R-squared	0.991848	Mean dependent var	4.256268	
Adjusted R-squared	0.991139	S.D. dependent var	0.162473	
S.E. of regression	0.015294	Akaike info criterion	−5.4146	
Sum squared resid	0.00538	Schwarz criterion	−5.26943	
Log likelihood	73.38978	F-statistic	1399.252	
Durbin-Watson stat	0.678112	Prob(F-statistic)	0	

Attached list M.3 Ireland's investment value model

Dependent Variable: *M*				
Method: Least Squares				
Sample(adjusted): 1983 2009				
Included observations: 27 after adjusting endpoints				
Convergence achieved after 37 iterations				
Variable	Coefficient	Std. Error	T-Statistic	Prob.
C	4289.686	7745.177	0.553853	0.5855
K	0.315808	0.112514	2.80682	0.0106
SHD/K^2	0.143621	0.033401	4.299849	0.0003
AR(4)	−2.17573	0.501658	−4.33709	0.0003
AR(3)	2.872362	0.43267	6.638689	0
R-squared	0.984708	Mean dependent var	29212.39	
Adjusted R-squared	0.981795	S.D. dependent var	14198.48	
S.E. of regression	1891.538	Akaike info criterion	16.06835	
Sum squared resid	75136248	Schwarz criterion	16.30832	
Log likelihood	−230.29	F-statistic	2770.283	
Durbin-Watson stat	1.257541	Prob(F-statistic)	0	
Inverted AR Roots	.91 −.22i	.91 +.22i	−.91 −1.27i	

Attached list M.4 The analysis of the resource allocation efficiency of production factors

Year	Efficiency	Waste rate of physical capital	Waste rate of labor	Waste rate of human capital
1981	0.77	0.00	0.25	0.13
1982	0.73	0.00	0.20	0.09
1983	0.68	0.00	0.15	0.04
1984	0.67	0.00	0.11	0.01
1985	0.68	0.00	0.10	0.00
1986	0.67	0.00	0.11	0.00
1987	0.69	0.00	0.11	0.00
1988	0.72	0.00	0.11	0.00
1989	0.75	0.00	0.11	0.00
1990	0.79	0.00	0.09	0.00
1991	0.78	0.00	0.10	0.00
1992	0.79	0.00	0.11	0.00
1993	0.79	0.00	0.10	0.00
1994	0.81	0.00	0.09	0.00
1995	0.85	0.00	0.05	0.00
1996	0.88	0.00	0.04	0.00
1997	0.93	0.00	0.03	0.00
1998	0.96	0.00	0.05	0.03
1999	0.99	0.00	0.04	0.03
2000	1.00	0.00	0.00	0.00
2001	0.99	0.00	0.01	0.00
2002	0.99	0.00	0.01	0.00
2003	1.00	0.00	0.00	0.00
2004	1.00	0.00	0.00	0.00
2005	1.00	0.00	0.00	0.00
2006	1.00	0.00	0.00	0.00
2007	1.00	0.00	0.00	0.00
2008	1.00	0.00	0.00	0.00
2009	0.98	0.00	0.00	0.01
2010	1.00	0.00	0.00	0.00

Appendix N
The Data and Model of Sweden's Economic Growth

(1) Data

Data Sources: The data of GDP, labor, compensation of employees, physical capital stock, investment in physical capital come from *Sweden Statistical Yearbook*, and databases of Groningen Growth and Development Centre, The World Bank, The Conference Board and United Nations Statistics Division. The data of average years of schooling of laborers come from *Does Human Capital Matter for Growth in OECD Countries? Evidence from Poole Mean-Group Estimates* written by Bassanini A and Scarpetta S, and Organization for Economic Co-operation and Development (OECD). The index of R&D expenditure comes from Organization for Economic Co-operation and Development (OECD) (Attached list N.1).

(2) Sweden's economic growth model (Add N.1)

$$Y = 0.06(HL)^{0.42}(SD/L)^{0.268} + 0.166K + 0.36SD/K + 9.5 \qquad \text{(Add N.1)}$$

Attached list N.2.
Attached list N.3.
Attached list N.4.

J. H. Liu and Z. H. Jiang, *The Synergy Theory on Economic Growth: Comparative Study Between China and Developed Countries*,
https://doi.org/10.1007/978-981-13-1885-6

Attached list N.1 The data of Sweden' economic growth (the prices at 2000, per billion Swedish krona; per thousand people; years)

Year	GDP (Billion Krones)	Physical capital stock (Billion Krones)	Investment in physical capital (Billion Krones)	The share of labor remuneration	R&D expenditure (Billion Krones)	Average years of schooling of laborers (years)	Labor (thousand people)
1980	1254.32	2341.93	217.66	0.6223	26.97	10.1	4,226
1981	1248.28	2412.33	204.50	0.6229	27.71	10.2	4,219
1982	1263.66	2472.82	205.80	0.6018	29.70	10.3	4,213
1983	1289.31	2533.98	211.65	0.5813	31.85	10.4	4,218
1984	1351.30	2598.55	228.44	0.5668	35.54	10.5	4,249
1985	1383.46	2674.78	244.80	0.5673	38.46	10.6	4,293
1986	1425.47	2757.66	247.97	0.5678	39.91	10.7	4,326
1987	1478.83	2844.30	268.69	0.5669	42.29	10.8	4,340
1988	1520.74	2939.18	285.97	0.5673	43.19	10.9	4,410
1989	1566.45	3051.74	321.54	0.5767	43.86	11	4,480
1990	1582.79	3170.79	321.69	0.5903	44.00	11.1	4,513
1991	1560.86	3259.91	293.62	0.5758	43.55	11.2	4,447
1992	1537.07	3305.95	259.54	0.5695	46.57	11.3	4,265
1993	1500.59	3317.12	221.07	0.55	49.07	11.3	4,028
1994	1571.83	3334.07	238.13	0.54	52.81	11.4	3,992
1995	1638.84	3386.20	262.71	0.53	57.36	11.5	4,056
1996	1662.03	3456.33	274.68	0.55	59.17	11.5	4,019
1997	1706.08	3523.48	276.04	0.55	62.61	11.6	3,973
1998	1776.80	3592.32	300.14	0.54	64.32	11.6	4,034
1999	1867.99	3672.08	327.88	0.54	68.18	11.65	4,117
2000	1955.66	3756.98	347.63	0.56	77.25	11.73	4,229
2001	1978.79	3831.94	348.82	0.58	84.49	11.88	4,310

(continued)

Attached list N.1 (continued)

Year	GDP (Billion Krones)	Physical capital stock (Billion Krones)	Investment in physical capital (Billion Krones)	The share of labor remuneration	R&D expenditure (Billion Krones)	Average years of schooling of laborers (years)	Labor (thousand people)
2002	2003.65	3865.53	340.15	0.57	73.13	11.94	4,393
2003	2053.34	3902.58	346.29	0.57	81.11	12.00	4,368
2004	2100.78	3949.60	359.23	0.55	84.03	12.06	4,337
2005	2188.88	4025.72	392.09	0.55	83.18	12.12	4,349
2006	2258.90	4127.22	423.56	0.53	81.32	12.18	4,422
2007	2356.04	4262.54	465.49	0.55	84.23	12.24	4,524
2008	2435.10	4412.56	491.03	0.55	86.67	12.30	4,565
2009	2419.29	4493.81	434.26	0.57	89.13	12.36	4,455
2010	2297.31	4548.66	414.35	0.55	78.04	12.43	4,509

Attached list N.2 Sweden's compensation of employees model

Dependent Variable: log *V*				
Method: Least Squares				
Sample(adjusted): 1981 2010				
Included observations: 30 after adjusting endpoints				
Convergence achieved after 11 iterations				
Variable	Coefficient	Std. Error	T-Statistic	Prob.
C	−1.21758	0.945719	−1.28746	0.2093
log *HL*	0.421269	0.1197	3.519383	0.0016
log *SD/L*	0.26853	0.033835	7.93648	0
AR(1)	0.662105	0.122427	5.408159	0
R-squared	0.983614	Mean dependent var	2.988117	
Adjusted R-squared	0.981724	S.D. dependent var	0.081915	
S.E. of regression	0.011074	Akaike info criterion	−6.04485	
Sum squared resid	0.003189	Schwarz criterion	−5.85802	
Log likelihood	94.67268	F-statistic	520.2523	
Durbin-Watson stat	2.124479	Prob(F-statistic)	0	
Inverted AR Roots	0.66			

Attached list N.3 Sweden's investment value model

Dependent Variable: *M*				
Method: Least Squares				
Sample: 1980 2010				
Included observations: 31				
Variable	Coefficient	Std. Error	T-Statistic	Prob.
C	9.506712	47.26736	0.201126	0.8421
K	0.165689	0.022861	7.247698	0
SD/K	0.35927	0.067124	5.352349	0
R-squared	0.97471	Mean dependent var	766.0677	
Adjusted R-squared	0.972903	S.D. dependent var	184.4307	
S.E. of regression	30.35932	Akaike info criterion	9.75585	
Sum squared resid	25807.27	Schwarz criterion	9.894623	
Log likelihood	−148.216	F-statistic	539.5713	
Durbin-Watson stat	1.0322	Prob(F-statistic)	0	

Attached list N.4 The analysis of the resource allocation efficiency of production factors

Year	Efficiency	Waste rate of physical capital	Waste rate of labor	Waste rate of human capital
1980	0.9596	0	0.3766	0.2147
1981	0.9316	0	0.3515	0.2017
1982	0.9203	0	0.3334	0.1926
1983	0.9156	0	0.3194	0.1862
1984	0.9323	0	0.3157	0.1861
1985	0.9258	0	0.3052	0.1825
1986	0.9249	0	0.2937	0.1773
1987	0.9285	0	0.2779	0.168
1988	0.9196	0	0.2662	0.163
1989	0.9117	0	0.2537	0.1571
1990	0.896	0	0.2379	0.1496
1991	0.8713	0	0.2096	0.132
1992	0.8551	0	0.1692	0.1029
1993	0.8306	0	0.1177	0.0571
1994	0.8566	0	0.1045	0.0488
1995	0.875	0	0.1054	0.0539
1996	0.8705	0	0.0846	0.0339
1997	0.8764	0	0.0627	0.0186
1998	0.8929	0	0.0599	0.0144
1999	0.9176	0	0.0609	0.0165
2000	0.9418	0	0.07	0.0289
2001	0.9447	0	0.0801	0.0489
2002	0.9475	0	0.0898	0.0622
2003	0.9594	0	0.0754	0.0522
2004	0.963	0	0.0527	0.0342
2005	0.9787	0	0.0337	0.0196
2006	0.978	0	0.0199	0.0103
2007	0.9853	0	0.0091	0.0041
2008	1	0	0	0
2009	1	0	0	0
2010	0.9381	0.0072	0	0.0047

Appendix O
The Data and Model of Finland's Economic Growth

(1) Data

Data Sources: The data of GDP, labor, compensation of employees, physical capital stock, investment in physical capital come from *Sweden Statistical Yearbook*, and databases of Groningen Growth and Development Centre, The World Bank, The Conference Board and United Nations Statistics Division. The data of average years of schooling of laborers come from *Does Human Capital Matter for Growth in OECD Countries? Evidence from Poole Mean-Group Estimates* written by Bassanini A and Scarpetta S, and Organization for Economic Co-operation and Development (OECD). The index of R&D expenditure come from Organization for Economic Co-operation and Development (OECD) (Attached list O.1).

(2) Finland's economic growth model (Add O.1)

$$Y = 1.235(HL)^{0.338}(SD/L)^{0.17} + 0.154K + 5HD/K^2 + 35.7 \qquad \text{(Add O.1)}$$

Attached list O.2.
Attached list O.3.
Attached list O.4.

J. H. Liu and Z. H. Jiang, *The Synergy Theory on Economic Growth: Comparative Study Between China and Developed Countries*,
https://doi.org/10.1007/978-981-13-1885-6

Attached list O.1 The data of Finland's economic growth (the prices at 2005, per hundred million euros; per thousand people; years)

Year	GDP (million euros)	Physical capital stock (million euros)	Investment in physical capital (million euros)	Compensation of employees (million euros)	R&D expenditure (million euros)	Labor (thousand people)	Average years of schooling of laborers (years)
1980	834		192	450		2355	9.6
1981	845	1827	197	465	9	2384	9.7
1982	871	1878	208	473	10	2411	9.7
1983	897	1935	215	484	10	2420	9.8
1984	925	1995	213	497	11	2435	9.9
1985	955	2048	221	525	12	2439	10
1986	981	2105	223	541	14	2431	10.1
1987	1015	2160	236	561	15	2445	10.1
1988	1068	2223	263	575	16	2469	10.2
1989	1122	2308	296	607	18	2493	10.3
1990	1128	2419	285	628	19	2481	10.4
1991	1060	2510	233	621	20	2341	10.5
1992	1023	2542	196	580	21	2176	10.6
1993	1015	2534	169	536	22	2046	10.7
1994	1052	2501	169	535	22	2017	10.8
1995	1094	2469	194	545	22	2053	10.9
1996	1133	2466	212	568	24	2082	11
1997	1203	2481	234	585	25	2153	11.1
1998	1263	2516	260	609	29	2193	11.2
1999	1313	2575	269	642	33	2247	11.3
2000	1383	2638	286	663	36	2293	11.4
2001	1414	2712	294	694	42	2324	11.5

(continued)

Attached list O.1 (continued)

Year	GDP (million euros)	Physical capital stock (million euros)	Investment in physical capital (million euros)	Compensation of employees (million euros)	R&D expenditure (million euros)	Labor (thousand people)	Average years of schooling of laborers (years)
2002	1440	2789	283	705	47	2346	11.7
2003	1469	2849	291	728	48	2348	11.9
2004	1530	2912	305	758	50	2357	12.1
2005	1574	2985	316	780	51	2389	12.3
2006	1644	3062	322	815	53	2433	12.5
2007	1731	3140	357	858	55	2486	12.7
2008	1737	3245	354	861	57	2550	12.9
2009	1588	3340	308	787	60	2484	13.1
2010	1641	3380	313	813	64	2482	13.3

Attached list O.2 Finland's compensation of employees model

Dependent Variable: log *V*				
Method: Least Squares				
Sample(adjusted): 1982 2010				
Included observations: 29 after adjusting endpoints				
Convergence achieved after 9 iterations				
Variable	Coefficient	Std. Error	T-Statistic	Prob.
C	0.091607	0.689107	0.132936	0.8953
log *HL*	0.338039	0.090078	3.75274	0.0009
log *SD*/*L*	0.169789	0.030751	5.521398	0
AR(1)	0.744177	0.147917	5.031032	0
R-squared	0.988604	Mean dependent var	2.799806	
Adjusted R-squared	0.987237	S.D. dependent var	0.077208	
S.E. of regression	0.008723	Akaike info criterion	−6.51838	
Sum squared resid	0.001902	Schwarz criterion	−6.32979	
Log likelihood	98.51649	F-statistic	722.9413	
Durbin-Watson stat	1.501231	Prob(F-statistic)	0	
Inverted AR Roots	0.74			

Attached list O.3 Finland's investment value model

Dependent Variable: *M*				
Method: Least Squares				
Sample(adjusted): 1982 2010				
Included observations: 29 after adjusting endpoints				
Convergence achieved after 7 iterations				
Variable	Coefficient	Std. Error	T-Statistic	Prob.
C	35.69238	110.9852	0.321596	0.7504
K	0.154275	0.053257	2.896794	0.0077
SHD/K^2	5.000958	1.327116	3.768291	0.0009
AR(1)	0.630374	0.213769	2.948852	0.0068
R-squared	0.97673	Mean dependent var	594.5793	
Adjusted R-squared	0.973937	S.D. dependent var	160.3802	
S.E. of regression	25.89161	Akaike info criterion	9.473157	
Sum squared resid	16759.39	Schwarz criterion	9.66175	
Log likelihood	−133.361	F-statistic	349.7795	
Durbin-Watson stat	1.551518	Prob(F-statistic)	0	
Inverted AR Roots	0.63			

Attached list O.4 The analysis of the resource allocation efficiency of production factors

Year	Efficiency	Waste rate of physical capital	Waste rate of labor	Waste rate of human capital
1981	0.84	0.00	0.33	0.17
1982	0.84	0.00	0.32	0.16
1983	0.84	0.00	0.31	0.15
1984	0.84	0.00	0.30	0.14
1985	0.85	0.00	0.28	0.13
1986	0.84	0.00	0.27	0.12
1987	0.85	0.00	0.26	0.10
1988	0.87	0.00	0.25	0.10
1989	0.88	0.00	0.24	0.08
1990	0.85	0.00	0.19	0.05
1991	0.79	0.02	0.14	0.00
1992	0.81	0.08	0.13	0.00
1993	0.85	0.12	0.13	0.00
1994	0.88	0.12	0.13	0.00
1995	0.89	0.09	0.13	0.00
1996	0.90	0.07	0.12	0.00
1997	0.92	0.04	0.12	0.00
1998	0.94	0.03	0.11	0.00
1999	0.94	0.02	0.10	0.00
2000	0.96	0.01	0.10	0.00
2001	0.96	0.02	0.09	0.00
2002	0.96	0.02	0.08	0.00
2003	0.96	0.02	0.06	0.00
2004	0.98	0.03	0.05	0.00
2005	0.98	0.02	0.03	0.00
2006	0.99	0.01	0.02	0.00
2007	1.00	0.00	0.00	0.00
2008	0.98	0.01	0.00	0.02
2009	0.92	0.06	0.00	0.03
2010	0.95	0.07	0.00	0.04

Uncited References

Román, P., Romero, D., & Torres-Ruiz, F. (2010). A diffusion process to model generalized growth patterns: fitting to real data. Journal of Theoretical Biology, 263(1), 59–69.

Small, H. (2014). Co-citation in the scientific literature: a new measure of the relationship between two documents. Journal of the Association for Information Science & Technology, 24(4), 265–269.

Song, X.F. (2004). Complex scientific research. Beijing: Science Press.

Swanson, D.R., Smalheiser, N.R., & Torvik, V.I. (2014). Ranking indirect connections in literature-based discovery: the role of medical subject headings. Journal of the Association for Information Science & Technology, 57(11), 1427–1439.

Wang, S.M., & Watada, Junzo. (2009). Modelling redundancy allocation for a fuzzy random parallel-series system. Amsterdam: Elsevier Science Publishers B.V.

Yang, K., Chen, J., Zhang, P., & Liang, Y. (2001). The knowledge discovery research of POL equipment based on regular taping. Logistics Technology.

Yang, M., & Jiang, Z.H. (2006). Cause analysis and prospect of Japanese-style economic growth trajectory. Research on Economics and Management, (03), 82–85.

Yang, S.P., & Shen, Y.J. (2003). Bifurcation and Singularity of lag nonlinear systems. Beijing: Science Press.

Zhao, X.P. (2006). Research and practice of automatic control and hydraulics simulation in yellow river diversion project. Beijing: China Water Resources and Hydropower Press.

J. H. Liu and Z. H. Jiang, *The Synergy Theory on Economic Growth: Comparative Study Between China and Developed Countries*,
https://doi.org/10.1007/978-981-13-1885-6

The manufacturer's authorised representative in the EU is Springer Nature Customer Service Centre GmbH, Europaplatz 3, 69115 Heidelberg, Germany. If you have any concerns regarding our products, please contact ProductSafety@springernature.com

Printed and bound by CPI Group (UK) Ltd, Croydon, CR0 4YY
30/09/2026
02225446-0014